AN INTRODUCTION TO BEHAVIOR THEORY AND ITS APPLICATIONS

1999

HARPER'S EXPERIMENTAL PSYCHOLOGY SERIES
under the editorship of H. Philip Zeigler

An Introduction to Behavior Theory and Its Applications

Robert L. Karen
San Diego State University

HARPER & ROW, PUBLISHERS
New York   Evanston   San Francisco   London

To My Mother and Father

110,314

Sponsoring Editor: George A. Middendorf
Project Editor: Robert Ginsberg
Designer: T. R. Funderburk
Production Supervisor: Robert A. Pirrung

AN INTRODUCTION TO BEHAVIOR THEORY AND ITS APPLICATIONS
Copyright © 1974 by Robert L. Karen.

Library of Congress Cataloging in Publication Data

Karen, Robert L.
  An introduction to behavior theory and its applications.

  (Harper's experimental psychology series)
  Includes bibliographical references.
  1. Conditioned response.   2.   Human behavior.
3.   Skinner, Burrhus Frederic, 1904–   I.   Title.
[DNLM: 1. Behavior.   2. Behavior therapy.   WM420
K165i 1974]
BF319.K27   150'.19'434   73-15419
ISBN 0-06-043527-5

CONTENTS

Chapter 3   Operant Behavior 47

Chapter 4   Operant Conditioning 66

Chapter 5   Operant Discrimination 94

Chapter 6   Chaining and Complex Behavior 128

APPLICATIONS

Chapter 13   Behavior Modification and Behavior Therapy 356

Chapter 14   Behavior Management in the Classroom 407

Chapter 15   Some Afterthoughts 450

Index 459

PREFACE

Presented in the following discussions is a compilation and distillation of ideas taken from many sources, although the primary source of information is the writings of B. F. Skinner and his students. The principal goals in the preparation of this material have been threefold. The first is to present some basic principles of behavior that the reader may find useful in his daily transactions, especially in the matter of behavior control and behavioral engineering. (Certainly the adequacy of psychology as a science, like that of other sciences, can be judged in part by how well its principles work in natural settings.) In Chapters 1–9, these basic principles are more often presented as generalizations than as raw experimental data, and they take the form of statements and examples in the context of the natural environment; in Chapters 10–15, the applications chapters, they are more apt to be presented as examples in the tables.

The second goal is to give the reader a distinct point of view from which to approach the analysis of behavior, and to introduce the technical language needed to discuss behavior theory. As the sophisticated reader will observe, no attempt is made to be impartial or to present relevant information from other contemporary viewpoints in psychology, but we have tried, whenever possible, to avoid the use of terms with connotations extraneous to the discussions. There are, however, some occasional references to the points of contact between the views expressed here and other views in psychology, especially in the matter of criticism. Most often these are dealt with in the footnotes.

Finally an attempt is made to give the reader an appreciation of some of the problems encountered in the study of behavior and how these problems may be dealt with. This is especially evident in the discussions on models and methods of research in psychology in the introductory chapter and in the chapter on behavior disorders where the consequences of current theory and practices are grave.

No attempt is made to document all the information presented in each chapter. For one thing, many of the statements, especially in the chapters on the applications of behavior theory, are educated guesses for which empirical verification is not available. However, when documentation is used, it is used to guide the student to original studies or reviews that may interest him and to acknowledge those scholars whose work is extensively used in developing ideas or illustrations in the text. Although only a small number of studies are presented in detail, they have been chosen because in the author's view they are classic works, because they illustrate interspecies generality of a procedure or a behavioral process (especially from infrahuman animals to man), and because they illustrate the usefulness of experimental procedures or the laws of behavior in dealing with human behavior problems.

The author wishes to express his gratitude to Drs. Carolyn K. Staats, Arthur W. Staats, and Israel Goldiamond for the marvelous stimulation they gave him during graduate study, an experience he will always value. Particularly deserving of appreciation is Dr. Jack L. Michael, whose knowledge, patience, and concern are especially appreciated and whose suggestions for the improvement of the manuscript have been the most helpful. Appreciation is also acknowledged to Drs. Edwin G. Aiken and Joseph Morrow for their helpful and constructive suggestions; to Dr. W. A. Hillix for his encouragement; to Dr. H. P. Zeigler, editorial consultant for Harper & Row, whose editorial comments assisted the author in clarifying his purposes and improving the style of his presentation; to Mr. Melvin Eisner for his suggestions and editorial assistance in the preparation of the manuscript; to Mrs. Mollie Harris for her assistance in securing supporting documentary material; and to Mrs. Simma Armenti Rifkin, who made possible vital first-hand experiences with retarded and disturbed patients. Particularly deserving of appreciation are the many students whose patience, constructive criticism, and questions provided new insights.

ROBERT L. KAREN

CHAPTER 1

INTRODUCTION

See if the following episode seems familiar:

After dinner John gets up from the dinner table, walks into the den, and sits in front of the TV in his favorite, overstuffed chair. On the table next to the chair are cigarettes, matches, an ashtray, and the television command switch box. John picks up the switch box, presses the television On button, and while waiting for the set to warm up, reaches for the pack of cigarettes. He pulls one cigarette out of the pack, puts it into his mouth, reaches for a match, strikes it, and then places the ignited match to the end of the cigarette and puffs. Very soon the tip of the cigarette glows red-hot. About that time the CBS News with Walter Cronkite appears on the television screen. John leans back in the chair, puffs slowly on the cigarette, lets out a sigh, and watches the news.

This sequence occurs night after night, and what is so striking about it is its regularity. John always seems to sit in his chair, turn on the TV, and smoke a cigarette while watching it. If we watched the episode every night, it might provoke us into asking a number of questions: Of what does John's smoking behavior actually consist? In what other situations does John smoke? In what situations does he not smoke? What are the causes of John's smoking? How can his smoking be eliminated? One question leads to another in rapid succession.

How might we find the answers to these questions? We could watch John some more and have others join us to make sure we don't miss anything. Our basic rule of observation would be to look for the behavior that seems to occur most often when John is smoking and least often when he is not. When we compare notes with the other observers, they may agree that the following sequence always seems to occur:

After John turns on the TV, he reaches for the pack of cigarettes, takes a cigarette out, puts it into his mouth, strikes a match, lights the cigarette while puffing on it, leans back and sighs, and continues to smoke while watching the TV.

One of the observers reports that John seems to be very relaxed while smoking. The observer goes so far as to suggest that this might even be the reason John smokes. He bases his conclusion on John's remark that smoking gives him a feeling of relaxation.

The possibility exists, therefore, that in addition to the locomotor responses, such as John's reaching for a cigarette, and the vocal responses, such as his sigh, smoking may also involve other important, but less obvious and less easily observed systemic events. These events might include specific changes in the activity of the circulatory and gastrointestinal systems, and these changes could be, in part, the basis for the reported feeling of relaxation.

With John's permission we may decide to study the changes that occur in his reflex activity, both when he is smoking and when he is not. This study requires the use of special equipment and it seems desirable to eliminate the TV as a possible source of stimulation. It is decided, therefore, to move John to an easy chair in a laboratory and to study:

1. Changes in his heart rate. These changes are observed by simply taking John's pulse.

2. Changes in his blood pressure. These changes are observed by means of a sphygmomanometer.

3. Changes in the dilation and constriction of the blood vessels in his skin (vasomotor changes). These changes are observed by means of a plethysmograph.

4. Changes in the hydrochloric acid content of his stomach. These changes are observed by taking samples of the gastric juices and analyzing them.

5. Changes in the smooth muscles (gastrointestinal tract motility). These changes are observed by means of an electrogastrogram, an instrument that records electrical potentials arising from the smooth muscles.

During a prolonged period of observation, we find that the following changes in John's reflexes occur when he is smoking: increased heart rate, blood pressure, constriction of the blood vessels in the skin, stomach acidity, and gastrointestinal motility. These changes are not necessarily due to the smoking alone, however. They could be due to his placing an object to his lips or to the breathing patterns characteristic of puffing or inhaling. However, this information about John's smoking behavior does provide a partial answer to our first question: Of what does John's smoking behavior actually consist?

What is perhaps more important, however, is that this example gives us some useful information about how other observations might be carried out. For example, we found out that:

1. It is frequently useful to observe an organism's behavior repeatedly in order to get an adequate description of it.

2. It is frequently useful to have others observe the behavior of interest, so that important events will not go unnoticed and others can check our observations.

3. Descriptions obtained from such observations may deal with the more easily observed, *overt behavior* of the organism. Examples include responses of the skeletal muscles and vocal mechanisms which are involved in locomotion and speech, respectively. Such responses are directly accessible to the senses of the observer, and they will be referred to in future discussions as *operant behavior.*

4. Such descriptions may also deal with less easily observed behavior of the organism, such as the responses of the cardiac and smooth muscle mechanisms, of the endocrine and exocrine glands, and of the associated structures. These are the responses that are involved in *reflex activity;* with the proper equipment, they are also directly accessible to the senses of the observer. They will be referred to in future discussions as *respondent behavior.*[1]

5. Typically, both operant behavior and respondent behavior occur at the same time. Thus they are concurrent behavioral events.

Our analysis of John's smoking behavior has been limited to what might be called *public events*—those events that can be directly and reliably observed (with or without special instruments) and that can be verified by different observers. It is the author's contention that further analysis of the public events occurring prior to and during smoking would also yield a description of the causes of smoking and perhaps even a description of a procedure for its elimination.

Some observers, however, would find an analysis of behavior based solely on public events wanting. They would assert that such an analysis *can never* reveal anything more than a description of the behavior itself. In order to

---

[1] Some operants may be of such small magnitude that they are covert and difficult to observe without special equipment (for example, subvocal speech), and some respondents may be overt and easy to observe (for example, pupillary dilation or eye blinks).

obtain the true causes of the behavior, they contend, a study must be made of the *private events* going on in the individual's psyche or mind—namely, his feelings, desires, wishes, thoughts, dreams, fantasies and so on. They would argue that an analysis of behavior based solely on public events deals with the symptoms rather than the causes of behavior.

Although such things as feelings, thoughts, and wishes are very real phenomena, they cannot be directly and reliably observed or verified by different observers. For this reason, private events, with a few exceptions to be noted later, are beyond the scope of our study.

Psychology, then, is the study of the behavior of organisms; in particular, it is the study of (1) the responses of the skeletal and vocal systems—operant behavior, (2) the responses of the cardiac and smooth muscles of the endocrine and exocrine glands, and of the associated structures of the organism—respondent behavior, (3) the concurrent patterns of operant and respondent behaviors, and (4) the possible interactions between these behaviors. It is essential to this study of behavior for the events under observation to be public events—events that are accessible to direct observation and confirmation by more than one observer, in short, events that can be observed objectively.

THE FUNCTIONS OF PSYCHOLOGICAL RESEARCH

To many observers the primary function of research in psychology is the discovery of empirical laws of behavior, which ultimately lead to the prediction, control, and understanding of behavior. Others assert that a major function of psychological research is the development of a systematic and logical account of behavior. This account would consist of empirical laws, axioms, postulates, and hypotheses that require experimental verification. In short, this account would be a theory of behavior.

Still other investigators regard a major function of psychological research as the development of a technology of behavior control, and in their daily work these investigators are concerned with behavior problems ranging from teaching Jimmy to read to controlling delinquent behavior in adolescents. These investigators are interested in developing procedures that will maximize behavior according to criteria as to what behavior is appropriate as determined by themselves and others.

Investigators differ widely in the area of behavior they choose to study, the species whose behavior they choose to study, and the conditions under which it is studied. One psychologist may study operant discrimination in the rat in a well-controlled laboratory setting, whereas another may be interested in modifying the behavior of a psychotic in a mental hospital. These varied interests reflect the educational history of the investigators. They also are related to the kinds of stimulation that go on in the investigator's environment where the observation actually occurs.

Regardless of the investigator's area of interest, of whether he is testing a hypothesis informally generated out of his experience or testing hypotheses generated deductively from a theory, or of whether or not he is developing a technology of behavior, both logic and experimentation are the essential tools.

DATA IN PSYCHOLOGY

It was suggested that psychology is the study of behavioral events that are accessible to observation. These behavioral events are also stimuli that control various types of responses in the observer, such as counting, timing, or giving verbal accounts of the events.

Suppose, for example, we want to study the lever-pressing behavior of the laboratory rat. We would probably put him in a Skinner box, which is a box that is closed off from uncontrolled sources of stimulation, present him with controlled stimuli, and then observe his responses to these stimuli. A Skinner box is illustrated in Figure 1-1. Suppose further that we decide to study the behavior of two different rats (rat A and rat B). At different times, each animal is placed in the box, and moments later we peek inside to see what is happening. We continue to look inside the box every hour on the hour for the next four hours. Thus we make five observations in all. Table 1-1 shows

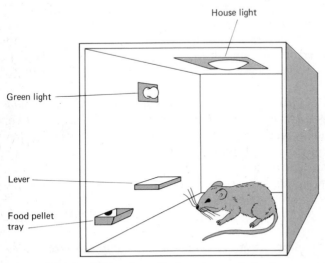

House light

Green light

Lever

Food pellet tray

FIGURE 1-1 The Skinner box. If the rat presses the lever or manipulandum when the green light is on, there is an immediate presentation of a food pellet in the food pellet tray, which serves as a reinforcement.

the data-recording operations we might use, the properties of the data we might obtain, the response dimensions, the units of measurement, and typical data obtained.

The operation of *verbally describing* the event is the most demanding for the observer. He could, of course, use a tape recorder or write notes. Verbal descriptions will vary from observation to observation and can be ambiguous. For example, if the observer reports that one rat is slower than the other, just *how much* slower is not clear and, of course, the behavior of the same rat may be described as "slow" by one observer and "very slow" by another. This example illustrates the difficulty encountered when one uses verbal descriptions of behavior, even when one is talking about public events.[2]

Rating the behavioral event is a more accurate method than verbally describing the event. With this procedure the observer assigns a number to the rat's performance, using standardized criteria. Not only does this number enable the observer to give more accurate descriptions of the rat's behavior, but at the same time, it gives us useful estimates of the differences between observers when compared with verbal descriptions such as "slow" and "slower."

An even more precise data-recording operation is *measuring the behavioral event*. With this procedure some specific aspect, or dimension, of behavior is observed by means of special, standardized equipment, and numbers are assigned to that aspect of the behavior. These numbers are in terms of standardized units of measurement. For example, the force with which the rat presses the level may be described as the response dimension of magnitude or amplitude, and the units of measurement are dynes or grams. Because this type of measurement involves the use of special, often very sensitive, equipment and because standardized units of measurement are used, the data obtained are usually far more accurate and reliable than those obtained with the first two methods.

Like measuring the behavioral event, *counting* and *timing the behavioral event* are also precise data-recording operations in which some aspect, or dimension, of behavior is specified (for example, the frequency, rate, latency, or duration of lever pressing) and numbers are assigned to it. Counting and timing operations can also be done with highly accurate, often high-speed, automatic data-recording equipment, for example, the cumulative recorder (see Figure 1-2), so that high-speed behavioral events (events in excess of four responses per second) such as lever pressing can be recorded accurately over long periods of time.

It is also possible, by means of special programming equipment, for various

---

[2] The reader can appreciate the difficulty encountered when one uses verbal descriptions of private events, as, for example, when one person tells another person that he feels frustrated and depressed because life has no meaning for him.

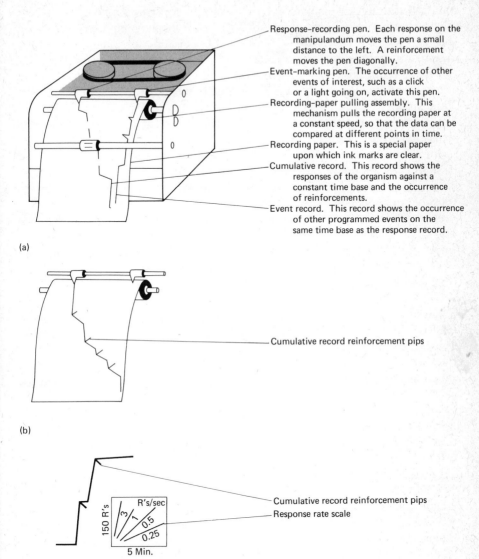

Response-recording pen. Each response on the manipulandum moves the pen a small distance to the left. A reinforcement moves the pen diagonally.

Event-marking pen. The occurrence of other events of interest, such as a click or a light going on, activate this pen.

Recording-paper pulling assembly. This mechanism pulls the recording paper at a constant speed, so that the data can be compared at different points in time.

Recording paper. This is a special paper upon which ink marks are clear.

Cumulative record. This record shows the responses of the organism against a constant time base and the occurrence of reinforcements.

Event record. This record shows the occurrence of other programmed events on the same time base as the response record.

(a)

Cumulative record reinforcement pips

(b)

Cumulative record reinforcement pips
Response rate scale

150 R's
R's/sec
3
1
0.5
0.25
5 Min.

(c)

FIGURE 1-2 The cumulative recorder, an automatic data-recording device, and some sample data. Figure 1-2(a) shows the basic recording equipment. The response pulses produced when the rat operates the manipulandum are fed into this machine. Figure 1-2(b) shows a close-up of the cumulative record, including the response slope and reinforcement pips. Figure 1-2(c) shows a segment of the cumulative record and a rate scale. To provide some idea of the rate of responding, the slope of the cumulative record shown in Figure 1-2(c) is compared with sample slopes shown in the rate scale. In this example the slope of the cumulative record exceeds the maximum rate of three responses per second shown in the rate scale.

kinds of stimulus events to be presented automatically to the rat and recorded at the same time. Such programming and recording equipment can be adapted to the study of all sorts of stimulus events (for example, auditory, visual, or shock stimulus presentations) or response events (for example, licking, lever or button pressing, or vocalizing). It is especially useful for those events that develop slowly and might not be observed during brief observation periods.

Table 1-1 shows that rat A performs differently from rat B, and that the behavior of each rat shows some variability over time as well. A portion of both *intersubject* variability (variability between two or more subjects) and *intrasubject* variability (variability within one subject) can be attributed to the data-recording operations themselves. In actual practice it is not always possible to know how much of the variability can be attributed to the recording operations. It seems obvious, however, that of the four operations shown in Table 1-1 those of verbally describing and rating the behavioral event are more apt to produce variability over and above the variability attributed to the organisms themselves (that is, to their individual differences). As we shall see, this variability of data causes some dispute among investigators.

TYPES OF VARIABLES ENCOUNTERED IN THE STUDY OF BEHAVIOR

A variable in psychology is either a stimulus or response event that can be manipulated, or observed, respectively, by the investigator. There is some dispute among psychologists over the types of variables that are essential to the study of behavior. The majority assert that there are three major classes of variables: independent variables, intervening variables, and dependent variables. These three types will be designated as S variables, O variables, and R variables, respectively.

The *independent*, or S *variables* consist of environmental events that can be described and manipulated by the experimenter. Independent variables may be roughly classified as (1) stimulus variables and (2) state variables. Hence the designation S *variable*. Stimulus variables include verbal instructions, the stimulus properties of the task and the surroundings, the investigator's characteristics if he is active in the experimental procedure, the amount and type of reinforcing or aversive stimuli, the trial duration, the frequency and duration of rest periods, and so on. State variables include an organism's deprivation condition, the organism's anatomic or physiological state, modifications of the organism, the organism's age, sex, or genetic background, and other specific historical-environmental factors affecting the organism's condition.

These variables are defined as independent variables because they are capable of relatively *precise description* and *manipulation* by the *investigator* and include such stimulus variables as the instructions, the task, and the reinforcers, and the state variables, such as deprivation, anatomic or physiological modification, and age. The investigator accomplishes this by engaging in a series of *procedures* or *defining operations.* These operations must be carried out in a manner that is explicit enough for others to repeat them. For example, to establish the definition of a "food-deprived rat," one could establish the free-feeding weight of a fully grown rat over a 2-week period, then deprive that rat of food until his weight is 80 percent of his free-feeding weight. This precise and explicit specification of procedures is called an *operational definition,* and it provides a basis for observers to check each other's observations by defining precisely the S variables under study.

The *dependent* or R *variables* consist of response classes (hence the designation R *variable*). They involve such dimensions of a response as frequency, rate, magnitude, duration, latency, and quality. Dependent variables must be amenable to a reasonably reliable observation procedure. As we have seen, the response class can involve respondents, operants, or both. Table 1-1 gives some idea of the possible ways to measure some dependent variables.

The third class of variables includes the *intervening,* or O, *variables.* Unlike either independent or dependent variables, these variables are not observed directly, even with special instruments. They are inferred from the relationship between the S variables and the R variables. In other words, they are inferred from the behavior changes observed in an organism that has been placed in a given experimental setting. That setting is defined in terms of a given set of measurement operations or procedures, which are specified for both S and R events. Intervening variables are organismic conditions (conditions within the organism) of either a psychic or physiological nature. Hence the designation O *variable.* Along with the S variables, O variables affect the organism's behavior (the R variable under study). Terms such as *need* (an organismic motivational factor) and *cortical irradiation* (an organismic neural excitation or inhibition process) are descriptive of these variables, and to the investigators who use these terms, they represent real, although not directly observed, psychic or physiological states or events that affect the organism's behavior.

BEHAVIOR FORMULATIONS IN PSYCHOLOGY

Psychologists differ in the manner in which they conceptualize the determinants of behavior. One group, by far the majority, asserts that there are three key elements that must be considered in the study of behavior. The first two elements consist of two sets of antecedents, or causes, designated as S and O events, and the last includes the consequences, or effects, designated as

Table 1-1 Data-Recording Operations, Properties of the Data, Response Dimensions, Units of Measurement, and the Typical Data in Psychological Research.

DATA-RECORDING OPERATION	PROPERTIES OF THE DATA	RESPONSE DIMENSION	UNITS OF MEASUREMENT	TYPICAL DATA
Verbally describing the event	Describes entire behavior over time, but without time reference points. Adequate for short-term observation. Words describe specific observable events about which observers can agree.	Response frequency Response latency	Integers expressing count	Rat A: "When the light goes on, the rat slowly walks over to the lever and presses it. He receives a food pellet for his lever-pressing response, and he then eats." Rat B: "When the light goes on, the rat rushes over to the lever, presses it, and eats the pellet on the tray."
Rating the event	Describes one aspect of the behavior, that is, the accuracy with which rat places paw in the center of the lever. Behavioral events are quantified. Numbers denote observable events.	Response precision or accuracy	Accuracy of performance rating: Center of lever = 3 Center of lever = 2 Center of lever = 1	Rat A: 3, 3, 2, 2, 3 Rat B: 1, 2, 1, 2, 3
Measuring the event	Describes one aspect of behavior, that is, the force with which rat presses the lever. Permits quantification of behavioral events. Numbers denote observable events.	Response amplitude or magnitude	Dynes, grams pressure/per response	Rat A: 5.1, 5.3, 5.0, 4.9, 5.5 Rat B: 7.2, 6.9, 7.5, 6.5, 6.7

Counting the event	Describes one aspect of behavior, that is, the occurrence of lever pressing when light is on. Permits quantification of behavioral events. Numbers denote observable events.	Response frequency Response rate	Integers expressing count Responses per sec., min., or hr.	Rat A: 3, 1, 2, 3, 2 Rat B: 5, 2, 3, 5, 4 Rat A: 200/hr., 190/hr., 205/hr., 210/hr., 198/hr. Rat B: 150/hr., 149/hr., 140/hr., 158/hr., 159/hr.
Timing the event	Describes either of two aspects of behavior: 1. The time it takes rat to press lever after the light goes on. 2. The time it takes rat to move the lever from beginning movements to its terminal position (execution time). Permits quantification of behavioral events. Numbers denote observable events.	Response latency Response duration	Sec., min., hrs.	Rat A: .8, .9, .6, .7, 1.0 sec. Rat B: 1.2, 1.3, .90, 1.4, 1.3 sec.

the R events. Collectively, these elements refer to the *three-stage model,* or S-O-R view. (See Figure 1-3.) In this model:

1. S refers to external, environmental, and directly observable events.
2. O refers to organismic events.
3. R refers to the organism's behavior.

If the organismic event is defined *solely* by the operations or procedures for measuring the S and R events, the inferred organismic event is called an *intervening variable.* The sequence, then, in the three-stage model is (1) the measurement of the S event, (2) the inferred O event, or intervening variable, and (3) the measurement of the R event. An example of an intervening variable is hunger drive, which can be defined by the measurement operations or procedures of putting the organism on food deprivation (an S event) and observing changes in his behavior (such as the frequency of lever pressing) when food is presented (an R event). Hunger drive, a motivational factor, is real (in the sense that it is believed to exist and to affect behavior), internal (organismic), and inferred. It is reducible to certain empirical operations—those involving the specification and measurement of the S and R events. There are, however, organismic events that are not defined by the measurement operations for S and R events; they are called hypothetical constructs. Examples of hypothetical constructs include intelligence (a faculty of the mind) and excitatory potential (a mental motivational factor), both of which are multiply determined, in addition to being real, internal (organismic), and inferred. Neither is anchored to either S or R events, but rather to other hypothetical constructs.[3]

Thus according to the S-O-R view, the behavior of an organism, or the R event, is the result of two sets of antecedent conditions—S events and O events.

The other major viewpoint is the *two-stage,* or S-R, *model.* (See Figure 1-3.) In this model:

1. S refers to the external, environmental, and manipulable events.
2. R refers to the organism's behavior.

Thus there is only one set of antecedents, S, to the behavior, R. No use is made of intervening variables or hypothetical constructs. The S and R events are anchored to each other by the measurement operations or procedures used in the experimental observation of the behavior.

The reader may well ask why some psychologists include inferred (intervening) organismic events in the study of behavior while others do not. There are several reasons, but it is sufficient to mention the major reason—the attempt to account for variability in the behavior of organisms.

---

[3] Psychological theory is replete with hypothetical constructs. For example, Freudians refer to the libido as an intrapsychic entity, and Hebb refers to cell assemblies as neurophysiological entities.

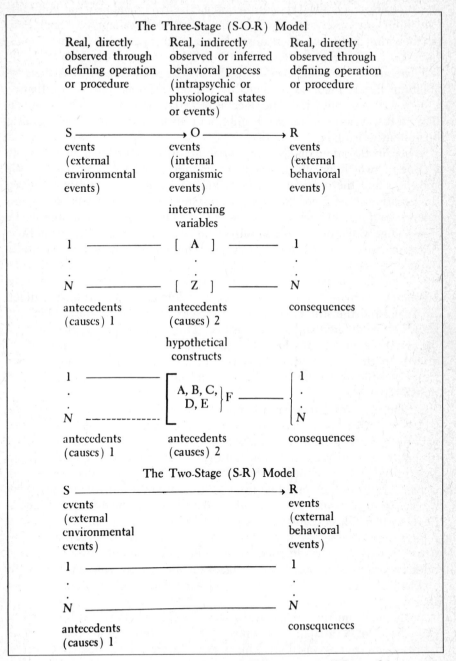

FIGURE 1-3 Diagram of the three-stage (S-O-R) and the two-stage (S-R) models.

In Table 1-1 the data reported for rat A are different from the data for rat B (intersubject variability). Furthermore, the data obtained for both rats vary from one observation to another (intrasubject variability). Such variability within and between organisms forces us to cope with two central questions. First, what causes the variability? Second, what are we to do about it?

There are two possible answers to the first question. One is that the variability in the data can be attributed to the observational procedures, that is, to how well controlled the experimental procedure was. The second answer is that no two organisms are exactly alike, and furthermore, any given organism is constantly changing.

When investigators observe this variability in behavior, they may tend to do one of two things. First, search for unnoticed but subtle changes in the apparatus and the observational procedure to see if they could have caused the variation in behavior. Suppose, for instance, that a rat is trained to press a lever for food, but when he is presented with colored visual stimuli, he shows large variations in his sensitivity to different hues. To explain these variations, we may search for flaws in the techniques of observation. The technique of observation may not have been exactly the same on the trial when the rat failed to respond to the visual stimulus. Since the rat is a freely moving animal, perhaps his head was in slightly different positions on the different trials, and the stimuli stimulated different areas of his retina, which are known to be differentially color sensitive. This, then, might be the basis for the variations in the rat's lever pressing when the colored stimuli were presented. In this case solution to the problem of the variability in the data focuses on the observational techniques and includes an examination of possible S variables.

Second, an investigator may attempt to explain behavior variability by postulating that other events (namely O events) are going on and have intervened with the S events to produce the observed behavior change. In real-life settings, for example, we may observe fraternal twins who show distinctly different degrees of speech development and attribute the difference to differences in maturation. Or we may observe that two children have different IQ's, despite what we believe to be similar environments, and assume that the difference is due to their native intelligence. Or when we notice that our rat varies in his response to colored visual stimuli, we may attribute this variation to the hypothetical construct "behavior oscillation potential"—an organismic event that is believed to cause variations in the behavior of organisms. In each case the solution to the problem of intersubject and intrasubject variability is the postulation of organismic events.

In the long run the student will have to decide whether it is better to explain behavioral variability in terms of the experimental procedures or in terms of intervening variables. This is rather a crucial decision, since it will determine how the student will behave as a scientist. Either he will increase his skill in observation and in the collection of reliable data or he will increase his skill in the development of psychological theory.

Of course, there are arguments in support of both approaches. Advocates of the S-O-R view point to the fact that in natural sciences, such as physics and chemistry, frequent use is made of hypothetical constructs, and they contend that this justifies the use of such constructs in psychology. In the long run, however, techniques in psychology must be justified by the extent to which they lead to the discovery of laws of behavior that enable one to predict, control, and understand behavior rather than by a comparison to the natural sciences. Unfortunately, *despite* extensive use of hypothetical constructs in psychology, psychological laws are few in number, and the prediction, control, and understanding of behavior is largely unaccomplished. Moreover, the observational techniques of the psychologist are not as precise as those of the physicist or the chemist, and variability of behavior resulting from observational procedures is still a major problem. As a result, some psychologists are acutely aware and critical of their observational techniques and are hesitant to assume that there are other sources of variability inside the organism.

THE NATURE OF LAWS IN PSYCHOLOGY

It has been suggested that a primary goal of psychological research is the discovery of laws of behavior. There are two major types of laws. The first type can be expressed by the general formula:

$$R_1 = f(R_2)$$

where R_1 = dependent variable 1; R_2 = dependent variable 2; and f = function of.

This kind of law relates two different behavioral measures (dependent variables 1 and 2). With the information provided by such laws, the investigator can predict individual behavior from grouped data on a probability basis. For example, suppose R_1, or dependent variable 1, consists of vocabulary test scores, and R_2, or dependent variable 2, consists of IQ. In a summary of twenty-one studies relating vocabulary test scores and IQ, Miner (1957) shows that there is a median correlation between R_1 and R_2 of +.83, and numerous approximations of this correlation confirm that a lawful relation between R_1 and R_2 does exist. By means of certain statistical procedures (the regression equation), the investigator can use this lawful relationship to predict an individual's behavior. Such a prediction is a probability statement, in which the value of R_1 (the individual's vocabulary test score) is predicted from R_2 (his IQ). To perform the appropriate calculations, one needs only (1) information on R_2 and (2) the value of the correlation coefficient.

Although such a law does allow the prediction of R_1 from a knowledge of

R_2, it does *not* reveal anything about the antecedents of R_1. The law does not reveal anything about the causes of either IQ or vocabulary test scores. In other words, even though we may be able to predict an individual's probable vocabulary test score from his IQ, the law does not tell us how we can systematically change or manipulate his test scores. One can *never* say that IQ causes vocabulary test performance.[4] One can only say that IQ and vocabulary test performance are related variables.

The second type of law can be expressed by the general formula:

$$R_1 = f(S_1)$$

where R_1 = dependent variable 1; S_1 = independent variable; and f = function of.

This kind of law relates a dependent variable (a consequence) to some independent variable (an antecedent) such that changes in the magnitude of S allow us to make predictions about the magnitude of R_1. Furthermore, not only does knowledge of the relationship between S and R_1 allow us to make predictions, but it also enables us to *control* R_1 by varying the magnitude of S. Finally, this type of law gives us an understanding of the relationship between S and R_1, because it provides us with a functional, or an antecedent-consequence, relationship.

The prediction and control of behavior based on the $R_1 = f(S_1)$ type of law is also expressed as a probability statement. For instance, suppose R_1 is the frequency of a subject's emitting a verbal operant response class consisting of personal pronouns such as *I* and *we* and S_1 is the frequency of the listener's presentation of a verbal gestural reinforcing event consisting of head nodding and saying, "*mm, hmm*," when the subject emits R_1. A number of studies in verbal conditioning, the original experiment having been done by Greenspoon in 1955, have shown that the frequency of a subject's emitting a verbal response class is a function of the schedule of response-contingent reinforcement (Salzinger, 1959; Williams, 1964; Holz and Azrin, 1966). These studies confirm that a lawful relationship exists between R_1, the frequency of emitting the verbal operant *I* or *we*, and S_1, the frequency of the presentation of a reinforcing event. Because this type of law involves a *functional relationship* between S_1 and R_1, not only can one *predict* that R_1 will become more or less frequent as a function of either presenting or taking away S_1, but one can also *control* the value of R_1 (its frequency) by the systematic manipulation of S_1. Finally, this law provides us with an *understanding* of the behavior of emitted speech for it provides us with a precise description of the conditions under which there is a functional relationship between the re-

---

[4] Psychologists who find such tests useful would be more likely to state that it is the individual's intelligence, as measured by the IQ, that causes or determines his vocabulary test performance. However, this usage is equally inappropriate, since as we shall see, knowledge of causation can come only from the discovery and verification of a law of causation.

sponse class (the verbal operant) and the manipulated independent variable (the reinforcement).

As has been emphasized, laws in psychology are essentially probability statements about the occurrence of some behavior. This is because the laws must take into account the variability of organisms from one observation to the next. Even though we may have discovered some lawful relationship, an organism's behavior on any given observation may or may not correspond to our prediction. It is this variability that forces us to make our prediction of behavior as a probability statement rather than as a description of the absolute frequency with which the behavior occurs.

Figure 1-4 shows the frequency of lever pressing in a rat trained in an operant discrimination. The rat was trained to press the lever when a green light is on (S^D) and not to press the lever when the light is off (S^Δ). Notice that the frequencies vary from session to session and do not exceed 125 lever presses during S^Δ presentations and 1,960 presses during S^D presentations. Even though this curve tells us quite a bit about the behavior of the rat, we would never be able to specify or predict *exactly* the *absolute frequency* of lever pressing during a given session (either S^D or S^Δ). We can say, however, that lever pressing, though variable, is much more probable during the light-on (S^D) condition. These relative frequencies can be used as measures of the probabilities of the occurrence of this behavioral event. In essence, this is an empirical law of the type $R_1 = f(S_1)$, in which R_1 is the occurence of lever pressing, and S_1 is the presentation of S^D. The law can be stated more for-

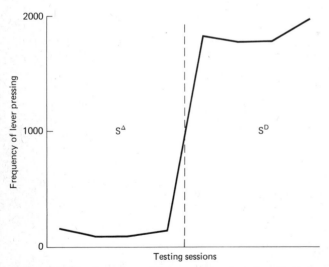

FIGURE 1-4 The frequency of lever pressing in a hypothetical rat trained in an operant discrimination. During training, lever pressing was reinforced when the green light was on (S^D); it was not reinforced when the green light was off (S^Δ).

mally as follows: Given an appropriate reinforcement history, 80 percent free-feeding weight (FFW) food deprivation, and food pellets as the reinforcing stimulus, if S^D is presented, R_i is more likely. This law refers specifically to the rat described, although we can make the assumption (or take an inductive leap) that it applies to other rats and perhaps other species as well.

A law, then, is a statement of the probability of occurrence of R_1, given either R_2 or S_1. Laws are seldom verified by a single crucial experiment, but rather by numerous experiments, which either confirm or deny the described relationship between two variables. Verification is laborious and requires extensive, well-controlled laboratory work. Laws may be *discovered* outside the laboratory, as in clinics, animal colonies, and other uncontrolled situations, but for a lawful relationship to be accepted, it must be verified in the laboratory under well-controlled conditions.

TWO TYPES OF EXPERIMENTS IN PSYCHOLOGY

There are two major traditions or views about how psychological experiments should be carried out. Both views assert that while the single independent variable of interest to the investigator is varied systematically, the other relevant independent variables presumed to affect the dependent variable under scrutiny should be held constant.

Beyond this, however, the similarity between the two viewpoints disappears. Of crucial importance to the differences between the two views are the questions of (1) how many subjects should be studied and (2) over how long a period they should be studied. The highly popular *traditional* view stresses the study of relatively large numbers of subjects over a relatively short period of time in the life-span of the organism. Samples of less than fifty are often viewed with skepticism and dismay, and the experimental sessions during which the subject actually responds, exclusive of instructions and so on, may be of 10 to 15 minutes duration. These figures are merely suggestive, and variations exist in both sample size and the actual duration of the observation.

During an investigation the investigator attempts to hold constant all variables affecting the organism's behavior except the one under study, but he recognizes that prior (historical) events may also affect behavior. For example, animals may have different genetic or handling backgrounds, which may affect the behavior observed during an experiment in a significant way. It is imperative, therefore, that procedures be developed that preclude the possibility of the investigator's confusing the effect of the experimental variable with the effects of previous (historical) background factors.

To offset these possible sources of confusion, the traditional approach to research requires (1) the random assignment of subjects to either the experimental or a control group, (2) the use of large rather than small numbers of subjects, and (3) the use of the group mean as the basic datum when the two groups are compared. Large numbers of subjects are used because the use of small samples of subjects would increase the likelihood of sampling error; that is, subjects might be assigned to either the experimental or the control group with significantly different (historical) behavioral characteristics. The experimental group receives the experimental treatment. That is, it is presented with the independent variable under study. The control group serves as a basis for comparison. It provides data on the amount of variation in the behavior of a group of subjects who do not receive the experimental treatment.

Two sources are presumed to contribute to the observed behavior change in the experimental group: One is the effect of other independent variables besides the one that is the experimental treatment, and the other is the sampling procedures used in assigning subjects to the experimental and control groups. Adequate experimental controls are presumed to offset the former type of variation, and adequate experimental design and statistical analysis are presumed to offset the latter type of variation. Both techniques add to the overall reliability of the obtained data. Although the variation in the experimental group can be attributed to two sources, the experimental treatment and the sampling procedure, the variation in the control group can be attributed only to the latter. When the mean of the experimental group is significantly different from the mean of the control group, the difference is attributed to the effect of the experimental treatment.

Analysis of data obtained by the traditional method seldom focuses on the behavior of the individual subjects in each group, since what is important is the *mean* of the group. The investigator usually evaluates the significance of the observed difference between the mean of the experimental group and the mean of the control group by means of a *statistical test of significance*.

The use of statistical tests, however, involves certain pitfalls:

1. The statistical test of significance specifies that the difference between the mean of the experimental group and the mean of the control group must exceed the difference to be expected by chance alone (the difference expected from a random sampling of subjects assigned to each group). When the observed difference between the two means falls short of the arbitrary statistical *level of significance*, the observed difference is attributed to chance. The investigator then assumes that the variable under study is not significant, and he may study the effects of another variable. If the observed difference falls *just* short of the level of significance and the investigator turns to the study of another variable, however, he may miss an opportunity for the discovery of a potentially significant variable.

2. Because of the difficulties in controlling the variables affecting a given behavior, the investigator may observe behavior over a short term. However, short-term observations are more sensitive to *weak* uncontrolled sources of

variation, and the intrusion of such uncontrolled sources of variation may conceal or offset the magnitude of the effect of the independent variable under study.

3. On occasion the effect of an independent variable may be statistically significant, but it may be of such low magnitude that its psychological significance is questionable.

4. When data are pooled by computing means from grouped data, the pooling may conceal psychologically significant variations in the behavior of the individual subjects attributable to the independent variable. As a result, a behavioral process may go unnoticed, a possibility to be explored in more detail later.

5. Investigators may accept individual differences as a given fact of nature and aim at their control by statistical rather than experimental means. However, better experimental control (through better procedures) and longer base lines of observation might effectively reduce the magnitude of these individual differences.

The second type of experiment, the *experimental analysis of behavior*, has developed from the methods of observation used in the biological sciences. This approach tends to stress the systematic, intensive study of fewer organisms. A handful of subjects, say, three to twelve, may be studied for prolonged periods, ranging from 40 or 50 hours to 1 or 2 years. Of course, these figures vary too, particularly the length of the time over which the study is made. This approach makes use of either the *reversal* or the *multiple base-line procedure*. (See Table 1-2.) In the reversal procedure only one dependent variable is observed, whereas the multiple base-line procedure involves two or more.

Table 1-2 A Comparison of the Reversal and Multiple Base-line Procedures for the Experimental Analysis of Behavior.

DEPENDENT VARIABLE		PHASE			
		1 *Base line*	*2* *Treatment*	*3* *Reversal*	*4* *Reinstatement*
Reversal Procedure	R_1	BL	TR	BL	TR
		Base line		*Base line and Treatment*	
Multiple Base-line Procedure	R_1	BL	TR		
	R_2	BL	BL	TR	
	R_3	BL	BL	BL	TR
	R_N	BL	BL	BL	BL

BL = observe behavior only—no treatment.
TR = observe behavior with treatment.

During phase 1 (the base-line phase) in both of these procedures the dependent variable S(s) under study is observed without the treatment (that is, without the introduction of the independent variable). This observation should yield behavioral data showing a minimum of variability, and because of this, the investigator may spend a great deal of time and effort modifying his observational procedures (by eliminating extraneous or uncontrolled sources of stimulation that may cause variations in behavior) until stability of behavior is achieved.

In phase 2 (the treatment phase) the independent variable under study is introduced to determine its effect on the dependent variable. In both the reversal and the multiple base-line procedures, a *single* dependent variable is treated by the introduction of the independent variable.

During phase 3 (the reversal phase) in the reversal procedure the treatment is removed in an effort to reverse the effects of the experimental treatment. In the multiple base-line procedure another dependent variable may be treated (R_2) while the remaining untreated dependent variables continue to serve as controls.[5]

Finally, during phase 4 (the reinstatement phase) in the reversal procedure an attempt is made to reinstate the treatment effect observed in phase 2 by reintroducing the treatment. In the multiple base-line procedure still another dependent variable is treated (R_3) while the remaining dependent variable continues to serve as a control as before.

Sometimes investigators use variations of these procedures. For example, instead of eliminating the treatment altogether during the reversal phase, the investigator may apply it to another response class. For example, the investigator may observe the frequency of lever pressing during base-line, treat lever pressing during training, and then during the reversal phase apply the treatment normally applied to lever pressing to another response class such as vocalizing. Subsequently, during the reinstatement phase he would treat lever pressing again.

Regardless of which procedure is used, the organism is always compared with *himself*. The investigator examines the organism's untreated and treated performances either for the *same* dependent variable (the reversal paradigm) or across dependent variables (the multiple base-line paradigm). Group comparisons involving group means are not used. Thus prior (historical) background factors are controlled; that is, since the organism is compared with himself rather than with others, the possibility of significant differences in background either masking or intensifying the treatment effects is eliminated.

---

[5] The multiple base-line procedure is most useful when one anticipates, because of prior evidence, that the effect of the treatment cannot be reversed, as when the treatment is removed but the behavior remains at the same level as in phase 2. Since in the multiple base-line procedure one or more dependent variables remain untreated, the investigator can compare the untreated and the treated behavior to assess the treatment effect.

Criticisms of this approach are as follows:

1. Because of the small number of subjects, such experiments, have limited generality.

2. Some experiments by their nature require analysis of grouped data (for example, an experiment evaluating the number of errors made by a group of subjects exposed to a course of programmed instruction).

3. Investigators may be interested in short-term or transient phenomena (for example, short-term learning), which would necessarily involve a brief exposure to the experimental condition.

In the interests of comparing the traditional approach and the experimental analysis of behavior, the reader should examine Figure 1-5. This figure shows hypothetical performance (the dependent variable Y) of three different experimental subjects (the values of Y) at different values of the independent variable (X) and illustrates some of the problems one encounters in the analysis of data from psychological experiments. These curves reveal the following:

1. When the data for the three subjects are plotted separately, all the subjects appear to be going through the same behavioral process (that is, the three curves have the same shape), although only one subject (S_1) shows the complete process in the range of values of X studied.

2. When the data are plotted separately, the maximum Y value is at a different level of X for each subject.

3. When the data are plotted separately, the choice of some values of X (for example, $X = 14$) will reveal a corresponding value of Y (Y_1, Y_2, and

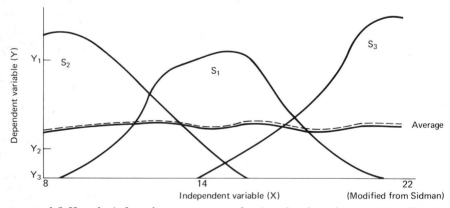

FIGURE 1-5 Hypothetical performance curves showing the dependent variable (Y) for three different subjects plotted both individually and as an average for each value of the independent variable (X) studied. After Murray Sidman, *Tactics of Scientific Research*, page 50. Copyright © 1960, Basic Books, Inc., New York. By permission of the author and Basic Books, Inc.

Y_3) for each subject, but it does *not* reveal the *maximum* value of Y for *any* of the subjects.

4. When a single curve is plotted for all three subjects, using the group means of Y for each value of X, the result is an almost flat curve throughout all values of X—a *rectangular function* that bears no similarity to the *curvilinear function* obtained when the data for each individual are plotted separately.

5. If a group mean of Y at any of the values of X is calculated, the obtained (statistical) average is different from any of the actual values of Y obtained for *any* subject throughout the *entire range* of X studied.

Although this example may be an exaggeration, it illustrates two important points. First, the study of limited values (or parameters) of an independent variable can prevent us from discovering a behavioral process. Second, when the data obtained for individual subjects are pooled and group means are computed, this can prevent the discovery of a behavioral process and give an erroneous impression of the function that best describes that process.

To sum up, the traditional view is the dominant view in psychological research. It stresses the brief observation of a large number of subjects. Some workers believe that this approach has failed to reveal many significant laws of behavior, despite frequent reports of statistically significant relationships among variables. They also believe that the experimental analysis of behavior, which stresses long-term observation of behavior, use of fewer subjects, and experimental rather than statistical control of variables, has been, and will be, a far more promising approach to the study of behavior.

A COMMENT ON THE RELATIVE MERITS OF BASIC RESEARCH AND APPLIED RESEARCH IN PSYCHOLOGY

Frequently, one hears basic researchers and applied researchers making critical comments about each other. The basic researcher often believes that only he can discover fundamental laws of behavior, and the applied researcher asserts that the basic researcher is naïve, laboratory-bound, and unappreciative of the complexities of behavior in its natural setting.

The difficulty is in defining what is basic research and what is applied research. In a crude way the distinction can be made in terms of the "cleanness" of the experiment (experimental control) and the immediacy of application of the obtained data to the solution of some human problem. However, even though these distinctions are in a way true, they are not, in the author's opinion, worth stressing. In the first place, truly clean experiments are hard to come by. In the second place, today's data from basic research may have meaning tomorrow for applied research and vice versa. An interesting example was reported by a colleague. In a basic research project, he was studying the electroencephalogram (EEG) patterns, or brain waves, of subjects who were stimulated visually. He observed that certain test patterns of visual stimuli produced characteristic EEG patterns. It suddenly occurred to him that a subject's visual acuity could be tested by the direct observation of his EEG patterns rather than by the usual procedure of recording the subject's verbal reports of the different-sized letters on a visual acuity test chart.

Finally, in mature sciences the successful application of the basic principles in natural settings adds to their credibility. This task, of course, is most often carried out by the applied workers in the field.

A COMMENT ON SCIENTIFIC METHOD IN PSYCHOLOGY

The scientific method is often described as a series of formal stages of investigation including formulating a hypothesis, designing an experiment, executing the experiment, analyzing the data, and rejecting or accepting the hypothesis. Essential to the scientific method, it is further suggested, is the use of quantification and the experimental method.

However, this view seems limiting and perhaps somewhat naïve. Not all scientific observations are made in the course of experimentation as a manipulative procedure, in testing a hypothesis formally arrived at, or even through quantification. Many highly legitimate sciences are not experimental in a manipulative sense (consider astronomy); not all employ hypothesis testing (consider vertebrate taxonomy) or quantification (consider parasitology). Some sciences are purely observational in character, and others may be manipulative.

Moreover, the importance of accidents in scientific research leading to significant discoveries must not be overlooked. An interesting illustration of this was the discovery of Ringer's solution—a standard reagent in biological research. It is now known that when heart tissue is placed in Ringer's solution, a solution containing salts, it will continue to beat longer than when placed in distilled water. This was discovered when a laboratory assistant mistakenly prepared a heart tissue perfusion fluid using tap water containing salts instead of distilled water and then placed the heart tissue sample in the fluid.

Sometimes important discoveries are made simply because an investigator changes his procedure for reasons of personal convenience. For example, over a period of several days B. F. Skinner (1956) gave a rat a food pellet every time he pressed a lever. Later Skinner planned to see what would happen to the rat's lever pressing when the pellets were eliminated. At one point it became apparent to Skinner that his pellet supply would soon be gone unless he spent the rest of that Saturday afternoon making up a new batch of pellets. Rather than do that, he decided to reinforce lever pressing once every minute.

Lo! Not only did he find that his supply of pellets lasted longer, but also that the rat's behavior stabilized into a new pattern—one characteristic of a fixed-interval schedule of reinforcement.

Then too, significant discoveries are made by serendipity—finding one thing while looking for something else, an example of which is also reported by Skinner (1956). He was trying to solve the problem of maintaining a constant level of food deprivation in the rat over long periods of time. The procedures he used did not produce the results he sought, but there was an unexpected pay-off—he discovered a characteristic pattern of lever pressing (a fixed ratio of reinforcement performance) that had not been observed before.

Although no one is advocating discovery by accident, goofing, convenience, or serendipity, such things do happen in scientific inquiry, and there is no single path to scientific discovery. Rather, it would seem that the scientific method encompasses a wide variety of procedures of observation, some of which may involve a systematic and logical process, others of which may not.

FACTORS AFFECTING THE INVESTIGATOR'S BEHAVIOR AND VIEWPOINTS

As with other scientists, the psychologist's behavior is acquired through and maintained by a number of complex factors. First, the graduate-training program gives him (1) investigative tools (a methodology), (2) a theoretical position about behavior, and (3) an area of specialization in the field. Furthermore, the data the investigator obtains during the observations he makes, the approval, attention, and interest he receives from his teachers during training and later from his colleagues, and the grades, degrees, publications, awards, and promotions that he receives in the course of his career all affect his behavior. As the reader may guess, they can serve to either strengthen or weaken the investigator's scientific behavior, depending on their nature. Thus psychologists, as we have seen, possess diverse points of view about behavior and its study, and these diverse viewpoints reflect important historical and contemporary influences.

SUMMARY

An attempt has been made to explore some of the problems and methods encountered in the study of behavior. Although it was recognized that there are different viewpoints as to what behavioral phenomena are of legitimate concern in psychology and what methods are appropriate for the study of these phenomena, it was stated that our inquiry will be primarily limited to public events—those events for which direct, reliable observation and verification is possible. These events include operant behaviors (responses of the locomotor and speech-producing apparatus) and respondent behaviors (responses of the autonomic nervous system, the endocrine and exocrine glands, cardiac muscles, and the smooth muscles of the gastrointestinal tract). All of these events are capable of direct, reliable observation and verification with or without special instruments and form the basis of the two-stage (S-R) model. Private events, such as wishes, thoughts, and feelings will be excluded from analysis. Furthermore, psychological theories that postulate hypothetical mental or neurophysiological organismic states which are essential features of the three stage (S-O-R) model will not be analyzed.

The traditional approach to research, which stresses brief observations, grouping the data of individual organisms into a commonly used statistic such as the mean, and statistical rather than experimental controls, was discussed, but a preference was indicated for the experimental analysis of behavior. This method of experimentation involves the long-term observation of a relatively few organisms under sufficiently well-controlled conditions to produce stable base-line observations. When these base-line observations have been obtained, the experimental (independent) variable of interest to the investigator is introduced, and its effect on behavior is observed. In the interests of demonstrating the prediction and control of the behavior, this sequence may be repeated. The goal of such investigations is the discovery of laws of the behavior of organisms that will give us the ability to predict, control, and understand behavior.

Now that the reader has been introduced to some of the background and the problems in the study of behavior, he is ready for a more detailed analysis. This analysis will be presented in two parts. Chapters 2 to 9 will present a foundation in behavior theory, including basic definitions and principles. Chapters 10 to 14 will illustrate the application of these principles to problems of the real world. It is hoped that by the time the student completes his study, he will be excited by the possibilities of psychology as both a science and an art.

STUDY QUESTIONS

1. State the logic behind the basic rule of observation described at the beginning of the chapter.
2. Compare and contrast the problems encountered in corroborating the observers' reports that John "reaches for the pack of cigarettes, takes a cigarette out, puts it into his mouth, strikes a match, lights the cigarette while puffing on it, leans back and sighs" and that "John seemed to be very relaxed while smoking."
3. Summarize the locomotor and vocal behaviors that seem to occur while smoking.

4. Summarize the reflex activity that seems to be characteristic of smoking.
5. Reread the changes in John's reflexes reported by the observers and suggest three things they have in common.
6. If you were studying the changes in John's reflex activities, how could you control the presence of other extraneous variables affecting his reflex activity while smoking?
7. Distinguish between operant and respondent behavior in terms of the following:
   a. Accessibility to direct observation.
   b. The response systems (structures) involved.
   c. The function of the response systems involved.
8. Why are private events regarded as being beyond the scope of the present study?
9. What are some of the functions of psychological research? Compare these functions and see if you can identify one function which is more essential or basic than the others cited.
10. What do investigators share in common regardless of their area of interest?
11. For each of the following data-recording operations give (1) the properties of the data, (2) the response dimension, (3) the unit of measurement, and (4) some typical data:
    a. Verbally describing the behavioral event.
    b. Rating the behavioral event.
    c. Measuring the behavioral event.
    d. Counting the behavioral event.
    e. Timing the behavioral event.
12. Give one criticism of the data-recording operations of verbally describing behavioral events and rating behavioral events.
13. Give three reasons for the superiority of measuring, counting, and timing as data-recording operations.
14. Distinguish between intersubject and intrasubject variability in behavior.
15. What are the three major types of variables that psychologists study? Give an example of each and cite its defining properties.
16. Describe the three key elements in the S-O-R behavior formulation to which most investigators subscribe.
17. What is the difference between an intervening variable and a hypothetical construct?
18. What two classes of antecedents are employed in the S-O-R view?
19. What is the difference between the S-O-R and the S-R view as far as antecedent-consequence relations are concerned?
20. Discuss the relationship between the question of variability in the behavior of organisms and the investigator's decision to use the three-stage or the two-stage model.
21. What two central questions must we ask concerning variability in behavior?
22. What two answers are often given to these questions about the variability of behavior?
23. What is the ultimate criterion or justification for the method of investigation and behavior formulation used in psychology?

24. State the formulas for the two major types of laws in psychology. Define each term in these formulas.
25. What are the characteristics of these two laws?
26. Explain why laws of behavior are statements of probability (relating the terms in the laws) rather than absolute statements.
27. Describe four characteristics of the traditional approach to research.
28. What two factors contribute to the changes observed in the dependent variable?
29. Describe the logic behind statistical controls. For which factor (see answer to preceding question) are these controls used?
30. In what ways are the reversal paradigm and the multiple base-line paradigm similar? Different?
31. Why is it important to secure stable base lines of behavior in the experimental analysis of behavior?
32. During the introduction of the experimental treatment, what serves as the control condition in the reversal paradigm? In the multiple base-line procedure? In the experimental analysis of behavior, how are prior (historical) background factors controlled?
33. Which approach generally requires longer periods of laboratory observation?
34. Give three criticisms of the experimental analysis of behavior.
35. Which approach stresses the prediction and control of the behavior of the individual? The group?
36. Examine Figure 1-5 carefully and then do the following:
    a. Draw a rectangular function.
    b. Present some hypothetical data for five values (parameters) of X for five subjects that fit the function.
37. What risk does an investigator take when he limits his investigation to a study of the effects of a few values or parameters of X? Explain why there is such a risk.
38. How can you tell which research approach is the best?
39. The view that the scientific method involves an orderly succession of steps or procedures probably ignores what aspects of research? Emphasizes what others?
40. What is serendipity?
41. Give examples of sciences that are quantitative and of sciences that are not.
42. Give an example of a purely observational science.
43. What criticisms are made of applied research? Of basic research?
44. What seems to most characterize
    a. the basic research project?
    b. the applied research project?
45. What is the author's viewpoint concerning the necessity of distinguishing between basic and applied research?
46. What factors in the scientist's environment serve to strengthen his scientific behavior? To weaken it?
47. Identify the following as either a public or a private event:
    a. A fantasy that one is rich.
    b. A death wish.
    c. Turning pale.

48. Identify the following as involving either respondents or operants:
    a. John's heartbeat quickens as he runs down the street.
    b. A salesman pushes a prospective customer's door back.
49. Identify the following as independent, intervening, or dependent variables or as hypothetical constructs:
    a. The presentation of a tone of 260 cps at 30 Db.
    b. Presentation of food pellets.
    c. A cubic centimeter of saliva.
    d. Thirst drive.
    e. Percentage of correct responses.
    f. A loud buzzer presented for .1 second.
    g. Pecking rate.
    h. Superego.
50. From the following, identify the response class and the response class dimension:
    a. The frequency of socking the victim's arm or thorax.
    b. Loudness of utterances "I" and "We."

REFERENCES

Baer, D. M., Wolf, M. W., and Risley, T. R. Some dimensions of applied behavior analysis. *Journal of Applied Behavior Analysis*, 1968, **1**, 91–97.

Bernard, C. *An introduction to the study of experimental medicine.* New York: Dover Publications, 1957.

Beveridge, W. I. B. *The art of scientific investigation.* New York: Vintage Books, 1950.

Goldiamond, I. Perception. In A. J. Bachrach (Ed.), *Experimental foundations of clinical psychology.* New York: Basic Books, 1962.

Greenspoon, J. The reinforcing effect of two spoken sounds on the frequency of two responses. *American Journal of Psychology*, 1955, **68**, 409–416.

Holz, W. C., and Azrin, N. H. Conditioning of human verbal behavior. In W. K. Honig (Ed.), *Operant behavior: Areas of research and application.* New York: Appleton-Century-Crofts, 1966.

Miller, N. E. Analytical studies of drive and reward. *American Psychologist*, 1961, **16**, 739–754.

Miner, J. B. *Intelligence in the United States.* New York: Springer, 1957.

Salzinger, K. Experimental manipulation of verbal behavior: A review. *Journal of Genetic Psychology*, 1959, **61**, 65–95.

Sidman, M. *Tactics of scientific research.* New York: Basic Books, 1960.

Skinner, B. F. Are theories of learning necessary? *Psychological Review*, 1950, **57**, 193–216.

Skinner, B. F. The analysis of behavior. *American Psychologist*, 1953, **8**, 69–79.

Skinner, B. F. A case history in the scientific method. *American Psychologist*, 1956, **11**, 221–223.

Skinner, B. F. The flight from the laboratory. In *Cumulative record.* (Enlarg. ed.) New York: Appleton-Century-Crofts, 1961.

Skinner, B. F. Operant behavior. *American Psychologist,* 1963, **18,** 503–515. (a)

Skinner, B. F. What is the experimental analysis of behavior? *Journal of the Experimental Analysis of Behavior,* 1966, **9,** 213–218. (b)

Spence, K. W. The postulates and methods of behaviorism. *Psychological Review,* 1948, **55,** 67–78.

Williams, J. H. Conditioning of verbalization: A review. *Psychological Bulletin,* 1964, **62,** 383–393.

FOUNDATIONS

CHAPTER 2

RESPONDENT BEHAVIOR

The activity of the autonomic nervous system, the endocrine and exocrine glands, cardiac muscle, the smooth muscle of the gastrointestinal tract, and certain skeletal muscles provide the anatomic and physiological basis for *respondent behavior*. Historically, the operations of these response systems have been viewed as reflexes that can be elicited by specific stimuli in the organism's environment. They play a vital role in the economy of the body, especially in the maintenance and preservation of a stable internal environment (homeostasis), which is essential to the organism's cellular activity and metabolism, as well as in the protection of the organism from harmful or irritating stimuli.

AN EXAMPLE OF RESPONDENT BEHAVIOR

Suppose that a food-deprived dog is presented with a chewy, crunchy dog biscuit. Observation will reveal that besides the food-approach responses of biting and chewing, there is a copious flow of saliva. Repeated presentations of the dog biscuit on several occasions seem to produce the same response—saliva flow. The saliva serves as a lubricant for the pieces of biscuit as they are swallowed. Along with biting and chewing, salivation aids the assimilation of the food and helps to maintain an internal environment. Food assimilation, in turn, is essential for life processes because it makes essential nutrients available to the body cells.

Other types of behavior that are viewed as being essentially reflexive are changes in blood pressure, pulse rate, respiration, gastrointestinal motility, gastric hydrochloric acid (HCl) secretion, lacrimal gland secretion, electric conductivity of the skin (or the galvanic skin response, abbreviated GSR), the pupillary and patellar reflexes, and the eye blink. All of these behaviors are presumed to facilitate the maintenance of an internal environment or to be protective reflexes against painful, noxious, or irritating stimuli.

RESPONDENT CONDITIONING

Respondent conditioning is based on the fact that respondent behaviors can be reliably *elicited* by certain classes of *prepotent stimuli*. Prepotent stimuli are stimuli that possess this elicitation function without any special training, and they are called *unconditioned stimuli*. The essential procedure in respondent conditioning is known as *stimulus pairing*. A previously neutral stimulus, called the *conditioned stimulus* (CS), is repeatedly paired with the prepotent, or unconditioned, stimulus (US) that functions as an elicitor of a particular response (r). After repeated pairings the response (r) is elicited by the conditioned stimulus (CS); prior to training it was elicited only by the unconditioned stimulus (US). This process, which is sometimes also called *stimulus substitution*, is illustrated in Figure 2-1.

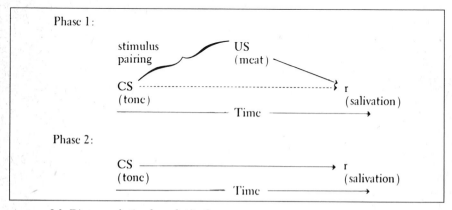

Phase 1:

stimulus pairing   US (meat)

CS (tone) ————→ r (salivation)

Time ————→

Phase 2:

CS (tone) ————————→ r (salivation)

Time ————→

FIGURE 2-1 Diagram of stimulus substitution.

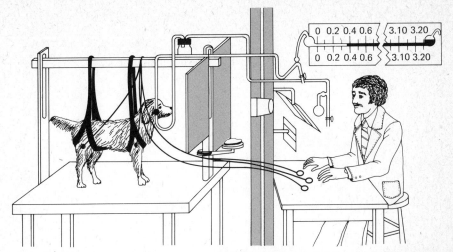

FIGURE 2-2 Pavlov's laboratory arrangement for the study of the digestive reflex of salivation. From I. P. Pavlov. *Lectures on conditioned reflexes,* page 271. Translated by W. H. Gantt and G. Volbarth. New York: International Publishers, 1928, by permission.

In phase I the previously neutral stimulus, the tone (CS), is followed immediately by the prepotent stimulus, the meat (US), which already has the capacity to elicit salivation (r) in a food-deprived organism. This sequence is repeated until finally in phase 2, the tone (CS) elicits the salivary response (r) in the absence of the meat (US). Because of limitations in the test equipment and variations in the test procedures used during such training, these tone presentations vary from trial to trial. Thus the tone, as a CS, refers to a *class* of *stimuli,* not to the presentation of a single stimulus. All of the tones are sufficiently similar to elicit the r.

To get some idea of how this process is studied in the laboratory, we may review some of the experimental work done by the discoverer of respondent conditioning—the famous Russian neurophysiologist Ivan Petrovich Pavlov. In a simple surgical procedure a dog's salivary gland duct was extruded through a small incision made in the dog's cheek. After recovery from the operation, the animal was placed in a special harness and housed in a laboratory cubicle. (See Figure 2-2.) The animal's salivary gland duct was connected to a tube, which, in turn, was connected to a graduated glass measuring tube containing a colored fluid. When salivary gland secretion occurred, the saliva displaced the colored fluid in the graduated tube. The amount of fluid displaced was read in drops or tenths of a drop. In this way, the dog's salivary gland secretion was simply and accurately observed by direct visual inspection of the tube.

Pavlov's basic plan was simple and consistent with the basic rule of observation described in Chapter 1. It was to study the amount, or magnitude, of saliva secreted by the dog's salivary gland (its volume in drops) during occasions of presentation and nonpresentation of *known, reproducible,* and often *quantitatively specifiable* stimuli. These stimuli included biscuit powder, different dilutions of hydrochloric acid solution, metronome beats of differing frequencies, and pure tones of tuning forks with different pitches. At first Pavlov studied the amount of saliva (in drops) as the dependent variable during presentations of various unconditioned stimuli such as the biscuit powder or hydrochloric acid. After his discovery of respondent conditioning, his interests broadened, and he studied, among other things, the effects of presentations of conditioned stimuli (metronome beats or pure tones) as independent variables, of variations in the duration or temporal relationships among these stimuli, and of presentations of compound stimuli. See Figure 2-3 for some typical data and a description of an experimental procedure.

In the respondent conditioning procedure, the response elicited by the unconditioned stimulus is known as the *unconditioned response* (Ur), and the response elicited by the conditioned stimulus is known as the *conditioned response* (Cr). Although the Ur and Cr are very similar, they are seldom identical. Typically, the Cr is a subtotal, or partial response, of the Ur and possesses other qualitative features that make it different from the Ur. Pavlov found, for example, that not only was there less saliva flow (Cr) in response to a tone (CS), but the saliva contained fewer enzymes. Thus, compared with the Ur, the Cr shows both quantitative and qualitative differences. It should also be noted that in respondent conditioning, a new response is not learned; rather, an old response gradually comes to be elicited by a new stimulus.

Procedure: A pure sound (637.5 vibrations per second) is presented for 5 seconds, then after 2 to 3 seconds a measured amount of biscuit powder is presented. After the dog finishes eating, a test of the strength of the CS (sound) is made by counting the number of drops of saliva secreted during a 30-second presentation of the sound.

WORKING DAYS	NUMBER OF PAIRINGS OF SOUND WITH THE UNCONDITIONED STIMULUS	REFLEX STRENGTH IN DROPS	LATENT PERIOD IN SECONDS
1	1	0	—
3	9	18	15
5	15	30	4
11	31	65	2
14	41	64	3
17	51	69	2

FIGURE 2-3 Experimental procedure and typical data in the study of respondent conditioning by Pavlov and his students. (Data from *Lectures on conditioned reflexes* by I. P. Pavlov. Translated by W. H. Gantt and G. Volbarth. New York: International Publishers, 1928, by permission.)

For maximum conditioning to occur, the presentation of the CS should precede the US by .5 second; and in general, the more occasions on which the CS is followed by the US, the stronger the response, as measured by its magnitude, latency (time elapsed before it occurs), or frequency. The strength of the response is generally proportional to the magnitude of the US; a strong stimulus will elicit more saliva, more quickly, and more frequently than a weak stimulus.

This is also true when the CS is followed by a US that is extremely noxious or irritating (for example, a loud noise). The following classic experiment conducted by John B. Watson and Rosalie Rayner in 1920 illustrates this situation:

When Albert was 8 months and 26 days old, it was established that by repeatedly striking a steel bar with a sharp blow from behind, the experimenters could induce a violent startle response in Albert. This response consisted of checked breathing, sudden, upward arm movements, puckering and trembling of the lips, and crying.

Later on, when Albert was 11 months and 3 days old, the loud noise as an auditory stimulus (a US) was paired repeatedly with presentations of a white rat as a visual stimulus (the CS). The experimenters simply presented the rat and struck the bar as Albert reached for it. After only *seven* such pairings, Albert cried violently even when the rat was presented alone. He also cried when presented with a rabbit, a dog, and a fur (seal) coat, and he avoided cotton wool. However, he did not cry when blocks were presented, but instead, smiled, giggled, and played with them.

Sometimes the CS will elicit the r even though there has been only *one* pairing of the CS with the US. Such is the case when the US is a particularly strong and noxious stimulus, for example, a strong electric shock.

In most conditioning situations, numerous changes take place in the autonomic nervous system and the *effectors* (the glands and muscles) it controls. The presentation of extremely noxious stimuli, such as a strong shock, elicits many respondents, including changes in blood pressure, respiration, cardiac activity, the digestive glands, the sweat glands, the blood vessels, and even the cellular and biochemical composition of the blood. Because it involves such widespread anatomic and physiological changes, this respondent pattern to strong irritating stimuli is known as the *activation syndrome*.

The presentation of food to a food-deprived animal elicits a different set of respondents involving other changes in these effectors. A typical respondent conditioning situation, therefore, involves a *pattern of respondents*. The eliciting stimuli for the pattern of respondents can be characterized along a positive–negative dimension. The stimulus dimension can be defined as positive or negative by the types of responses elicited by the stimuli. For example, stimuli that elicit strong escape, or avoidance, responses are negative, and those that elicit strong approach responses are positive. When such patterns of respondents are elicited by the conditioned stimulus, they are referred to as either positive or negative *conditioned emotional responses* (CEr).

It has been suggested that various stimuli are, by their nature, prepotent elicitors of respondents, without special training of the organism. Among these unconditioned stimuli are loud sounds, bright lights, electric shocks, rotation of the subject, mechanical blows, food, and water. Other stimuli are essentially neutral but can come to function as conditioned stimuli through their association with a given US. Among these stimuli are buzzes and pure tones, lights, patterns of visual stimuli, odors, and other objects in the organism's environment that possess visual, tactile, or olfactory stimulus properties. Even the spoken or written word is an auditory or visual stimulus. The word *bad*, for example, will elicit a negative CEr for many of us, because in the past it has been followed by a US such as a slap. Similarly, the word *good* will elicit a positive CEr because it has probably been followed by food or a hug, which involves both tactile stimulation and stimulation of the warmth receptors.

Normally, the capacity of the CS to elicit the response is derived from its pairing with the US. There are occasions, however, when the initial presentation of the neutral stimulus that is to be used as a CS will elicit the response without being paired with the US. This phenomenon is known as *pseudoconditioning*, or *sensitization*. An infant's sucking can be elicited by placing a nipple into his mouth (a US) or by presenting a tone that has been repeatedly paired with the US. On occasion, however, the mere presentation of the tone, without any history of its being paired with the nipple, will also elicit sucking—a form of pseudoconditioning (Lipsitt and Kaye, 1964). In order to establish that respondent conditioning has occurred and that a particular CS has acquired its elicitation function because of respondent conditioning, it is customary to present a potential CS by itself both prior to and after occasions of stimulus pairing. The CS is presented alone prior to the pairings so the experimenter can observe its strength as an eliciting stimulus. Otherwise, he would not know later on, after the pairings had occurred, whether the CS elicited the r simply because of pseudoconditioning or sensitization effects or because of respondent conditioning.

RESPONDENT EXTINCTION

Repeated presentations of the CS without the US will result in a decline in response strength (decreased response magnitude, longer response latency, lower response frequency). This procedure is known as *respondent extinction*. Table 2-1 shows the data obtained with repeated presentations of metronome

Table 2-1 Data Obtained with Repeated Presentations of Metronome
Beats (CS) Without Paired Presentations of Meat Powder (US)

TRIAL	SECRETION OF SALIVA IN DROPS DURING 30 SECONDS	LATENT PERIOD IN SECONDS
1	10	3
2	7	7
3	8	5
4	5	4
5	7	5
6	4	9
7	3	13

From I. P. Pavlov, *Conditioned reflexes*. Translated by G. V. Anrep. Copyright © 1928, International Universities Press, Inc., New York, p. 49.

beats (the CS) without paired presentations of the meat powder (the US). As shown in the table, there is an increase in the response latency of the reflex (salivation) and a decrease in the response magnitude (drops of saliva).

Even though all measures of response strength (magnitude, latency, and frequency) decline during extinction, response strength will be greater at the beginning of any given extinction session than it was at the end of the preceding extinction session. This increase in response strength at the beginning of an extinction session is known as *spontaneous recovery*.

SECONDARY OR HIGHER ORDER CONDITIONING

Once a conditioned stimulus has acquired its eliciting stimulus function through repeated pairings with a US, it can be paired with other neutral stimuli to make them conditioned stimuli. This phenomenon is known as *secondary*, or *higher order, conditioning* and involves the two-stage process shown in Figure 2-4. During stage 1 the tone (the CS) is repeatedly paired with the food (the US) until it becomes a conditioned elicitor of salivation. During stage 2 the same tone is used as the eliciting stimulus and is repeatedly paired with the black square (the new CS) until it becomes the conditioned elicitor of the salivation. However, Cr's obtained at the conclusion of stage 2 procedures tend to be very weak (less response magnitude, longer response latency) and short-lived, compared with those obtained at the conclusion of stage 1 procedures. When a negative US (shock) is substituted for the positive US (food) in stage 1 the Cr's obtained at the conclusion of stage 2 procedures are stronger.

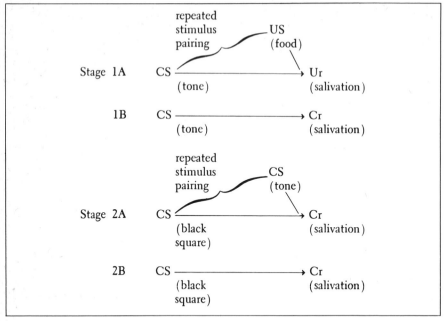

FIGURE 2-4 Diagram of secondary conditioning.

A very common and significant variation of secondary, or higher order, conditioning occurs when words that are previously conditioned stimuli are paired with other neutral stimuli, making them conditioned elicitors. These other neutral stimuli with which a word is paired may be objects or events in the organism's environment. When, for example, a mother says, "Bad!" as she shows baby his dirty hands, she is pairing his dirty hands, a visual stimulus, with the word *bad*, an elicitor of a negative CEr.

There are also occasions when words are joined in a *subject–predicate relationship* or sentence so that a previously neutral word through pairing with either a positive or negative word stimulus, also becomes an eliciting stimulus. For example, the sentence "John is good" pairs the positive eliciting stimulus *good* with *John* (the neutral stimulus), so that the word *John* by itself becomes a positive eliciting stimulus. Similarly, when the word *bad*, an elicitor of a negative CEr, is paired in the sentence "Bill is bad," the word *Bill*, formerly a neutral stimulus, becomes an elicitor of a negative CEr. This form of *language conditioning*, as we shall see, can be especially significant in the acquisition of positive or negative CEr's toward certain objects or events in the individual's environment, for example, toward minorities or social legislation. Such language conditioning may occur during exposure to printed or graphic media in which words, as negative eliciting stimuli, are paired with the names of minority groups (in sentences) or are contiguous with pictures of minority groups (in graphics). Subsequently, when the individual reads or sees (turns to look at) such stimuli, it amounts to the *self-presentation* of such stimulus pairings.

To sum up, through a process of stimulus pairing, a previously neutral stimulus (CS) may acquire the capacity to elicit a response in the same way that a prepotent stimulus (US) does. It is characteristic of both the CS and US that they will generally elicit a pattern or class of responses, rather than a single response. Such patterns are called positive or negative conditioned emotional responses.

DISCRIMINATION AND GENERALIZATION

Suppose that we were to study the amount of saliva secreted by a food-deprived dog that has been presented in random order from trial to trial with either (1) a pure tone auditory stimulus of 260 cps or (2) a pure tone auditory stimulus of 400 cps immediately followed by the presentation of a dog biscuit. At the very beginning of such a *respondent discrimination training procedure* both tones are *neutral stimuli*, but as training progresses and the number of stimulus pairings increases, the dog consistently salivates a great deal to the 400 cps tone presentations and very little to the 260 cps tone presentations. In other words, the 400 cps tone, by virtue of its pairing with the dog biscuit, acquires an eliciting stimulus function for salivation. On the other hand, the 260 cps tone, which is never paired with the presentation of a dog biscuit, does not acquire this eliciting stimulus function. The increased amounts of salivation to the 400 cps tone presentations and the virtual absence of salivation to the 260 cps tone presentations reveal that an important behavioral process, namely, *respondent discrimination*, has occurred.

Sometimes a stimulus that was not originally paired with the US and was not present during training will elicit the conditioned response. When this phenomenon occurs, it is known as *stimulus generalization*. Whether or not a stimulus that was not originally paired with the US, and therefore did not become a member of the stimulus class CS, will possess such an eliciting function depends, among other things, on the similarity between the CS and the stimulus in question and the number of times the CS and US have been paired.

Stimulus generalization is greatest when the stimuli in question are similar to the CS. For example, a child will be afraid (negative CEr) of a dog (CS) after having been bitten (US) by that dog. At the same time other furry animals, such as cats and even stuffed-animal dolls, may also elicit the negative CEr, even though they were not paired initially with the US. In this instance of stimulus generalization, the negative CEr is elicited by a stimulus that is similar to the CS.

THE ELIMINATION OF CONDITIONED EMOTIONAL RESPONSES

Suppose that one day a toddler is playing in the yard and a strange dog runs up to him and bites him, drawing blood. From that time on, let us say, he is deathly afraid of that dog and other dogs as well. Because the dog, as a visual and perhaps auditory stimulus, was paired with the presentation of a painful US, the bite, the dog functions as a CS. Whenever the dog is near the child, it elicits negative conditioned emotional responses consisting of the child's turning pale, crying, and screaming. Through stimulus generalization, other dogs are also elicitors of this negative CEr. In a sense, the child might be characterized as having a dog phobia.

Suppose further that you are the helpful sort, and the child's parents ask you how his phobia might be eliminated. Although there are a number of procedures that can be used, some of which will be presented later, two procedures worthy of mention at this point are *extinction* and *counter-conditioning*.

In respondent extinction, as was noted earlier, the CS is repeatedly presented without the US until the CS no longer elicits the conditioned emotional response. In a respondent extinction procedure to eliminate the child's fear of dogs, the dog (CS) would be presented to the child, but under no circumstances would the dog again be allowed to bite the child. When such presentations of the dog to the child are repeated over and over again, the dog as a CS will gradually elicit the negative CEr less and less. However, if the magnitude of the child's negative CEr to the dog is great, an immediate and close presentation of the dog may overwhelm the child. Besides showing the characteristic negative conditioned emotional response, the child may also show escape or avoidance (operant) behavior. If attempts are made to restrain him, further respondent conditioning may take place, which will defeat the original purpose of the training (that is, to reduce the child's fear of dogs). A sensible alternative procedure would be to introduce the dog at some distance from the child and make initial exposures to the dog quite brief. The dog would then be gradually moved closer and closer to the child and presented for longer and longer intervals, until the child no longer showed his phobic response.

An alternative to extinction is counter-conditioning, a procedure that contains (1) a component of extinction (presentation of the CS without the old US) and (2) a component of respondent conditioning (presentation of the CS with a new US). The goal of this procedure is to make the CS (the former elicitor of the negative CEr) an elicitor of a pattern of respondents that is incompatible with the negative CEr. That is, the CS becomes the elicitor of a positive CEr. For example, the dog as an elicitor of the negative CEr would become, through counter-conditioning, the elicitor of a positive CEr.

This could be accomplished by presenting the dog (as the CS) without the bite (the US), and at the *same time* pairing the presentations of the dog (again as the CS) with presentations of cookies or candy (as the new US and a prepotent elicitor of positive respondents). The first part of the procedure would be the extinction component of training, and the second part would be the respondent conditioning component. Repeated presentations would make the dog a new CS, capable of eliciting a positive CEr. As in the extinction procedure, care should be taken during the initial presentations of the dog not to elicit excessive disruptive behavior of the type described earlier. Furthermore, successful use of this procedure requires that the new US be sufficiently strong to elicit respondents that are incompatible with those elicited by the CS.

VERBAL INSTRUCTIONS AND THE MODIFICATION OF RESPONDENT BEHAVIOR

Ordinarily, the modification of reflex strength (its magnitude, latency, and frequency) is a slow process, involving either repeated pairings of the CS and the US (as in respondent conditioning), the repeated presentation of the CS alone (as in respondent extinction), or both pairings of the old CS with a new US and presentation of the CS without the old US (as in respondent counter-conditioning). However, there are occasions when reflexes can be abruptly modified by the introduction of *verbal instructions*. For example, Grings (1965) found that the magnitude of galvanic skin responses can be abruptly and substantially *increased* by verbally telling the subject that he will be (but has not yet been) shocked. Grings also found that the magnitude of this reflex can be abruptly and substantially *decreased* by telling the subject that the US (a shock) will no longer be presented. The frequency of the eye blink reflex can be modified in the same manner.

However, conditioned emotional responses are not as easily modified by the presentation of verbal instructions, and verbal instructions can only be used in the modification of the reflexes of some, not all subjects—perhaps only those with certain histories. One possible reason for this variation among individuals is that for some individuals appropriate reflexive behavior in the presence of appropriate verbal instructions may have been followed in the past by strengthening consequences (reinforcements). (This matter will be discussed in Chapters 5 and 6.) Thus, telling subjects that "I will no longer present the air blast to your eyelid, only sound the buzzer" will bring an immediate reduction in the buzzer-elicited eye blink in some individuals, because for those individuals such instructions have been followed by strengthening consequences in the past.

ORGAN NEUROSES

There are occasions when respondents malfunction, producing what is often called *organ neuroses* or *psychosomatic disorders*. In such cases it can be established by careful medical examination that for a particular individual there may be powerful environmental stimuli, rather than anatomic or physiological factors, that affect a particular organ's function (the respondent). For example, an individual may show high blood pressure (essential hypertension) or a skin rash due to changes in the circulation of the blood in the skin (neurodermatitis) because of environmental stimuli. Such stimulation may involve events preceding or following the respondent behavior. Events preceding the behavior would be eliciting stimuli; those following it, as we shall see in Chapter 3, are called consequences. In any case, recent research work, to be described later, reveals that such disorders can also be overcome by the manipulation of environmental stimuli.

EMOTIONAL BEHAVIOR

In the literature of psychology workers have used terms such as *emotional behavior* and *affective behavior* to describe what we have called patterns of respondent behavior. Although so-called emotional or affective behaviors (for example, distress, excitement, fear, and rage) often involve more than the mere occurrence of reflexes (for example, changes in speech patterns and flight movements), the characterization of emotional behavior as essentially reflexive, or respondent, behavior has historical origins. A more modern view regards emotional behavior as concurrent respondent *and* operant behaviors that occur in the presence of provocative or emotion-producing stimuli.

In this chapter the emphasis has been placed on the importance of stimuli occurring before the response. However, responses are also affected by the stimulus events following them, a matter to be discussed in more detail later.

STUDY QUESTIONS

1. Which anatomic and physiological response systems (effectors) are involved in respondent behavior? What are the functions of these systems?
2. Define and give an example of each of the following:
   a. CS.   c. r.
   b. US.
3. Identify the following as either a CS, a US, or an r:
   a. Shock.   d. A nipple in the mouth.
   b. Galvanic skin response.   e. A slap.
   c. Tone.   f. The word *bad*.

4. What is the essential procedure in respondent conditioning?
5. In what ways do the CS and US differ
   a. prior to conditioning?   b. following conditioning?
6. In what ways do the Ur and Cr differ?
7. Basically, which changes in respondent conditioning, the stimulus or the response?
8. When is respondent conditioning likely to occur in one trial?
9. What two major factors determine the strength of a response?
10. Describe three response dimensions that can be used as measures of reflex or response strength.
11. What defines a positive or negative CEr?
12. Describe the activation syndrome.
13. How can you determine whether a US is positive or negative?
14. What is pseudoconditioning? How does it create a problem in verifying that respondent conditioning has taken place?
15. What is the procedure for respondent extinction? What is the effect of respondent extinction on the reflex?
16. What is spontaneous recovery? Give an account of its occurrence.
17. Give some examples of commonly used conditioned stimuli. Commonly used unconditioned stimuli.
18. Describe how a word can become an elicitor of respondent behavior.
19. What is language conditioning? What forms may it take?
20. Discuss the relationship between language conditioning and prejudice.
21. Describe a program of language conditioning aimed at overcoming prejudice against blacks.
22. Describe the procedure known as respondent discrimination.
23. Describe the procedure known as stimulus generalization.
24. Cite two important variables affecting stimulus generalization.
25. In terms of respondent conditioning principles, describe how a child might acquire a phobia.
26. Specify and describe in detail two respondent conditioning procedures that would be suitable for the elimination of a negative CEr.
27. What is the inherent danger in a therapy program designed to eliminate a negative CEr in which the patient is immediately confronted with the CS? How can this danger be avoided?
28. What two procedures are involved in counter-conditioning?
29. What is the goal of counter-conditioning?
30. In what ways can verbal instructions modify the strength of a reflex?
31. Cite two limitations to the effectiveness of verbal instructions as a method for the modification of a reflex, and suggest a reason for these limitations.

REFERENCES

Anrep, G. V. Pitch discrimination in the dog. *Journal of Physiology*, 1920, **53**, 365–385.

Grings, W. W. Verbal-perceptual factors in the conditioning of autonomous responses. In W. F. Prokasy (Ed.), *Classical conditioning.* New York: Appleton-Century-Crofts, 1965.

Holland, J. G., and Skinner, B. F. *The analysis of behavior.* New York: McGraw-Hill, 1961.

Kaplan, M. *Essential works of Pavlov.* New York: Bantam Books, 1966.

Kimble, G. A. *Hilgard and Marquis' conditioning and learning.* (2nd ed.) New York: Appleton-Century-Crofts, 1961.

Lipsitt, L. P., and Kaye, H. Conditioned sucking in the human newborn. *Psychonomic Science,* 1964, **1**, 29–30.

Mowrer, O. H. *Learning theory and symbolic processes.* New York: Wiley, 1960.

Pavlov, I. P. *Conditioned reflexes.* Translated by G. V. Anrep. New York: International Universities Press, 1928.

Pavlov, I. P. *Lectures on conditioned reflexes.* Vol. 1. Translated and edited by W. H. Gantt and G. Volbarth. New York: International Publishers, 1928.

Staats, A. W., and Staats, C. K. *Complex human behavior.* New York: Holt, Rinehart and Winston, 1964.

Watson, J. B., and Rayner, R. Conditioned emotional reactions. *Journal of Experimental Psychology,* 1920, **3**, 1–14.

CHAPTER 3

OPERANT BEHAVIOR

Operant behavior has its basis in the skeletal muscles and the mechanisms of speech, which in turn produce movement and vocal responses. Responses of the skeletal system are called *motor operants*, and responses of the vocal system are called *vocal operants*.

AN EXAMPLE OF OPERANT BEHAVIOR

Consider the situation in which a food-deprived rat has been trained to "work for a living" inside a Skinner box. The rat's work consists of pressing a lever during a green-light-on condition, and this action activates a food-delivery system. The rat's living consists of food pellets, which are delivered only when the food-delivery system is activated. The box has been arranged so that the food pellet mechanism works only when the green light inside the box is turned on. Thus lever presses during the green-light-on condition will produce food pellets, but lever presses during the green-light-off condition will not. Our rat will be observed to move around inside the box, sniffing, preening itself, standing on its hind legs, and from time to time, approaching the lever and pressing it. If we watch him long enough, we will observe that the lever-approach responses and lever-pressing responses are more likely to occur when the green light is on, and sniffing, preening, standing, and moving about are more apt to occur when the green light is off. However, all of the rat's actions are examples of *motor operant behavior*.

THE ESSENTIAL FEATURE OF OPERANT BEHAVIOR

If we were to study the rat long enough in many different situations, we would probably notice that his operant behavior acts, or operates, on his environment in such a way as to bring about certain environmental events. These events are known as *consequences*, and they have varied and widespread effects on his behavior. As we shall see, certain of these consequences will strengthen or make more frequent the behavior that preceded them, and others will weaken or make less frequent the behavior that preceded them.

Operant behavior involves an ongoing, transactional process between the organism and its environment. This can be illustrated as follows:

$$\text{Response} \longrightarrow \text{Consequences}$$

Relating this illustration to the behavior of the rat, we have the following:

$$S^D \longrightarrow R \longrightarrow \text{Consequences}$$
$$\text{(green light on)} \quad \text{(lever press)} \quad \text{(food pellet)}$$

When the green light is on (S^D) and the rat presses the lever with sufficient force (R), a consequence follows, consisting of the delivery of a food pellet.

The consequence affecting the rat's lever-pressing behavior is the presentation of a food pellet—a *stimulus event*. But, as we shall see, certain classes of the rat's behavior, as *response events*, may also be consequences affecting the rat's lever pressing.

STIMULUS EVENTS THAT FUNCTION AS CONSEQUENCES

There are several major classes of stimulus events that function as consequences. All of these events are defined by their effect on the behavior preceding them. The first major class includes *positive reinforcing stimuli*. Some frequently observed types are:

1. *Unconditioned positive reinforcing stimuli*. These are stimuli, such as food and water, that function to strengthen the behavior that precedes them without special training.

2. *Conditioned positive reinforcing stimuli*. These are stimuli that have

been paired with unconditioned positive reinforcing stimuli.[1] Examples include the click of a food pellet magazine that precedes the presentation of the unconditioned reinforcing stimulus (the food pellet), and the word *good* presented along with an unconditioned positive reinforcing stimulus such as candy.

3. *Generalized positive reinforcing stimuli.* These include various types of stimuli that acquire their positive reinforcing function by being paired with many different types of reinforcers appropriate to many different conditions of deprivation. A mother's smile, for example, may be paired with the presentation of food, water, or tactile stimulation, and would therefore become a generalized positive reinforcing stimulus. Words of praise and such tactile affectional responses as hugs and kisses are other examples of generalized positive reinforcers.

4. *Token reinforcing stimuli.* These are commonly used stimuli that can be exchanged for other types of reinforcers or for the termination of aversive stimuli. Some common examples are poker chips, money, grades, and a diploma. All of these stimuli acquire their reinforcing properties through being paired with other reinforcers. The development of behavior in a "token culture" typically requires that the individual first be trained to work with unconditioned reinforcers, then with conditioned reinforcers—especially generalized positive reinforcers—and finally, with token reinforcers.

5. *Stimulus change.* There is evidence that stimuli that differ in some way from ongoing stimuli may function as positive reinforcers. For example, Lockard (1963) reports that rats will press a lever to turn on a light in a darkened box.

6. *Novel stimuli.* Many novel stimuli with which the organism has had little or no contact may possess reinforcing properties. For example, Lindsley (1962) found that psychotic patients would pull a lever for the opportunity to observe a hungry kitten lap milk from a dish or to see slides of nude human figures. Then, too, many novel edibles (foods, candies, and drinks) are reinforcers, perhaps because they possess stimulus properties that are similar to other reinforcers with which one is already familiar or because they are paired with other reinforcers and thus have become conditioned reinforcers.

A second major class of stimulus events is generally referred to as *negative reinforcing stimuli.* These are stimulus events whose *termination* or *removal* *strengthens* the operant behavior that immediately precedes them. The ter-

---

[1] The conditions that are necessary and sufficient for making a neutral stimulus into a conditioned positive reinforcing stimulus are a matter of dispute. Most psychologists agree that repeated pairing of the neutral stimulus with the unconditioned reinforcer is sufficient (Blough and Millward, 1965; Kelleher and Gollub, 1966). However, some maintain that it is essential for the neutral stimulus to become a discriminative stimulus (S^D) first (Keller and Schoenfeld, 1950; Bijou and Baer, 1966; Lovaas, Freitag, Kinder, Rubenstein, Schaeffer, and Simmons, 1966). This question will be discussed in detail later.

mination of sustained shocking or slapping will strengthen the behavior preceding their termination, and these stimuli are examples of unconditioned negative reinforcing stimuli. Similarly, the termination of sustained yelling will strengthen the behavior preceding its termination, and this stimulus is an example of a conditioned negative reinforcer. A child, for example, can terminate his parents' yelling at him by making responses that differ from the behavior occurring during the yelling, thus making the behavior that terminates the yelling more probable.

A third major class of stimulus events that function as consequences is known as *aversive stimuli*. These are stimulus events whose *presentation weakens* or *makes less frequent* the operant behavior that preceded their presentation. Some frequently observed aversive stimuli are:

1. *Unconditioned aversive stimuli.* These are stimuli that weaken or make less frequent the behavior that preceded them, without any special training. Common examples are a slap, a loud noise, and a shock.

2. *Conditioned aversive stimuli.* These are stimuli that weaken or make the behavior preceding them less frequent as a result of having been repeatedly paired with unconditioned aversive stimuli. Examples include a buzzer or light that goes on before or during shock and a parent's scolding or yelling at a child before or while spanking him.

To avoid confusion later on, it is worthwhile to mention that, depending on the conditions of presentation, the same stimulus event can either weaken behavior (as in a punishment operation) or strengthen behavior (as in a reinforcement operation). For example, the immediate presentation of an electric shock after some response has a weakening effect on that response and is, therefore, an aversive stimulus that is being used in a punishment operation. On the other hand, if the electric shock is removed immediately after some response, the shock termination has a strengthening effect on that response and is, therefore, a negative reinforcer being used in a reinforcement operation. The same is true of food pellets, which are ordinarily regarded as positive reinforcers. For example, if the food pellet is removed immediately after some response, it will have a weakening effect on that response because it is being used in a punishment operation. On the other hand, the presentation of the food pellet immediately after some response has a strengthening effect on that response (an effect that is consistent with the definition of a food pellet as a positive reinforcer). In this case, however, the food pellet as a positive reinforcer is being used in a reinforcement operation.

RESPONSE EVENTS THAT FUNCTION AS CONSEQUENCES

So far the discussion has stressed the importance of stimuli that follow operant behavior and that function as consequences, either strengthening or weakening the behavior. David Premack and his colleagues (1959, 1965), however, found that under certain conditions an organism's own behavior may function as a consequence.

First, they observed that female rats spent a great deal more time running in an activity wheel than drinking water from a tube when given an equal opportunity to do both. Of this pair of behaviors, then, the running was the more probable behavior, and the drinking was the less probable behavior.

Next, they introduced a brake on the activity wheel. The brake was released only after the rat had licked the drinking tube a specified number of times. In other words, the situation was such that the rat had to engage in the low-probability behavior (LPB) of drinking before she could engage in the high-probability behavior (HPB) of running. Although the specified number of licks required to release the brake was varied, the rats were required and did make as many as three hundred licking responses in order to release the brake. This represented increases over initial licking frequencies of from 1.5 to 6 times. Running, then, as a high-probability behavior served to strengthen drinking, a low-probability behavior. This observation has become known as the *Premack principle* and can be stated more formally as follows: If one of an organism's behaviors is less probable than another behavior, the less probable behavior can be strengthened (or made more probable) by making the occurrence of the more probable behavior contingent on it.

The Premack principle can also be used to weaken or make less frequent some behavior. One need only reverse the order of events, so that the high-probability behavior is followed by the low-probability behavior. In this case the low-probability behavior functions like an aversive stimulus, suppressing the behavior that preceded it.

OPERANT CONDITIONING

Table 3-1 gives the different types of events that function as consequences, their behavioral effects, and the notation that will be used in the analysis of operant behavior and the discussions to follow. As we shall see, behavior can be changed or modified significantly when it is followed by the types of events shown in Table 3-1 in an experimental operation known as *operant conditioning*. However, finding stimulus and response events that function as consequences is one of the major problems in operant conditioning. Although careful observation of an organism may reveal stimulus events potentially capable of functioning as consequences for that organism, an empirical test is always required, since an event is defined as a consequence because of its effect on the behavior preceding it. It is the outcome of this empirical test that determines whether or not a stimulus event that has been chosen as a consequence does in fact function as one, either strengthening or weakening

Table 3-1 Events that Function as Consequences, Their Behavioral Effects, and the Notation Used in the Analysis of Operant Behavior.

EVENTS THAT FUNCTION AS CONSEQUENCES	BEHAVIORAL EFFECTS	NOTATION
Unconditioned positive reinforcer	Strengthens (makes more frequent or probable) the behavior that precedes it.	SR+
Conditioned positive reinforcer		Sr+
Generalized positive reinforcer		Generalized Sr+
Token reinforcer		Token Sr+
Stimulus change		SC
Novel stimuli		NS
Unconditioned negative reinforcer		Terminate SR−
Conditioned negative reinforcer		Terminate Sr−
High-probability behavior		HPB
Unconditioned aversive stimulus	Weakens (makes less frequent or probable) the behavior that precedes it.	SR−
Conditioned aversive stimulus		Sr−
Low-probability behavior		LPB

the behavior preceding it. Similarly, although careful observation will reveal an organism's response events (high- and low-probability behaviors), the effects of these response events have to be defined as consequences that either strengthen or weaken the behavior preceding them. The procedure for conducting this test will be elaborated in Chapter 4. Meanwhile, in the discussions to follow, the more generalized term *consequation* will be used to refer to the consequences (stimulus or response events) that the trainer arranges in specific applications of operant conditioning as a means of modifying a trainee's behavior.

CONDITIONS RELEVANT TO THE PRESENTATION OF CONSEQUENCES

Deprivation

The term *deprivation* refers to the operations performed by a trainer in which there is a reduction in the availability of a reinforcer. The effect of this reduction is to increase the effectiveness of the reinforcer, the systematic presentation of which may be used by the trainer later on, to modify the organism's behavior. The use of food as a reinforcing event is more effective when the organism is deprived of food, and the use of water as a reinforcing event is more effective when the organism is deprived of water.

The food-deprivation operation can be measured in two ways: first, by withholding the reinforcing stimulus (food) from the organism for a fixed interval of time, such as 24 hours, or second, by reducing the organism's body weight by a fixed amount from its normal ad-lib or free-feeding weight. In rats or pigeons, for example, reduction to 80 percent of free-feeding weight is sufficient to make food pellets or grain effective reinforcers for lever pressing or pecking.

Ferster and Skinner (1957), for example, studied the effects on pecking of several different levels of food deprivation defined as a percentage of the subject's "inactive weight" (the ad-lib feeding weight at which little or no pecking occurs), and they found that the effect of food as a reinforcer is the greatest under conditions of maximum deprivation and the least under conditions of minimum deprivation. Although seldom done in psychological experiments, depriving human subjects of food or water has a comparable effect—it makes food or water presentations into powerful reinforcers.

Similarly, prolonged exposure to *sensory deprivation* (a monotonous, routinized sensory environment) will make various types of visual, tactual, auditory, olfactory, and somesthetic stimuli into effective reinforcers, and *social deprivation* has comparable effects on social reinforcers (Gerwitz and Baer, 1958). Figure 3-1 shows the effects of either a brief period of social deprivation (20 minutes of isolated play), nondeprivation (nonisolation), or satia-

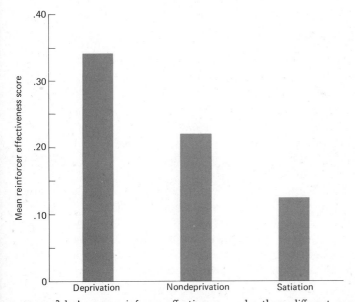

FIGURE 3-1 Average reinforcer effectiveness under three different conditions: deprivation, nondeprivation, and satiation. From J. Gerwitz and D. M. Baer, Deprivation and satiation of social reinforcers as drive conditions. *Journal of Abnormal and Social Psychology*, 1958, **57**, 165–172. Copyright © 1958 by the American Psychological Association and reproduced by permission.

tion (20 minutes of social interaction involving frequent presentations of praise and admiration) on a subsequent test of reinforcer effectiveness. Presentations of praise and approval to the young children who were subjects were the most powerful following the period of deprivation and the least powerful following the period of satiation.

For many effective reinforcers there are no obvious deprivation conditions. Examples of such reinforcers include candy, novel foods, toys, trinkets, and a host of conditioned and token reinforcers. All of these stimuli have been reported to function as reinforcers in the absence of a systematically arranged deprivation condition.

Behavior can also be maintained in the absence of any deprivation condition when it terminates a situation containing aversive properties. Behavior can also be maintained in the absence of any deprivation condition when it produces stimuli that are discriminative for reinforcement. Such was the case reported by Ferster and Skinner (1957), who found that pigeons will continue to peck at a disk even without food deprivation (when their weight is 100 percent of their free-feeding weight), provided they have had sufficient training. Some stimuli may acquire their reinforcing properties because of their contiguous relationship to other reinforcers. These, too, can be sufficiently powerful to maintain operant behavior in the absence of any deprivation condition, a matter to be discussed later.

Amount of Reinforcement

If, on a given reinforcement occasion, an operant is followed by a greater amount of the reinforcing stimulus than previously, it will tend to have a shorter response latency and will show less variability. On the other hand, if on a given reinforcement occasion an operant is followed by a decrease in the amount of the reinforcing stimulus, there is an increase in both response latency and response variability. Figure 3-2, from a study by Stebbins (1962), shows the relative frequency of different reaction times (the time it takes for a rat to push a lever when a light goes on) under three different amounts of liquid reinforcement (20, 5, and 0 percent sucrose solutions). Notice that response latency is the shortest, and the variability the least, for all four subjects when they are presented with the 20 percent sucrose solution. When the subjects are reinforced by smaller amounts of sucrose solution (5 percent and 0 percent solutions), both response latency and variability show increases in proportion to decreases in the amount of reinforcement.

Response-Contingent Consequences

When the reinforcing or aversive stimuli occur immediately after the emission of some operant and at no other time, the consequences are defined as

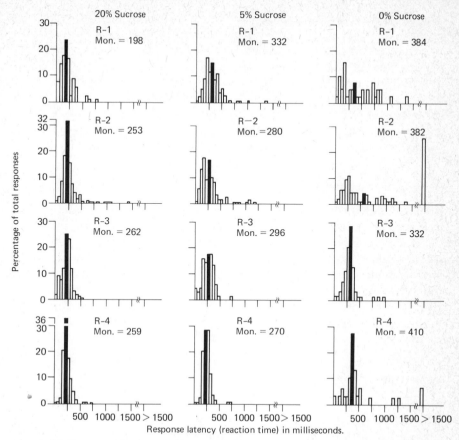

FIGURE 3-2 Response latency (reaction time) in milliseconds and response variability under three different amounts of reinforcement (20, 5, and 0 percent sucrose solution) for four subjects (R1, R2, R3, and R4). The value following the expression MDN. is the median reaction time and the interval containing that interval is shaded. From W. C. Stebbins, Response latency as a function of the amount of reinforcement, *Journal of the Experimental Analysis of Behavior*, 1962, **5**, 305–307. Copyright © 1962 by the Society for the Experimental Analysis of Behavior, Inc., and reproduced with permission.

response-contingent. For example, the rat described earlier can obtain a food pellet only after lever pressing, and not at any other time. Thus his obtaining the food pellet is response-contingent. On other occasions, however, and especially in the natural environment, reinforcing or aversive stimuli may occur or be presented irrespective of the operant behavior preceding them, in which case the consequences may be said to be *non-response-contingent.* A rat may be given food pellets even though he is in a resting position, or a mother may spontaneously reach out and hug her child. If we consider that the presentation of such consequences may strengthen or weaken the behavior immediately preceding their presentation, it becomes apparent that response-contingent consequences are more apt to strengthen or weaken behavior that is *relevant* to the goals of training, and non-response-contingent consequences are likely to strengthen or weaken behavior that, from the trainer's point of view, is *irrelevant behavior*. The mother who gives her child almost everything he wants, regardless of what the child does (spoils the child), is using non-response-contingent consequences. In so doing the mother not only inadvertently strengthens irrelevant or even inappropriate behavior, but she may, in addition, reduce the baby's deprivation level to a point where she may be forced to search for other strengthening consequences.

Delay in Consequences

Consequences occurring some time after an operant has been emitted may have the same effect as non-response-contingent consequences and may, from the trainer's point of view, inappropriately affect some irrelevant operant. The parent who spanks the child some time after his misdeed is, in effect, suppressing some later occurring operant (the behavior immediately preceding the spanking) rather than the actual misdeed. Following appropriate and intensive training, however, organisms will tend to respond in a manner consistent with the goals of training, despite long delays in the presentation of the consequences.

Verbal Instructions

When a trainer presents *verbal instructions* to a trainee, these instructions typically possess complex stimulus properties (either discriminative or reinforcing) that can be used to reduce, or attenuate, the effect of delays in the presentation of consequences. For example, a boss may say to his employee, "Finish the job and I'll pay you." If the employer does in fact pay the employee when the job is completed, the employer's verbal instructions serve to maintain job-appropriate operants and to reduce the effect of delayed reinforcement. Other, nonverbal stimuli, such as lights and sounds, may also possess comparable stimulus functions that attenuate delays in reinforcement, if only because of their temporal relationship to other reinforcers through chaining—a complex process to be discussed later.

SCHEDULES OF REINFORCEMENT

The details of the relationship between behavior and its consequences, the *schedule of reinforcement*, is of primary importance in determining the effects of those consequences on operant behavior. Schedules of reinforcement can be separated into two basic groups: those that are nonintermittent and those that are intermittent.

Nonintermittent Schedules of Reinforcement

There are two major types of *nonintermittent schedules*. The first is the *continuous-reinforcement schedule* (CRF), in which the emission of each appropriate response is followed by the reinforcing stimulus (consequence). The second type of nonintermittent schedule is the *extinction schedule* (EXT), in which none of the emitted responses is followed by the reinforcing stimulus (consequence). It is easiest to arrange nonintermittent schedules in laboratory situations, where the investigator has complete surveillance of the operant and can provide for the immediate delivery or nondelivery of the reinforcing stimulus following every occurrence of the appropriate operant.

Intermittent Schedules of Reinforcement

There are a number of different types of *intermittent schedules*. What is common to all of them is that some responses are followed by the reinforcing stimulus and others are not. Intermittent schedules, by definition, contain a *component of reinforcement and a component of extinction*. Although both nonintermittent and intermittent schedules of reinforcement can be arranged and studied in the laboratory, intermittent schedules are the most commonly occurring schedules in the natural environment. Four major types of intermittent schedules are:

1. *Fixed-Ratio (FR) Schedules.* In FR schedules there is a systematic relationship between the number of times an appropriate operant is emitted and the number of times the reinforcing stimulus is presented. For example, FR 2 means that the second appropriate response is followed by the reinforcement, and FR 200 means that only the two-hundredth emitted appropriate response is followed by the reinforcement. On an FR 200 schedule, the first 199 appropriate responses are on extinction (nonreinforcement), and only the last appropriate response—the two-hundredth—is reinforced. FR schedules are similar to those pay schedules in industry known as piecework, in which the employee is paid a certain amount per unit of work, but usually does not receive payment until a certain number of units has been produced.

2. *Variable-Ratio (VR) Schedules.* In VR schedules a variable number of appropriate responses must be emitted prior to any given occasion of reinforcement. The value expressing the VR ratio between the number of appropriate responses emitted and the occasions of reinforcement is the *average of the total number of appropriate responses required for reinforcement for all occasions*. For example:

REINFORCEMENT OCCASION	TOTAL NUMBER OF RESPONSES REQUIRED FOR EACH OCCASION OF REINFORCEMENT
1	3
2	5
3	4
4	4
5	3
6	5

$$\text{VR} \begin{pmatrix} \text{Average number of} \\ \text{responses required} \\ \text{for each occasion} \\ \text{of reinforcement} \end{pmatrix} = \frac{\begin{array}{c} \text{Total number of responses} \\ \text{required for all occasions} \\ \text{of reinforcement} \end{array}}{\begin{array}{c} \text{Total number of reinforce-} \\ \text{ment occasions} \end{array}}$$

$$\text{VR} = \frac{24}{6}$$
$$\text{VR} = 4$$

Notation: VR 4

The ratios for each reinforcement occasion were arbitrarily chosen by the investigator from an arithmetic progression (3, 4, 5), although geometric progressions are also used. The ratios are usually presented in random order. In the natural environment pay schedules in which different amounts of work are produced before payment is received would be analogous to laboratory versions of the VR schedule. For example, on some occasions a bill collector may make two or three collections in a row, and on other occasions collections may be few and far between.

3. *Fixed-Interval (FI) Schedules.* In FI schedules the *first appropriate response occurring after a fixed time interval has ended is reinforced.* Responses occurring prior to the end of this time interval are on extinction. (They are not reinforced.) The interval is usually specified in seconds or minutes. In an FI 60-second schedule the first appropriate response emitted following a 60-second interval is reinforced. Similarly, in an FI 5-minute schedule the first appropriate response following a 5-minute interval is reinforced. Although at first glance hourly, weekly, and monthly pay schedules would seem to be fixed-interval schedules, they are not. Unlike a fixed-interval schedule, an hourly, weekly, or monthly pay schedule provides reinforcers for work occurring *during* the interval rather than for work occurring after the termination of the interval.

4. *Variable-Interval (VI) Schedules.* In a VI schedule variable intervals of time elapse before each occasion of reinforcement. As in the FI schedule, appropriate responses emitted prior to the end of the interval are not reinforced. Only the first appropriate response emitted after the end of the inter-

val is reinforced. The VI is computed as an average interval in a manner similar to that described for VR schedules. One need merely substitute seconds or minutes for the number of responses required for the reinforcement occasion. Let us refer to the discussion of VR schedules and substitute the appropriate figures: On the first reinforcement occasion, the first appropriate operant emitted following a 3-minute interval is reinforced, then a 5-minute interval, and so on. The average interval would then be 4 minutes, and would be expressed as VI 4 minutes. As in the VR schedules, the intervals are presented in random order. The types of payoff schedules encountered by fishermen and hitchhikers are analogous to the laboratory version of the VI schedule.

When an investigator programs only one of the preceding schedules of reinforcement for a single response class, he is using a *single schedule*. For example, a lever-pressing response might be followed by the presentation of a food pellet on a CRF, FR, VR, FI, or VI schedule. A schedule of reinforcement, then, specifies the relationship between an operant and its consequences—the single schedule being the simplest case.

Differential Reinforcement Schedule

It is also possible to specify still other relationships between an operant and its consequences by introducing the variable of time in what are called *differential reinforcement schedules*. The most common differential reinforcement schedules are:

1. *Differential Reinforcement of Low Rates (drl)*. Drl schedules specify that a response is not to be reinforced unless a minimum time interval has elapsed since the preceding response. A drl 5-second contingency would, for example, require that the second response be reinforced only if 5 seconds had elapsed since the preceding response. Responses occurring during the drl interval would be extinguished and would start the interval over again. This contingency is often combined with other schedules. For example, in a CRF-drl 3-second schedule, every response is reinforced only if it occurs at least 3 seconds after the preceding response.

2. *Differential Reinforcement of High Rates (drh)*. In drh schedules a response is reinforced only if a certain number of responses has occurred during the interval preceding that response. For example, a reinforcer may follow a response only if it has been preceded by at least four responses in the preceding second, or a response may be reinforced only if five responses have occurred and the inter-response times (IRT's) between the preceding four responses did not exceed 25 seconds. As with the drl schedule, drh schedules are often combined with other schedules.

3. *Differential Reinforcement of Other Behaviors (dro)*. In dro schedules reinforcements are presented in the absence of some response within a given

time interval. Thus, CRF dro would simply mean that the reinforcer would be presented immediately following each interval specified by the investigator in which the response did not occur. If the response did occur during the interval, it would not be reinforced during that interval.

It is also possible to arrange two or more single schedules in various ways to produce what are known as *compound schedules*. In such schedules, each component operates independently, and the components can be arranged to occur simultaneously or successively, with or without stimuli that mark the onset of the component schedule. Among the more common compound schedules are the following:

1. *Multiple (MULT) Schedules.* These consist of two or more component schedules that are presented alternately or in random sequence. The onset of each component schedule is preceded by a (correlated) stimulus, and each schedule is followed by reinforcement. Thus in a MULT FR 10 FI 10-minute schedule, a red light may precede the FR 10 component, and a green light may precede the FI 10-minute component. Reinforcement would follow the tenth response made in the presence of the red light and the first response made after the green light had been present for 10 minutes.

2. *Mixed (MIX) Schedules.* These schedules are essentially the same as multiple schedules except that all components of the schedule are presented without the presence of correlated stimuli. In a MIX FR 10 FI 10-minute schedule, reinforcement would follow the tenth response on some occasions, and it would follow the first response made after a 10-minute interval on other occasions.

3. *Chained (CHAIN) Schedules.* These schedules contain two or more components that are in a sequence. Each component has its own correlated stimulus, and only the last component of the schedule is followed by the reinforcing stimulus. A CHAIN FR 2 FI 5-minute schedule would require, for example, that following the presentation of the first correlated stimulus, a red light, two lever presses must be made (FR 2). The second lever press turns on the second correlated stimulus, a green light, and the first lever press made after the green light has been on for 5 minutes is then reinforced (FI 5-minute).

4. *Tandem (TAND) Schedules.* These schedules are essentially the same as the chained schedules except that all components of the schedule are presented without the presence of correlated stimuli. Thus, in a TAND FR 5 FI 15-second schedule, the fifth response (FR 5) starts the clock for the fixed interval of 15 seconds. The first response after this interval has elapsed is then reinforced.

5. *Concurrent (CONC) Schedules.* Although the definition of the concurrent schedule varies, in the present discussion a concurrent schedule consists of two or more schedules operating at the same time, each programmed for a

different response class. For example, in a CONC FR 5 FI 60-second schedule, the first operant is reinforced after the fifth response, and the second response is reinforced only when it is emitted after a 60-second interval. In many respects concurrent schedules are the most like those encountered in everyday living situations. For example, a mother may reinforce her child's vocalizations having affectional content (for example, "I love you, Mommy!") on a VR schedule, and at the same time she may punish the child's vocalizations having an unpleasant content (for example, "I hate you, Mommy!") on a CRF schedule. Since both consequences are in effect at all times and are programmed for two different response classes they are concurrent schedules.

All of these schedules, either singly or in combination, generate characteristic performances, some of which will be described in Chapter 4. Furthermore, there are sequential effects between schedules. For example, if a schedule of reinforcement is presented in which reinforcement occurs infrequently, a characteristic low rate of responding will occur. If, following the organism's exposure to this schedule, a second schedule is presented that provides for a higher rate of reinforcement, changes in the organism's behavior will be observed. Under this second schedule the rate will be higher and the latency of responding shorter than they would be without the preceding schedule of reinforcement in which a low rate of reinforcement was programmed. Such an increase in rate and decrease in response latency attributable to transition from a lean to a rich schedule of reinforcement is called *behavioral contrast.*

Even though the consequence most commonly cited in the foregoing discussion was positive reinforcement, other consequences can be used just as easily. For example, an aversive stimulus could be presented on a VR or FI schedule or as a component of a compound schedule.

THE RESPONSE CLASS

In operant conditioning the investigator generally selects an easily observable response that is (1) a member of a class of responses and (2) followed by certain consequences. This class of responses, abbreviated R, will possess several different dimensions, such as form or topography, frequency, rate, duration, and magnitude or force, any one of which can be studied.

Suppose, for example, that the investigator chooses to study a button-pushing response and selects as his basic datum the frequency with which the response occurs. Aside from his major concern with the response class dimension of frequency, the investigator also specifies the characteristics of some of the other response class dimensions, such as topography, duration, and magnitude. Furthermore, while reinforcements are made contingent on a certain frequency of button-pushing responses, they may also be contingent on a certain topography (for example, pushing the button with the tip of the forefinger rather than with the knuckle).[2] The investigator may also specify that the button-pushing response have a certain duration and be of a certain magnitude.

As the study progresses, careful and long-term observation will reveal that the response class dimension of frequency shows the least amount of change over time, and the response class dimensions of topography, magnitude, and duration show considerable change over time. Of course, the button design will set the limits on the variability of these dimensions, and unless they are explicitly controlled these latter dimensions will be more variable than the dimension under study, namely frequency.

It is possible for several different responses, occuring at the same time and followed by the same consequences, to become members of the same response class. For example, a response class may consist of the vocal and motor operants involved in standing erect and talking at a lectern. Although these behaviors involve different response systems (speech and motor coordination mechanisms), each having different response topographies, they are members of the same response class because they *occur at the same time and are followed by the same consequences*. In fact, a response class may contain multiple component responses consisting of many vocal and motor operants.

SUMMARY

Three major elements in operant behavior have been discussed: (1) the various types of consequences that follow operant behavior and affect that behavior, as well as other related factors such as deprivation, delays in consequences, and the presence of stimuli correlated with those consequences, (2) the specific relationship between behavior and its consequences, generally referred to as the schedule of reinforcement, and (3) the (operant) response class, which is followed and affected by the consequences. Together these three elements constitute the *reinforcement contingency*. The reinforcement contingency is a precise description of the response class, the temporal relationship between the response class and the reinforcing stimulus, and the nature of the reinforcing stimulus. More simply stated, the reinforcement contingency can be said to be *the conditions under which the reinforcing stimulus is available*.

---

[2] Instead of using operant conditioning procedures to obtain this response topography, the investigator might make a simple change in the physical environment. For example, he might place a vertical tube around the button, so that contact with the button would not be possible unless the subject first placed his finger in the tube.

STUDY QUESTIONS

1. What anatomic structures and systems are involved in operant behavior? What two major types of responses characterize these systems?
2. Identify the response system involved in the following:
   a. Pushing a button.   b. Saying "Hi."
3. What is the essential relationship between an organism's operant behavior and its environment?
4. What are the two major *effects* of consequences that follow operant behavior?
5. What are the two major *types* of consequences following operant behavior?
6. What is the effect of a positive reinforcing stimulus?
7. Define and give examples of the following:
   a. Unconditioned positive reinforcer.
   b. Conditioned positive reinforcer.
   c. Generalized positive reinforcer.
   d. Token reinforcer.
   e. Negative reinforcer.
   f. Unconditioned aversive stimulus.
   g. Conditioned aversive stimulus.
8. What is the Premack principle?
9. Identify the following as either a stimulus event or a response event and indicate its effect as a consequence:
   a. Generalized positive reinforcer.
   b. Novel stimuli.
   c. A shock.
   d. Conditioned aversive stimulus.
   e. Stimulus change.
   f. Low probability behavior (drinking).
10. How can one best determine whether or not an event functions as a consequence for a particular organism?
11. What is the significance of deprivation for the presentation of consequences?
12. Give an operational definition of deprivation, and cite a reinforcer appropriate to your definition.
13. Distinguish between response-contingent and non-response-contingent consequences.
14. What are the possible behavioral effects of non-response-contingent consequences?
15. What is meant by *satiation?* What is its probable effect on the training situation?
16. Delays in the presentation of consequences can have what effects on behavior?
17. In what way can non-response-contingent consequences and delayed consequences have comparable effects on behavior?
18. Besides increasing the frequency of the behavior preceding its presentation, what is the effect of the amount of reinforcement?
19. What two stimulus functions may verbal instructions possess?
20. Give an example of how verbal instructions can be used to attenuate the effects of delays in reinforcement.

21. Define and give examples of the following schedules:

a. CRF	f. VI	k. MIX
b. EXT	g. drl	l. CHAIN
c. FR	h. drh	m. TAND
d. VR	i. dro	n. CONC
e. FI	j. MULT	

22. What is the essential difference between nonintermittent and intermittent schedules of reinforcement?
23. Which schedule of reinforcement (see Study Question 21) would you expect to be most prevalent in real-life situations?
24. How many response classes are involved in a single schedule? In a compound schedule? In concurrent schedules?
25. What is behavioral contrast? Under what conditions does it occur?
26. Cite five response class dimensions frequently studied by investigators.
27. Which response class dimension(s) will normally show the least variability?
28. Give two reasons why the term *response class* seems to be more descriptive of the behavior followed by consequences than the term *response*.
29. Under what conditions can behaviors involving different response systems become members of the same response class?
30. What is meant by the term *reinforcement contingency*?

REFERENCES

Bijou, S. W., and Baer, D. M. Operant methods in child behavior and development. In W. K. Honig (Ed.), *Operant behavior: Areas of research and application.* New York: Appleton-Century-Crofts, 1966.

Blough, D. S., and Millward, R. B. Learning: Operant conditioning and verbal learning. In P. R. Farnsworth, O. McNemar, and Q. McNemar (Eds.), *Annual review of psychology.* Palo Alto, Calif.: Annual Reviews, 1965.

Catania, A. C. *Contemporary research in operant behavior.* Glenview, Ill.: Scott, Foresman, 1968.

Ferster, C. F., and Skinner, B. F. *Schedules of reinforcement.* New York: Appleton-Century-Crofts, 1957.

Gewirtz, J., and Baer, D. M. Deprivation and satiation of social reinforcers as drive conditions. *Journal of Abnormal and Social Psychology* 1958, 57, 165–172.

Holland, J. G., and Skinner, B. F. *The analysis of behavior.* New York: McGraw-Hill, 1961.

Kelleher, R. T., and Gollub, R. T. A review of positive conditioned reinforcement. *Journal of the Experimental Analysis of Behavior,* 1962, 5, 543–597.

Keller, F. S., and Schoenfeld, W. N. *Principles of psychology.* New York: Appleton-Century-Crofts, 1950.

Lindsley, O. R. Operant conditioning methods in diagnosis. In the *First Symposium on Psychosomatic Medicine.* Philadelphia: Lea and Febiger, 1962.

Lockard, R. B. Some effects of light upon the behavior of rodents. *Psychological Bulletin,* 1963, 60, 509–529.

Lovaas, O. I., Freitag, G., Kinder M. I., Rubenstein, B. D., Schaeffer, B., and Simmons, J. Q. Establishment of social reinforcers in two schizophrenic children on the basis of food. *Journal of Experimental Child Psychology*, 1966, 4, 109–125.

Premack, D. Toward empirical behavior laws: I. Positive reinforcement. *Psychological Record*, 1959, 66, 219–233.

Premack, D., Schaeffer, R. W., and Hundt, A. Reinforcement of drinking by running: Effect of fixed rates and reinforcement time. *Journal of the Experimental Analysis of Behavior*, 1965, 7, 91–96.

Stebbins, W. C. Response latency as function of amount of reinforcement. *Journal of the Experimental Analysis of Behavior*, 1962, 5, 305–307.

CHAPTER 4

OPERANT CONDITIONING

The principles of operant conditioning can be used for either the acquisition, maintenance, or elimination of operant behavior. Whatever its aim, the successful application of operant conditioning presents two major problems. First and foremost is the necessity of precisely specifying the response class with which the trainer is concerned.[1] Second is the necessity of choosing a procedure that will have the desired effect on the response class in question.

As we have seen, one class of procedures is aimed at strengthening operant behavior. Application of these procedures requires that we distinguish be-

[1] The trainer may decide what response class to deal with, or he may be directed by an individual's caretaker or others in the community. An illustration of the former would be a golf "pro" who offers diagnostic services and training to students. An example of the latter would be a classroom teacher, who is guided by the course curriculum and curriculum specialists, members of the board of education, and ultimately the community. Other workers called upon to decide what response class should be dealt with are psychiatrists, psychologists, social workers, jurists, criminologists, speech therapists, and the like. Individuals having such influence in the development of behavior are called, collectively, the *verbal community*.

tween operant acquisition and operant maintenance. In the former, the operant is not normally a part of the organism's repertoire but, for reasons determined by the trainer, should be. In the latter, the operant is already a part of the organism's repertoire, but from the point of view of the trainer it occurs too infrequently. The other class of procedures is aimed at weakening or eliminating previously acquired operants. In this case, the response class occurs too frequently, from the trainer's point of view, and its frequency must be reduced.

Whether the trainer's goal is the acquisition, maintenance, or elimination of an operant, some concern must be given to the definition of the operant as a response class, the consequences following the emitted response class, and the frequency with which these consequences follow the operant (the schedule of reinforcement)—in short, to the reinforcement contingency.

THE RESPONSE CLASS—INITIAL CONSIDERATIONS

When the goal of operant conditioning is the acquisition of some response class, it is assumed that the probability of the organism's emitting the particular response class prior to the onset of conditioning is zero. Thus prolonged observation of the organism's behavior during a *base-line*, or *pretraining, period* will reveal that the relative frequency of the response class is also zero. Of course, in order to observe the presence or absence of a response class at any phase (either base-line or training), the trainer must have specifically defined the response class in question, as well as some measurable dimension(s) of it.

Suppose, for example, that the trainer is concerned with the acquisition of a verbal operant consisting of the vocalized response class "Ma." Suppose further that the measurable dimension that is of primary concern to the trainer is the frequency with which the child emits the vocalization "Ma." Nevertheless, at the beginning of training other dimensions of the final performance are also involved. Not only must the response class become more frequent, but it must also possess a certain magnitude ("Ma" should be emitted at sufficient volume to be heard by others), a certain duration (it should last long enough to be intelligible), and a certain form or topography (the qualitative aspects of the response class which make it intelligible). Consequently, the final performance of the operant must be defined or specified in a number of different ways. Furthermore, not only must the trainer have some idea of the response class dimensions, but during training he must continually compare the trainee's performances with the desired (terminal) performance requirements.

OPERANT ACQUISITION

A major decision in operant conditioning involves the choice of consequences used to strengthen operant behavior, as well as the frequency with which these consequences follow the operant. When acquisition of an operant is the goal of operant conditioning, consequences must be chosen from those types of stimulus events that strengthen the operant. The Premack principle, in which an operant is followed by a response event (high-probability behavior), can also be used, but stimulus events can often be presented with greater rapidity and convenience.

Stimulus events that strengthen operant behavior include unconditioned positive reinforcers (food and water), conditioned positive reinforcers (the click of a food pellet magazine), generalized positive reinforcers (affectional responses such as a hug), token reinforcers (money), negative reinforcers (sustained yelling), stimulus change, and novel stimuli. Not all of these are equally powerful in their effect on operant behavior, and so our choice will be determined, at least in part, by how rapidly we wish the operant conditioning to take place. Our decision will also be determined by (1) the ease with which we can arrange for deprivation, (2) the availability of the reinforcing stimulus, (3) the ease with which it can be presented, contingent on the organism's emitting the proper response, and (4) the sophistication of the subject. The operant behavior of completely naïve subjects will be insensitive to conditioned reinforcers, and unconditioned reinforcers should be used. In human subjects initial training may be aimed specifically at making their behavior sensitive to conditioned reinforcers, then generalized reinforcers, and finally, token reinforcers. (For a more detailed discussion of these procedures, see Chapter 6.)

In any case, a test will be required to determine whether or not the stimulus event being presented is actually a reinforcer. This test consists of observing the immediate effects of the reinforcing stimulus on the response class that precedes it. Although the reinforcer may affect several different dimensions of the response class, the dimension of frequency is often the easiest to observe initially. Contingent reinforcement should produce an observable increase in the frequency of the operant, as, for example, when the reinforcements are presented contingent on an approach response, a behavior that is already part of the subject's repertoire. If, indeed, the stimulus chosen as a reinforcer is functional and if indeed the approach response is already part of the subject's repertoire, then the subject will readily approach the trainer and even follow him around. Using an operant that is already part of the subject's repertoire to test the effectiveness of a reinforcer saves time and effort on the part of the trainer.

Since training is most rapid under a continuous reinforcement (CRF) schedule, let us assume, for the purposes of this discussion, that a CRF schedule is being used. (The effects of various schedules of reinforcement on operant behavior will be discussed in detail later.)

The acquisition of an operant requires that the trainer make use of two essential procedures—*differential reinforcement* and *successive approximation*. These two procedures result in a behavioral process known as *operant differentiation*. Since the probability of the subject's emitting the desired response class is initially very low, the trainer may begin by strengthening response classes that are only remotely similar to the form, or topography, to the operant in the final performance.

It was suggested earlier that we train a baby to say, "Ma." Such training would take advantage of the primitive utterances occurring around the fifth month (during babbling), at which time infants with normal hearing will make all of the rudimentary (vowel and consonant) speech sounds characteristic of Indo-European languages. It is from these primitive beginnings that the more complex performances arise. To begin our training program, we would strengthen these primitive vocalizations by following them with positive reinforcing stimuli, while at the same time not reinforcing (extinguishing) other, irrelevant vocalizations. The emitted response class that is followed by the reinforcing stimulus is known as the R^D. The emitted response class that is followed by nonreinforcement, or extinction, is known as the R^Δ. The procedure whereby the trainer simultaneously uses positive reinforcement to strengthen a given response class and extinction to weaken others is known as differential reinforcement.

The vocalization "Ma" is a combination of two rudimentary sounds. "MM" and "AH" (ä). Thus training starts with the sound "MM" as follows:

TRIAL

1		R^D (Baby says, "mm.") ————	Generalized Sr^+
2	,	R^Δ (Baby is silent.) ————	EXT
3		R^D (Baby says, "mm.") ————	Generalized Sr^+
4		R^Δ (Baby is silent.) ————	EXT

Thus the vocalization "mm" is the response class followed by reinforcement (the R^D), and silence is the response class followed by extinction (the R^Δ). The reinforcement makes the sound "mm" more frequent, and extinction makes the silence less frequent. This differential reinforcement procedure is, then, aimed at strengthening the response class consisting of the vocalization "mm" and, particularly, its dimension of frequency.[2]

[2] In actual practice the trainer would first make the utterance "mm" himself. Then he would wait for the child's response and reinforce it. This procedure would lead to the acquisition of the echoic response. (See Chapter 7.)

So far, then, the child's utterance has been made more frequent by means of differential reinforcement. Suppose though that the child's vocalization of "mm" is barely audible—it is of minimal magnitude or volume. Suppose further that it has been decided that the magnitude of the "mm" sound must be increased before it can be blended with the "ah" sound. To increase the volume, the trainer presents reinforcements only for increasingly louder vocalizations:

TRIAL

5	R^Δ (Baby says, "mm.")	——— EXT
6	R^D (Baby says, "MM.")	——— Generalized Sr^+
7	R^Δ (Baby says, "mm.")	——— EXT
8	R^D (Baby says, "MM.")	——— Generalized Sr^+

Notice that the former R^D, the vocalization "mm," has become an R^Δ, and the new R^D is the louder vocalization "MM." Although not shown here, changing the magnitude of the child's vocalization involves a progression of steps toward a final performance of a sufficiently audible "MM" sound. In each step of this series the R^D has to be a little bit louder than its predecessor. In this way, the magnitude of the child's vocalization is increased by selectively reinforcing only those responses that are more and more like the final performance. This procedure of successively reinforcing only those responses that are more and more like the final performance is called successive approximation or *shaping*.

Although shaping can be used to increase or decrease the response class dimension of magnitude, it is most often used to change the response class dimension of form, or topography. Thus to teach our child to say "AH" (ä), we may have to start by reinforcing the vocalization "aa" (a) and then, through shaping procedures, change the response topography of the utterance from "aa" (a) to "AH" (ä), as follows.

TRIAL

9	R^Δ (Baby says, "aa.")	——— EXT
10	R^D (Baby says, "AH.")	——— Generalized Sr^+
11	R^Δ (Baby says, "aa.")	——— EXT
12	R^Δ (Baby says, "aa.")	——— EXT
13	R^D (Baby says, "AH.")	——— Generalized Sr^+
14	R^D (Baby says, "AH.")	——— Generalized Sr^+

As before, this illustration telescopes the actual situation. It does not show the many steps in the transition from the initial R^D ("aa") to the final performance R^D ("AH").

Once the vocalization "AH" has been attained, the "MM" and "AH" sounds can be chained together to form the expression "MA." Reinforcements would be made available only on the occurrence of the two responses in that order. However, reinforcements would be given even when there is some delay between the two responses, that is, "MM . . . . AH." Gradually, however, that delay would be reduced to "MM . . . AH," then to "MM . . AH," then to "MM . AH," until the final performance—"MMAH" ("Ma")—is obtained. This can be done by giving reinforcement only for performances containing shorter and shorter intervals between the "MM" and the "AH."

To use differential reinforcement and successive approximation in speech training, the trainer must be particularly skilled in listening to the subject's utterances, since he must compare each utterance with past performances and decide whether it is better, the same, or worse than preceding performances, and then reinforce or extinguish it immediately after it occurs.[3]

Organisms can be trained in the same way to make precise locomotor responses, such as those required in small deflections of a lever. For example, Herrick (1964) arranged a situation such that at the beginning of training lever-press deflections of large magnitude were within the reinforcement zone (the R^D was lever-press deflections in positions 1–8). Then, more and more precise lever-press deflections were reinforced, and all others were extinguished (the R^Δ's were lever-press deflections in positions 2–8, then 2–7) until the final performance was obtained (the R^D was lever presses in position 5). The histograms (bar graphs) in Figure 4-1 show the differentiation of increasingly more precise lever-pressing response topographies (on the right) from increasingly more imprecise responses (on the left). Notice that as the R^D changes, there is a corresponding change in the percentage of responses to each lever until the greatest percentage of lever presses are made in position 5—the final performance.

A review of the conditions defining the R^D in both the speech-training and the lever-pressing examples reveals that the R^D changed from one *occasion* of training to the next. In each instance, a "better" performance was required for reinforcement (R^D), and "poorer" performances (R^Δ's) were extinguished. This change in operant behavior by selectively applying consequences is known as operant differentiation, and is the very basis of operant acquisition.

Two features of operant differentiation should be particularly noted. First, thousands of trials may be required to modify an organism's behavior, de-

---

[3] In speech training it is customary also to monitor visually the subject's lip and tongue movements, so that the trainer's monitoring of the subject's response is based on both auditory and visual cues.

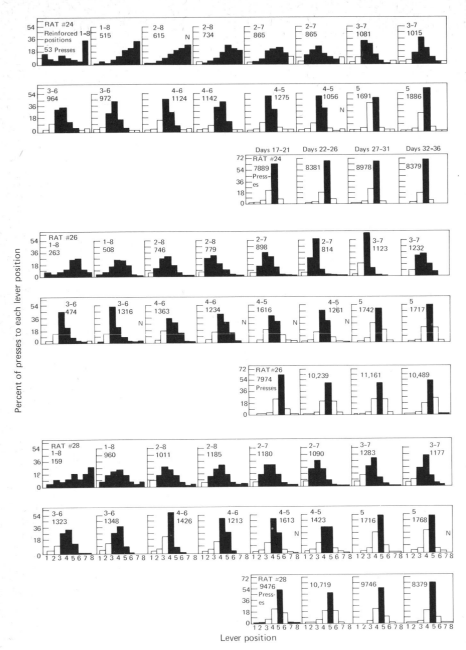

FIGURE 4-1 The differentiation of precise lever-pressing response topographies. Each bar graph (histogram) shows the lever position responses that are either reinforced (R^D's, the shaded bars) or extinguished (R$^\Delta$'s, the light bars), the days, and the percentage of responses to each lever position. The figures in the upper left-hand corner of each graph designate the reinforced lever position and the total number of responses during that session. From R. M. Herrick, The successive differentiation of a lever displacement response. *Journal of the Experimental Analysis of Behavior*, 1964, 7, 211–215. Copyright © 1964, by the Society for the Experimental Analysis of Behavior, Inc., and reproduced by permission.

pending on its sophistication at the onset of training and the nature of the final performance. Second, operant differentiation from simple to more complex performances depends on the variability of the organism's behavior. Two things contribute to that variability. First, over time a well-learned response will show a characteristic "drift," or changes in the response topography, from one occasion to the next. Second, when successive approximations are used, the responses that are first reinforced and then subsequently extinguished become increasingly variable. This variability increases the probability of novel performances, and these novel responses may become new R^D's, which, in turn, become more frequent through differential reinforcement.

A question that frequently arises is whether or not operant acquisition procedures must necessarily deal with *overt* operant behavior. They need not. Subvocal or covert (weak) muscular responses can also be affected by the events that follow them. Hefferline, Keenan, and Harford (1959) studied thumb muscle twitches of such low magnitude that they had to be amplified 1 million times to be observed. Subjects were wired with several sets of electrodes, one of which was attached to the base of their left thumb. Music was then presented through the subjects' headphones, and their thumb muscle twitches, indicated by needle deflections on a meter, were observed over a 10-minute base-line period. During conditioning, whenever the experimenter observed a needle deflection of sufficient magnitude, he presented the subject with 15 seconds of noise termination (music without noise) or 15 seconds of noise postponement. Over a 1-hour conditioning period, there was an increase in the rate of muscle twitches. Although there was a small decline in the rate during a 10-minute extinction period (continuous noise regardless of thumb muscle twitches), it was greatest during a final 10-minute base line during which only music was presented. Although some of the subjects were told what muscles to flex, most of them were not, and even after the experiment was over, they remained unaware that it was their thumb muscle twitches that stopped the noise.

Given the appropriate equipment, then, it is possible to make accurate measurements of subvocal or covert responses and even to consequate them. Moreover, as we shall see later, an individual can be trained to consequate his own covert responses as a form of self-control or self-managed behavior. Unless a means of reliable observation of covert behavior is available, however, the introduction of such events into the analysis of behavior leads to speculation and confusion, since their verification is not possible.

OPERANT MAINTENANCE

When an operant is already part of a subject's repertoire, shaping the operant is not required unless, for some reason, the subject's contemporary performance does not measure up to the final performance demanded by the trainer, as when the subject's emitted response class is deficient in the dimension of magnitude, duration, or topography. If, on the other hand, the subject's performance is adequate but occurs too infrequently, procedures would be directed at strengthening the response class dimension of frequency and nothing else. The operant maintenance procedure would simply require that the trainer reinforce the subject's current performances often enough to increase their frequency.

OPERANT ELIMINATION

If, from the trainer's point of view, an operant occurs too frequently, procedures that have a weakening effect on the operant are required. Among the procedures available are: (1) arranging for consequences to follow the operant that will have a weakening effect on it (either aversive stimuli or low-probability behavior), (2) manipulating consequences in such a way as to strengthen another operant that is incompatible with the undesired operant, (3) manipulating the schedule of reinforcement, and (4) certain other procedures to be described.

The choice of procedures necessarily depends on such considerations as (1) the availability of consequences, (2) the ease with which they can be presented, (3) the sophistication of the subject, and (4) the ease with which the trainer is able to manipulate other relevant features of the subject's environment.

Punishment

Punishment includes the use of two procedures, each involving a major type of stimulus event and each making the operant that preceded the stimulus event less frequent. In the first procedure, whenever the operant to be eliminated occurs, the trainer *removes a positive reinforcer*. For example, as the child reaches out and twists the television control knob, his mother removes the all-day sucker he holds in his other hand. The second procedure involves the *presentation of an aversive stimulus*. In this case, the mother abruptly slaps the child's hand when he reaches out and twists the television control knob. Both procedures employ response-contingent consequences in the form of stimulus events, the defining properties of which are such that their presentation reduces the frequency of the operant that immediately preceded them. As in the case of positive reinforcers, when the trainer anticipates using stimulus events in the elimination of an operant, he must establish that they are punishers. He does this in an empirical test in which it is shown that the stimulus events reduce the frequency of the behavior producing them.

There has been a tendency to avoid the use of punishment as a means of behavior control for the following reasons:

1. Punishment procedures elicit strong emotional responses that are incompatible with the operant to be eliminated and hence serve merely to disrupt it momentarily.

2. Punished behavior can provide cues, in the form of conditioned aversive stimuli, that elicit strong disruptive, emotional behavior which is incompatible with the operant to be eliminated. On future occasions, for example, the child's own behavior of merely reaching for the television may produce these incompatible emotional responses through the visual and proprioceptive cues it produces.

3. Other, more remote stimuli tend to become conditioned to the aversive stimuli in the situation, so that they may be avoided. The television and the room, for example, will acquire cue properties that also elicit the emotional behavior that is incompatible with the operant.

4. Since any behavior that terminates an aversive stimulus will be strengthened, operants that are undesirable and incompatible with the goals of training may be strengthened. For example, a child may run away (escape) from the room in which he was punished or even refuse to enter it (avoid it).

5. Procedures used in punishment may have unanticipated effects. For example, punishment may actually strengthen the behavior it was designed to suppress, especially when it becomes a discriminative stimulus for positive reinforcement, as when a mother slaps her child and immediately follows the slap with heavy doses of affection, a generalized positive reinforcer.

6. When punishment procedures are terminated, the previously punished behavior is increased in what has been called *punishment contrast*. For example, pecking in pigeons following termination of shock punishment was increased above that characteristic of no punishment at all (Azrin, 1960).

Strengthening Incompatible Responses

Another approach to the elimination of an operant consists of strengthening, through the presentation of response-contingent positive reinforcement, a response class that is incompatible with the operant to be eliminated. Suppose a child shows a pattern of hyperactivity consisting of continuously moving about, shouting, and waving his hands. The goal of the procedure here would be to strengthen a different response class—those operants, let us say, that are involved in modeling clay while the child is seated at a table. The child's behavior, of course, would have to be shaped into sitting at the table and working with the clay. Positive reinforcement would be contingent on successive approximations to that kind of final performance. Sitting and modeling clay would thus become more frequent, and hyperactivity would become less frequent. In a sense it would be displaced by the behavior incompatible with it.

Extinction

An extinction schedule of reinforcement can also be used to reduce the frequency of an operant. In this case, the consequences that normally follow and maintain an operant are no longer presented. During extinction, for example, a rat's lever presses would not result in the delivery of a positive reinforcing stimulus (that is, a food pellet). Similarly, a child's tantrum behavior would no longer be followed by the parent's presenting the child with a piece of candy to "shut him up." Initially, the effect of extinction procedures is to make the response topography of the operant more variable; then, gradually, the effect is to reduce the operant's frequency.

There are two major difficulties in the use of extinction procedures to eliminate operant behavior. First, it is not always easy to determine which reinforcing stimuli actually maintain the operant. Second, once the reinforcing stimuli have been determined, the trainer may have trouble manipulating the environment in such a way as to remove them. It is frequently difficult to exercise sufficient control over the natural environment to arrange an extinction schedule. A child may emit funny faces and sounds (the response class) in a classroom, thus producing laughter among the other pupils (the reinforcing stimulus). To use an extinction procedure in such a setting, one would have to have sufficient control over the entire class to prevent the pupils from laughing at the child's "cutting up."

Time-Out (TO) Procedures

Still another approach to reducing the frequency of an operant is the use of any of the following *time-out (TO) procedures*, all of which are designed to prevent the trainee from emitting the behavior in question:

1. The trainee is removed from the situation in which the operant occurs. For example, the child who twists the television control knob is removed from the room containing the television set.

2. The manipulandum is removed from the situation in which the operant occurs. For example, the television set is removed from the room containing the child.

3. The "house lights" are turned off. For example, the room with the child in it is made completely dark.

4. A stimulus is introduced that has been present in the past during occasions when the operant was followed by nonreinforcement. For example, when the child's father is in the room, the television set never works because

the father disconnects the television, and therefore the set fails to produce the sounds and images that are probably reinforcing to the child.

Satiation

Satiation is another procedure that reduces the frequency of an operant. In this case the trainee is given complete access to the reinforcing stimulus. For example, the child is permitted to twist the television control knob as much as he wants, producing continuous variation in the sounds and images coming from the television set. Use of this procedure requires that there be an abundance of reinforcing stimuli as well as ease in presenting them to the trainee.

Stimulus Change

Stimulus change can also be used to reduce the frequency of an operant. This procedure consists of introducing a new stimulus, responses to which have never before been reinforced. Holz and Azrin (1963) studied the effect of the presentation of a novel stimulus on pigeons' pecking for grain under a drl 30-second schedule of reinforcement, and their results are shown in Figure 4-2. Notice that over a 60-minute period the initial effect of the change is the disruption of the pecking response. Comparable effects on behavior under the control of other schedules of reinforcement, such as FI and VI schedules, have also been reported. A somewhat analogous procedure for the child who plays with the television set would be the introduction of a completely new control knob.

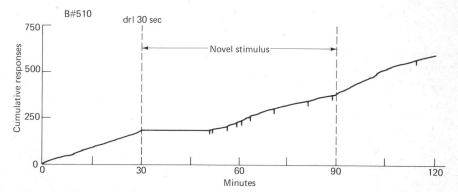

FIGURE 4-2 The effect of stimulus change (the presentation of a novel stimulus) on pecking for grain under a drl 30-second schedule of reinforcement. The change consisted of changing the color of the pecking key from white to green. From W. C. Holz and N. H. Azrin, A comparison of several procedures for eliminating behavior. *Journal of the Experimental Analysis of Behavior*, 1963, 6, 399–406. Copyright © 1963, by the Society for the Experimental Analysis of Behavior, Inc., and reproduced by permission.

Table 4-1 The Effectiveness of Procedures Used to Eliminate Operants

PROCEDURE	IMMEDIATE EFFECT	ENDURING EFFECT	COMPLETE SUPPRESSION	IRREVERSIBLE EFFECT
Punishment (shock)	Yes	Yes	Yes	Yes
Extinction	No	Yes	No	No
Satiation	Yes	Yes	No	No
Physical Restraint*	Yes	Yes	Yes	No
Stimulus Change	Yes	No	No	No

* Physical restraint is analogous to the time-out procedure in which the trainee is removed from the situation in which the operant occurred.
From W. C. Holz and N. H. Azrin, A comparison of several procedures for eliminating behavior. *Journal of the Experimental Analysis of Behavior,* 1963, 6, 399–406. Copyright © 1963 by the Society for the Experimental Analysis of Behavior, Inc. and reproduced by permission.

The Relative Effectiveness of Operant Elimination Procedures

There are, then, a number of procedures available that can be employed to reduce the frequency of an operant, including punishment, strengthening of incompatible responses, extinction, time-out, and satiation. Not all of these procedures are equally effective, and the relative effectiveness of any one procedure depends on the conditions under which it is used.[4] Weak aversive stimulation, as a punishment procedure, may actually possess facilitative properties rather than suppressive properties under certain conditions of presentation. Consequently, when any procedure is chosen, it must be tried out in the setting in which it is to be employed. Table 4-1 summarizes the effectiveness of several different procedures for eliminating behavior.

Application of these procedures in natural situations may actually involve two or more behavior elimination techniques. For example, incompatible responses may be reinforced, while at the same time undesirable operants are punished under a concurrent (CONC) schedule.

It should be mentioned that although there is a tendency to avoid punishment procedures, such procedures are not always detrimental to the organism. In fact, in certain situations, they may increase the organism's control over its environment. For example, during the base-line phase of a study by Holz and Azrin (1963), pigeons were reinforced for pecking at a white disk with grain presented on a CRF drl 30-second schedule of reinforcement. Thus the

[4] Azrin and Holz (1966), for example, suggest that the actual implementation of an extinction schedule in a natural setting requires a degree of environmental control seldom attainable. In such cases, punishment may be more effective. A more detailed discussion of this will be presented later.

first peck occurring 30-seconds after the last reinforced peck was reinforced, and pecks occurring during the drl interval were extinguished. Subsequently, several different procedures for the elimination of behavior, including punishment (pecking-contingent shock), satiation, and extinction, were introduced, and their effects on pecking rate and the interval between pecks or inter-response times (IRT's), were observed. Figure 4-3 shows the changes in the

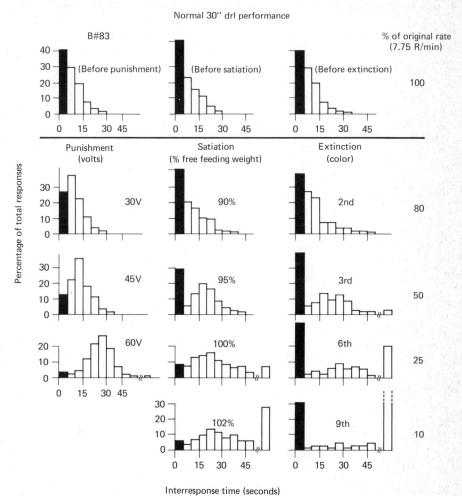

FIGURE 4-3 Normal (base-line) pecking rates and IRT distributions under a CRF drl 30-second schedule of reinforcement and following exposure to three different behavior elimination procedures: (1) punishment (30, 45, 60 volts of pecking-response-contingent shock), (2) satiation (90, 95, 100, and 102 percent FFW), and (3) days 2, 3, 6, and 9 of extinction. From W. C. Holz and N. H. Azrin, A comparison of several procedures for eliminating behavior. *Journal of the Experimental Analysis of Behavior*, 1963, **6**, 399–406. Copyright © 1963, by the Society for the Experimental Analysis of Behavior, Inc., and reproduced by permission.

rate of pecking and the percentage of total responses having different inter-response times under different amounts of punishment (shock), satiation, and exposure to an extinction schedule. All three procedures reduced the rate of responding and produced changes in the distribution of IRT's (the per-centage of the total responses occurring within each interval). The punish-ment procedure produced the most efficient pattern of responding under the drl 30-second schedule. It eliminated the very short IRT's (those that nor-mally occur within the drl interval and are followed by extinction). As a result, a much greater percentage of the total responses had IRT's approach-ing that required under the drl 30-second schedule. In other words, before punishment was introduced, only 1 percent of all of the pigeon's pecking responses produced reinforcements, and afterward about 28 percent did. It is in this kind of situation—one in which the organism's behavior persists de-spite the fact that it does not act on the environment to produce appropriate consequences—that a punishment procedure may strengthen the organism's repertoire and increase its chances for survival.

SCHEDULES OF REINFORCEMENT DURING ACQUISITION

Whenever possible, acquisition training should begin with a continuous re-inforcement (CRF) schedule. This schedule generally produces the quickest changes in the frequency of the R^D. When the operant occurs sufficiently often, a gradual transition to an intermittent schedule of reinforcement can be introduced. Since intermittent schedules contain a component of extinc-tion, the introduction of such a schedule intensifies the operant, making it more variable even though it is still technically a member of the same re-sponse class and an R^D. For example, when a response class that was pre-viously reinforced is followed by extinction, the response class dimensions of both rate and magnitude will change.

The transition from a nonintermittent schedule (CRF) to an intermittent schedule (FR, VR, FI, VI) should be made gradually. The schedule changes should be made (1) in small increments and (2) over a relatively long period of time. For example, in going from a CRF schedule to an FR 10 schedule, the trainer can introduce a progression consisting of FR 2, FR 4, FR 6, and so on.[5] Similarly, in going from a CRF schedule to an FI 3-minute schedule, the trainer can introduce a progression such as FI 5 seconds, FI 10 seconds, FI 20 seconds, and so on. These schedule values are merely examples of how such transitions can be made, and larger steps are often possible. However,

[5] The reader can obtain some idea of the time required for such a progression from the fact that a rat can be trained to work on an FR 10 schedule for a lever-pressing task in 10 to 20 minutes, provided he has worked on a CRF schedule for approximately 5 to 10 minutes.

if the change from a nonintermittent schedule to an intermittent schedule is made too abruptly, emotional responses (such as wing flapping in pigeons and various vocalizations and motor responses in man) occur along with greater variability in the operant; and in the long run these reactions may prove to be detrimental to the performance goal set by the trainer.

The subject's performances provide a possible guide to the rate at which schedule changes can be introduced, and these performances can be monitored by the trainer. Variability in the operant is directly observable as schedule changes occur. Even though changes in the R^D are observed, these variations need not exceed the limits set by the trainer for satisfactory performance. If the variations observed in the operant are too large, attempts can be made to adjust the schedule and thereby "recover" the operant.

Schedule changes, then, ordinarily involve a series of stages. First, there is a period during which performance is acquired and stabilized under a CRF schedule. Second, there is a transition period, during which schedule changes are introduced and changes in the organism's behavior are observed—especially changes in its rate of responding and in the frequency and duration of pauses. Third, there is a final, or terminal, stage, during which performance is acquired and stabilized under the terminal schedule. Figure 4-4 presents some data from a study by Ferster and Skinner (1957) and shows performances under a CRF schedule, under transition to an FR 22 schedule, and under the final FR 22 schedule. A progression from FR 22 to a higher ratio schedule would also involve a transition period as would progressions from a CRF to a VR, FI, or VI schedule. During the transition, characteristic rate changes, frequencies and duration of pauses, and training times necessary to reach the final performance would be observed, and these would be unique to each terminal schedule.

If training is begun under an intermittent, rather than a CRF, schedule, the operant will be infrequent, poorly differentiated, and, as we shall see, poorly discriminated from the beginning.

CHARACTERISTIC PERFORMANCES UNDER VARIOUS SCHEDULES OF REINFORCEMENT

Once an operant has been acquired and stabilized under a CRF schedule, there will be a high rate of responding followed by a pause when the organism receives the reinforcer. This presentation of reinforcement marks the *post-reinforcement period* during which schedule changes may be introduced that result in a characteristic performance on the new schedule. Performances on the various schedules have been reported for various species, including rats, pigeons, monkeys, chimpanzees, and humans, both children and adults. These reports are summarized in the form of a cumulative record, which

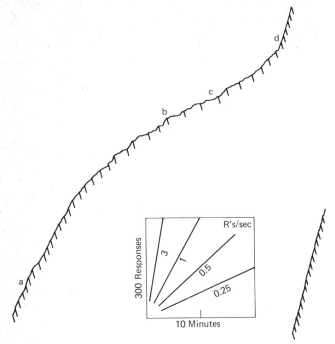

FIGURE 4-4 Initial, transitional, and final performances occurring during changes in the schedule of reinforcement from CRF to FR 22. The typical CRF performance is shown at point a. This typical CRF performance is followed by a gradual decline in rate and pauses, shown at point b, a low rate of responding, shown at point c, and a gradual acceleration in rate until an FR 22 performance is obtained at point d. The FR 22 final performance is shown next to the response rate meter. From *Schedules of Reinforcement* by C. B. Ferster and B. F. Skinner. Copyright © 1957. By permission of Appleton-Century-Crofts, Educational Division, Meredith Corporation.

shows, against a common time base, the characteristic performance of the organism, the occurrence of the reinforcing stimulus, and other investigator-presented stimulus events. As the student studies the main features of the performances under each of the following schedules, he should relate the features of the record described in the text to the actual cumulative records, and he should compare the records obtained for different species under each schedule.

Single Schedules

As we have already observed (see Chapter 3), a single schedule specifies the rules under which a single response class is reinforced. Most of the descriptions to follow are from Ferster and Skinner (1957) and reveal the typical performances generated by these rules.

FIXED-RATIO (FR) SCHEDULES

When compared with a response rate scale (when available), the slopes of Figure 4-5 (a–d) show that the FR schedule produces high rates of responding. In the pigeon, for example, more than ten responses per second have been reported under certain schedules. Each reinforcement is followed by a *post-reinforcement pause*, which is shown at point y in Figure 4-5(d). There is a reason for this pause. Under the rules of the FR schedule, a response occurring immediately after the reinforcement is not reinforced. Thus during the transition from a CRF to an FR schedule, responses occurring immediately after reinforcement are extinguished. Because of this, the presentation of the reinforcer and the possession of the reinforcer (food in the mouth) are events correlated with extinction; thus they become cues for nonresponding. The post-reinforcement pause increases as the FR increases. Pauses on an FR 60 schedule tend to be quite brief, lasting only a few seconds before they are followed by the terminal rate, whereas pauses of 10 minutes have been reported under an FR 120 schedule. FR schedules, like the VR schedules to be discussed shortly, provide for the differential reinforcement of high rates. This is because high rates of responding (with short IRT's) produce a greater probability of reinforcement. In other words, on an FR schedule the probability of reinforcement is determined by the number of responses, and when a number of responses occurs in rapid succession, the probability of reinforcement is high. The effect of this schedule is to reinforce a run of responses having short IRT's. When the FR schedule is a component of a compound (tandem) schedule containing a time-out (TO) contingency and there is an increase in the ratio requirements, pigeons can be trained to peck consistently as many as 875 times to get one reinforcer. There are, however, limits to the size of the ratio. Beyond this limit, performance ceases.

FIXED-INTERVAL (FI) SCHEDULES

In FI schedules long pauses are observed immediately following reinforcement, as shown by Figure 4-5 (e–h). The duration of this pause is determined by the FI requirement. Low rates of responding are followed by increased responding (acceleration in rate) until the terminal rate that precedes reinforcement is reached. This response pattern produces the characteristic FI "scallop," which is shown in Figure 4-5 (f or g). Sometimes a high terminal rate of responding occurs during the first part of the FI interval ("running through"), throughout the entire FI period, or the last part of the interval. Early in the FI period, when there is minimal responding on the manipulandum, a number of other behaviors may occur such as "mediating," "collateral" behavior, for example, preening in the rat and counting in humans. As larger intervals, such as FI 17, are approached, scalloping becomes much less distinct, and there is a more linear performance, which

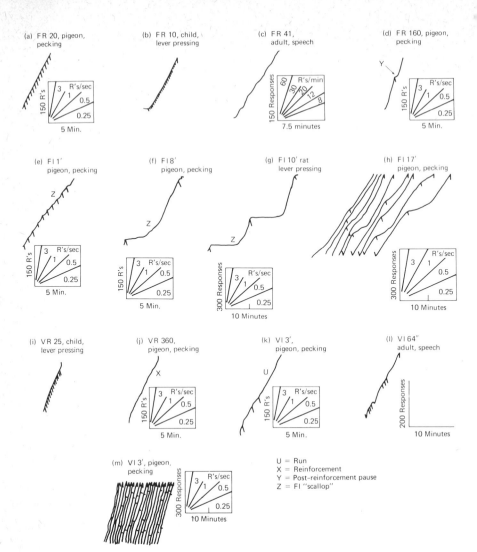

FIGURE 4-5 Cumulative records of a pigeon, rat, child, and adult under different schedules of reinforcement and for different operants. Some records do not show the reinforcements because they have been reduced, and others show finer detail because they have been enlarged. Rates were obtained directly from the sources of the records when available.

Figures 4-5(a), (d), (e), (f), (g), (h), (j), (k), and (m) from *Schedules of Reinforcement,* by C. B. Ferster and B. F. Skinner. Copyright © 1957. By permission of Appleton-Century-Crofts, Educational Division, Meredith Corporation. Figures 4-5(b) and (i) from R. Orlando and S. Bijou, Single and multiple schedules of reinforcement in developmentally retarded children. *Journal of the Experimental Analysis of Behavior,* 1960, **3**, 339–348. Copyright © 1960 by the Society for the Experimental Analysis of Behavior, Inc. and reproduced by permission. Figure 4-5(c) from D. Witters, Fixed ratio performance of psychiatric patients' verbal behavior in a small group. Unpublished manuscript, 1964; Figure 4-5 (l) from H. L. Lane and P. G. Shinkman, Methods and findings in an analysis of a vocal operant. *Journal of the Experimental Analysis of Behavior,* 1963, **6**, 179–188. Copyright © 1963 by the Society for the Experimental Analysis of Behavior, Inc. and reproduced by permission.

often shows irregularities in the form of sudden bursts or pauses giving the record a "rough grain," as shown by Figure 4-5 (h). These bursts or pauses may occur throughout the entire FI interval and even after reinforcement, suggesting that performance under longer FI's is quite unstable, an observation that is also shown in Figure 4-5(h).

VARIABLE-RATIO (VR) SCHEDULES

In VR schedules sustained runs at high rates of responding are observed, although the rate is variable. See Figure 4-5(i–j). Like the FR schedule, the VR schedule provides for the differential reinforcement of high rates, and reinforcement is more likely to occur following high rates of responding (more responses per unit of time). In VR schedules, runs after reinforcement are more apt to occur and are like those observed in VI schedules. (See Figure 4-5(k).) These runs at a high rate may be followed by a slower rate or by a pause, which in some cases may be of very long duration. Such a change in rates reflects changes in the density of reinforcement. When a series of small ratios is programmed, the rate goes up, and when a series of large ratios is programmed, the rate goes down. Compared with other schedules, the development of the VR final performance from a CRF initial performance is very rapid.

VARIABLE-INTERVAL (VI) SCHEDULES

In VI schedules uniform and high rates of responding over long periods of time occur with brief post-reinforcement pauses. See Figure 4-5(k–m). Higher rates are frequently noted immediately after reinforcement, but the overall performance is at a high rate and quite stable. This is clearly shown in Figure 4-5(m), which is for a VI 3-minute performance with a very stable rate. During the 14-hour session that provided the data for Figure 4-5(m), the pigeon made over 87,000 responses on an average of about two responses per second. This is the pattern with VI schedules despite the fact that the schedule rule specifies that the reinforcer be made available only for a response made after the passage of time—a feature of all interval schedules, which, as we noted earlier, provides for the differential reinforcement of low rates. It is a characteristic of the VI schedule, however, that the duration of the interval is variable and random, the overall effect of which is to produce both a relatively high rate of responding for an interval schedule and a stable rate. These characteristics make the VI an ideal schedule for the acquisition of operant behavior among human subjects.

Compound Schedules

Although a detailed review of the organism's behavior under compound schedules is beyond the scope of the present discussion, it is necessary to point out that there is extensive literature available. Studies have been made of the various possible combinations of single schedules with and without correlated stimuli for each component, and with and without programmed consequences for each component. When there is a correlated stimulus for each component of a compound schedule, the behavior of the organism can be made extraordinarily complex. For example, Ferster and Skinner (1957) trained pigeons on a multiple schedule containing the following components, each with a correlated stimulus in the presence of which appropriate responses were reinforced: FI 2, FI 11, FR 50, FR 250. The final performances after thirty-eight sessions are shown in Figure 4-6. Each of these performances is appropriate to the schedule requirements; that is, the programmed interval schedule components, both large and small, show some scalloping, and the programmed ratio components, both large and small, show high rates and post-reinforcement pauses. Moreover, even when the correlated stimuli are eliminated from the compound schedule, resulting in a mixed schedule, for example, MIX FI 10 FR 40, a pigeon's performance conforms reasonably well with the characteristics of the schedule; that is, the pigeon's record shows runs and post-reinforcement pauses characteristic of the FR component, and pauses in responding during the initial phase of the FI component.

Although the multiple and mixed schedules contain programmed reinforcements following each component in the schedule, in tandem and chain schedules only the last programmed component is followed by the reinforcing event. Nevertheless, with tandem and particularly chain schedules that contain a correlated stimulus for each component, protracted and elaborate

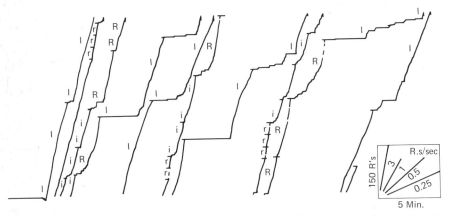

FIGURE 4-6 A multiple-schedule performance after thirty-eight sessions under a schedule having the following components: FR 50, FR 250, FI 2, and FI 11. R and r designate the large and small fixed ratios, and I and i designate the long and short fixed intervals. From *Schedules of Reinforcement* by C. B. Ferster and B. F. Skinner. Copyright © 1957. By permission of Appleton-Century-Crofts, Educational Division, Meredith Corporation.

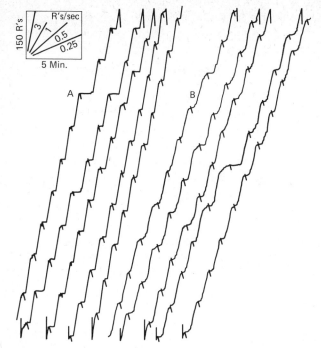

FIGURE 4-7 Performance of two subjects (A and B) under a CHAIN FR 95 CRF drl schedule of reinforcement. From *Schedules of Reinforcement* by C. B. Ferster and B. F. Skinner. Copyright © 1957. By permission of Appleton-Century-Crofts, Educational Division, Meredith Corporation.

performances are possible. Figure 4-7, for example, shows a CHAIN FR 95 CRF drl performance that is under good control of the stimuli correlated with the two major components of the chain schedule.

What is surprising, then, is that under both single and compound schedules, nonhuman organisms can be trained to engage in a large number of responses or to delay in responding, despite infrequent reinforcements.

CHARACTERISTIC PERFORMANCES DURING EXTINCTION

Ferster and Skinner (1957) also found that following training on a given schedule of reinforcement, characteristic performances emerge during extinction.

Fixed-Ratio (FR) Schedules

At first during extinction, the FR rate is maintained, but with increasingly longer pauses. The longer pauses and shorter runs result in a decline in the overall response rate. The changes from the high rates of responding to the pauses are abrupt. (See Figure 4-8.) Higher rates of responding occur mostly at the beginning of each session (spontaneous recovery).

Fixed-Interval (FI) Schedules

At first high rates are reached during the terminal portion of the FI interval, as during the reinforcement schedule. The rate drops to zero, followed by another buildup, ending in a slower terminal rate. The rate of responding continues to decline, and the scallop becomes less distinct as pauses occur more and more often. This is shown in Figure 4-9.

Variable-Ratio (VR) Schedules

Like the FR, sustained runs at high rates occur early in extinction, followed by long pauses characteristic of performances during reinforcement. The pauses between short bursts of responding grow longer and longer as extinction continues. Even though the pauses grow increasingly longer, however, the bursts tend to continue at high rates.

Variable-Interval (VI) Schedules

At first, sustained, high rates of responding, characteristic of VI performances during reinforcement, are observed. Then, longer and longer pauses occur, along with a decline in rate, which remains variable. Despite longer pauses and lowered rates during extinction, reinforcement on a VI schedule produces the most prolonged period of resistance to extinction of any type of schedule. Indeed, a single reinforcement following extinction may reinstate

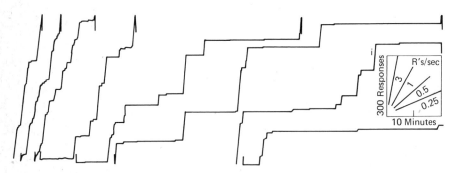

FIGURE 4-8 Extinction of pecking in the pigeon following seven hundred reinforcements on FR 60. High rates of responding are abruptly followed by pauses, which are of longer and longer duration. From *Schedules of Reinforcement* by C. B. Ferster and B. F. Skinner. Copyright © 1957. By permission of Appleton-Century-Crofts, Educational Division, Meredith Corporation.

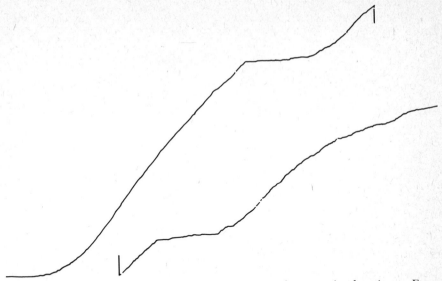

FIGURE 4-9 One session of extinction of an FI 45 performance in the pigeon. From *Schedules of Reinforcement* by C. B. Ferster and B. F. Skinner. Copyright © 1957. By permission of Appleton-Century-Crofts, Educational Division, Meredith Corporation.

the high rate of responding observed earlier during reinforcement. This is illustrated in Figure 4-10, which shows the low rate occurring during extinction, one occasion of reinforcement, and the resumption of a rate comparable to that observed before extinction.

SUMMARY AND CONCLUSION

Operant acquisition is the most rapid under a CRF schedule. However, plans should be made for an eventual transition to an intermittent schedule, preferably a VI schedule, which produces sufficiently high rates of stable responding and, in the long run, requires the fewest reinforcers to maintain the performance. Similarly, when one wants to eliminate an operant, a CRF schedule will produce maximum effects when punishment is used.

The data on the behavioral effects of the different schedules of reinforcement clearly show that stable patterns of operant behavior can be controlled and maintained over long periods of time and under conditions of infrequent or delayed reinforcement. When changes in the pattern of responding (for example, in the rate, frequency, and duration of pauses) correspond to changes in the schedule of reinforcement, the organism's behavior is said to be under *schedule control*. When behavior occurs only in the presence of certain stimuli, which have been correlated with certain consequences, and

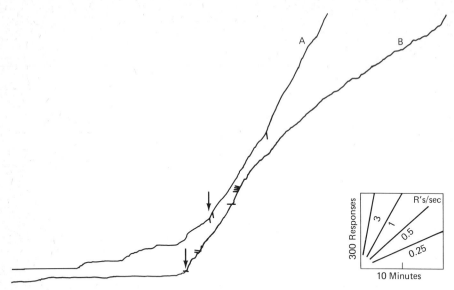

FIGURE 4-10 Recovery of extinguished VI performance in two pigeons (A and B) following the presentation of a single reinforcer. Arrow shows pips on record where reinforcers were presented. From *Schedules of Reinforcement* by C. B. Ferster and B. F. Skinner. Copyright © 1957. By permission of Appleton-Century-Crofts, Educational Division, Meredith Corporation.

does not occur in the absence of these stimuli, the organism's behavior is said to be under *stimulus control*. At any given point in time operant behavior may be under schedule control, stimulus control, or both. Ordinarily, the occurrence of reinforcing consequences (for schedule control) and/or correlated stimuli (for stimulus control) is sufficient to maintain considerable amounts of behavior over long periods of time in the natural environment as well as in the laboratory.

STUDY QUESTIONS

1. With what two major questions must the trainer concern himself if his attempts at operant conditioning are to be successful?
2. As far as the trainer is concerned, what situation characterizes operant acquisition? What situation characterizes operant maintenance?
3. What is the purpose of observing the organism's behavior during the baseline, or pretraining period?
4. Defining the response class involves consideration of what dimensions?
5. What types of consequences can be used to strengthen operant behavior?
6. What four conditions are relevant to the choice of a reinforcer?
7. What is the advantage of using stimulus events, instead of response events, to strengthen operant behavior?

8. What kinds of reinforcers are probably unsuitable for use with naïve subjects? What kinds are suitable for use with naïve subjects?
9. In testing the effectiveness of a reinforcer, what advantage does the trainer obtain by using an operant that is already part of the subject's repertoire?
10. What does the trainer do when he uses the following procedures?
    a. Differential reinforcement.
    b. Successive approximations.
11. Distinguish between an R^D and an R^Δ.
12. Operant differentiation involves what two procedures?
13. What does the trainer do when an emitted operant is deficient in some dimension of performance, such as form, or topography, or magnitude?
14. What does the trainer do if the trainee's performance is adequate but occurs too infrequently?
15. With which dimension of the response class are procedures aimed at operant elimination probably concerned?
16. What two procedures are used in punishment?
17. What defines a stimulus event as a punisher?
18. What are the six major objections to using punishment?
19. Removal of a punisher has what effect on the previously punished operant? What is this phenomenon called?
20. Explain how an operant can be eliminated by dealing with a response that is incompatible with it.
21. Describe the procedures involved when an extinction schedule is used.
22. What two major difficulties are encountered when an extinction schedule is used in natural situations to eliminate behavior?
23. What is the general function or purpose of time-out (TO) procedures?
24. Of the basic time-out (TO) procedures, which ones seem most applicable to natural situations?
25. Describe the procedure involved in the use of satiation. Cite two limiting conditions in the use of satiation.
26. Why must a test be made in the setting in which a behavior control procedure is to be used before the procedure can be finally adopted?
27. Contrast the following behavior elimination procedures in terms of their immediate, enduring, suppressive, and irreversible effects on an operant:
    a. Punishment (shock).　　　　d. Stimulus change.
    b. Extinction.　　　　　　　　e. Satiation.
    c. Physical restraint.
28. Defend the proposition that punishment can strengthen an organism's repertoire of behaviors.
29. Suggest some long-term and short-term consequences to an organism when only 1 percent of its behavior produces reinforcement.
30. Jimmy, a 5-year-old in kindergarten, socks his playmates 4 or 5 times a day. Select a set of procedures you would use to eliminate this behavior.
31. Why is it suggested that extinction alone is inadequate as a behavior elimination technique in natural situations?
32. Which schedule of reinforcement will produce the most rapid operant acquisition?

33. Transition from a CRF schedule to an intermittent schedule of reinforcement has what effects on the operant? Why? Suggest two response class dimensions that are particularly sensitive to this change.

34. What effect does a too-abrupt transition from a nonintermittent to an intermittent schedule of reinforcement have on an operant?

35. A transition that is too abrupt is apt to produce what types of emotional behavior in pigeons? In man?

36. What two important changes occur in operant behavior during transition from a CRF to an FR schedule of reinforcement?

37. What characterizes an operant that was acquired initially under an intermittent schedule of reinforcement?

38. In what way does an FR schedule provide for the differential reinforcement of high rates?

39. In the FR schedule, what important event occurs during the post-reinforcement pause?

40. What effect does this have on behavior under an FR schedule and why?

41. In what way does a pigeon's stable performance on an FR schedule show exceptional self-control?

42. In what way does an FI schedule provide for the differential reinforcement of low rates?

43. Schedules in which the response-reinforcement rule involves the passage of time (that is, an FI schedule), rather than the occurrence of a number of responses, have been observed to possess a drl characteristic. This is not true, however, of a VI schedule, even though this schedule is based on the passage of time. Why?

44. What evidence in Figures 4-6 and 4-7 and in the discussion in the text suggests that pigeons are capable of performing rather complex behavior without making many mistakes?

45. Draw a sample of the cumulative record in Figure 4-8 that shows evidence of the pigeon's spontaneous recovery of pecking during extinction of an FR 60 performance.

46. Which schedule produces performances that are the most stable and durable and the easiest to recover during extinction? Be able to pick out evidence from Figures 4-5 and 4-10 respectively, to show this.

47. Which schedule is the most effective in the elimination of an operant by punishment?

48. Suggest a reason for the occurrence of mediating or time-filling behavior observed under an FI schedule of reinforcement.

49. Describe the following and find evidence of them in the cumulative records presented in Figure 4-5:

   a. Post-reinforcement pause.
   b. Other pauses.
   c. Reinforcement.
   d. Run.
   e. Scallop.
   f. Stability in the record.
   g. Irregularity, or graininess, in the record.

50. What major change in performance seems common to any single schedule during extinction?

51. What is the difference between the stimulus control and schedule control of behavior?

REFERENCES

Azrin, N. H. Sequential effects of punishment. *Science*, 1960, **131**, 605–606.

Azrin, N. H., and Holz, W. C. Punishment. In W. K. Honig (Ed.), *Operant behavior: Areas of research and application.* New York: Appleton-Century-Crofts, 1966.

Ferster, C. B., and Skinner, B. F. *Schedules of reinforcement.* New York: Appleton-Century-Crofts, 1957.

Hefferline, R. F., Keenan, B., and Harford, R. A. Escape and avoidance conditioning in human subjects without their observation of the response. *Science*, 1959, **130**, 1338–1339.

Herrick, R. M. The successive differentiation of a lever displacement response. *Journal of the Experimental Analysis of Behavior*, 1964, **7**, 211–215.

Holland, J. G., and Skinner, B. F. *The analysis of behavior.* New York: McGraw-Hill, 1961.

Holz, W. C., and Azrin, N. H. A comparison of several procedures for eliminating behavior. *Journal of the Experimental Analysis of Behavior*, 1963, **6**, 399–406.

Keller, F. S. *Learning: Reinforcement theory.* (2nd ed.) New York: Random House, 1969.

Lane, H. L., and Shinkman, P. G. Methods and findings in an analysis of the vocal operant. *Journal of the Experimental Analysis of Behavior*, 1963, **6**, 179–188.

Morse, W. H. Intermittent reinforcement. In W. K. Honig (Ed.), *Operant behavior: Areas of research and application.* New York: Appleton-Century-Crofts, 1966.

Orlando, R., and Bijou, S. Single and multiple schedules of reinforcement in developmentally retarded children. *Journal of the Experimental Analysis of Behavior*, 1960, **3**, 339–348.

Witters, D. R. Fixed ratio performance of psychiatric patients' verbal behavior in a small group. Unpublished manuscript, 1964.

CHAPTER 5

OPERANT DISCRIMINATION

Operant behavior inevitably occurs in the presence of various types of stimuli, some of which precede the operant, others of which follow it. We have already seen that the stimulus (and response) events that follow an operant and affect it are called consequences. Consequences can affect the operant in two ways. First, they tend to either strengthen or weaken it, making it either more or less likely to occur on future occasions. Second, consequences function to bring the operant under the control of the stimuli preceding it. The present discussion deals with the latter process—the manner in which stimuli that precede an operant come to control it.

EXAMPLES OF OPERANT DISCRIMINATION

Operant discrimination, both as a behavioral process and in the procedures necessary to produce it, reveals some of the conditions under which operant behavior occurs. For example, we observed earlier that the rat who was trained to work for a living by pressing a lever for food pellets did his work only under certain conditions. He pressed the lever primarily when the green light was on, and he seldom pressed the lever when the green light was off. This selective lever pressing (lever pressing controlled by the green light), in which the operant is only emitted following a certain stimulus event, is an example of a *discriminated operant.*

Still another example is behavior under the control of verbal instructions. The teacher says, "recess" and her pupils get up from their seats and run out of the room and onto the playground. Thus the teacher-presented event ("recess") controls the operant chain consisting of getting up from the seat, running out of the room, and running onto the playground. The occurrence of this operant chain is much more probable following the presentation of the verbal instruction "recess" than it is during the instruction's absence.

In nature there are very large numbers of nonverbal stimuli (warning lights, buzzers, alarms, signals, and signs) and verbal stimuli (instructions, commands, requests, suggestions) that have gained their stimulus control function over operant behavior through a process called operant discrimination.

CLASSICAL OPERANT DISCRIMINATION TRAINING

In *classical operant discrimination training* (sometimes called the differential reinforcement procedure), the trainer arranges a situation in which the occurrence of an operant is reinforced in the presence of certain stimuli and not reinforced in the absence of these stimuli. When an operant is reinforced in the presence of certain stimulus events, these events are called events marking the occasion of some consequence or correlated stimuli, and in the classical operant discrimination training procedure, they are presented in a systematic manner. For example, Herrick, Myers, and Koropotkin (1959) trained a rat to press a lever only when a light inside his box was on and not to press it when the light was off. The food-deprived rat who served as a subject was placed in the box and trained through successive approximations to press the lever for a food pellet. During this training the light inside the box was off. Then, the light-on condition was introduced as an event marking the occasion for, or correlated with, reinforcement—a discriminative stimulus for reinforcement, or S^D. The light-off condition was used as an event marking the occasion for, or correlated with, extinction or nonreinforcement—a discriminative stimulus for extinction, or S^Δ. Hence we have:

$$S^D \longrightarrow R \longrightarrow SR^+$$
$$\text{(light-on)} \qquad \text{(lever press)} \qquad \text{(food pellet)}$$

$$S^\Delta \longrightarrow R \longrightarrow EXT$$
$$\text{(light-off)} \qquad \text{(lever press)}$$

The rat was then exposed to occasions when the light was on (the S^D) and occasions when it was off (the S^Δ). Lever presses in the presence of the S^D were reinforced, and lever presses in the presence of the S^Δ were extinguished. Training was carried out for 45 minutes a day. As it progressed over a 40-day period, there was a gradual increase in the rate of responding (responses per minute) in the presence of the S^D and a gradual decrease in rate of responding in the presence of the S^Δ, as shown in Figure 5-1. By the last day of training the rate under the S^D condition was about sixty-five responses per minute, and under the S^Δ condition it was about five responses per minute.

This procedure can also be used to train a child to make a final performance consisting of a naming or labeling verbal response, for example, saying "ball" when being shown a ball:

S^D ─────────────→ R ───────────── Generalized Sr^+
(A ball, an object, is   (Child says, "ball.")   (The trainer
presented to child.)   says, "Good!")

S^Δ ─────────────→ R ───────────── EXT
(The ball is absent—   (Child says, "ball.")   (No response from
no ball presented.)   the trainer)

In this situation, just as in the lever-pressing example, there are two kinds of discriminative stimuli. One stimulus, the S^D, is followed by response-contingent reinforcement. When the child says, "ball" following presentation of the ball as an object (the S^D), he is reinforced by the trainer's expression, "Good!" When the child says, "ball" in the absence of the ball (the S^Δ), his response is followed by extinction, or nonreinforcement.[1]

Following repeated and systematic presentations of the S^D and S^Δ and appropriate consequences, operant discrimination will occur. In the case of the rat, the light-on condition will become a controlling stimulus for lever pressing in the sense that when the light is on, the rat is more likely to press the lever. Similarly, when the ball, as an object, is presented to the child, it will become a controlling stimulus for the verbal operant "ball" in the sense that the child is more likely to say "ball" when the ball is presented. The occurrence of such discriminated operant behavior following operant discrimination training is, therefore, stated in terms of probabilities. The behavior controlled by the S^D is simply more probable in the presence of S^D than in its absence (or in the presence of the S^Δ). In Figure 5-1, for example, there was some S^Δ responding even after 40 days of training. However, there was a great deal more S^D responding.

---

[1] In actual practice several other elements are often involved in such training. For example, S^D may consist of several different objects and may be presented along with verbal instructions such as "What is this?" Correct labeling responses in the presence of the objects would be reinforced, and incorrect ones would be weakly punished, as when the trainer says, "no." See Chapters 7 and 8 for a more extended discussion of this.

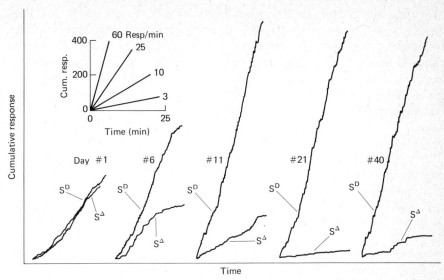

FIGURE 5-1 The development of an operant discrimination through the use of the classical operant discrimination training procedure, in which lever-pressing responses in the presence of the S^D are reinforced, and lever-pressing responses in the presence of S^Δ are extinguished. From R. M. Herrick, J. M. Myers, and A. L. Koropotkin, Changes in S^D and S^Δ rates during the development of an operant discrimination. *Journal of Comparative and Physiological Psychology*, 1959, **52**, 352–363. Copyright © 1959, by the American Psychological Association and reproduced by permission.

There are four things about the classical operant discrimination training procedure that should be emphasized.

First, the response class (for example, emitting the verbal operant "ball") is already a part of the subject's repertoire and must necessarily be so in order for a discrimination to develop.

Second, besides the necessity of response-contingent reinforcement, the subject must make errors during training—for example, say "ball" in the presence of the S^Δ. Because error responses (emitting R in the presence of S^Δ) are followed by extinction, they tend to produce the kinds of emotional behavior ordinarily observed during the presentation of an extinction schedule. Both errors and the emotional behavior they produce are unfortunate aspects of the classical procedure. It can be argued, however, that organisms subjected to the procedure acquire "frustration tolerance"—that is, they show minimum emotional behavior and disruption during extinction.

Third, even though this type of training produces predominantly S^D responding, S^Δ responding is never entirely eliminated, even when training is completed.

Fourth, this example described the classical discrimination training procedure involving only one relevant stimulus event, the presentation or nonpresentation of a ball. If a stimulus object were to be presented that possessed many different stimulus features or dimensions (such as color, size, or texture), any one dimension could conceivably become an S^D. For example, if we had used a large, red, leather-bound book as the stimulus object, discrimination training could have aimed at the acquisition of a verbal operant under the stimulus control of the book's color or size or the texture of the binding. The verbal operant would then be descriptive of these dimensions.

To sum up, classical operant discrimination training requires that there be instances of reinforced and extinguished responses in the presence of the S^D and the S^Δ, respectively. An undesirable concomitant of this procedure is the unavoidability of the subject's emitting error responses and the attendant emotional behavior that follows them as a result of their being followed by extinction. Finally, it should be emphasized that discriminated operant behaviors, whether they be motor or verbal, arise from a history of training. Without such training neither the light on nor the ball would possess discriminative stimulus functions. Whether or not a stimulus event is a discriminative stimulus depends on its effect on the organism's behavior, and this, in turn, reflects the organism's reinforcement history.

ERRORLESS OPERANT DISCRIMINATION TRAINING

There are two major objections to any training procedure that involves extinction-produced emotional behavior. They include the difficulty in maintaining the operant behavior during extinction and the necessity for prolonged training to establish the discrimination. An alternative procedure has been developed in which errors seldom occur or are eliminated altogether. This procedure is known as *errorless operant discrimination training*.[2]

Suppose, for example, that the goal of training is the development of an operant discrimination in which a child can tell the difference between the letters of the alphabet. The response class is a button-pushing response, which, through discrimination training, comes to be controlled by letters in the alphabet. Correct (reinforced) button-pressing responses occur during the presentation of S+, and incorrect (extinguished) button-pressing responses occur during the presentation of S-.

$$S^+ \longrightarrow R \longrightarrow SR^+$$
$$\text{(button press)}$$

$$S^- \longrightarrow R \longrightarrow EXT$$
$$\text{(button press)}$$

---

[2] For a more comprehensive discussion of the errorless discrimination training procedure, see Terrace (1963).

Training consists of presenting a matching-to-sample discrimination task. The trainee is presented with two or more stimuli, one of which is a match to the sample stimulus (S⁺) and one or more of which are not (S⁻). The steps in the errorless discrimination training procedure are as follows:

First, the child is presented with the sample, S⁺.

Second, he is presented with S⁺ and S⁻ together and must decide which one matches the sample S⁺, which appears above the two stimuli. He indicates his choice by pushing a button located below either S⁺ or S⁻. During this stage S⁺ and S⁻ differ from one another as much as possible and across various stimulus dimensions so as to obscure the relevant stimulus dimension of S⁻ leaving only S⁺. This makes the correct matching response (S⁺) highly probable.

Third, following the subject's repeated responding to S⁺, the magnitude of differences between S⁺ and S⁻ across the possible stimulus dimensions is gradually reduced or faded until S⁺ and S⁻ differ from one another along *a single stimulus dimension*.

A simplified version of this procedure, as it was used in actual practice by Moore and Goldiamond (1964), is as follows:

Phase 1

The child is first presented with a sample stimulus, S⁺, consisting of the letter A.

Phase 2

The child is then presented with two stimuli, the letter A (S⁺) and the letter B (S⁻). The relevant stimulus dimension of S⁺ (A) is form, and the relevant stimulus dimensions of S⁻ (B) are form and brightness. In the beginning of training, the form of S⁻ (the letter B) is not distinguishable because S⁻ is presented at such a low brightness level that its form is obscured. Below each stimulus in the stimulus pairs is a button, which the child presses to indicate which stimulus matches the sample stimulus. This is illustrated in Figure 5-2.

Phase 3

There are repeated presentations of the sample stimulus (S⁺) and the stimulus pair (S⁺ and S⁻). Responses to the button under the S⁺ are always reinforced, and responses to the button under S⁻ are always extinguished. Gradually, the brightness level of S⁻ is increased, so that the magnitude of the difference between S⁺ and S⁻ is reduced and the form of S⁻ (the letter B) becomes visible to the child. Operant discrimination training is completed when most, if not all, button-pressing responses are made to S⁺, even though the brightness level presentations of S⁻ are now comparable to the brightness level presentations of S⁺ and thus the form of the letter B shows

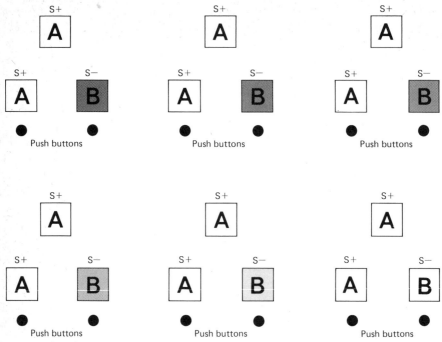

FIGURE 5-2 A schematic diagram illustrating the errorless discrimination training procedure in a matching-to-sample task. The subject must push the button under the correct matching stimulus (S+, the letter A) to be reinforced. S- is completely darkened, concealing the letter B. As training progresses (from left to right), the brightness difference between S+ and S- is faded until S+ and S- differ only in form. In actual practice, the positioning (from left to right) of the pairs of stimuli (S+, S-) is random.

clearly. When satisfactory performance is reached, other letters can be introduced in the same manner.

Modifications of this procedure have been used successfully with animals, children, and adults in many different situations ranging from color or form discriminations to applications in programmed instruction. It is essential to the procedure to make S- as different as possible from S+, and to introduce S- early in training, with brief, repeated exposures as the irrelevant stimulus dimensions are faded out and the relevant stimulus dimension is faded in. The major benefits of the procedure are: (1) sustained performances, (2) the absence of errors, (3) the absence of emotional responses, and (4) more rapid acquisition of the operant discrimination. There are no major disadvantages to the procedure. Moreover, even though classical operant discrimination training procedures build frustration tolerance in the subject by putting some responses on extinction, it does not necessarily follow that the errorless discrimination technique makes the subject more prone to frustration. The errorless operant discrimination technique can be modified so that there are occasions when correct responses are followed by extinction. For example, at the beginning of training, all responses to S⁺ are reinforced (a CRF schedule). Subsequently, a gradual shift in the reinforcement schedule is introduced ending with a VI schedule. In this way, performance is maintained even though the probability of reinforcement is diminished.

THE IDENTIFICATION OF THE DISCRIMINATIVE STIMULUS: A PRACTICAL PROBLEM

The knowledge we have about operant discrimination training procedures has both practical and theoretical significance. Its practical significance arises from the fact that many investigators, in both basic and applied research, are interested in studying the organism's sensitivity to various types of investigator-presented stimuli. There is an obvious question that arises from such study. How does one know when an organism is sensitive to such stimulus presentations? The answer is, of course, that the investigator looks for some sort of response that the organism makes consistently when the stimulus is presented. In lower animals the response is typically a motor response, and in humans it may be either motor or verbal, depending on the sophistication of the subject.

Suppose, for example, we are interested in studying the sensitivity of our favorite pigeon to visual stimuli—particularly, we want to know the minimum amount of light energy that the pigeon's visual system is sensitive to, or the *absolute threshold*. Besides getting a pigeon for our study, we need to select appropriate visual stimuli. The specification of these stimuli can be quite precise if we describe them in terms of standard units of light intensity (footlamberts) and wavelength (angstroms). After specifying the visual stimuli, we have to pick a response class that can be observed during occasions of presentation and nonpresentation of these stimuli. Of course, such stimulus presentations will possess a neutral stimulus function until the pigeon has been exposed to some kind of operant discrimination training procedure.

Fortunately, the details of the necessary training procedure have already been worked out by Blough (1958). The procedure is illustrated in Figure 5-3. In essence, our pigeon is shaped to place his head inside the stimulus-viewing hole and to peck at key A and key B. See Figure 5-3(a). Then, the pigeon is reinforced for pecks on key A when light of a known wavelength and varying intensity is presented in the test-stimulus-viewing patch or for pecks on key B when the test stimulus patch is dark. During testing, pecks on key A reduce the light intensity values appearing in the test stimulus patch and thus provide a descending series of light intensity values. Pecks on key B (when the test stimulus is dark) increase the light intensity values appearing in the test stimulus patch and thus provide an ascending series of light intensity values. See Figure 5-3(b). Thus the S^D for pecking on key A is the appearance of light of varying intensity in the test stimulus patch, and the S^D for pecking on key B is the appearance of darkness in the test stimulus patch. During testing, records are kept of (1) pecking in the presence and in the absence of test stimuli (light of varying intensities),

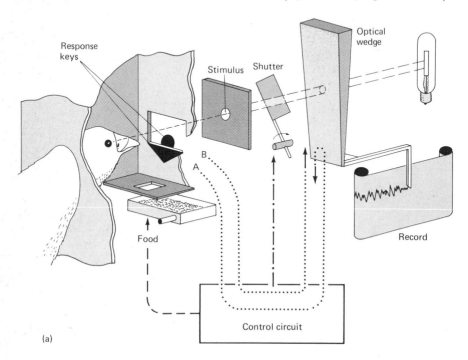

(a)

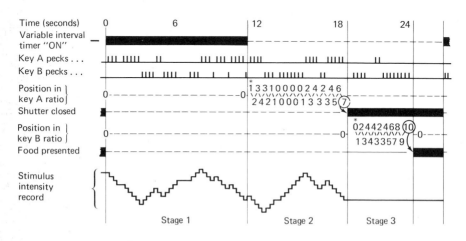

(b)

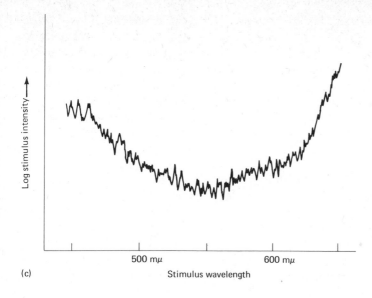

FIGURE 5-3 The Blough technique for obtaining visual thresholds in the pigeon. Figure 5-3(a) shows the apparatus used in establishing the minimum amount of light energy that the pigeon is sensitive to (the absolute threshold). Figure 5-3(b) presents a schematic summary of the procedure, and Figure 5-3(c) presents a function that describes the pigeon's sensitivity to . different wavelengths. From D. S. Blough, A method for obtaining psychophysical thresholds from the pigeon. *Journal of the Experimental Analysis of Behavior*, 1958, 1, 31–43. Copyright © 1958 by the Society for the Experimental Analysis of Behavior and reproduced by permission.

(2) occasions of reinforcement, and (3) readings of the light intensity values during the presentation of the ascending and descending series. See Figure 5-3(b). The absolute threshold is obtained by averaging the light intensity values above which the pigeon pecked 50 percent of the time when the test patch was illuminated.

Thus by carefully applying our knowledge of the procedures involved in operant discrimination training and using automatic stimulus programming and recording equipment, we can obtain reliable data on the sensitivity of a nonverbal organism to stimulus presentations consisting of light intensities of different wavelengths. Such knowledge can also be used to assess the sensitivity of human subjects. For example, suppose a retarded child is brought to the laboratory for examination. Although he possesses no intelligible speech, he is able to move freely about in the physical environment without hazard. It is suspected that he is deaf, but in order to be sure, we must check his sensitivity to auditory stimuli. To do this, we must again make two decisions.

First, we must decide what auditory stimuli to present, and second, we must choose the response to be observed following presentations of these stimuli. Of course, we could make a crude test of the child's sensitivity to auditory stimulation by simply yelling at him or striking a mallet against a metal pan when he is not looking, and then watching for some reaction—perhaps a startle or turning-around pattern. However, a much more careful and less traumatic test would seem to be in order, and Michael and Myerson (Michael, 1967) have adapted the procedures Blough used in training and testing the pigeon to the problems of training and testing nonverbal human subjects for auditory sensitivity.

First, they used pure tone auditory stimuli having frequency and intensity characteristics that are well within the range of auditory sensitivity of normal-hearing subjects and that are within the range of frequencies (from 100 to 3,000 cps) and intensities (from 0 to 65 decibels) used in speech and conversation. The use of these stimuli enabled the investigators to compare the performance of the subject with the performance of those with normal sensitivity to auditory stimuli. By means of special equipment (an electronic auditory signal generator), they were able to specify precisely the frequency and intensity characteristics of the stimuli presented.

Second, they used a lever-pressing response (a motor operant), because the subject's speech was unintelligible and erratic and because lever pressing and magazine training can be acquired quickly. (In magazine training the subject must learn how to obtain edibles from a tray. The procedure will be discussed in detail in Chapter 6.) From then on the testing procedure was aimed at ultimately bringing the child's lever-pressing response under the discriminative control of the auditory stimuli. Figure 5-4 shows the laboratory setup and procedure the investigators used. During phases 1 and 2 of the training, the procedure consisted of making both a light-on condition and a tone-on condition S^D's for lever pressing by reinforcing lever pressing in their presence and making their absence S^Δ's by extinguishing lever pressing in the presence of the tone-off and light-off conditions. A reinforcement schedule was used that maintained a great deal of behavior with minimum reinforcements (VR 8). During phase 3, left and right lever pressing were reinforced in the presence of the appropriate S^D (the light-on or the light-on and the tone-on conditions, respectively). During testing, the light above each lever was faded out entirely leaving only the tone presentations on the right lever in the presence of which responses were reinforced. Left-lever presses during the light-off condition were not reinforced. In essence then, the procedure consisted of making the auditory stimulus into an S^D for pressing the right lever by (1) reinforcing lever pressing in the presence of auditory stimuli and (2) extinguishing lever pressing in their absence. To obtain information on the minimum intensity levels (absolute thresholds) of tones that had acquired the S^D function, the investigators presented different tones at different intensities. They expected that after the subject was trained, the probability of lever-pressing responses in the

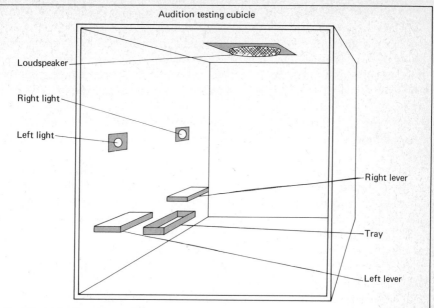

Audition testing cubicle

Loudspeaker

Right light

Left light

Right lever

Tray

Left lever

Audition-Testing Procedure:

1. Reinforcements are made available according to the following schedule.

2. Simultaneous operation of both levers or rapid alteration between levers is never reinforced.

3. Training:

	LEFT LEVER	RIGHT LEVER
Phase 1	Light and tone presentations off	Light and tone presentations on
	Lever presses not reinforced	Lever presses reinforced, VR8
Phase 2	Light only presentation on	Light and tone presentations off
	Lever presses reinforced, VR8	Lever presses not reinforced
Phase 3	alternation between:	
	Light only presentation on	Light and tone presentations on
	Lever presses reinforced, VR8	Lever presses reinforced, VR8
4. Testing:	Light faded out	Light faded out, tone only presentation on, lever presses reinforced, VR8 Tone frequency varied, and within a given frequency, the tone intensity is varied

FIGURE 5-4 The physical layout and procedure for testing the audition of a retardate used by Michael and Myerson (Michael, 1967).

presence of tone presentations of minimum intensity would decrease appreciably, and the probability of lever-pressing responses to higher intensities would increase appreciably. Further they expected one of the three following interpretations to be possible after extensive training in all phases of the procedure but particularly from tests in phase 4:

1. If pressing the right lever is more probable during the different tone presentations than during their absence, the tones are S^D's, and the child can hear.

2. If the child presses both levers about equally, presses them less and less frequently, and never systematically presses the right lever immediately after the tone presentations, even at the highest intensities for all frequencies, the tones are not S^D's, and the child shows *conductive deafness*.

3. If pressing the right lever is more probable during *certain* tone presentations (tones of certain frequencies and intensities) than in their absence, some of the tones are S^D's, but not all of them. The child is only partially deaf and possesses *nerve deafness*.

It was expected, then, that in general a child with normal hearing would press the right lever each time a tone was presented (the S^D condition) and make a *hit*, and that he would not press the right lever when a tone was not presented (the S^Δ condition) and make a *quiet*. Sometimes, however, he would fail to press the lever when a tone was presented and make a *miss*, and sometimes he would press the right lever when a tone was not presented and make a *false alarm*.

The child's sensitivity to these presentations of stimuli depends on two very important factors: First, the anatomic and physiological integrity of the child's auditory system. Second, the extent to which his training has made essentially neutral stimuli (the tones) into discriminative stimuli—in essence, *his reinforcement history*.

It is possible to arrange a training situation so that there is a greater probability of false alarms and misses occurring during testing than of hits and quiets occurring. This is a matter of operant discrimination training, only reinforcements are contingent on lever pressing in the *absence* of a tone presentation (the S^D condition) and no lever pressing in the presence of the tone (the S^Δ condition). In short, the reinforcement contingencies required to increase the probabilities of false alarms[3] and misses are the *reverse* of the reinforcement contingencies required to increase the probabilities of hits and quiets.

Sometimes such contingencies occur in the natural environment, and when an individual whose behavior has been controlled by them is studied, special

---

[3] When false alarms consist of verbal reports of the presence of sounds, noises, or voices when, in fact, such forms of stimulation are not present, such behavior is often described by clinical psychologists and psychiatrists as hallucinatory.

testing procedures are necessary, as the following case reported by Grosz and Zimmerman (1965) illustrates:

The patient was a 40-year-old married male whose father ran away when the son was eleven. Although the patient quit school at the age of sixteen because he said he liked to work better, his work history was sporadic. When he was twenty-three, he entered the service for a 3-year period, during which he developed dendritic keratitis of the right eye. Although there was good recovery, he did sustain a loss in vision (acuity of 20/80), which entitled him to a small disability pension upon discharge. While in the service he was involved in an auto accident in which a civilian was seriously injured, an event that he failed to recall. He himself was not injured. From 1945, when he was discharged from the service, until 1957, his adjustment was poor, and he was frequently out of work. This necessitated financial assistance from his family and the welfare department.

In 1957, while he was Christmas shopping with his wife and mother-in-law, who were reported to be very demanding, he suddenly became blind in both eyes. He was admitted to the veterans hospital, and neurological and ophthalmological examinations were performed. The results of both were negative. At this time he did not seem upset about his blindness, but rather showed an attitude of forbearance. His blindness continued on and off over a period of 8 years.

In the course of his receiving an examination, his sight was recovered just as suddenly as it was lost. An important element of this examination was operant discrimination training. When he was tested during periods of blindness, he failed to report verbally the presence of visual acuity test stimuli. He also used a blind man's tapping stick while walking (ostensibly to avoid collisions with obstacles), and he failed to recognize the faces of others when directly confronted by them. However, during these periods he was observed eating with utensils and successfully reaching for small objects. On one occasion, he confided to a nurse that he was beginning to see, but that she should not tell anyone about it. On another occasion, he told the same nurse that he was so experienced that he would never have to work hard again. Probably it is significant that he received a disability pension for his blindness, that the welfare department had known his family as "moochers" for over 20 years, and that the patient had two aunts who were blind late in life. What is more, even after he recovered his sight and began to work, his blindness returned some 8 months later. In 1965 (when he was blind), his "earnings" from Social Security and disability payments were $4,200. His best year's earnings from work were $3,800. His total earnings from 1937 to 1951 were less than $7,000.

The problem faced by anyone examining him was to determine whether or not he could see and whether or not the reported blindness was attributable to hysteria (a form of neurosis) or malingering.

A testing apparatus and procedure were devised to determine whether or not the patient's behavior during a period of reported blindness was actually under the control of visual stimuli. The patient was seated before a console containing three windows. A triangle was projected through each window, and below each window there was a lever. One triangle was inverted and two were upright. The patient was told to look at the three windows and, when the buzzer sounded, to press one of the levers. (His hand was directed until it touched each of the three levers. He was told that if he pressed the correct lever, the buzzer would stop. Otherwise, the buzzer would continue to sound for 5 seconds. After this, he would hear clicks for 10 seconds, and then the buzzer would again sound. He was instructed to make as many correct responses as he could and told that on any trial any one of the switches could be correct. He was also told that in any given session all three of the switches would be correct about the same number of times. He was *not* told that each session consisted of 120 trials, nor was any mention made of the fact that visual stimuli were involved, although he was told sessions would last about 30 minutes.

At the end of each session a record was obtained of the total number of correct responses (pressing the lever under the inverted triangle) and the cumulative response latency (the interval of time between the onset of the buzzer and lever depression). There were 132 daily sessions. During sessions 1, 2, 3, and 9 triangles were not presented thus making these sessions a control and a base line. (These sessions were a control in the sense that when no triangles were presented, none could be seen —a condition analogous to being blind.) It was expected that by guessing alone the subject would be correct one-third of the time. On the other hand, should the number of correct responses fall below twenty-seven, an event that occurs by chance alone only one time in a hundred, it would indicate that the patient could see and that he deliberately avoided pressing the lever under the inverted triangle. Should the number of correct responses exceed fifty-three, another event that occurs by chance only one time in a hundred, then it would be proved beyond chance that he could see the triangles.

The results are shown in Table 5-1. During the control sessions in which there were no visual stimuli, the number of correct responses fell well within the chance range. During sessions involving presentations of the triangles, the number of correct responses dropped well below the chance range, suggesting that the patient could see the inverted triangle but avoided pressing the lever under it.

Then, following two control sessions (sessions 122 and 123) and five sessions with the triangles (sessions 124–128), a social manipulation

Table 5-1 The Number of Correct Responses Made by the Patient During Presentations Without and With Triangles.

SESSION	CONDITION	NUMBER OF CORRECT RESPONSES
1	Control—no triangles	39
2	Control	46
3	Control	49
4	Triangles	38
5	Triangles	28
6	Triangles	23
7	Triangles	20
8	Triangles	19
9	Control—no triangles	35
10	Triangles	21
11	Triangles	18
12	Triangles	12
13	Triangles	11
14	Triangles	12
15	Triangles	8
16	Triangles	7
17	Triangles	9
18	Triangles	10
122	Control—no triangles	37
123	Control	34
124	Triangles	20
125	Triangles	20
126	Triangles	18
127	Triangles	23
128	Triangles	20
	Social Manipulation	
129	Triangles	43
130	Triangles	49
131	Triangles	42
132	Triangles	36

From H. J. Grosz and J. Zimmerman, Experimental analysis of hysterical blindness: A follow-up report and new experimental data. *Archives of General Psychiatry*, 1965, **13**, 255–260. Copyright © 1965, American Medical Association and reproduced by permission.

was introduced. The experimenter's assistant established rapport with the patient by sympathizing with him, complaining about his own lot as an assistant, and expressing hostility toward the doctors examining the patient. The assistant then told the patient that the doctors believed he could see, for they knew that if he were really blind, he would make about 40 correct responses in each session. Following these revelations, there were four more sessions. The results are also shown in Table 5-1. This social manipulation clearly had a powerful effect on the patient's behavior. Not only were the number of correct responses for sessions 129–132 abruptly increased to a point where they were clearly within the number range expected by chance (that is, the number range expected if the subject were truly blind), but there was also a large increase in the response latencies.

There are several things that should be emphasized about this example. First, despite the subject's virtually normal sense-organ anatomy and physiology, his history prior to testing maximized the likelihood of his making misses during testing. Second, over and above the mere presentation of test stimuli, other stimulation going on during testing had a powerful effect on the subject's behavior. Both the presentations of the triangles and the social manipulation (the verbal instruction from the experimenter's assistant) as discriminative stimulus presentations modified the subject's behavior. Finally, this effect was not possible if the patient had not had a reinforcement history for following such instructions.

The procedures derived from behavior theory are quite useful, then, not only in creating discriminative stimuli from neutral stimuli, but also in the identification of discriminative stimuli. We cannot, however, always specify the *specific aspect or dimension* of a stimulus that possesses discriminative properties for a particular organism. For example, although we can make a colored disk an S^D for pecking, we cannot be sure that the pecking isn't controlled by some other stimulus dimension such as the disk's brightness or form. Of course, a knowledge of a particular pigeon's reinforcement history will give us a partial answer to this question (since reinforcement variables are important in the development of a discriminative stimulus). However, other factors, perhaps innate or genetic factors, may also be involved. Species do differ in their sensitivity to stimuli because of their anatomic and physiological characteristics, and this may make some organisms more sensitive to certain stimulus dimensions and less sensitive to others.

THE IDENTIFICATION OF THE DISCRIMINATIVE STIMULUS: A PROBLEM OF THEORETICAL SIGNIFICANCE

In our previous discussions we studied some of the practical problems one encounters in trying to make neutral stimuli into discriminative stimuli and in trying to devise tests that establish that these stimuli actually do function as discriminative stimuli. In the context of traditional approaches in psychology, these are problems in perception. We also found some of the solutions to these problems, even though we limited our analysis to observable environmental, or S, events (such as the amount and kind of reinforcement, the schedule of reinforcement, and physical specification of the visual or auditory stimulus) and to observable behavioral, or R, events (for example, the lever-pressing response).

A more traditional analysis, however, would conceptualize the problem of the identification of the discriminative stimulus within the context of a three-stage model, as follows:

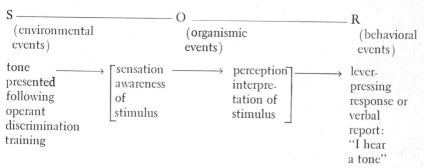

S	O	R
(environmental events)	(organismic events)	(behavioral events)

Between the observable and verifiable S and R events are the inferred organismic, or O, events. These are (1) the sensation, which is perhaps an awareness of the stimulus (tone), and (2) the perception, which is perhaps an interpretation of the stimulus.[4] This perception, in turn, produces the perceptual response, consisting in this case of lever pressing or perhaps a verbal report that the stimulus is present. Furthermore, according to those workers who employ the three-stage (S-O-R) model, the perceptual response is affected by perceptual processes, as intrapsychic states themselves, and still other intrapsychic states or events such as repression or drive. So according to this view, the perceptual response may be determined by a host of O events, in addition to the S event presentations occurring during testing. Moreover, it is quite common for the investigator to use the individual's perceptual response (that is, his verbal report) to make inferences about the individual's psychic state (his perceptual processes and other events affecting them, such as repression and drive).

An example is provided by the well-known Rorschach inkblot test. Figure 5-5 shows a card from this test. The marked areas represent the male

---

[4] Workers by no means agree on the definitions of the terms *sensation* and *perception*. The usage above tends to stress intrapsychic states or processes, but many observers would prefer to refer to underlying physiological processes. For example, a sensation may be regarded as the response of a sense organ (in this case the discharge of the auditory or visual sense receptors), and perception may be regarded as the activation of the central nervous system caused by the sensation. Although the physiological processes that underlie perceptual processes can often be observed precisely, the extent to which they can be systematically and functionally related either to the intrapsychic states or processes involved in sensation and perception or to the so-called perceptual response (lever pressing or verbally reporting the presence of the stimulus) is not precise.

Sex areas

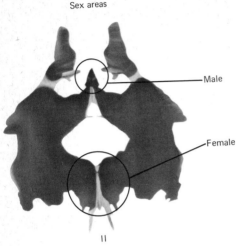

Male

Female

II

FIGURE 5-5 Sample card from the Rorschach inkblot test. Marked portions of the plot show the male and female sex areas. From B. Klopfer and H. H. Davidson, *Individual record blank: The Rorschach technique: An introductory manual.* Copyright © 1962, Harcourt Brace Jovanovich, New York and reproduced by permission.

and female sex areas, and when an individual fails to use these areas in developing his concepts about the inkblot (that is, in giving the examiner his verbal report of what he sees in the blot), this perceptual response is considered to reveal repression of sexual impulses. When an individual does use these areas of the blot to develop concepts (for example, when he reports that the female area looks like a vagina or a butterfly), he is regarded as accepting of his sexual impulses and is, therefore, regarded as more normal.[5]

However, these responses, like other perceptual responses (for example, verbally reporting the presence of a tone presented during an audiometric test), are a function of the subject's reinforcement history. Individuals who use portions of the blot other than the sexual area to develop their concepts do so simply because those portions possess a form, color, texture, or shading characteristic that controls the perceptual response (through stimulus generalization—a matter to be discussed shortly. And, of course, the same is true of those who use the sexual areas of the blots in the development of their concepts.

What is important, then, is (1) the subject's prior exposure to situations involving visual stimuli having a form, color, shading, or texture charac-

---

[5] It may have occurred to the reader that there is an element of circular reasoning involved in this interpretation. The investigator (1) observes the individual's perceptual response (his failure to use the sexual area of the blot), (2) infers from the response that sexual repression has occurred, and (3) attempts to prove that the repression has occurred by pointing to the individual's perceptual response.

istic of the sex anatomy, (2) whether or not perceptual responses to such stimuli have been reinforced, and (3) the similarity of those stimuli to the stimulus properties of the sexual areas of the inkblot. Most of us have been given little or no training in giving verbal (perceptual) reports to sexual stimuli, so it is not surprising that when we are presented with an inkblot containing such stimuli (as visual stimuli), we aren't very likely to report them verbally. If, on the other hand, one has had a great deal of such training, it would not be surprising if he were to give such reports. Either way, it becomes a matter of *response bias*—the likelihood of the person's making a certain perceptual response because of the extent of his prior (operant discrimination) training in making that response. Thus it is not necessary to extend our analysis beyond those observable and verifiable historical and contemporary events that produce the perceptual response.

STIMULUS CLASS AND STIMULUS GENERALIZATION

Stimulus presentations during discrimination training are rarely identical. They are, however, sufficiently similar to acquire stimulus control (through the operant discrimination training procedure) of a response class. When similar stimuli have stimulus control over a response class, they are said to be members of the same *stimulus class*.

One phenomenon for which the concept of stimulus class has implications is *perceptual constancy*. The size or color of an object, for example, an orange, varies from one presentation to the next. On some occasions it may be viewed close up, and on others, farther away. On still other occasions, it may be viewed under illumination that gives it a varying color. Despite these variations, however, the orange will be reported to have the same size and color, a matter of size and color constancy, respectively. Some observers attribute this size and color constancy to a basic intrapsychic process—a tendency for perceptual constancy, or tendency to see the world in a stable manner.

Another interpretation, however, stresses the observer's reinforcement history and present environmental (stimulus) variables. Suppose, for example, you are asked to look at a dinner plate from the edge of a table rather than from directly above it and that someone asks you its shape. Despite the fact that the plate forms an elliptical rather than round image on the retina of your eye, you are very likely to say it is round, an example of shape constancy. The chances are that you have been repeatedly reinforced for saying "round" in the presence of (1) a plate presented at varying angles (forming both round and elliptical images on your retina), and (2) the question "What shape is the plate?" Furthermore, the chances are that you've never been reinforced for saying "elliptical" in the presence of a plate presented at an angle (forming an elliptical image on the retina) and the question "What shape is the plate?" Of course, there is no reason why you couldn't have been trained to provide a more accurate description of the plate's shape. For example, you could have been reinforced for reporting "round" when you viewed the plate from directly above and "elliptical" for all views of the plate at an angle. Ordinarily, however, we are not given such precise training in the shape of objects or for that matter in their size or color, even though such constancies can be analyzed in the same way.

Then there is the possibility that stimuli not originally involved in the operant discrimination training procedure control the response class involved in the original training through *stimulus generalization*. For example, when a child whose training has progressed to a point where he will reliably call the letter E an "E" is presented with the letter F, he may call it an "E." In this instance the vocal response "E" is controlled by the new visual stimulus, the letter F, through stimulus generalization.

When stimulus generalization is studied, three distinct steps are involved. First, operant discrimination training is given in which some behavior of the organism is brought under the control of a particular stimulus. Second, when the S^D reliably controls the response class of concern, the schedule on which the consequences were presented is changed to an intermittent schedule, usually a VI schedule. This tends to maintain the discriminated behavior for prolonged periods despite only occasional reinforcements. Third, tests are performed in which stimuli not used during training are presented to the subject so the investigator can see how much stimulus control they possess over the operant used during training. The data obtained from these tests can then be used to plot a curve called a *generalization gradient*. This curve shows the relative probability of the subject's responding to the various stimuli presented during the tests of generalization as well as the probability of his responding to the original stimulus.

In one classic study by Guttman and Kalish (1956), pigeons were first trained to peck at a disk through which monochromatic light was shown for a period of 60 seconds (the original stimulus). Pecks on the disk in the presence of this light produced grain in the food hopper on a VI schedule. At the end of each minute of exposure to the monochromatic light in the disk, both the light inside the box and the disk light were turned off for 10 seconds. This 10-second lights-out condition was used later as a means of presenting the test stimuli. It was introduced during training so that the conditions of testing would be the same as those during training (except for the introduction of the test stimuli). Thus the lights-out condition did *not* serve as a cue for the beginning of the testing period.

Four different groups of pigeons were used, and each group was presented with a different monochromatic light. The original training stimuli included the following wavelengths: 530, 550, 580, and 600mμ. During the tests of

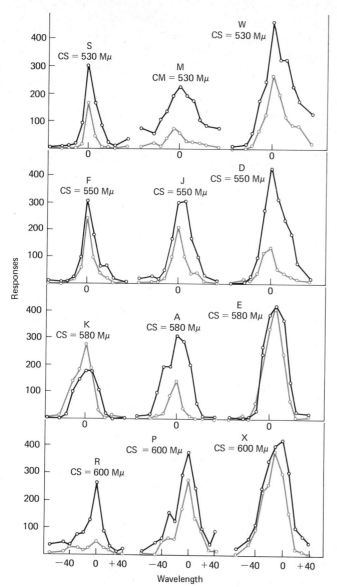

FIGURE 5-6 Generalization gradients obtained for twelve pigeons. Each group of four was trained with a different original training stimulus (lights of 530, 550, 580, and 600mμ). Each training stimulus is designated as zero on the abscissa. From N. H. Guttman and H. I. Kalish, Discriminability and stimulus generalization. *Journal of Experimental Psychology*, 1956, **51**, 79–88. Copyright © 1956, by the American Psychological Association and reproduced by permission.

generalization an extinction schedule was presented and ten different additional stimuli were presented in random order to see how much pecking they controlled. During these tests none of the pecking responses were reinforced. Figure 5-6 shows the generalization gradients obtained for each of the twelve subjects. Notice that during extinction the greatest number of responses were to the original stimuli (those designated by the zero on the abscissa). Notice too that generalization (the percentage of responses) is the greatest to test stimuli that were the most like the original training stimuli. For example, during the first test, when the original training stimulus was 600mμ, the subjects made from 280 to 540 responses. When the test stimuli were 40mμ above or below the original stimulus (640 and 560mμ, respectively), the number of responses ranged from about 10 to 50. On the other hand, when the test stimuli were only 10mμ above or below the original training stimuli, the subjects made from 140 to over 400 responses. Figure 5-6 also shows that the data for the second generalization test were comparable to the first generalization test, and that the gradients for all subjects were surprisingly similar.

However, the kind of generalization gradient that occurs depends on a number of other important conditions, for example, whether or not the operant discrimination training procedure prior to the tests of generalization involved the occurrence of errors (S^Δ responding). Terrace (1966) found that when training does involve the subject's making errors (as in the differential reinforcement procedure), there is a shift in the peak of the generalization gradient away from S^+ to S^-. On the other hand, when such training is errorless, there is no peak shift. See Figure 5-7.

What these generalization gradients show, then, is that there are stimuli that possess discriminative (stimulus) control over the organism's behavior *even though* the organism has *never had any training* with *them*. In general, those stimuli that are most like the original training stimulus are the most apt to possess this function. There are, however, important exceptions.

If discrimination training has provided exposure to both S^D and S^Δ and has involved the subject's making errors, then maximum generalization is to stimuli that lie beyond the S^D on the S^D–S^Δ stimulus intensity continuum (Pierrel and Sherman, 1960). If, for example, the stimulus intensity of the S^D, a tone, is 30 decibels and the stimulus intensity of the S^Δ is 10 decibels, there is almost as much lever pressing during tests of generalization to a tone having a stimulus intensity of 40 decibels as there is to the original tone of 30 decibels. Maximum generalization can occur when the test stimulus is below the stimulus intensity of the S^D, provided that the intensity of the S^Δ stimulus exceeds that of the S^D. See Figure 5-8. What this suggests is that it is the subject's reinforcement history more than the mere intensity of a stimulus that determines the subject's sensitivity to the stimulus (as revealed by the gradient of generalization).

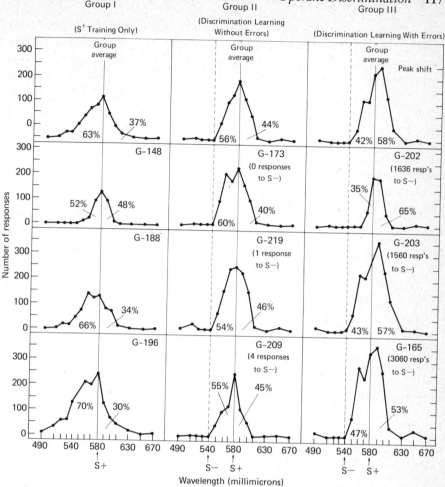

FIGURE 5-7 The generalization gradients obtained with and without errors in the training procedure. Notice the peak shift of the gradient obtained with the classical operant discrimination training procedure. From H. S. Terrace, Wavelength generalization after discrimination learning with and without errors. *Science*, 1964, **144**, 78–80. Copyright © 1964 by the American Association for the Advancement of Science and reproduced by permission.

The generalization gradients also show that discrimination is the sharpest or the most precise (that is, most of the organism's responses are under the control of the stimuli that are the most like S⁺) when the discrimination was acquired under the errorless procedure rather than the classical operant discrimination training procedure. The classical operant discrimination training procedure yields gradients in which there is more responding to stimuli other than the original training stimulus (the S⁺), but such training affects the response rate and latency as well. After training using the differential reinforcement procedure in which responses in the presence of the S⁺ are reinforced and responses in the presence of the S⁻ are extinguished, the presentation of S⁺ right after the presentation of S⁻ increases response rate to S⁺ (Reynolds, 1961) and the response latency to S⁺ (Jenkins, 1961). These changes in response rate and latency to S⁺ following exposure to S⁻ and the opposite effect, which occurs when the order of presentation of S⁺ and S⁻ is reversed, are known as *behavioral contrast*. Such contrast effects occur only following operant discrimination training in which presentations of S⁺ and S⁻ have been correlated with reinforcement and extinction (or rich and lean reinforcement schedules), respectively. The effect does not occur in sequential presentations of S⁺ or S⁻ following errorless discrimination training (Terrace, 1963).

Although the emphasis in stimulus generalization is on the stimulus control of new test stimuli that are like the original training stimulus, there are occasions when an operant can be brought under the control of a single,

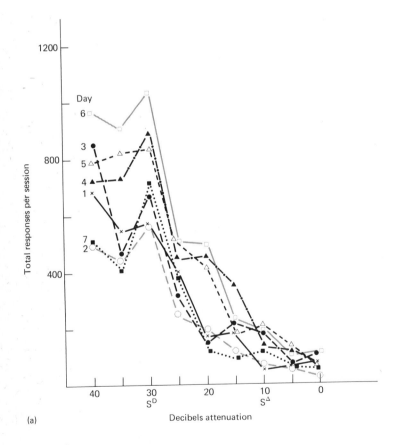

(a)

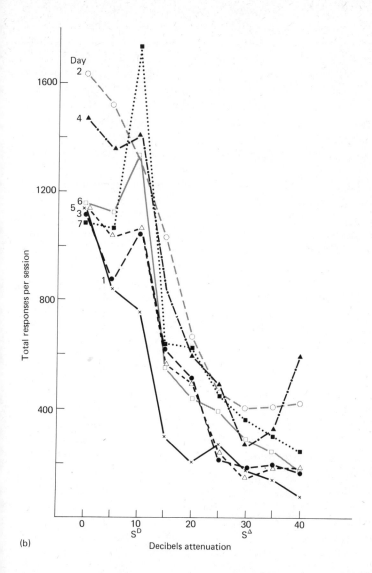

(b)

FIGURE 5-8 Generalization gradients following classical operant discrimination with both S^D and S^Δ presentations. Stimuli that lie at the S^D end of the S^D–S^Δ stimulus intensity continuum control the greatest amount of lever pressing, even though the stimuli beyond S^D may be of either higher (5-8a) or lower stimulus intensity (5-8b) than the S^D. From R. Pierrel and J. G. Sherman, Generalization of auditory intensity following discrimination training. *Journal of the Experimental Analysis of Behavior,* 1960, **3**, 313–322. Copyright © 1960 by the Society for the Experimental Analysis of Behavior, Inc., and reproduced by permission.

stimulus *element* that is common to various discrete and somewhat different stimuli. When such control exists, the organism is said to have formed a concept, or an abstraction. Consider, for example, the concept of the human being—a class of entities varying remarkably: Some are fat, others skinny; some are tall, and some are short; some are white, and others are black, brown, red, or yellow; some may be dressed, while others are undressed; some are children, and others are adults; and some may be standing, while others are seated or lying down. Despite this remarkable variation from one person to the next, a person is still a member of a class of entities we call human beings. This is because at one time or another, we have been reinforced for saying "human being" in the presence of people, and we have not been reinforced for saying "human being" in their absence.

Herrnstein and Loveland (1964) used a reinforcement procedure to teach pigeons the concept of the human being. The differential response in their procedure was pecking at a high rate in the presence of black-and-white and colored 35-mm. slides of human beings, which were projected on a screen inside the birds' box. There were over eighty training slides. Half of the slides had people in them, photographed against landscapes, water scenes, meadows, and the like, and the other half did not have people in them. Even though the people in the slides came in all sizes, shapes, and colors, the birds did form a concept, or abstraction, of the human being. Pecking rate was the highest in the presence of the human beings and the lowest in their absence. What is more, when the pigeons erred, the human being in the picture was usually obscured in some way by other details in the photograph.

Finally, when two or more stimuli are presented simultaneously, organisms can also be trained to perform an operant discrimination based on the *relationship between* the *stimuli*. The procedure involved in such training is described in Figure 5-9. During phase 1 two circles of unequal size are presented, and button-pushing responses to the larger of the two circles are reinforced, thus making the larger circle an S^+. Button-pushing responses to the smaller of the two circles are not reinforced, thus making that circle an S^-. During phase 2 the subject is again exposed to two circles, one of which was the larger circle of the first pair (formerly the S^+) but is now the smaller circle of the new pair (and is now an S^-). However, the subject will push the button under the larger of the two circles even though he has *never been reinforced* for doing so. In other words, *transposition* has occurred in which the subject's button-pushing response is under the control of the relationship between two new stimuli (the larger of any pair of circles), not just the absolute size of a circle. In this test of generalization, sometimes called the *transposition experiment*, the subject is responding to the *relationship between* the *two stimuli* rather than to the absolute size of the individual stimuli. When other pairs of unequally sized circles are presented, he will tend to respond to the larger of the two. Subjects given extensive training

Procedure:

1. During phase 1 reinforcements are presented following button presses for S⁺ (the larger circle) but not for S⁻ (the smaller circle).

2. During phase 2 the investigator makes a test of generalization by observing the subject's responses to a new pair in which the S⁺ of phase 1 (formerly the larger circle) is now the S⁻, or the smaller of the pair.

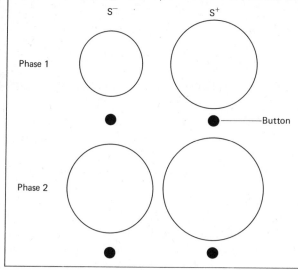

FIGURE 5-9 The training procedure for the acquisition of an operant discrimination based on the relationship between two stimuli.

with different pairs of circles (in phase 1) are trained, in effect, to respond to a single stimulus property of two somewhat different stimuli. In this case, it is the relative size of the two stimuli (an abstraction) that controls the button-pressing response.

VERBAL INSTRUCTIONS AS Sᴰ'S

Much of what is done in the way of behavior control in natural situations consists of presenting some form of *verbal instructions* to the subject whose behavior one seeks to control. These verbal instructions occur in many contexts, including, for example, test instructions and instructions in psychological experiments, directions presented orally in the classroom and in lectures, and the suggestions a psychotherapist makes to his patient. Regardless of where they occur, these verbal instructions can be viewed as stimuli possessing possible discriminative stimulus (Sᴰ) functions.

As individuals engage in social interactions, it is common for one person to administer verbal instructions (as S^D's) to another person, and then follow the instructions with reinforcement when the appropriate response occurs. For example:

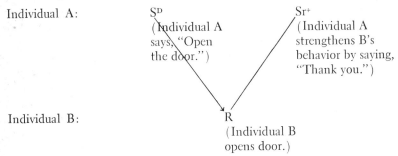

Individual A:

S^D
(Individual A
says, "Open
the door.")

Sr^+
(Individual A
strengthens B's
behavior by saying,
"Thank you.")

Individual B:

R
(Individual B
opens door.)

In this example individual A administers the verbal instructions (S^D) "Open the door"; B opens the door; and A reinforces B by thanking him. Such a sequence involves response-contingent reinforcement in the presence of the instructions, the effect of which is operant discrimination training. B would be more apt to open the door and then to be thanked when A asked him to (the S^D condition) than when A did not ask him to (the S^Δ condition), and on future occasions B will probably follow A's instructions. Of course, this training sequence is simplified. In reality, A would probably have presented another set of consequences to B had B failed to follow A's instructions (perhaps punish him). In any case, *it seems fairly clear that B's skill in following instructions is related to his prior exposure to an appropriate S^D (determined by his previous trainers) and to his prior reinforcement history.*

Other examples include the reader of an instruction manual who is reinforced when he performs the appropriate manipulative responses and makes the equipment work, the patient who feels better following the doctor's instructions, and the pupil who is reinforced for making the correct responses on a test.

However, should a subject fail to follow instructions by performing the appropriate behavior, several explanations are possible:

1. Appropriate S^D's were never presented to the subject. For example, a child may never have been exposed to a ball; yet he is expected to be able to name it.

2. The subject never emitted the appropriate response class in the presence of the S^D. For example, the ball was presented, but the verbal operant was not emitted.

3. The subject received appropriate S^D's and emitted the appropriate R; but he was never or infrequently reinforced, he was punished for following instructions (the work of an erratic trainer no doubt), or reinforcement was

delayed, thus strengthening some other irrelevant operant. For example, the ball was presented and the child emitted the operant; but either he was rarely or never reinforced, or his response was followed by punishment.

4. The subject was presented with the appropriate S^D, but he emitted some other inappropriate response class, which was strengthened and is incompatible with the appropriate response class. For example, the ball was presented, and the child said, "circle" and was then reinforced.

Whether or not verbal instructions possess appropriate discriminative stimulus functions depends, then, on a number of conditions, and even when these conditions have been fulfilled, the instructional control of behavior tends to be limited to the S^D and operant in question. In order for a child to show extensive ability in following instructions, he would have to have been trained to follow a multitude of instructions presented by a variety of trainers in a variety of situations.

The importance of adequate operant discrimination training in the development of sustained and complex behavior cannot be overstated. Simply following the verbal instructions of others is a case in point. Whether or not one follows instructions depends on the stimulus control such instructions acquire in the operant discrimination process. Of course, many of the prolonged and sustained performances shown by organisms in the absence of any obvious consequences are occasions of stimulus control.[6] For example, a child prodigy may seat himself before the piano, arrange his music, and practice piano by himself for 6 hours a day. Such a performance arises out of past occasions of operant discrimination training, in which there has been a thinning out of the schedule of consequences so that there are far fewer occasions of reinforcement than occurred earlier in training. The child's behavior, then, would be described as being primarily under stimulus control rather than schedule control.

Then there is the matter of *contingency contracts*. These are agreements between a trainer and a trainee, and they take the form of a verbal instruction that specifies the response sought by the trainer and the consequences

---

[6] It seems reasonable to assume that the behavior induced in a specific setting by verbal instructions would not be the same as the behavior induced through shaping procedures. In the latter, the reinforcements are only made available contingent on the occurrence of some response class having particular dimensional properties. For example, if a subject in a psychological experiment is told to push a button when he detects a target on a screen (instructional control over his behavior), the response class dimension of particular concern is frequency. On the other hand, if this response class is induced by shaping, the reinforcement contingency affects not only the frequency of the button-pushing response, but also its topography, its force, and its duration. Although there are undoubtedly occasions in psychological research when it is useful to induce behavior in the subject through verbal instructions, one cannot always assume that the verbal instructions as S^D's possess the same kind of precise control over the operant for a particular subject that shaping procedures would possess. Nor can one assume that all subjects have a common history of operant discrimination training—a matter to be discussed further in Chapter 11.

to be made available to the trainee contingent on the occurrence of that response. The mother may say, for example, "Do your homework (the behavior), and then you can watch TV" (the consequence). If, in fact, the child does get to watch TV after doing his homework, the mother's instructions ("Do your homework, then you can watch TV") become a stimulus in the presence of which the child's behavior is reinforced. Once this contract has been repeated successfully, the formal statement of the contract can be slowly faded out, as the child's behavior comes to be more and more under the control of the study situation. Eventually, the verbal instructions are no longer needed. As we shall see, such contracts are an important form of behavior control.

The examples in this chapter stressed the presentation of positive consequences immediately following the emitted operant in the presence of S^D. Illustrations could also have been used in which aversive consequences followed the emitted operant in the presence of the S^D. Furthermore, in most of the examples a single stimulus event was described as an S^D. As we shall see later, a given situation may, in fact, contain a number of stimulus elements, all of which combine to possess a controlling stimulus function.

STUDY QUESTIONS

1. Give two examples of discriminated operant behavior.
2. With what event is an S^D correlated? An S^Δ?
3. What are the basic characteristics of the classical operant discrimination procedure?
4. What is the behavioral significance of making errors in discrimination training? (Hint: With what event are errors correlated, and what is its effect on behavior?)
5. Cite two criticisms of the classical discrimination training procedure.
6. With what event is S^+ correlated? S^-?
7. Describe the essential features of the matching-to-sample task.
8. Cite one advantage of the classical discrimination procedure.
9. Describe the major features of the errorless discrimination training procedure.
10. In the example of the child learning the alphabet,
    a. initially what were the relevant stimulus dimensions of S^+ and S^-?
    b. what stimulus dimension of S^- changed during training?
    c. what were the relevant stimulus dimensions of S^+ and S^- at the conclusion of training?
11. What are the major advantages of the errorless discrimination training procedure?
12. How can frustration tolerance be increased in the errorless discrimination procedure?
13. Look over Figure 5-1 and find evidence that supports the assertion that "be-

havior controlled by an S^D is simply much more probable than behavior in its absence."

14. In what ways may the interests and activities of animal and child psychologists be the same? In what sense might both types of psychologists be applied psychologists?

15. When designing a test situation to determine an organism's sensitivity to stimuli, what two questions must we ask?

16. In the method for obtaining the absolute threshold in the pigeon,
    a. what is the reinforcer maintaining pecks on key A? On key B?
    b. what is the range of sensitivity in wavelengths of the pigeon to light stimuli?

17. Give three criticisms of the crude procedure for testing the retardate's auditory sensitivity described on page 104.

18. What were the three possible outcomes of the audition-testing procedure, and how were they interpreted? What kinds of responses would a child with normal hearing make to the presentation or the nonpresentation of the tone?

19. What finally defines the tone as a discriminative stimulus?

20. Distinguish between a hit, a miss, a quiet, and a false alarm, giving the conditions of stimulation and the subject's responses to them.

21. In the case of the hysteric-malingerer,
    a. how did sessions 1–3 serve as both a control and a base-line observation?
    b. why was it difficult to determine whether or not the patient was a hysteric or a malingerer?

22. Describe two major limiting factors in the identification of the discriminative stimuli in a particular case and how they might possibly be overcome.

23. How does a traditional approach to behavior deal with the problem of the identification of the discriminative stimulus?

24. a. Of what value is the perceptual response to those of a traditional persuasion?
    b. Using the Rorschach test as an example, describe how the perceptual response is used in the observation of the psyche. Suggest some limitations to this procedure.
    c. Offer an alternative account of such perceptual responses. (Hint: What is response bias?)

25. Define stimulus class and discuss its utility in accounting for the notion of perceptual constancy.

26. What happens in stimulus generalization? Describe the steps involved in studying stimulus generalization in the pigeon or the rat.

27. What is revealed by a gradient of generalization?

28. What is the difference between the generalization gradients obtained after classical discrimination training procedures and those obtained after errorless discrimination training procedures?

29. For precision in discrimination, what is the training procedure of choice? Find evidence for this choice in the figures in this chapter.

30. What stimulus sequences lead to behavioral contrast effects? Suggest a mode of training to avoid contrast effects.

31. Explain how an operant can be controlled by:
    a. Stimuli that are different from one another.
    b. The relationship between stimuli. (Hint: Distinguish between abstraction and transposition.)
32. What is the basis for viewing a verbal instruction as an S^D?
33. How is the view that verbal instructions are S^D's related to the notion of a contingency contract?
34. What four explanations are possible when a child fails to follow instructions?
35. What probably characterizes the history of a child who shows a good ability to follow instructions? Describe a program of training to make a child skillful at following instructions.
36. Behavior at one moment may be under both schedule and stimulus control. Describe the effects on a discriminated operant of suddenly removing (a) an S^D (stimulus control) and (b) the consequences (schedule control).
37. Suggest some reasons why behavior under instructional control may be different from behavior acquired by shaping.

REFERENCES

Allen, R. M. *Student's Rorschach manual*. New York: International Universities Press, 1966.

Blough, D. S. A method for obtaining psychophysical thresholds from the pigeon. *Journal of Experimental Analysis of Behavior*, 1958, **1**, 31–43.

Blough, D. S. The study of animal sensory processes by operant methods. In W. K. Honig (Ed.), *Operant behavior: Areas of research and application*. New York: Appleton-Century-Crofts, 1966.

Brady, J. P., and Lind, D. L. Experimental analysis of hysterical blindness. *Archives of General Psychiatry*, 1961, **4**, 331–339.

Goldiamond, I. Perception. In A. J. Bachrach (Ed.), *Experimental foundations of clinical psychology*. New York: Basic Books, 1962.

Grosz, H. J., and Zimmerman, J. Experimental analysis of hysterical blindness: A follow-up report and new experimental data. *Archives of General Psychiatry*, 1965, **13**, 255–260.

Guttman, N., and Kalish, H. I. Discriminability and stimulus generalization. *Journal of Experimental Psychology*, 1956, **51**, 79–88.

Herrick, R. M., Myers, J. L., and Koropotkin, A. L. Changes in S^D and S^Δ rates during the development of an operant discrimination. *Journal of Comparative and Physiological Psychology*, 1959, **52**, 359–363.

Herrnstein, R. J., and Loveland, D. H. Complex visual concept in the pigeon. *Science*, 1964, **146**, 549–551.

Holland, J. S., and Skinner, B. F. *The analysis of behavior*. New York: McGraw-Hill, 1961.

Jenkins, H. M. The effect of discrimination training on extinction. *Journal of Experimental Psychology*, 1961, **61**, 111–121.

Klopfer, B., Ainsworth, M. C., Klopfer, W. G., and Holt, R. R. *Developments in the Rorschach technique*. Yonkers, N.Y.: World Book Company, 1954.

Klopfer, B., and Davidson, H. H. *The Rorschach Technique: an introductory manual.* New York: Harcourt Brace Jovanovich, 1962.

Michael, J. L. The relevance of animal research. In R. L. Schiefelbusch, R. H. Copeland, and J. D. Smith (Eds.), *Language and mental retardation.* New York: Holt, Rinehart and Winston, 1967.

Moore, R. A., and Goldiamond, I. Errorless establishment of visual discrimination using fading procedures. *Journal of the Experimental Analysis of Behavior,* 1964, 7, 269–272.

Pierrel, R., and Sherman, J. G. Generalization of auditory intensity following discrimination training. *Journal of the Experimental Analysis of Behavior,* 1960, 3, 313–322.

Reynolds, G. S. Behavioral contrast. *Journal of the Experimental Analysis of Behavior,* 1961, 4, 57–71.

Skinner, B. F. *Verbal behavior.* New York: Appleton-Century-Crofts, 1957.

Skinner, B. F. Operant behavior. In W. K. Honig (Ed.), *Operant behavior: Areas of research and application.* New York: Appleton-Century-Crofts, 1966.

Terrace, H. S. Discrimination learning with and without errors. *Journal of the Experimental Analysis of Behavior,* 1963, 6, 1–27.

Terrace, H. S. Generalization gradients after discrimination learning with and without errors. *Science,* 1964, 144, 78–80.

Terrace, H. S. Stimulus control. In W. K. Honig (Ed.), *Operant behavior: Areas of research and application.* New York: Appleton-Century-Crofts, 1966.

CHAPTER 6

CHAINING AND COMPLEX BEHAVIOR

In previous discussions we have tended to deal with single response classes and some of their characteristics. For example, we studied some of the response classes characteristic of operant behavior and some of the response classes characteristic of respondent behavior. We also studied some of the response class dimensions characteristic of both types of behavior. Most particularly, we studied the kinds of stimulus events that precede and follow these response classes and the manner in which these stimulus events affect these response classes. By limiting our study primarily to the characteristics of a single response class, we have been able to obtain a great deal of useful information.

In these discussions we described the response class as if it were an event independent of our definition of it. Our definition asserted that responses occurring at the same time and followed by the same consequences were members of the same response class. Consider the case of the rat approaching the lever and pressing the lever (events that are followed by a pellet magazine click—Sr+) and the rat approaching the food cup and biting the food pellet (events that are followed by the food pellet—SR+). From this array of events the investigator chooses a *single aspect* for study. For although the rat presses the lever and stands on his hind legs at the same time (and both operants are followed by reinforcement and are thus members of the same response class), we chose to study only a single aspect of the entire class—the lever pressing. This choice is entirely arbitrary and is largely a matter of convenience.

We could have chosen to study the rat's behavior preceding the lever-pressing response. In that case we would also have had to define some single aspect of the entire response class, such as the time when the rat lifts his paw off the floor, when his paw changes direction and moves toward the lever, or when his paw first comes in contact with the lever. Again our choice is arbitrary and is a matter of convenience. In any case, since these response units themselves contain subdivisions of responses that are sequenced, they are also chains, even though they are part of the larger response unit of lever pressing, which is itself part of an *operant behavior chain* (that of approaching the lever, then approaching the food cup and eating the food pellet).

Thus the study of the organism's behavior over time reveals that its behavior consists of response classes that are linked together to form chains. Also, at any given moment the organism's behavior consists of a number of response classes that form a pattern of *concurrent behavior*. Although these chained and concurrent behaviors consist of both operant and respondent response classes, we will first discuss operant behavior chains in order to clarify our analysis. Later we will discuss the possible relationhips between operant and respondent response classes, both as chains and as concurrent events.

EXAMPLES OF OPERANT BEHAVIOR CHAINS

A relatively simple operant behavior chain was described earlier—the case of the rat who pressed a lever for food pellets when a green light was on. The lever press itself caused an audible click in the pellet magazine system, which was then followed by the rat's approaching the food cup and getting the food pellet.

A much more complicated chain has been observed in a highly educated rat named Rodent E. Lee. He (1) goes through a door, (2) runs up a spiral staircase, (3) runs across a drawbridge, (4) runs up a ladder, (5) rides a cable car, (6) climbs another staircase, (7) plays a toy piano, (8) crawls through a tunnel, (9) pulls a chain and rides an elevator down to the first floor of the "circus box," and finally (10) presses a lever that actuates the food pellet delivery system. This behavior chain is illustrated in Figure 6-1.

Another example of an operant behavior chain familiar to most of us is using a pay telephone to make a telephone call. This involves: (1) walking

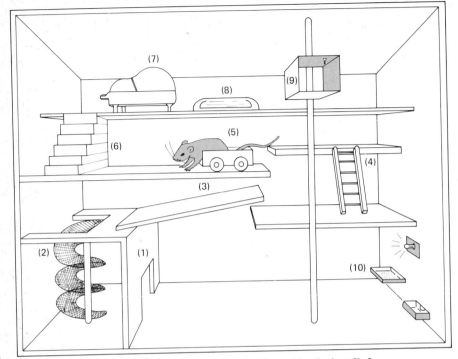

FIGURE 6-1 The ten-link operant behavior chain performed by Rodent E. Lee.

into the phone booth, (2) reaching for the phone book, (3) opening the book, (4) scanning the pages, (5) turning to the right page, (6) reaching into one's pocket, (7) producing change, (8) sorting through the change, (9) picking out a dime, (10) lifting the receiver and placing it against one's ear, (11) inserting the dime in the coin slot, (12) listening for the dial tone, (13) looking at the first number in the series of numbers one wishes to dial, (14) inserting one's finger into the dial and rotating it, (15) looking at the next number, (16) dialing it, and so on. Such an operation may require a sustained performance lasting up to 5 or 10 minutes or even longer.

SOME SIGNIFICANT FEATURES OF
OPERANT BEHAVIOR CHAINS

An operant behavior chain consists of one or more response classes that are temporally or sequentially related to one another. The following chain is for the rat who was trained to press a lever for food pellets when a green light goes on:

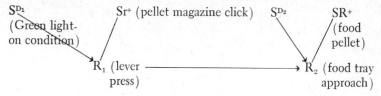

Notice that this chain contains two response classes (R_1, lever pressing, and R_2, food tray approach), two S^D's (S^{D_1}, the green light-on condition, and S^{D_2}, the pellet magazine click), and two sets of consequences (Sr^+, the conditioned reinforcer or the pellet magazine click, and SR^+, the unconditioned positive reinforcers or the food pellets). Although this illustration represents the simplest case (two response classes sequentially or temporally related), it shows an important characteristic of all operant behavior chains: *The stimuli in operant chains typically possess a dual function, consisting of discriminative and reinforcing functions.* In the discriminative function a stimulus (for example, S^{D_2}, the pellet magazine click) controls the operant that follows it (R_2, food-tray-approach responses), while in the reinforcing function the stimulus (again S^{D_2}, the pellet magazine click) strengthens the operant that preceded it (R_1, lever pressing). The reinforcing function of the click is due to its temporal relation to the reinforcing stimulus at the end of the chain—namely the unconditioned reinforcing stimulus (SR^+), or the food pellet. Although the reinforcing stimulus at the *end* of a chain may be unconditioned or conditioned, *the stimuli possessing both discriminative and reinforcing functions in operant behavior chains are conditioned reinforcers* (Sr^+). However, there are occasions when a component stimulus in an operant behavior chain possesses either the discriminative or reinforcing stimulus function, but not necessarily both.

Chains may be either homogeneous or heterogeneous. A *homogeneous chain* consists of *either* environmental (*exteroceptive*) stimuli or movement-produced (*proprioceptive*) stimuli. A *heterogeneous chain* consists of *both* environmental (exteroceptive) and movement-produced (proprioceptive) stimuli. For example, a homogeneous chain involves a single response topography, such as lever pressing, which is followed by successively different exteroceptive stimuli, such as colored lights. Heterogeneous chains are the most common. They involve successively different response topographies, such as lever-pressing and food-cup-approach responses. These two responses are followed by the pellet magazine click (an exteroceptive stimulus) and food pellet chewing (a proprioceptive stimulus), respectively.

The development of the organism's behavior over time in the form of either homogeneous or heterogeneous operant behavior chains is possible, then, only because the organism's responses produce exteroceptive or proprioceptive stimuli that acquire discriminative and/or reinforcing stimulus functions. Thus a chained performance is a matter of both stimulus control and schedule control. Although we have already described the procedures of operant discrimination training that will make a stimulus event into a discriminative stimulus (see Chapter 5), we have not yet examined the procedures involved in making a stimulus event into a conditioned reinforcer.

THE DEVELOPMENT OF A CONDITIONED REINFORCER

An understanding of the conditions under which a stimulus event becomes a conditioned reinforcer comes from a detailed examination of the events involved in *magazine training*.[1] In the previous example the rat approached the food cup after he had pressed a lever in the presence of a green light and his lever pressing had produced a pellet magazine click. This pellet magazine click served two functions. First, it was a discriminative stimulus (S^D) for food-cup-approach responses, and second, it was a conditioned reinforcer (Sr^+) for the lever-pressing response. It acquired its reinforcing function sometime during the rat's history of magazine training, which probably went something like this:

1. The rat was first food-deprived, then placed into a box containing only a food cup.

2. He was then given two or three food pellets gratis, each preceded by the pellet magazine click. Eventually, the sniffing and exploring food-deprived rat found the food cup and ate the pellets.

3. Later, when the rat stood near the food cup, a dozen more food pellets were presented, one at a time.

4. Still later, another dozen or more pellets were given (again, one at a time), but this time only when the rat was standing farther and farther away from the food cup.

At the conclusion of such magazine training, the rat approached the food cup whenever the pellet magazine click occurred, even though he might be standing some distance away from the food cup.

Two procedures are involved in this type of training, either of which may be involved in the development of the pellet magazine click as a conditioned reinforcer.

First, magazine training involves an element of stimulus pairing, in which a neutral stimulus is paired with an unconditioned positive reinforcing stimulus in a manner similar to the procedures of classical conditioning. The magazine click immediately precedes the presentation of the food pellet in much the same way that the CS precedes the US in respondent conditioning, the effect of which is to make the click a conditioned reinforcer, as follows:

[1] For a more detailed description of the laboratory procedures involved in magazine training and other related experiments, see Michael (1963).

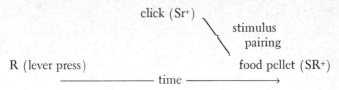

Second, magazine training involves an element of operant discrimination training. Part of the magazine-training procedure involved the rat's approaching the cup and the reinforcement of the food-cup-approach responses in the presence of the pellet magazine click and the nonreinforcement of such responses in its absence. In other words, the pellet magazine click also became a discriminative stimulus for food-cup-approach responses, as follows:

$$S^D \longrightarrow R \longrightarrow SR^+$$

(pellet   (food cup   (food
magazine   approach)   pellet)
click)

Thus a second procedure going on during magazine training, which may be involved in making the pellet magazine click a conditioned reinforcer, is operant discrimination training. The pellet magazine click becomes an S^D in an operant behavior chain consisting of the following: food-cup approach, nosing out the food pellets, and biting, chewing, and swallowing them.

Actual attempts to make a neutral stimulus into a conditioned reinforcer both in the experimental laboratory and in applications with human subjects provide evidence in support of both procedures. For example, when a tone is repeatedly paired with electrical intracranial stimulation (ICS) of the "reward center" of a rat's brain, the tone itself can become a conditioned reinforcer, which can subsequently be used to strengthen lever pressing (Stein, 1958). However, Lovaas and his co-workers (1966) found that mere stimulus pairing was not successful in making the neutral stimulus "good" into a conditioned reinforcer useful in the operant conditioning of schizophrenic children. The initial attempt to make the vocalization "good" into a conditioned reinforcer involved repeated paired presentations of the neutral stimulus with food (the unconditioned reinforcer). The vocalization was then used as a reinforcing stimulus to strengthen another operant—lever pressing. The procedure was ineffective, and an alternative procedure emerged in which the trainer presented to S (the subject) both the neutral verbal stimulus ("good") and the unconditioned reinforcer (food) on a response-contingent basis. The S had to approach the trainer to receive the reinforcement. As the training progressed, the S's view of the trainer was concealed by a partition, so that the S had to actively seek out the trainer. In other words, the trainer's vocalization "good," like the click of the pellet magazine in magazine training, became an S^D for approaching the trainer.

Conditioned reinforcers are more durable reinforcers when they are presented without the unconditioned reinforcers (that is, during extinction) and if they themselves were developed under an intermittent schedule. For example, early in training, Zimmerman (1957) preceded each presentation of water to water-deprived rats with the sound of a buzzer (a CRF schedule). Later in training, the water followed the buzzer on the average of only one time in ten (a VR 10 schedule). Even then, the rat approached the water-delivery area each time the buzzer sounded. During testing (extinction), a lever was introduced, and the first six times the lever was pressed it produced the buzzer (a CRF schedule) but no water. Subsequently, lever pressing produced the buzzer on an FI 1-minute schedule. Figure 6-2 shows the rate of responding under these schedules, under a second extinction period, and during a period of reinstatement of the buzzer, and finally, a terminal extinction period. Lever pressing occurred with remarkable vigor long after the removal of the unconditioned reinforcer—the water.

In conclusion, it should be emphasized that, like the unconditioned reinforcer, the conditioned reinforcer strengthens the behavior preceding it. It can, therefore, be used without presentation of unconditioned reinforcers (during extinction) to maintain a previously acquired operant, or it can be used in the acquisition of an operant that is not already part of the organism's repertoire—a matter to be discussed next.

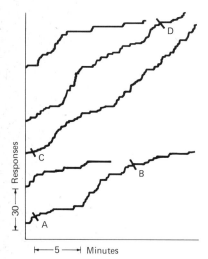

FIGURE 6-2 Lever pressing in the rat maintained by a conditioned reinforcer, a buzzer, under the following conditions: A (origin), CRF; A–B, FI 1; B–C, EXT; C–D, FI 1 minute; D on, EXT. The two bottom records were obtained on the first day and the remaining records were obtained on the second day. From D. W. Zimmerman, Durable secondary reinforcement: Method and theory. *Psychological Review*, 1957, **64**, 373–383. Copyright © 1957, by the American Psychological Association and reproduced by permission.

HOW OPERANT BEHAVIOR CHAINS ARE FORMED

Inasmuch as operant chains consist of two or more links, each of which contains an appropriate S^D, an appropriate R, and some consequence, training an organism to perform a chain requires that *each link be learned separately*. This means that the trainer will have to work out, in advance, (1) the essential elements (that is, the S^D, the R, and the consequences) that will control and maintain each link in the chain and (2) the terminal consequences that will maintain the entire chain.[2]

Suppose, for example, that we wish to train a rat to (1) push a certain key on a toy piano and (2) press a lever five times. The two response classes will be:

R_2, pushing the piano key.

R_1, pressing the lever five times.

Notice that the terminal performance of lever pressing is designated as R_1 (the *last* response in the chain), and pushing ("playing") the key on the piano is designated as R_2 (the first response in the chain):

$$R_2 \text{————} R_1$$

(pushing key   (pressing a lever
on piano)   five times)

Now consequences must be specified for each response class. The choice of what are appropriate consequences for the subject depends on (1) the sophistication of the subject (the rat) and (2) the temporal relationship of the response class to the other links in the chain. As we shall see, the consequences for each link will consist of either an unconditioned reinforcer (for example, food pellets as SR^+'s) or a conditioned reinforcer (that is, stimuli in the links of the chain that function as Sr^+'s). Suppose further that we choose to use a light-on condition as an S^D for lever pressing (R_1) and a light-off condition as an S^D for pushing the piano key. We now have:

$$S^{D_2} \text{————————→} R_2 \text{ (push piano key)}$$

(light-off condition)

$$S^{D_1} \text{————————→} R_1 \text{ (press lever five times)}$$

(light-on condition)

If our rat has already been magazine trained, we can start training by working on either R_1 or R_2. Our choice does not matter. However, if we have a completely naïve rat, the rat will first have to be magazine trained.

Suppose we start by training the rat to press the lever (R_1). The lever

[2] Some observers believe that some types of behavior chains are the result of phylogenetic programming—an innate or genetic serial ordering process, the effect of which is to order a sequence of individual response units into longer chained performances. This matter will be included in the discussions of the development of verbal behavior.

would be placed in the box; the "house lights" would be turned on; and we would then shape the lever pressing response (by reinforcing successive approximations of it). Since five lever presses are required, training would begin by strengthening lever presses on a CRF schedule until lever-pressing responses occurred frequently. Under these conditions the rat would (1) press the lever, (2) run over to the food cup, and (3) eat the food pellet. Reinforcers would not be delivered unless the rat pressed the lever at least once. Then, a gradual change in schedule would be introduced. At first, every other response would be reinforced, then every third response, and finally, every fifth response.

The next step involves classical operant discrimination training procedures, in which responses on the lever would be reinforced in the light-on condition and extinguished during the light-off condition. Following the fifth lever-pressing response, the light would go off. From then on the rat would have to wait for the light to go on again before lever presses would be reinforced. The sequence is now:

$$S^D \longrightarrow R \longrightarrow S^{R+}$$
$$\text{(light on)} \qquad \text{(lever press)} \qquad \text{(food pellet)}$$
$$S^\Delta \longrightarrow R \longrightarrow \text{EXT}$$
$$\text{(light off)} \qquad \text{(lever press)}$$

The final performance evolving from this training procedure is the last link (link 1) in the operant chain:

$$S^D \longrightarrow R \longrightarrow S^{R+}$$
$$\text{(light on)} \qquad \text{(press lever five} \qquad \text{(food pellet)}$$
$$\text{times)}$$

Training the rat to press the piano key (the response class in link 2) begins by (1) turning the house lights off, (2) introducing the piano, and (3) shaping the piano-key-pushing response[3] (through the reinforcement of successive approximations).

If the light-on condition is a sufficiently strong conditioned reinforcer, it can be used to strengthen the piano-key-pressing response by simply making presentations of the light-on condition contingent on the occurrence of some approximation to the final performance of pushing the piano key. For example, first any movement the rat makes toward the piano would cause the house lights to be turned on, then only contact of the rat's body with the piano, then only contact of the rat's paws with the piano, and so on. If the light-on condition is, indeed, a conditioned reinforcer, such a sequence could be shaped in this manner until we have:

[3] A toy piano that contains only one moving key is often used in this demonstration. The other keys are immovable. However, it is entirely possible to train an animal to press certain keys in a sequence.

S^{D_2} ⟶ R_2 ⟶ S^{D_1} ⟶ R_1 —— SR⁺
(light off)   (press piano   (light on)   (press lever   (food pellet)
          key)   five times)

A more exact description of the essential features of this operant chain would be:

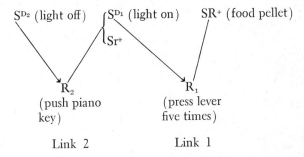

Link 2   Link 1

This diagram shows (1) that there are two links in the operant chain, each consisting of its respective S^D's, R's, and consequences, and (2) that a conditioned reinforcer (the light-on condition) maintains R_2 (the piano-key-pushing response), and the unconditioned reinforcer (the food pellet) maintains R_1 (the five lever-pressing responses). In this example, the light-on condition possesses both discriminative and reinforcing stimulus functions. That is, it reinforces the piano-key-pushing response and is a discriminative stimulus for pressing the lever five times.

One problem must be taken into account when this procedure is used. If we intend to use the light-on condition as a conditioned reinforcer, considerable initial training is necessary so that the final link in the chain, pressing the lever, is strengthened and brought under the control of the light-on condition. Then, subsequently, when the light-on condition is used as a conditioned reinforcer for the piano-key-pushing response, for its strength to be maintained, each training trial must involve the *entire* sequence—that is, the presentation of the light-off condition, the piano-key-pushing response, the presentation of the light-on condition, the five lever-pressing responses, and the presentation of the food pellet. Otherwise, the last link in the chain, lever pressing under the control of the light-on condition as a discriminated operant, would be extinguished.

If we wish to shorten training time (by avoiding training on the entire sequence) or the light-on condition is too weak a reinforcer to use in the chain schedule, an alternative procedure can be used, in which the light-on condition is not used at all to strengthen the piano-key-pushing response. Rather, the house lights are left off altogether, and training on the piano-key-pushing response is given using pellets as reinforcers, under the following *multiple schedule:*

$$S^D \xrightarrow{\hspace{1.5cm}} R \xrightarrow{\hspace{1cm}} SR^+$$
(lights off)   (piano-   (food pellet)
              key push)

$$S^D \xrightarrow{\hspace{1.5cm}} R \xrightarrow{\hspace{1cm}} SR^+$$
(lights on)   (press   (food pellet)
              lever five
              times)

Then, when the piano-key-pushing response is strong, the multiple schedule can be changed to the chain schedule by simply substituting the light-on condition (a conditioned reinforcer) for the food pellet presentation (an unconditioned reinforcer) after the piano-key-pushing response, so that we again have:

$$Sr^+$$

$$S^{D_2} \xrightarrow{\hspace{1cm}} R_2 \xrightarrow{\hspace{1cm}} S^{D_2} \xrightarrow{\hspace{1cm}} R_1 \xrightarrow{\hspace{1cm}} SR^+$$
(lights off)   (piano-   (lights on)   (press   (food
              key push)   lever five   pellet)
                                  times)

Notice that by substituting the light-on condition for the food pellet presentation we have shifted from using an unconditioned reinforcer to using a conditioned reinforcer in maintaining the piano-key-pushing response. Moreover, the light-on condition is a controlling stimulus for lever-pressing responses. Thus the light-on condition provides schedule control for the response preceding it (piano-key pushing) and stimulus control for the response following it (lever pressing). *It is this characteristic of the organism's response-produced stimuli, whether they be exteroceptive or proprioceptive, that makes elaborate chains possible.*

Finally, whether or not a conditioned reinforcer, such as the light-on condition, is used depends on the trainer's estimate of its strength as a reinforcer, and ultimately this is determined by an empirical test. The trainer chooses a behavior for which the conditioned reinforcer is response-contingent and observes that behavior before and following its repeated presentation, watching for changes in some response class dimension. In human applications, as in work with infrahuman organisms, one cannot always be certain that the organism's behavior is sensitive to conditioned reinforcers or to generalized reinforcers that are essential to the formation of chained performances. As in animal training, what is required therefore, is an empirical test of the strength of stimulus events as conditioned reinforcers. If this test reveals that the subject's behavior is not sensitive to conditioned or generalized reinforcers, especially verbal and gestural stimuli presented by the trainer (such as the word *good* or a smile), then training making the organism's behavior sensitive to these types of reinforcers is in order.

THE DEVELOPMENT OF OPERANT CHAINS IN HUMAN BEHAVIOR

Among the many types of complex performances that humans are capable of are those in which mathematical expressions are manipulated and solved. Like many other complex performances, such performances can be viewed as operant chains possessing links, each of which contains appropriate S^D's, R's, and consequences.

The following classroom episode provides an example:

The teacher says, "Expand this expression," and then presents the following:

$$(a + b)^2 =$$

The student probably learns how to do this as follows:

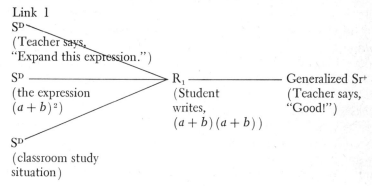

On another occasion the teacher will tell the student to solve

$$(a + b)(a + b) =$$

Link 2

S^D
(Teacher says, "Solve . . .")

S^D ──────────→ R_2 ────────── Generalized Sr⁺
(the expression (Student Teacher says,
$(a + b)(a + b)$) writes, "Good!")
$(a^2 + 2ab + b^2)$

S^D
(classroom study situation)

In this illustration the student actually learns two distinct operants, each of which is reinforced. Of course, each link contains the three essential elements: S^D's, R's, and consequences.

On still another occasion the following occurs:

S^D
(Teacher says,
"Expand and
solve . . .")
S^D
(expression
$(a+b)^2 =$)
S^D
(classroom study
situation)

Sr^+
(student-written
text
$(a+b)(a+b)$)
R_1
(Student
writes,
$(a+b)(a+b)$)

S^D

R_2
(Student
writes,
$a^2 + 2ab + b^2$)

Generalized Sr^+
(Teacher says,
"Good!")

Link 1   Link 2

Several things about the preceding sequence are worthy of note. First, *each link is learned separately* in much the same manner as the sequence described earlier, in which a *chain schedule of reinforcement* was used as a means of *transition from the acquisition of an individual operant* to the *acquisition of an operant chain.* Second, only *conditioned* and *generalized reinforcers* were used in training, namely the response-produced stimulus in the form of the student-written text $(a+b)(a+b)$ and the teacher's praise. Third, the *links are chained together by a common response-produced visual-textual stimulus* —the "self-produced expression" $(a+b)(a+b)$. This expression possesses two stimulus functions. First, it is a conditioned reinforcer for the operant R_1, writing $(a+b)(a+b)$. At the same time, it functions as an S^D for R_2, writing $(a^2 + 2ab + b^2)$. It is important to emphasize that the student's own behavior provided the conditioned reinforcement that ties link 1 to link 2 in the chain.

Many types of human behavior involve this type of *self-stimulation* in the form of response-produced controlling stimuli (the S^D's in the situation) and the self-administered consequences that are a result of monitoring one's own performance (the Sr^+'s in the situation). In many ways, such a sequence and the analysis we have made of it can be related to the problem of self-control, particularly if we are willing to define "self-control" as a situation in which one sequence of the individual's responses provides response-produced stimuli that make some behaviors, those controlled by these stimuli, more likely than other behaviors that are not controlled by these stimuli. The precocious student of the piano who seats himself before the piano, the keyboard, and music and practices for four hours shows remarkable self-control just because his playing well does provide response-produced stimuli that control his behavior. And, of course, in the beginning the piano student, like the student of algebra, was particularly sensitive to generalized positive reinforcers (the teacher's expression of approval, "good"), which served to strengthen and maintain the student's performance until such time as the skillful performance itself, through its pairing with other reinforcers, became reinforcing.

An interesting aspect of such behavior is that each link and the entire chain involve a teacher-defined, *culturally appropriate*, and *conventional performance*. Examples of other culturally appropriate and conventional performances acquired in the same manner are those involved in the more complex mathematical derivations, logical analyses (deductive reasoning), and problem solving in mechanical, technological, or scientific work.

Novel, or unusual, performances can also be acquired through the same behavioral processes. For example, by making reinforcements contingent on the occurrence of a behavior never before reinforced, Pryor, Haag, and O'Reilly (1969) taught Huo, the porpoise, to perform some strikingly novel performances. The actual implementation of this reinforcement rule was carried out as follows:

A bell was sounded to mark the beginning and the end of each training session, and no food deprivation was used. Reinforcers consisted of food (the unconditioned reinforcer) and the sound of a whistle (the conditioned reinforcer). Over each of thirty-two sessions occurring from two to four times daily, each lasting from 5 to 20 minutes, an attempt was made, though not completely adhered to, to reinforce only one behavior. The trainer and two observers visually monitored Huo's behavior and tape-recorded both the judges' and the trainer's verbal accounts of Huo's movements and the sound of the whistle. Any reinforceable act had the following characteristics:

1. It was a movement not normally part of animal's swimming actions.

2. It was sufficiently sustained or protracted through time and space to be reliably reported by the observers.

This tended to limit the types of behavior to the more gross, obvious types of movements (for example, tail movement rather than eye rolling). Two judges observed and recorded Huo's performance and inter-judge reliability was established from comparisons of transcripts of the tape recordings, comparisons of "position sketches" made by the judges, and comparisons of these sketches with filmed sequences.

To establish the range of normal behavior and to establish categories of genuine novelty, twelve trainers of this species of porpoise and related species were given diagrams of the sixteen behaviors that were reinforced under the novel response reinforcement rule and asked to rank these behaviors according to the frequency of their occurrence in an untrained animal.

Figure 6-3 shows diagrams of four of Huo's novel performances. Beaching and back flip were acquired by contingent reinforcement, and tail walk and the inverted tail slap (upslap) required some shaping. Besides these behaviors, Huo was also trained to spit, swim downward in a corkscrew pattern, wave his tail, spin, back porpoise (leap smoothly out of the water once or twice

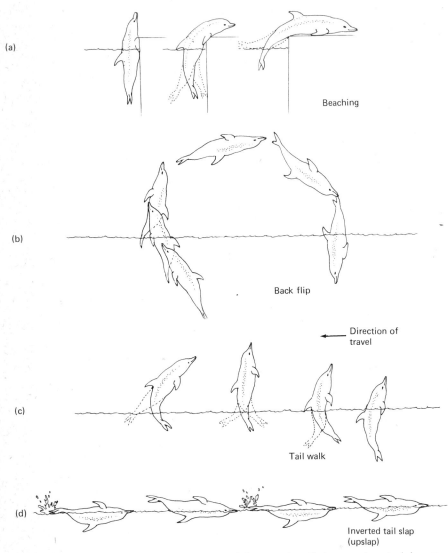

FIGURE 6-3 Some novel performances acquired by porpoises that were given training consisting of the presentation of reinforcements contingent on the occurrence of behavior never before reinforced ((a) and (b)) and, in addition, shaping ((c) and (d)). (From K. W. Pryor, R. Haag, and J. O'Reiley, The creative porpoise: Training for novel behavior. *Journal of the Experimental Analysis of Behavior*, 1969, 12, 653–663. Copyright © 1969, by the Society for the Experimental Analysis of Behavior, Inc., and reproduced by permission.)

backwards), flip forward, and make an inverted flip. The remaining six behaviors (breaching, jumping to the air and coming down sideways, porpoising, inverted swimming, tail slap, and sideswipe) had been observed by the judges as occurring spontaneously in porpoises without such training. So, by means of this novel response-contingent reinforcement rule, the investigators taught eleven different behaviors to this "creative" porpoise. Moreover, at one point in this study Huo's behavior became so elaborate that inter-judge agreement was no longer possible. The movements involved in his new forms of behavior could not be reliably observed.

Since such training is apt to occur in situations already having some stimulus control over the subject's preexisting behavior the procedure of only reinforcing responses that have never been reinforced before requires that the (preexisting) behavior already under stimulus control of the situation be extinguished. Thus in addition to generating novel behavior, this procedure also generates some emotional behavior. Although such procedures are seldom used systematically in human training situations, students can be reinforced for combining links in a chain in ways that are considered novel, unusual, or even in some cases, creative by the teacher or others in the verbal community. Unusual combinations of color or form in a painting, unusual dance performances, or unusual combinations of musical notes into musical selections are, perhaps, illustrative of this.

To sum up, both animals and men emit extremely elaborate, protracted, conventional or novel operant performances in the form of operant chains. These chains may be controlled and maintained by self-produced stimuli that are the result of the emitted operants of which the chain is composed. The strength of any operant behavior chain, however, is a function of a number of factors, including the amount and kind of reinforcer at the end of the chain and the schedule of reinforcement at the end of the chain. When the terminal link in a chain is followed by extinction, the other component links are also weakened. The effects of such an extinction procedure are greater variability of the response class(es), emotional responses, and a reduction in the frequency of the response classes of which the chain consists. Finally, the strength of the conditioned reinforcers in an operant behavior chain varies, so that those that are the most contiguous to the terminal reinforcer are the strongest, and those that are the least contiguous are the weakest.

THE RELATIONSHIP BETWEEN VERBAL INSTRUCTIONS, SUSTAINED OPERANT PERFORMANCES, AND CONSEQUENCES

There is an interesting relationship between verbal instructions (used as S^D's) and the maintenance of operant behavior over prolonged periods of time and under conditions of delayed reinforcement. For example, the boss instructs his workers that when they have finished their work assignment, the somewhat routine task of grape picking, they will be paid. However, since the task requires sustained performance and involves delayed reinforcement, the boss may check the progress of the workers and offer further instructions and reinforcement, as follows:

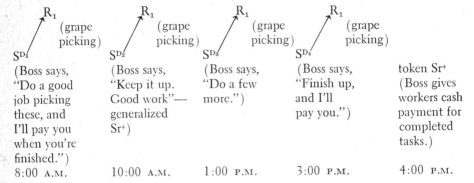

R_1 (grape picking)	R_1 (grape picking)	R_1 (grape picking)	R_1 (grape picking)	
S^{D_1} (Boss says, "Do a good job picking these, and I'll pay you when you're finished.")	S^{D_2} (Boss says, "Keep it up. Good work"— generalized Sr^+)	S^{D_3} (Boss says, "Do a few more.")	S^{D_4} (Boss says, "Finish up, and I'll pay you.")	token Sr^+ (Boss gives workers cash payment for completed tasks.)
8:00 A.M.	10:00 A.M.	1:00 P.M.	3:00 P.M.	4:00 P.M.

At 8:00 A.M. the task instructions (S^{D_1}) are given, and work begins (R_1). At 10:00 A.M. the boss checks the work, giving further instructions (S^{D_2}, "Keep it up") and positive reinforcement (generalized Sr^+, "Good work"). At 1:00 P.M. the boss checks the work again and presents instructions (S^{D_3}, "Do a few more"). At 3:00 P.M. the boss checks the work and provides a final instruction (S^{D_4}, "Finish up, and I'll pay you"). From time to time, too, the boss may merely move up and down the rows of grape vines, watching the grape pickers but saying nothing. Then, at 4:00 P.M., with the job completed, the workers are paid.

In this example the sustained performances are maintained by a combination of instructions (S^{D_1}–S^{D_4}) and positive reinforcement (generalized Sr^+, token Sr^+) for a period of 7 hours. Particularly important here is the presentation of the generalized positive reinforcement ("good") and, of course, the terminal reinforcement (the money). Often, too, the boss's presentation may be gestural rather than verbal, as when he looks at the employees in an approving or disapproving manner. Ordinarily, the boss would make use of other instructions and consequences when performance lags (for example, "Hurry up," an S^D, or "You're fired," a combination of Sr^- and permanent time-out). Thus the boss would employ a concurrent schedule. Of course, in situations where employees have worked in the same facility for a long enough period of time, both verbal instructions and supervisor-presented consequation occur infrequently, since the employees' behavior is maintained by the stimulus control of the work situation itself (the grape vines, the cutting shears, the occasional appearances of the boss, and the like) and the delayed consequation in the form of a paycheck (token reinforcer).

The significance of this analysis is twofold. It describes the conditions under which prolonged or sustained performances are emitted, and it describes the conditions under which delays in reinforcement can be sustained without a disruption of performance.

CHAINING AND IRRELEVANT OR SUPERSTITIOUS OPERANT BEHAVIOR

In many training situations the organism is reinforced for some final performance, and other irrelevant operants occurring just before the final performance is emitted may get chained to them. When this happens, the reinforcer that follows the terminal operant not only strengthens the required final performance, but it also strengthens the operant(s) that preceded the final performance:

$$R_3 \underbrace{\rule{3cm}{0.4pt} R_2 \rule{3cm}{0.4pt}} R_1 \rule{3cm}{0.4pt} Sr^+ \text{ (reinforcer)}$$

(irrelevant operants)		(required final performance— relevant operant)

————————————————— Time —————————————————

Suppose, for example, a student in an English class is asked to read the word *antidisestablishmentarianism*. Just prior to being called upon, he was drumming his fingers on the desk, and just before that he was scratching his cheek. His performance is deemed "very good" by the teacher. This sequence can be described as follows:

$$R_3 \rule{1.5cm}{0.4pt} R_2 \rule{1.5cm}{0.4pt} R_1 \rule{1.5cm}{0.4pt} Sr^+$$

(cheek scratching)	(finger drumming on desk)	(Student reads, "antidisestablish- mentarianism")	("very good")

This illustration shows that the irrelevant operants (R_3, cheek scratching, and R_2, finger drumming) are in a sense hooked to the terminal operant because of their temporal relationship to the reinforcement that followed R_1. On similar occasions in the future, the student will be more apt to emit cheek scratching (R_3), followed by drumming his fingers on his desk (R_2) before reciting in class (R_1).

One might describe these responses as a type of superstitious behavior that is accidentally chained to the appropriate performance. Even though they are not relevant to the final performance (that is, they are not functional or instrumental to the performance), they may become part of the S's repertoire because of their temporal relationship to the relevant, instrumental reinforced operant.

RELATIONSHIPS BETWEEN OPERANT AND RESPONDENT BEHAVIOR

In our previous discussion some rather clear-cut distinctions were made between operant and respondent behavior. These distinctions were made on the basis of three essential features:

1. The response systems involved. Operant behavior involves the skeletal muscles and the mechanisms of speech, and respondent behavior involves the activity of the autonomic nervous system, endocrine and exocrine glands, cardiac muscle, and the smooth muscle of the gastrointestinal tract.

2. The functions these response systems perform in the overall survival of the organism. Operant behavior functions to produce changes in the organism's external environment, and respondent behavior functions to regulate and maintain the organism's internal environment and to protect the organism from noxious and irritating stimuli.

3. The behavioral characteristics of these response systems. Operant behavior is particularly sensitive to the stimulus events that follow it, and respondent behavior is particularly sensitive to the stimulus events that precede it.

Although such distinctions seem reasonable enough, and have frequently proved to be quite useful, the last one in particular is somewhat misleading. There is considerable evidence to show that a wide range of response classes normally viewed as reflexive or respondent and elicited by stimuli that precede them are also sensitive to the consequences that follow them and may, therefore, behave as operants.

For example, Miller (1969), using rats as Ss, took measurements of both the magnitude of their intestinal contractions and their heart rates during a base-line period. Then, in a period of training, positive reinforcement, in the form of intracranial (electric) stimulation (ICS) of the reward center of the brain, was presented contingent on either increases or decreases in intestinal contractions or heart rate. To prevent spurious changes in these measures resulting from skeletal muscle movement or stimulation arising from the brain, the rats were given an injection of curare, a powerful poison that produces a deep paralysis. Respiration was maintained by a resuscitator. The results of this training are presented in Figure 6-4, which shows intestinal contraction scores and heartbeats per minute during base line and training with the reinforcements. Not only do the curves show that large changes in both the magnitude of intestinal contractions and the heart rate, both upward and downward, can be produced by making reinforcement contingent on these changes, but the curves also show that the effect of these reinforcements is specific to the reflex change upon which they are contingent. In other words, it is possible to use reinforcements to produce significant increases or decreases in the activity of one reflex without affecting other reflexes.

Besides intestinal contractions and heart rate, such classical reflexes as eye blink, salivation, kidney secretion, and the amount of blood flow to the stomach mucosa and the skin have been found to be sensitive to positive reinforcers (such as water, electric stimulation of the reward center of the brain, and money) and negative reinforcers (such as shock termination). What is even more interesting is that many of these reflexes are involved in psychosomatic diseases or organ neuroses. This suggests that reinforcements arising from the physical and especially the social environment that strengthen the

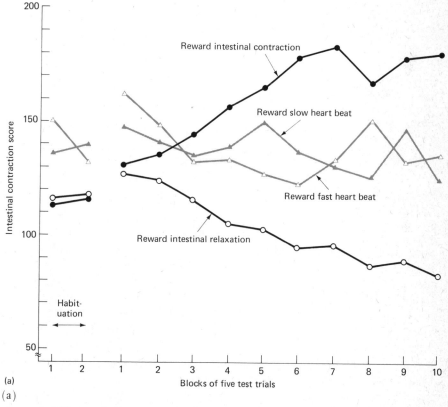

(a)

FIGURE 6-4 Changes in the magnitude of (a) intestinal contractions and (b) heart rate during base line (habituation) and following contingent reinforcements in the form of ICS. From N. E. Miller, Learning of visceral and glandular responses. *Science*, 1969, **163**, 434–445. Copyright © 1969 by the American Association for the Advancement of Science and reproduced by permission.

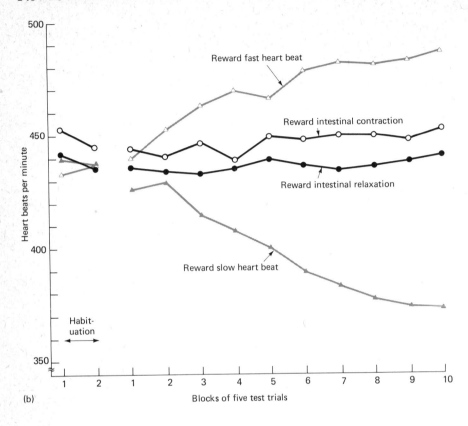

FIGURE 6-4 (Continued)

individual's verbal and motor operant behavior may, at the same time, strengthen his respondent behavior, resulting in a diseased condition, such as tachycardia (too rapid heartbeat) or essential hypertension (high blood pressure). Most reflexes tend to be covert and are, therefore, difficult for others to monitor. Thus they may be strengthened as a kind of concurrent superstition —that is, they may just happen to occur when reinforcements are presented by other people for other ongoing behaviors. For example, the mother who quiets her frightened and crying baby by hugging him may be strengthening increased heart rate (in addition to strengthening crying). This sensitivity of reflexes to the consequences following them can, as we shall see, provide a basis for the treatment of the so-called organ neuroses.

Just as respondents are affected by the consequences following them, many of the response classes normally viewed as operant can be elicited by the stimuli preceding them. For example, a rat's aggressive attack behavior, consisting of locomotor approach responses and biting and pulling the victim, can be elicited by a strong stimulus, such as shock, in a pattern sometimes called *unconditioned, reflexive,* or *respondent* aggression. Responses of the rat's vocal apparatus, such as cries or squeaks, can also be elicited by painful or noxious stimuli.

One reason for the apparent interchangeability of certain response classes may be that some investigators have studied response classes containing multiple component responses that have been too broadly defined. Crying, for example, consists of several component responses, some of which seem to be clearly respondent (that is, lacrimal gland secretion), others of which seem to be clearly operant (that is, facial expressions and sounds emitted during crying).

Still another reason for this apparent interchangeability is that certain response classes are made up of single component responses that are sensitive to stimulus events both preceding it *and* following it. Such might be the case with the human eye blink, a single component response that is sensitive to both eliciting and consequating stimuli and would thus appear to behave according to the laws of both respondent and operant behavior.

Finally, the apparent interchangeability of certain response classes may involve interactions between, or chaining of, operants and respondents—a complex phenomenon that will be described later.

At any rate, a comprehensive description of the response classes that show this interchangeability is beyond the scope of the present discussion. The essential point is that although our previous distinctions between operant and respondent behavior may have been useful and expedient, we can now see that in certain ways it was an oversimplification.

INTERACTIONS BETWEEN OPERANT AND RESPONDENT BEHAVIOR

Because respondent and operant behaviors are dynamic, ongoing processes, it is not uncommon for an *operant–respondent chain* to form, such as the following:

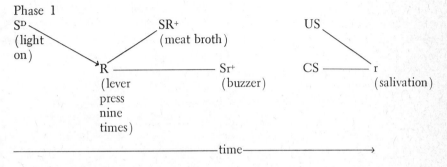

Phase 1
S^D (light on) → R (lever press nine times) → SR^+ (meat broth)

$S r^+$ (buzzer)

US → r (salivation)

CS → r

———————————————————time———————————————————→

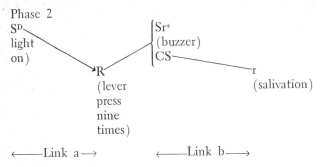

Phase 2

(lever
press
nine
times)

(salivation)

←——Link a——→   ←——Link b——→

In this diagram the light-on condition functions as an S^D controlling an operant (pressing a lever nine times), and the buzzer is a CS eliciting a respondent (salivation). Phase 1 illustrates the procedures that were used to achieve this kind of chain, and phase 2 describes the end result. Training began by simply pairing the buzzer (the CS) with the meat broth (the US). Then, the CS was not presented until the lever had been pressed at least once. Subsequently, lever presses in the light-on condition were followed by the buzzer, and presses during the light-off condition were not. Once the light-on condition became an S^D for lever pressing, the subject was required to make more and more lever presses in order to turn on the buzzer until nine presses were necessary. Once stabilized, as illustrated in Phase 2, the lever pressing was reinforced by the buzzer, which, in turn, was a conditioned elicitor for salivation. As shown by Figure 6-5, Ellison and Konorski (1964) found that the two links in the chain were quite distinct in the sense that there was virtually no salivation during the occurrence of the lever pressing (link a) and virtually no lever pressing during salivation (link b) on successive time samples.

In addition to the component links of the chain (lever pressing and salivation with their respective controlling stimuli), an essential feature of the chain is the delay introduced between the operant and the meat broth presentation (the SR$^+$) and between the buzzer (the CS) and the meat broth presentation (the US). These delays served to separate the two responses into two distinct links of a chain. It is also possible to arrange a training situation for the acquisition of a respondent–operant chain.

The preceding example illustrates that in certain types of training situations, there may be significant interactions between operants and respondents. The operant (lever pressing) ultimately elicited the salivation (a respondent) through the conditioned stimuli produced by the lever pressing. So even though the respondent of salivation is a reflex, it is actually induced by the organism's own operant behavior and, therefore, involves a kind of self-control. As we have seen, these conditioned stimuli can be objects, events, or even words. For example, a child's operant verbalization of "candy" when candy is sighted may function as an elicitor for the respondent salivation.

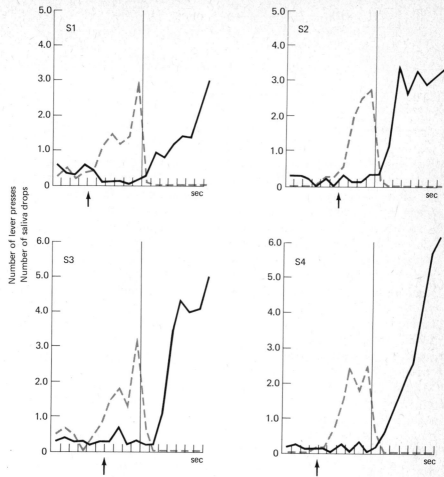

FIGURE 6-5 The number of lever presses and drops of saliva in successive time samples of an operant–respondent behavior chain for four Ss. The broken line is the presses per second, and the continuous line is the drops per second. The CS onset is shown by the vertical line, and the arrows indicate the median time for the S^D onsets. From G. D. Ellison and J. Konorski, Separation of the salivary and motor responses in instrumental conditioning. *Science*, 1964, **146**, 1071–1072. Copyright © 1964 by the American Association for the Advancement of Science and reproduced by permission.

CONCURRENT RESPONDENT–OPERANT BEHAVIOR

Another type of relationship between operant and respondent behavior is a *concurrent respondent–operant behavior pattern*. Suppose we arrange a situation such that lever presses made by a dog produce a biscuit on an FI 90-second schedule of reinforcement, as follows:

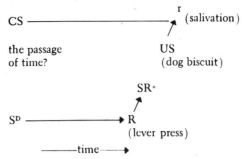

Under the FI 90-second schedule the first lever-pressing response after the 90-second interval produces the dog biscuit. Also the dog biscuit possesses a dual stimulus function. It is an unconditioned positive reinforcer for the lever pressing (an operant), and at the same time it is an unconditioned stimulus for salivation (a respondent). Furthermore, under the FI schedule both the operant and the respondent appear to be controlled by a temporal cue (the passage of time), so that during the early part of the fixed interval there tends to be neither lever pressing nor salivation. See Figure 6-6. However, as the end of the interval approaches, both lever pressing and salivation increase. Kintsch and White (1962), who performed this experiment, found that lever pressing was acquired and came to be under the control of the FI 90-second schedule more rapidly than the conditioned salivation. Nevertheless, there is sufficient parallelism between the two behaviors to regard them as a pattern consisting of concurrent operant and respondent behavior.

The effect of such relationships as this one is a pattern of behavior consisting of concurrent respondents and operants that can be controlled by various stimuli (which, themselves, become both conditioned and discriminative stimuli). It is this total pattern of concurrent respondent and operant behavior that underlies what is often described as emotions. Some emotions, such as joy, excitement, and surprise, are positive—patterns under the control of positive stimuli (food, a hug, an expression of adoration). Others such as fear, depression, and anger are negative—patterns under the control of negative stimuli (a shock or a slap, disapproval, extinction).

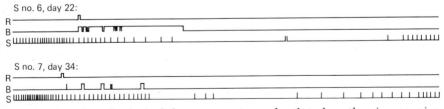

FIGURE 6-6(a) Records obtained from an event recorder that show the pips occurring during a single occasion of the reinforcing event (R), bar pressing (B), and salivation (S) for two Ss. These records should be read from right to left. The reinforcer occurred sometime after 90 seconds. At 0 time and beyond some unconditioned salivation is shown.

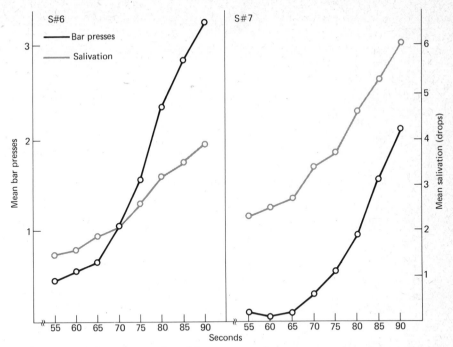

FIGURE 6-6(b) The mean number of bar presses and the mean number of drops of saliva under an FI 90-second schedule of reinforcement. From W. Kintsch and R. S. White, Concurrent conditioning of bar press and salivation responses. *Journal of Comparative and Physiological Psychology*, 1962, **55**, 963–968. Copyright © 1962 by the American Psychological Association and reproduced by permission.

In summary, then, although it is frequently useful to distinguish between operant and respondent behavior, there are often occasions in which such distinctions may be somewhat misleading. Some response classes seem to be interchangeable in that they can be described in terms of the behavioral characteristics of the laws of both operant and respondent behavior. There are several possible explanations for this, including multiple component response classes that have been too broadly defined, single component responses that are sensitive to stimulus events both preceding them and following them, and chains or interactions that have formed between the operant and respondent components. Related to these phenomena is a pattern of behavior known as a concurrent respondent–operant behavior pattern.

STUDY QUESTIONS

1. In what way is the investigator's definition of a response class arbitrary?
2. In what sense is any response class chosen for study by an investigator a chain?

3. In the simplest case how many response classes are there in an operant chain?
4. What are the two R's, S^D's, and reinforcers in the illustration of the rat pressing the lever for food pellets? What was the unconditioned reinforcer? The conditioned reinforcer?
5. What are the essential functions of stimuli in an operant chain?
6. Describe tests that can be used to determine whether or not stimuli in a chain do possess the necessary functions.
7. What stimulus in the illustration of the rat pressing the lever possessed the necessary functions?
8. What kind of reinforcer(s) can be found at the end of a chain? In other links of the chain?
9. What is a heterogeneous chain? A homogeneous chain?
10. Identify the type of chain involved in the following: Pecking at a disk that changes color from time to time.
11. What stimulus events are produced by the organism's own responses? What are their possible functions?
12. In magazine training how can one tell whether or not the pellet magazine click is an S^D? An S^{r+}?
13. Discuss *all* the possible implications for the animal's behavior and for the adequacy of the training situation when all of the reinforcements in magazine training are given at once.
14. By what two procedures are conditioned reinforcers developed?
15. Suggest an account or explanation that would tie together the conflicting observations regarding the necessary and sufficient conditions to make a stimulus event into a conditioned reinforcer (that is, review the details of the two procedures described in the text and develop your explanations from them).
16. In what way was the procedure used to make "good" a conditioned reinforcer for schizophrenic children like the magazine-training procedure?
17. Devise a procedure that can be used to (a) develop *durable* conditioned reinforcers for naïve human Ss. (Hint: Study carefully the procedures used in obtaining the data shown in Figure 6-2) and (b) test the effectiveness of these reinforcers.
18. If an organism is to be taught an operant behavior chain, what must be worked out in advance for each link?
19. When a rat is trained to press a lever when a light goes on, which actually occurs first, operant differentiation or discrimination?
20. When a rat is taught to play the piano, then press a lever, what stimulus event is used initially to reinforce piano playing? Explain why the procedures described on pages 135–136 involve a chain schedule, whereas those on pages 137–138 involve a multiple schedule.
21. After the rat has been trained, what events maintain (a) the piano-key-pushing response and (b) the lever pressing? What stimulus possesses both discriminative and reinforcing functions?
22. Why would training the rat to press the piano key (link 2 in the chain)

using only the light-on condition as a reinforcer, without going through the entire chained sequence, extinguish the discriminated lever pressing?

23. What three S^D's were involved in the operant chain in which the child learned the algebra problem?

24. What visual-textual stimulus functioned as both an S^D and an Sr^+ in the solution of the algebra problem? Why did it?

25. Give a definition of self-control. How does the analysis of the behavior in the solution of the algebra problem relate to this definition?

26. What are the differences and similarities between conventional and novel performances? Give examples of each.

27. Suggest two different procedures for the acquisition of novel performances.

28. What was the unconditioned reinforcer in the training of Huo? The conditioned reinforcer?

29. Describe an unfortunate aspect of the procedure used in generating novel behaviors in porpoises.

30. Which conditioned reinforcers are the strongest, those most contiguous or least contiguous to the terminal reinforcers?

31. Explain how prolonged performances can be maintained under conditions of delayed reinforcement. Give an example of such a situation from your experience.

32. In the example describing how the boss maintains control over his workers, what would happen to future performances if the boss failed to pay the workers to his S^D and Sr^+ presentations?

33. What is meant by an irrelevant operant? Give an example of one.

34. On what three grounds can distinctions be made between operant and respondent behavior? On what grounds are such distinctions open to question?

35. See if you can find an example in the text of what might be called shaping a reflex? Give an example of shaping a reflex.

36. Describe the conditions under which a caretaker could inadvertently strengthen an organ neurosis in someone in his charge.

37. A man shows a disturbingly rapid eye blink. Describe how you would modify this behavior to a point where the eye blink is not noticeable.

38. How would you define a multiple component response class?

39. Cite three possible explanations for the apparent interchangeability of operant and respondent behavior.

40. What is meant by an interaction between an operant and a respondent? Give an example of such an interaction, and describe the experimental procedures necessary to produce it.

41. What is meant by concurrent respondent–operant behavior? Give an example of such a behavior pattern.

42. Suggest a reason why in the concurrent operant–respondent behavior pattern described on pages 151–153, the acquisition of conditioned salivation lagged behind the acquisition of discriminated lever pressing under a training procedure involving an FI 90-second schedule of reinforcement.

43. From your experience and observation of behavior in the natural environment,

suggest some reasons why emotions involve concurrent operant and respondent behaviors.

REFERENCES

Azrin, N. H., Hake, D. F., and Hutchinson, R. R. Elicitation of aggression by a physical blow. *Journal of the Experimental Analysis of Behavior*, 1965, 8, 55–57.

Bijou, S. W., and Baer, D. M. Operant methods in child behavior and development. In W. K. Honig (Ed.), *Operant behavior: Areas of research and application*. New York: Appleton-Century-Crofts, 1966.

Blough, D. S., and Millward, R. B. Operant conditioning and verbal learning. In R. R. Farnsworth (Ed.), *Annual review of psychology*. Palo Alto, Calif.: Annual Reviews, 1965.

Catania, A. C., and Cutts, D. Experimental control of superstitious responding in humans. *Journal of the Experimental Analysis of Behavior*, 1963, 6, 203–208.

Creer, R. W., Hitzing, E. W., and Schaeffer, R. W. Classical conditioning of reflexive fighting. *Psychonomic Science*, 1966, 4, 89–90.

Ellison, G. D., and Konorski, J. Separation of the salivary and motor responses in instrumental conditioning. *Science*, 1964, 20, 1071–1072.

Etzel, B. C., and Gewirtz, J. L. Experimental modification of caretaker-maintained high-rate operant crying in a 6- and 20-week-old infant (infans tyranotearus). Extinction of crying with reinforcement of eye contact and smiling. *Journal of Experimental Child Psychology*, 1967, 5, 303–317.

Holland, J. G., and Skinner, B. F. *The analysis of behavior*. New York: McGraw-Hill, 1961.

Keehn, J. D., Lloyd, K. E., Hebes, M., and Johnson, D. Operant eyeblink conditioning without awareness: A preliminary report. *Psychonomic Science*, 1965, 2, 357–358.

Kelleher, R. T. Chaining and conditioned reinforcement. In W. K. Honig (Ed.), *Operant behavior: Areas of research and application*. New York: Appleton-Century-Crofts, 1966.

Kelleher, R. T., and Gollub, L. R. A review of positive conditioned reinforcement. *Journal of the Experimental Analysis of Behavior*, 1962, 5, 543–597.

Keller, F. S., and Schoenfeld, W. N. *Principles of psychology*. New York: Appleton-Century-Crofts, 1950.

Kimble, G. A. *Hilgard and Marquis: Conditioning and learning*. New York: Appleton-Century-Crofts, 1961.

Kintsch, W., and White, R. S. Concurrent conditioning of both bar press and salivation responses. *Journal of Comparative and Physiological Psychology*, 1962, 55, 963–968.

Lovaas, O. I., Freitag, G., Kinder, M. I., Rubinstein, B. D., Schaeffer, B., and Simmons, J. O. Establishment of social reinforcers in two schizophrenic children. *Journal of Experimental Child Psychology*, 1966, 4, 109–125.

Michael, J. L. *Laboratory studies in operant behavior*. New York: McGraw-Hill, 1963.

Miller, N. E. Learning of visceral and glandular responses. *Science.* 1969, **163**, 434–445.

Pryor, K. W., Haag, R., and O'Reilly, J. The creative porpoise: Training for novel behavior. *Journal of the Experimental Analysis of Behavior.* 1969, **12**, 653–663.

Staats, A. W., and Staats, C. K. *Complex human behavior.* New York: Holt, Rinehart and Winston, 1964.

Stein, L. Secondary reinforcement established with subcortical reinforcement. *Science*, 1958, **127**, 466–467.

Zimmerman, D. W. Durable secondary reinforcement: Method and theory: *Psychological Review*, 1957, **64**, 373–383.

CHAPTER 7

VERBAL BEHAVIOR

Usually our behavior is influenced in some way by others, and the nature of this process will be described in greater detail in Chapter 9. The present analysis focuses on language—the utterances, gestures, and movements of a speaker as he transacts with a listener.[1]

More often than not, we take for granted the degree of control we have over our environment through language. For example:

A child walks into the kitchen, where his mother is preparing dinner. She is cutting up carrot sticks, and the child spies them. He looks at his mother, tugs at her skirt, points at a carrot stick, and says, "Carrot stick, Mommy." His mother continues her work. The child again tugs at his mother's skirt, points at the carrot stick, looks up imploringly, and this time says, "Please, Mommy. May I have a carrot stick?" and this

---

[1] The author recognizes that to many observers language more properly refers to the linguistic practices of the community—the rules of semantics, grammar, and syntax. As defined here, language refers to the actual behavior of the speaker.

time she gives him one. He then says, "Thank you" and walks out of the room munching on his carrot stick.

When an analysis is made of such a social situation, the basic data with which all observers must deal are the objectively observed and verifiable phenomena of language—that is, the child's utterance "Please, Mommy. May I have a carrot stick?" and the gesture or movement of tugging at his mother's skirt. These are events for which we can prepare a rather accurate description.

The analysis of language must, however, progress beyond a mere description to an explanation, and it is here that there are real differences in the manner in which investigators conceptualize and study language for the purposes of giving an account of it.

Traditional researchers regard language as an expression of something else. It is the result of a transformation of an idea, an image, or a desire in the mind of the speaker into another product—the words, sentences, gestures, or movements of the speaker. The child's utterance of "Please Mommy. May I have a carrot stick?" is a transformation of a private event occurring in the child's psyche or mind, perhaps a desire, and his use of language is attributed to the presence of this desire and his ability to choose words and syntax to represent it.

Other observers, especially those with an interest in behavior theory, conceptualize and study language in terms of public events—particularly those changes in the speaker's environment that are mediated by a listener and that the language produces. For example, the child is far more likely to get his carrot stick following occasions of tugging on his mother's dress and saying, "Please Mommy. May I have a carrot stick?" than he is following occasions when he does neither of these.

Then, too, the speaker's utterance, gesture, or movement, because of its sensitivity to the consequences following it, comes under the control of stimuli in the presence of which the speaker has been reinforced. These stimuli include:

1. The presence of the listener who mediated the consequences.
2. Incidental stimuli that precede the speaker's response.

Not only is the child's tugging and asking for a carrot stick more likely in the presence of his mother, but it is also more likely to occur when he has gone through a period of carrot stick deprivation, when he is in the presence of a carrot stick or in the kitchen, and so on. These incidental stimuli and the presence of a listener become discriminative for the child's utterance, gesture, or movement.

Although the speaker may seem to benefit most obviously from a social transaction with a listener (as in the case of the child's receiving a carrot stick), the listener is also a beneficiary. When the mother gives her child a carrot stick, she terminates the somewhat insistent tugging at her dress and the child's verbal request, and she also receives the thanks of her child, perhaps a particularly powerful form of reinforcement.

In his classic work *Verbal Behavior* (1957) (the primary source for the following analysis), B. F. Skinner suggests that the term *verbal behavior* be used to describe those utterances, gestures, and movements that a speaker acquires *only* because of *listener-presented consequences*. Such behavior is under the stimulus control of the listener and incidental stimuli in the presence of which the speaker has been reinforced. Moreover, Skinner suggests that the listener himself has been conditioned to present these consequences to the speaker (contingent on the occurrence of the speaker's verbal behavior). This means that in the course of social transactions between a speaker and a listener, there are events going on that affect the behavior of the speaker and the listener and serve to make them both beneficiaries of these transactions.

TYPES OF VERBAL BEHAVIOR

In the following discussion a brief survey will be presented. The purpose of this survey is to describe possible functional relationships between the speaker's verbal behavior (as a dependent variable) and the discriminative and consequating stimuli (as independent variables) controlling or maintaining his behavior. As the reader surveys the different types of verbal behavior, he will notice differences along two major lines. First, there are major differences in the stimuli that control the verbal behavior. Second, there are major differences in the response systems involved (whether the verbal behavior is vocal or motor), the form or topography of the behavior, the size of the response unit, and the probability of behavior's occurrence. There are also differences in the magnitude or intensity of the operant and its speed and duration. The former tends to reflect differences in the culture and community of the speaker, and the latter tends to reflect differences in the history of development of the individual.

The Mand

The *mand* is a type of verbal behavior that is strengthened by the consequences following it—particularly the presentation of a positive reinforcer or the removal of an aversive stimulus. It is, therefore, under the functional control of a deprivation state (appropriate to the positive reinforcer) or an aversive stimulus. However, it is not clearly under the control of a prior stimulus, nor can it be defined alone by the formal properties of its response topography. Rather, it is defined by the (controlling) conditions under which it occurs. For example:

Situation 1:

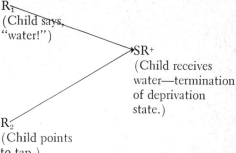

R₁
(Child says,
"water!")

SR⁺
(Child receives
water—termination
of deprivation
state.)

R₂
(Child points
to tap.)

Situation 2:

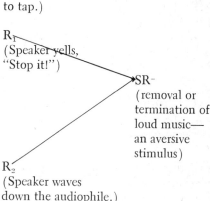

R₁
(Speaker yells,
"Stop it!")

SR⁻
(removal or
termination of
loud music—
an aversive
stimulus)

R₂
(Speaker waves
down the audiophile.)

In these examples two sets of responses occurred, each forming a single response class that was strengthened either by the listener-presented SR⁺ (water, a reinforcer appropriate to the child's water-deprivation state) or by the listener's removal of SR⁻ (the termination of the loud music).

Situation 1 (R₁, saying "water"; R₂, pointing to the water tap) is an example of a mand having both vocal and gestural operant components producing listener-presented strengthening consequences (in the form of water presented to a water-deprived child). Situation 2 (R₁, yelling "Stop it"; R₂, waving down the audiophile) is also an example of a mand having vocal and gestural operant components (R₁ and R₂) both of which are members of the same response class. In this case, however, the mand is maintained by the negative reinforcement that occurs when the very loud music is terminated by the listener.

Should either R₁ or R₂ in *either situation* occur by itself, it would also be a mand. For example, under the control of the Sᴰ (water-deprivation state), the child may merely say, "Water" (R₁), or he may merely point (R₂).

Thus a mand benefits the speaker because of the listener-presented consequences it produces. At the same time, events may follow the occurrence of the mand that serve to maintain the listener's behavior. Although not shown in the diagram, the speaker would probably thank the listener for the presentation of the water (situation 1) or for the termination of the loud music (situation 2), and such thanks would serve to strengthen the behavior of the listener.

In infancy and early childhood when cries of distress and discomfort are strengthened by the reinforcements following them, they are mands. In the adult more sophisticated forms of vocal and gestural expression are observed. In some instances an adult may say, "Shut up!" in an attempt to terminate a sarcastic or upsetting harangue. In polite society, however, the mand may consist of a much more subtle response class. For example, a dirty look may suffice to terminate the sarcastic remarks of others, the effect of which is to negatively reinforce the speaker (the one giving the dirty look). Both "shut up!" and the dirty look function in the speaker's repertoire as mands. The same is true when a speaker gives someone who is a constant source of irritation a "talking to" or a "dressing down." In such situations the mand, as a response unit, may be quite large.

The *extended mand* occurs when the speaker mands the behavior of someone he has never had contact with before (a stranger or someone who cannot reply, for example, an infant). The mother who pleads with her baby to stop crying, even though on no occasion in the past has the baby stopped crying following such a request, is using the extended mand. Such behavior may have been used successfully with older children and thus represents an occasion of stimulus generalization, in which the discriminative properties of the crying baby are sufficiently similar to those encountered earlier with the older children to control the same response class.

The Echoic Response

A vocal expression under the control of the immediately preceding sound of someone else's voice (or one's own voice), and whose response pattern is like the stimulus pattern preceding it, is called an *echoic response*. For example:

$$S^D \xrightarrow{\hspace{2cm}} R_1 \xrightarrow{\hspace{2cm}} \text{Generalized}$$

S^D	R_1	Generalized Sr^+
(Mother says, "Say 'baby.' ")	(Child says, "baby.")	(Mother says, "Good boy!" and smiles.)

The mother's vocalization "baby" produces an auditory S^D, in the presence of which the child's vocalization "baby" is reinforced. In other words, the child repeats or echoes what his mother has said. In this example, the mother, as the listener, is actively training the child (the speaker) by making the presentation of a generalized positive reinforcer contingent on the occurrence of a response that matches her response. By providing educational reinforcement in this manner, she strengthens one response from which (we shall see later) even more complex responses can be derived. Moreover, it seems reasonable to assume that the child's acquisition of the echoic "baby" is an event that serves to reinforce the mother's behavior as a listener.

Self-produced sounds, through the auditory stimulation they produce, may also function as S^D's, so that the first self-produced "baby" controls the second self-produced "baby" and so on. This happens when an echoic response has been extensively reinforced. Furthermore, because these sounds have been paired with listener-presented reinforcement, they will themselves acquire value as conditioned reinforcers, so that the sound of the second echoic serves to reinforce the occurrence of the first one. It is important to emphasize, however, that the second response, which produces a reinforcing sound, can be regarded as an echoic response only if it was preceded by the sound of the first response. In other words, the first response-produced sound must have been the S^D for the next (echoic) response (which produced the reinforcing sound).

Sometimes, an echoic response is maintained by events occurring long after its acquisition. For example, most of us have been reinforced, at least occasionally, for repeating to a second party what a first party has said. On still other occasions we may repeat an order as a means of guaranteeing its execution. For example, someone may give us the combination of a lock, such as "three, fifteen, twenty-one." Subsequently, we may repeat this over and over again until the lock can be worked and opened.

Then there are occasions when a speaker is *echolalic,* a situation where most, if not all, of his speech consists of echoic responses.

The development of the echoic response typically involves a situation in which the speaker's vocalization is a *match* to the listener's vocalization, the *sample.* This matching-to-sample characteristic of the echoic is reminiscent of the situation in which a trainee is said to *imitate* the performance of a model. This practice has an obvious benefit for the listener: Once the speaker has acquired an echoic response, the listener can immediately make the speaker produce it; then, additional training can be started, the goal of which is to bring the response under the control of other prior stimuli. For example, when the listener says, "Say 'baby,' " a child with such training will immediately say, "baby." Subsequently, the trainer may bring the response "baby" under the control of an object—a baby in the speaker's environment.

The Intraverbal Response

Vocal or gestural operants under the control of prior spoken or written stimuli, but whose pattern is different from these stimuli are known as *intraverbal responses.* For example:

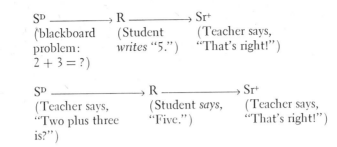

The first problem is presented to the student in written form and is, therefore, a visual S^D. In the second example the problem is presented to the student vocally and is, therefore, an auditory S^D. Intraverbal responses can also be spoken or written, so that various combinations of visual and auditory S^D's and responses are possible and are common to the reinforcement history of most of us. For example, most of us can either write or say "five" in answer to the written problem "$2 + 3 = ?$" Similarly, most of us can also write or say "five" in answer to the teacher's query "two plus three is?" The reinforcements maintaining such behavior come from two sources. Initially, the teacher's response (as a listener) of "That's right," "good," or "yes," serves to strengthen the speaker's intraverbal response. Later on, just having the right answer is reinforcing. And, of course, in educational situations the listener (teacher) is reinforced when the speaker gives the right answer—an event that at least in part serves to maintain the teacher's behavior.

Written or spoken answers to questions and written or spoken answers to interview presentations are common forms of the intraverbal response. Other examples are counting, arriving at conclusions through reasoning or formal logic, reciting the alphabet, the grammatical ordering of words as in "They are" instead of "They is," and even making small talk. The unit size of such responses may be quite small, as when the speaker answers the question "What is the first letter in the alphabet?" by replying "A," or large, as in the recitation of a long poem.

The Tact

A *tact* is a verbal operant under the control of a physical object or event or a property of an object or event. For example:

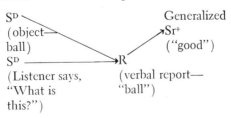

In effect, the speaker labels or names the object; that is, the speaker is much more likely to say "ball" in the presence of a ball than in its absence. The S^D is the presence of a listener who says, "What is this?" and the ball itself (an object). The response class is the verbal report "ball." As in the case of the intraverbal response, the tact can be either spoken, written, or gestural (as in the case of the deaf).

The reinforcing event strengthening the tact also arises from educational situations, and in those speakers whose performances have been reinforced frequently, a skilled performance may be automatically reinforcing. The listener's behavior of reinforcing the speaker for correct tacts comes from the increased environmental control he obtains when the speaker correctly tacts an object or event, or a property of an object or event, of concern to the listener. For example, when the mother of a child says to him, "Go see who is at the door" and the child replies, "It's daddy," she is spared from having to find out for herself.

When confronted with a new object or event that shares some of the properties of other stimuli controlling a previously emitted and reinforced tact, a speaker may respond with an *extended tact*. This, like the extended mand, is simply an instance of stimulus generalization. One form of the extended tact is the *generic extension*, as when the speaker sees an ashtray of new and unusual design and says, "ashtray." The *metaphorical extension* of the tact occurs, for example, when the hungover speaker says, "My head pounds like a jackhammer." Here, the pounding of the speaker's head possesses stimulus properties comparable to controlling stimuli for an earlier reinforced response of "a pounding jackhammer."

A tact may take the form of a written, spoken, or gestural response under the stimulus control of a *class of objects*, or *events*, or of the *properties of objects*, or *events*. Such a tact is an *abstraction*. Stated differently, an abstraction is a tact that is under the control of a number of different stimulus objects, all possessing a *common stimulus element or property*. For example, although all dogs are not exactly alike, they are sufficiently similar (they are furry, have four legs, a tail, and so on) to be grouped as a stimulus class that has common stimulus properties and controls the spoken or written response of "dog."

Finally, although the tact is an important part of the repertoire of all of us, it is a particularly vital aspect of the verbal behavior of the scientist. His skills in observing and studying the phenomena of nature and in reporting them are manifest in the extensiveness of his repertoire of tacts.

The Textual Response

The *textual*, or *reading*, response is verbal behavior under the control of a written or printed visual stimulus (except in the case of the blind, for whom the stimulus is tactual). For example:

$$S^D \longrightarrow R \longrightarrow \text{Generalized}$$

(the printed	(Student says,	Sr^+
word *dog*)	"dog" aloud.)	(Teacher says,
		"good")

The S^D in this example is the printed word *dog* (a textual stimulus), and the response class is the vocal operant—saying "dog" aloud. Usually, such responses are acquired after the speaker has already learned to make the response (R), or at least subunits of it, as some other form of verbal behavior. For example, the child may first be reinforced for saying "dog" only after his mother has said, "dog" (an echoic response). Then later the child may be reinforced for saying "dog" after the dog comes into the room (a tact). Still later the child is presented with the textual or printed stimulus; and reinforcers are presented for correct textual or reading responses in its presence, and extinction or punishment is presented for emitting the response in the absence of the appropriate textual (word) or in the presence of another textual stimulus. This process is essentially operant discrimination training, and as a result of it the child will be more likely to say "dog" in the presence of the word *dog* (the S^D) than in its absence (the S^Δ) or in the presence of another word (S-).

Once single-word responses are brought under the control of the textual stimulus, they can be combined or sequenced into longer units. For example, reading training may initially involve learning words or suffixes separately. Once they are mastered, they are then presented in appropriate juxtaposition so that the student is not reinforced unless he reads each unit in its proper order, as in the case of *himself* ("him ... self"), or *walking* ("walk ... ing").

The reinforcing events in reading are extremely complex. It is easy to see how various verbal reinforcers (generalized positive reinforcers in the form of praise) may strengthen textual responses when they are administered in educational settings. However, long sequences may be maintained by automatic reinforcement. That is, reading materials may provide a type of *stimulus change* or *novel stimulation* that functions as a reinforcer. In other cases textual responses may be chained to other reinforcers, as when one reads while eating. On still other occasions reading responses may be reinforced by some terminal consequences, as when one reads an instruction manual in order to operate some equipment successfully. Finally, textual responses are initially made aloud, the effect of which is to permit the listener to monitor and to respond to them appropriately. However, as the speaker's reading skill progresses, the listener provides reinforcements for silent textual or reading behavior, except in certain situations (a dramatic reading, for example).

Audience Control

All of a speaker's verbal behavior is sensitive to the influence of an audience, at least to the extent that it is controlled by and maintained by the presence of a listener. More specifically, however, *audience control* refers to a group of responses under the stimulus control of a particular listener. Listeners vary in the degree to which they control certain classes of verbal behavior in the speaker and in the degree to which they maintain these classes of behavior through reinforcement. For example:

Situation 1:

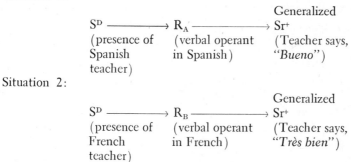

Situation 1:

$$S^D \longrightarrow R_A \longrightarrow \overset{\text{Generalized}}{Sr^+}$$

(presence of Spanish teacher) (verbal operant in Spanish) (Teacher says, *"Bueno"*)

Situation 2:

$$S^D \longrightarrow R_B \longrightarrow \overset{\text{Generalized}}{Sr^+}$$

(presence of French teacher) (verbal operant in French) (Teacher says, *"Très bien"*)

In this example the speaker shows appropriate spoken Spanish or French conversation in the presence of the appropriate listener, either the Spanish or the French teacher. Because the language teachers provide reinforcements for appropriate conversation, they themselves become S^D's for that conversation (since it was in their presence that the speaker was reinforced). The speaker is, therefore, more apt to speak Spanish with the Spanish teacher than with the French teacher and, of course, vice versa.

Besides the control over our foreign language repertoires that our language teachers possess, others may control different groups of responses. For example, we may talk only with certain people about our personal problems, and of course, we are especially apt to talk to those who are particularly interested, understanding, and sympathetic. Similarly, we may talk in a *particular manner* to certain people and in a different manner to others. We may be particularly polite to our elders and show them respect (address them appropriately, and never be argumentative with them), lest we be punished by them.

Audience control may also occur through the use of insignias, badges, or forms of dress. We are most apt to ask a policeman for help in some law enforcement problem or ask a person wearing a badge that says INFORMATION for information.

A special case of written audience control is letter writing, but because listener- (correspondent-) presented reinforcements tend to be weak and necessarily delayed, letter writing often tends to occur infrequently.

Sometimes, too, the speaker will talk to himself in a self-audience control response—a type of behavior that is commonly suppressed by others. ("What are you talking to yourself for? What's the matter? You crazy or something?")

Finally, the audience control response is sensitive to certain physical aspects of the speaker's environment. Such aspects of the environment become discriminative for the audience control response simply because a listener has presented the speaker with consequences in the presence of these stimuli. For example, a young college student is talking to his girl friend and suddenly drops his voice as he enters the library, because in past conversations in the library his girl friend has put her fingers on her lips and said, "Shh."

The Transcription Response

The *transcription response* is verbal behavior consisting of a motor operant that produces written or printed material in a form comparable to the printed or written stimulus that controls it.

The S^D is, then, some kind of written or printed material, and the response class consists of manual, manipulative, motor operants such as those in cursive handwriting and in printing. The former requires that S emit a *continuous* or *smooth response topography*, and the latter requires a more *discrete response topography*. For example:

$$S^D \longrightarrow R \longrightarrow \text{Generalized}$$
(S is given the   (S writes the Sr^+
sample letter *a*.)   letter *a*.)   ("good")

or

$$S^D \longrightarrow R \longrightarrow \text{Generalized}$$
(S is given the   (S prints the Sr^+
sample letter *A*.)   letter *A*.)   ("good")

The letter A in the form of a sample of cursive handwriting or of manuscript printing is a visual S^D for a comparable transcription response (cursive handwriting or manuscript printing, respectively).

The reinforcer involved in the acquistion of the transcription response is most often a generalized reinforcer. This is presented by a listener when the speaker produces a transcription response that matches a sample cursive or printed verbal stimulus or when the speaker copies a drawing. Such reinforcement usually occurs in educational, business, or technical settings, where the transcription is valued. Once the speaker has become skillful, the transcription response, like many other forms of verbal behavior, may become automatically reinforcing. There are occasions, too, when the speaker who is making a transcription response is able to use special writing materials that provide some reinforcement (for example, a felt-tipped pen, special colored ink, or a pastel crayon).

Like textual responses, transcription responses are often acquired in units (*a, b, c,* or *A, B, C*) and then later combined into sequences (*cab* or *CAB*). Finally, the size and complexity of the unit of the transcription response varies widely. Transcribing a period, a word, a sentence, and a paragraph and copying a drawing involves increasingly larger and more complex response units.

The Dictation Response

The *dictation response* is a motor or written response under the control of an *auditory stimulus* in the form of the speech of others. For example:

$$
\begin{array}{ccc}
& & \text{Generalized} \\
\text{S}^{\text{D}} \longrightarrow & \text{R} \longrightarrow & \text{Sr}^{+} \\
\text{(Teacher says,} & \text{(Child writes} & \text{(Teacher says,} \\
\text{``Write dog.'')} & \text{``dog.'')} & \text{``That's right.'')}
\end{array}
$$

The dictation response consists of the child's written expression "dog" under the stimulus control of the teacher's utterance "dog," an auditory stimulus. Moreover, the teacher (as a listener) reinforced the child's (the speaker's) performance.

Relationships Between Each Type of Verbal Behavior

The relationships and the correspondence between the stimulus dimension of the S^{D}, the response form, and the stimulus dimension of the response product of each type of verbal behavior (with the exception of the mand) are summarized in Table 7-1. For example, the stimulus dimension of the echoic is auditory; the echoic response form is spoken; and the stimulus dimension of the echoic response product is auditory. Thus the stimulus dimension of the echoic S^{D} is the same as the stimulus dimension of the echoic response product (both are auditory), and there is formal correspondence between the echoic stimulus and the echoic response product—that is, the echoic response product is physically the same as the stimulus producing it.

In the dictation response, the stimulus dimension of the dictation S^{D} is auditory; the dictation response form is written; and the stimulus dimension of the dictation response product is visual, so that the stimulus dimension of the S^{D} is different from the stimulus dimension of the dictation response product. (The former is auditory, and the latter is visual.) There is, however, *point-to-point correspondence* between the dictation stimulus and the dictation response, so that the beginning and end of the dictation response is controlled by the beginning and the end of the dictation stimulus. Thus the occurrence of the child's dictation responses "A" ... "B" ... "C," are from moment to moment under the control of the teacher's utterances "A" ... "B" ... "C" as dictation stimuli.

In the intraverbal response, the stimulus dimension of the intraverbal S^{D} can be either visual or auditory; the intraverbal response can be either spoken or written; and the stimulus dimension of the intraverbal response product can be either auditory or visual. For example, the intraverbal stimulus "How old are you?" can be presented as an auditory or visual stimulus; the response of "five" can be either spoken or written; and the stimulus dimension of the

Table 7-1 Characteristics of Various Types of Verbal Behavior.

TYPE OF VERBAL BEHAVIOR	STIMULUS DIMENSION OF THE S^D	RESPONSE FORM	STIMULUS DIMENSION OF THE RESPONSE PRODUCT	RELATIONSHIP BETWEEN THESE STIMULUS DIMENSIONS	CORRESPONDENCE BETWEEN THE STIMULUS AND RESPONSE PRODUCTS
The Echoic Response	auditory	spoken	auditory	same	formal correspondence (actual physical similarity)
The Intraverbal Response	visual auditory	spoken written spoken written	auditory visual auditory visual	different same same different	none
The tact	visual somesthetic auditory olfactory gustatory	spoken written	auditory visual	same in two cases, different in all the rest	none
The Textual Response	visual	spoken	auditory	different	point-to-point correspondence
Audience Control	visual auditory	spoken written spoken written	auditory visual auditory visual	different same same different	none
The Transcription Response	visual	written	visual	different	formal correspondence (actual physical similarity)
The Dictation Response	auditory	written	visual	different	point-to-point correspondence

response product can be either auditory or visual. There is neither formal nor point-to-point correspondence between the intraverbal stimulus ("How old are you?") and the response product (a spoken or written response of "five"). The reader should carefully examine the remainder of this table to familiarize himself with the characteristics of the remaining types of verbal behavior.

The Autoclitic Response

It has been suggested that the types of verbal behavior described are under the control of specific environmental events (stimuli that uniquely control them in the presence of a listener). There are, however, occasions when the speaker's behavior functions to modify his verbal productions through the responses his behavior controls in himself. In other words, the *speaker becomes his own listener.* When the speaker functions as a self-listener, the responses are called *autoclitic responses.* Such responses allow for the self-manipulation of one's own verbal behavior. Autoclitic responses are manifest in a variety of ways, some examples of which are *descriptive autoclitics* and *relational autoclitics.* Descriptive autoclitics include verbal statements that describe the speaker's past or present behavior ("I am now writing"), qualifying remarks that describe the strength of the speaker's response ("I guess," "I believe"), statements that describe the relationship of a response to the other verbal behavior of a speaker or a listener and which serve to modify or qualify that behavior ("I mean to say"), statements that describe the speaker's motivational state ("I am sorry to say"), and the verbal statement "I wish" when it is followed by a response that specifies how the listener ought to behave ("I wish you would go") or merely a condition ("I wish it would rain"). Relational autoclitics are verbal behaviors involved in the grammatical ordering of the speaker's verbal production—a kind of self-editing function. For example, when the speaker makes a noun and verb agree ("boys are" instead of "boys is") or uses proper word order ("good chocolate" instead of "chocolate good"), he is performing a relational autoclitic.

VERBAL BEHAVIOR: A MATTER OF MULTIPLE CAUSATION

At any one moment a speaker's verbal behavior is dynamic and the strength of any reponse (probability of occurrence) is a function of *multiple causes.* First, a given response unit may be under the control of *several different discriminative stimuli.* For example, the word *candy* may be under the control of (1) a candy deprivation state (and is, therefore, a mand), (2) candy as an object (and is, therefore, a tact), or (3) a question such as "What is your favorite food?" (and is, therefore, an intraverbal response).

Second, there is the effect of *multiple audiences,* each of which possesses characteristic stimulus control that determines the strength of the speaker's response. A dirty joke told to a colleague may be completely suppressed by the intrusion of another audience, say, the colleague's girl friend.

Third, subunits of a given total verbal response unit have their own controlling stimuli. While in the preceding example the response "candy" may have had diverse controlling stimuli (a deprivation state, an object, or an intraverbal stimulus), "can," a subunit of the total response unit ("candy"), may be, by itself, under the control of still other discriminative stimuli (as an intraverbal response, it might be controlled by a personal pronoun such as *I* or *we* [can]).

Then, too, the influence of the verbal community may at different times and in different situations strengthen a number of *different but related responses*. The word *food*, a mand under functional control of a food-deprivation state and ordinarily reinforced by the verbal community, is only one of the many possible responses reinforced under comparable conditions. Others might be the words *meat*, *eat*, and *dinner*, and these, too, may be under the functional control of a food-deprivation state.

It would seem, then, that the controlling conditions of verbal behavior may, in a given instance, be complex, and that a given unit of verbal behavior may function in the speaker–listener relationship in many different ways.[2] What is more, the sources of control of verbal behavior often change in subtle ways, giving the behavior a particular dynamic and variable quality.

THE DEVELOPMENT OF VERBAL BEHAVIOR

It has been suggested that verbal behavior develops from social transactions that take place between a speaker and a listener, that the listener's responses can function as consequences for a speaker, and that the reverse is also true, making both parties beneficiaries of the transaction. Parents, siblings, peers, and teachers function as both listeners and agents of the verbal community in the course of social transactions with a speaker. They are the ones who are able to provide the speaker with sample performances, who monitor the speaker's performances, and who follow those performances with appropriate consequences. The effect of such transactions is the speaker's acquisition of verbal behavior.[3]

This process of operant acquisition begins with the acquisition of small, usually single-component, unit responses, from which larger and more com-

---

[2] For further discussion of verbal behavior as a matter of multiple causation, see Skinner, 1957.

[3] Analyses of the behavioral processes involved in the acquisition of verbal behavior are presented in Chapters 4, 5, 6, and 9.

plex response units derive. The infant's initial vocalizations fall into two classes:

1. Whines and cries elicited by noxious, irritating, or painful stimuli (respondents).

2. An array of sounds including vowels and consonants, to which are added gestures and later movements. All of these operants are affected by the consequences following them from which the child's verbal behavior develops.

Early in life as the child produces speech sounds (and gestures and movements), they are followed by listener-presented strengthening consequences and come under the control of these consequences; forming a minimum identifiable response unit of verbal behavior from which larger and more complex combinations can be made. The single response units "m" as in "met" (a consonant sound) and "ä" as in "car" (a vowel sound) are early speech sounds called *phonemes*, and they can be chained together to form the expression "ma." As a response unit, the derivative expression "ma," when brought under the control of a particular stimulus, becomes a larger verbal response unit, called a *morpheme*. This, in turn, can be combined with other morphemes to form longer and more complex *chained sequences*, which can also be brought under the control of a discriminative stimulus, as, for example, in intraverbal behavior. A child's reply, "I like Mama," to a query about who he likes involves three essential events. First, the words are differentiated from their more rudimentary precursors, probably as echoic responses that are gradually brought under other forms of stimulus control besides the sample utterance of the listener.[4] Initially, the child may be reinforced by the listener for emitting the echoic response "Mama" after being presented with the listener's sample utterance "Mama." Later on, the child is more likely to be reinforced for saying "Mama" when his mother is in the room, this reinforcement leading to the acquisition of a tact. Second, each separately acquired response is chained in a manner such that the response class "I" serves as an S^D for the response class "like," and this, in turn, functions as an S^D for the response "Mama," and so on. Finally, concurrent with, or subsequent to, the acquisition of this chained sequence, the sequence must be brought under the stimulus control of the question "Who do you like?" and the person asking the question.

When motor response components are added to the analysis, the speaker's verbal behavior acquires functional significance in the speaker's manipulating his environment. For example, a speaker may first acquire the textual unit responses "Open" "the" "red" "box," with each response unit under the control of a textual (printed) stimulus. These unit responses are then chained

---

[4] An echolalic speaker would presumably have a history of training limited to the acquisition of the echoic response. For various reasons, the listener would have stopped training the speaker before the controlling stimuli for the tact, the textual response, and so on, were presented.

together and brought under the control of the sentence "Open the red box." Subsequently, appropriate motor responses (opening the red box) are reinforced when they occur in the presence of the textual stimulus ("Open the red box"). Thus a new and identifiable functional unit of verbal behavior, under the control of a textual stimulus, is formed.

There is one other point worthy of mention. It is *not* necessary to base our analysis of the conditions under which verbal behavior develops on the lexical or grammatical properties of the speaker's responses. Rather, the emphasis is on the functional relationships between the identifiable response units of the speaker's verbal behavior and the variables controlling these units. For example, in the case of the child wanting a carrot stick, it is likely that on some earlier occasion a smaller and topographically different unit of verbal behavior, perhaps merely grunting and pointing to the carrot stick, would have been sufficient to produce it. It is also likely that the mother, as a member of the verbal community, changed the reinforcement contingency several times, with each change requiring a topographically different and larger unit of verbal behavior. Although the child's pointing and grunting may have served at one time to produce the carrot stick, it did not conform to any lexical or grammatical rule. The same can be said about the child's utterance of "Carrot stick! Mommy!" In the two cases the unit of verbal behavior was different, even though both units were mands and both were under the functional control of a carrot stick deprivation and the presence of a listener who had provided reinforcements in the past.

Such training, in which reinforcements are initially used to strengthen single-unit responses, then to strengthen longer chained sequences of responses that are then brought under the control of a stimulus, leads to the acquisition of verbal performances that are noted for their length, complexity, variety, and reliability. In fact, so impressive are these performances that some observers believe the emission of speech is really a matter of "choice behavior" on the part of the speaker. That is, the speaker selects the appropriate rules for his utterance, and the task of the listener is to detect these rules. These observers also believe that the grammatical ordering of the speaker's unit responses, as they occur in a sentence, is due to an innate tendency—that is, the organism's nervous system imposes a serial order on the organism's responses.[5] This is, of course, an inference about a hypothetical antecedent of

[5] For example, Chomsky (1959) asserts that the fact "that all normal children acquire essentially comparable grammars of great complexity with remarkable rapidity suggests that human beings are somehow specially designed to do this, with data-handling or 'hypothesis-formulating' ability of unknown complexity." He states further:

There is nothing essentially mysterious about this. Complex innate behavior patterns and innate "tendencies to learn in specific ways" have been carefully studied in lower organisms. Many psychologists have been inclined to believe that such biological structure will not have an important effect on acquisition of complex behavior in

behavior and is difficult if not impossible to prove or disprove. It might be pointed out that there are children who, according to routine medical and clinical tests, show no nervous system pathology, yet are lacking in speech. For example:

Dee was a 3½-year-old girl with delayed speech. Her physical exam was negative. She possessed a normal speech apparatus and normal hearing functions. The problem was that she seldom spoke, and when she did, it consisted of a vowel-like inhalation, [a], that sounded like a gasp of surprise and whining. Most often, she made gestures, which others had learned to follow. For example, when she wanted a drink, she simply went to the sink and pointed at the faucet. On the Stanford-Binet Intelligence Test and the Leiter, she was found to be mildly mentally retarded. Probably it is significant that her mother was a heart patient, who had been warned to get plenty of rest. During the first 2½ years of Dee's life, Dee spent better than half a day in her crib until her mother awakened (around 1 P.M.) and fed her lunch. In the morning her father or her 12-year-old brother or 10-year-old sister fed her cereal and put her back in the crib with plenty of toys. She remained there each weekday morning until her mother got up to feed her. Unfortunately, there are many children just like Dee at the clinic, although they have different diagnoses ranging from retardation to infantile autism. Dee is now showing good progress with operant conditioning speech therapy.

One may interpret this case in one of two ways. First, Dee's lack of speech can be attributed to some kind of nervous system pathology, which current methods of examination failed to reveal but, nevertheless, affects her speech development. An alternative view, and one that the author finds much more plausible, is that she did not receive adequate training for speech and did receive adequate training for silence and perhaps for emitting mands (such as pointing to the faucet).

Language consisting of chained units in appropriate syntactical relationships (sentences) is by no means universal in humans, nor is it limited to them.[6] Even if it were universal in humans, it could just as easily be attributed to reinforcement contingencies that are common to the various verbal communities as to an innate tendency. Members of the verbal community define the reinforcement contingency so that when the child is old enough, utterances are not strengthened until they occur in the proper order or sequence.

---

higher organisms, but I have not been able to find any serious justification for this attitude. Some recent studies have stressed the necessity for carefully analyzing the strategies available to the organism, regarded as a complex "information processing system." [p. 57].

[6] See pages 176–179 and Figure 7-1 for a discussion of the procedures used to train a chimpanzee to write sentences.

Although the mother of the child who wanted a carrot stick might have been willing to give him a carrot stick for such utterances as "carrot" or "me carrot" when he was a toddler, she probably would not have been willing to give him one for "me carrot" or for "carrot me" when he was much older. Unfortunately, there is no easy way to prove unequivocally either account of the serial ordering of language, and so the author will let the reader decide for himself.

Whatever the cause of a speech problem in an individual case, training programs based on operant conditioning principles are useful in the acquisition of expressive language (as when the speaker uses symbols in communicating with the listener, for example, when he says, "two" in answer to the listener's query regarding the number of eyes he has) and of receptive language (as when the speaker follows the listener's verbal instructions or directions, for example, nods his head when so directed).

Premack (1970) developed a program for teaching Sarah, a chimpanzee, both forms of language. Even though this program is for a chimpanzee and strengthens motor rather than vocal responses,[7] the procedures can be and have been used in training children. The details of the training program are outlined in Figure 7-1.

At the beginning of Sarah's training, food reinforcers were made available contingent on the emission of a single-unit correct "writing" response. That response consisted of Sarah's picking up a word (a plastic symbol of particular color, size, and shape) for a particular piece of fruit, such as a banana, and placing it on a board. (A metal board and magnetic plastic cards were used.)

Next, the reinforcers were made contingent on the emission of *two-unit responses* in *sequence*. That is, Sarah had to write the name of the donor of the fruit (by placing the word for that donor on the board) and the name of the fruit in proper order. For example, she would write "Mary banana."

Later, food reinforcers were made contingent on the emission of *several response units* in *sequence*. For example, Sarah had to write sentences using the words that described the relationship between actual objects as they were arranged by the trainer. For example, if the trainer had placed a green card on a red card, Sarah would write "green on red." (This is an example of expressive language.) Sarah also learned to arrange the cards according to trainer-specified directions written as sentences with the words on the board. For example, when the direction said "red on green," Sarah arranged the cards so that the red card was on the green card. (This is an example of receptive language.)

Still later, food reinforcers were made contingent on the emission of motor behavior consistent with the trainer's instructions. For example, she would

---

[7] There have been several attempts to teach chimpanzees to use vocal expressive language but with limited success (Kellogg, 1968).

1. Elements: A trainer (E) who serves as a listener, a trainee who serves as a speaker (S), stimuli to function as S^D's, and appropriate consequences.
2. General Procedure: Bring E and S together in an appropriately arranged training situation, select a response class (placing plastic objects on a board), select objects to function as S^D's, and provide magazine training.
  A. *Using words.* Specific Procedures:
  In order to receive reinforcements, S must "write" the correct name of the reinforcement on the board (she must place the plastic symbol that is the referent (word) for the reinforcement on the board), as follows:

S^{D_1} ——————— R ——————— SR^+
(plastic symbol   (S writes "banana"—   (Speaker is given
for banana)   that is, picks up banana   banana by
   symbol and puts   listener.)
   it on the board.)

S^{D_2} ——————— R ——————— SR^+
(plastic symbol   (S writes "apple"—   (Speaker is given
for apple)   that is, picks up apple   apple by E.)
   symbol and puts
   it on the board.)

  Subsequent training involves presentations by different trainers of different words (symbols) and reinforcements.

  B. *Using sentences—expressive language.* Specific Procedures:
  1. Two-Unit Responses in Sequence—In order to receive reinforcements, S must write a sentence specifying the donor and the name of the object received from the donor by using the appropriate words (plastic symbols) in a proper syntactical relationship. Sentences (chains) in which the words (links) are out of order (for example, "banana Mary") are not reinforced.

S^D ——————— R ——————— S^D ——————— R ——————— SR^+
(situation in   (S writes   (word *Mary*   (S writes   (Speaker is
which Mary is   "Mary"—puts   on board)   "banana"—puts   given banana
the donor, the word   symbol for   symbol for   by E.)
is *banana*, and   Mary on board.)   banana on
the banana is   board.)
the reinforcer)

  2. Several Unit Responses in Sequence. Specific Procedures:
  E places green card on red card, S writes sentence with words in proper order describing E's presentation (green or red) in order to be reinforced.

S^D ——— R ——————— S^D ——— R ——————— S^D ——— R ——— SR^+
(green card   (S writes   (symbol for   (S writes   (symbol   (S writes   (E gives
placed on a   "green"—puts   green on   "on"—puts   for *on*   "red.")   speaker
red card)   symbol for   board)   symbol for   on board)   banana.)
   green on   *on* on board.)
   board.)

FIGURE 7-1 Outline of procedure used in teaching Sarah language.

Subsequent training involves different E's, words (symbols), and reinforcements. Only chains containing correct links in proper order are reinforced.

C *Using sentences—receptive language.* Specific Procedures:

In order to receive reinforcements, S must make appropriate motor responses to the instructions "written" with plastic symbols on the board by the E. E may assist S in making the response by successive approximations or by a putting-through procedure. For example, E may put the green card in S's hand and then guide her hand over the red card, reinforcing S when the green card is on the red card.

S^D	R	SR^+
("Green card on red card"—a sentence on the board made up of words [plastic symbols])	(S picks up green card and places it on top of red card.)	(Listener gives speaker banana.)

S^D	R	SR^+
("Sarah insert banana dish.")	(S puts banana in dish.)	(Listener gives speaker banana.)

Additional training involves different fruits (words) the containers (words). *One sentence is presented at a time.* Placing the correct fruit into the correct container is reinforced. For example, the four sentences:

"Sarah	"Sarah	"Sarah	"Sarah
insert	insert	insert	insert
banana	apple	banana	apple
dish."	pail."	pail."	dish."

are presented vertically, at one time, and in all possible combinations.

Then the four sentences are presented in a series of three phases. Each phase involves a single pair of sentences arranged vertically. Subsequently, words in the two sentences are faded out. All combinations of sentences are eventually presented in this manner. Sarah is reinforced for making two correct responses to each pair in a sequence (a chain).

	words faded out $\longrightarrow$	
"Sarah	"Sarah	"Sarah
insert	insert	insert
banana	banana	banana
pail."	pail	pail
"Sarah	insert	apple
insert	apple	dish."
apple	dish."	
dish."		

FIGURE 7-1 *(Continued)*

178

D. *Metalanguage*. Specific Procedures:

S's reinforcements contingent on writing sentences using plastic words that describe the objects they represent. Training involves word–object pairs on the board. Between the word and the object the S places other words that indicate whether or not the word names the object. For example, S writes, "Apple (word) name of apple (fruit)."

S^D	R	SR+
(The word *apple* and the object placed on board)	(S writes "name of"—puts plastic word *name of* on the board between the word *apple* and the object apple.)	(E gives speaker apple.)

Additional procedures involve the introduction of variations in the word–object pairs and the use of phrases that describe the relationship between the word and the object. Training is also given in answering questions on the board—such as "Apple (word name of apple (object)?"—by S's answering Yes or No (picking up the word *yes* or *no* and putting it on the board).

FIGURE 7-1 *(Continued)*

follow the instruction "Sarah insert banana dish" by putting a banana into a dish, or even the instruction "Sarah insert banana pail apple dish" by putting a banana into a pail and an apple into a dish. When Sarah was trained to follow the latter instruction, she was first taught to follow each single set of instructions (that is, "Sarah insert banana dish," "Sarah insert apple pail"). Then the two sentences were aranged in sequence and parts of the two sentences were faded out to make them into a compound sentence (that is, "Sarah insert banana dish apple pail"). Sarah promptly learned to do this. (Again this is an example of receptive language).

Finally, Sarah learned to use language to describe other language (metalanguage). Reinforcers were made contingent on Sarah's writing sentences with plastic words that described the objects they represent. For example, the instructor placed the word *apple* and the actual fruit on the board, and Sarah wrote "Apple (word) name of apple (object)" by placing the correct plastic words between the word *apple* and the object, or if the instructor used the word *apple* and a banana, Sarah wrote "Apple (word) not name of banana (object)." Sarah also wrote "no" in answer to the trainer's written question "Apple (word) name of banana (object)?"

Sarah's training always involved the strengthening through positive reinforcements of single-unit and multiple-unit responses in trainer-defined sequences and in the presence of trainer-arranged S^D's. Incorrect responses were extinguished. In many ways, these procedures are remarkable, since they provide a rich source of information about language acquisition, and the student would do well to study them carefully.

In the earlier examples of the speech training of children and even in the case of training Sarah, it is presupposed that an adequate speaker–listener relationship exists. There is no guarantee, however, that a child *will* develop such sophisticated performances, unless conditions favoring their acquisition are explicitly arranged. A child exposed to minimal listener–speaker relationships may be expected to acquire a minimal verbal repertoire, consisting primarily of mands. The reason for this, of course, is that children are most likely to secure the attention of a listener by using mands and the termination of a mand may prove particularly reinforcing to the listener.

The other types of verbal behavior described earlier would be absent from the child's repertoire. Fortunately, however, such minimal speaker–listener relationships are rare in our culture, although for most of us this speaker–listener relationship is seldom as good as it could be. Listeners are not always able to provide good sample performances, to monitor carefully the speaker's behavior, or to consequate that behavior appropriately. Moreover, the acquisition of certain types of verbal behavior may be particularly difficult because the stimuli controlling the behavior is highly detailed and "fine-grained." This is particularly true of reading (textual) behavior. The majority of us, then, have speaker–listener relationships with members of the verbal community that produce verbal repertoires consisting of all the various types of verbal behavior. However, although some of these verbal behaviors are strong and we become extremely skillful with them, we prove to be less skillful with others.[8] The repertoires that characterize the verbal behavior of individuals are unique to each individual and reflect unique training histories.

THE MEANING OR UNDERSTANDING OF VERBAL STIMULI

When we say that a child understands or knows the meaning of a verbal stimulus, we have observed that the child emits some type of verbal behavior under conditions defined as appropriate or conventional by the verbal community. Suppose, for example, we observe a child emit the verbal expression "five" in the presence of a listener under the following conditions:

1. S^D ——————————————→ R   (a tact)
   (The listener shows   (Child says, "Five.")
   the child five fingers
   and says, "How many?")

---

[8] Often such variations in skill are mistakenly attributed to brain damage. For example, an individual who is able to write the word *dog*, as a transcription response under the control of a visual S^D, may *not* be able to write the word *dog* as a dictation response under the control of an auditory S^D. Viewing these skills as distinct types of verbal behavior, each having specific controlling stimuli and unique reinforcement histories, does a great deal to reduce the mystery and make the variations in skill more understandable.

2. S^D ─────────────→ R   (an intraverbal response)
(Teacher says, "How   (Child says, "Five.")
old are you?")

3. S^D ─────────────→ R   (a textual response)
(The word *five* is   (Child says, "Five.")
presented, and the
teacher says,
"Read this.")

4. S^D ─────────────→ R   (an echoic response)
(Child's mother   (Child says, "Five.")
says, "Say five.")

5. S^D ─────────────→ R   (an incorrect tact)
(Mother points to   (Child says, "Five.")
chair and says,
"What's that?")

6. S^D ─────────────→ R   (an unknown S^D,
(?)   (Child says, "Five.")   perhaps an audience
control response)

In examples 1 through 3 the verbal operant "five" was emitted under conditions that may be said to be conventional for our society. (It was emitted in the presence of appropriate S^D's.) Observing the child's behavior, we would probably say that he knows or understands the meaning of the various types of S^D's presented to him (that is, the five fingers, the question "How old are you?" and the printed word *five*), because in these examples the child's verbal response "five" was appropriate. In example 4 (the echoic response) the child's response would probably be characterized as being *imitative* and *shallow*, since the child may be said to have shown a "lack of understanding," especially if we have not observed the child emit the operant under the other stimulus conditions. In examples 5 and 6 it may be assumed that not only *doesn't* the child understand or know the meaning of the word *five*, but he also shows a *cognitive disorder*—that is, behavior that seems to be characteristic of a disturbed or mentally ill person.

What needs emphasis, and what is germane to our entire discussion, is that when an organism shows understanding or knows the meaning of a particular stimulus, his behavior is such that *he emits an appropriate operant in the presence of an appropriate stimulus*, as defined by the verbal community in which his verbal behavior was acquired. Therefore, understanding or knowing the meaning of a stimulus would necessarily involve operant differentiation training and operant discrimination training (that is, training in emitting an appropriate differentiated response (R^D) under the control of an appropriate S^D).

The more likely a child is to emit appropriate or "correct" behavior under a variety of possible stimulus conditions, the more likely he is to be characterized by his teachers and others as being capable of understanding meaning.

Conversely, the less likely he is to emit appropriate or "correct" behavior under these various conditions, the more likely is he to be characterized by those people as slow, stupid, lacking in understanding, or untrainable.

In summary, then, understanding the meaning of verbal stimuli involves emitting appropriate behavior in the presence of appropriate stimuli. This process is a direct function of one's history of training and of his history of reinforcement. Consequently, when one plans a program for the training of understanding, he should give serious consideration to these facts.[9]

SOME IMPLICATIONS OF THE FOREGOING ANALYSIS FOR READING TRAINING

Reading skills, which we have defined as textual responses, are essential for the acquisition of other verbal behaviors. However, they frequently present extremely difficult problems for the student as well as for the teacher in charge of reading training. When reading problems are encountered, they are often viewed as evidence that an individual has failed to reach a proper level of growth or maturity, or they are seen as being caused by perceptual difficulties. By contrast, skilled readers are viewed, perhaps erroneously, as possessing special capacities. In *Verbal Behavior* (1957) Skinner says: "Reading is not an ability or a capacity, but a tendency. When we say that a person is 'able to read,' we mean that he will behave in certain ways under circumstances involving a non-auditory stimulus" (p. 66).

As discriminated operants, textual responses very often require extremely fine discriminations. Compare the following:

LIST A	LIST B
There	House
Three	Short
Then	Start
Their	Green
They	Ridge

The words in list A show a high degree of *formal similarity*. Three or more letters are the same, and two or three are presented in the same order. Thus a very careful inspection of each letter in each word is necessary for accurate

---

[9] It has been demonstrated that even animals can be trained to understand the meaning of verbal stimuli, despite the fact that the appropriate S^D's and R^D's have been defined by the human verbal community rather than their own animal community. This has been demonstrated by Ellen Reese (1965) in a film entitled "Behavior Theory in Practice: Part III: Learning, Motivation, and Discrimination." In the film a pigeon is trained to make appropriate differential responses to human verbal stimuli. When the word *peck* is presented to the pigeon through a window in the box, the pigeon pecks; when the word *turn* is presented, the pigeon turns in circles, thereby showing understanding of the stimuli (or at least receptive language).

discriminations to be made. By contrast, the items in list B show a high degree of formal dissimilarity, and less fine-grained discriminations are required. It would not be surprising, then, for a subject to make more errors on a test with list A than on a test with list B, even if he had had the same amount of training on both lists. In short, the difficulty can be attributed to the formal properties of these textual stimuli rather than to the perceptual problems of the reader.

Another frequently reported perceptual difficulty is the *order reversal* of words such as *was* and *saw* (emitting the textual response "saw" to the textual stimulus "was" or vice versa). What is needed here is additional training to strengthen the left-to-right direction of the reader's "attack" of the textual stimulus. (The word *was*, for example, when read from right to left, is *saw*.)

A failure to remedy such difficulties or to improve an already poor reading performance may profoundly affect a child's performance in other scholastic endeavors. What is more, poor scholastic performance and its consequence— failure (extinction, punishment)—are events occurring in the presence of classroom stimuli (books, the reading study, the teacher, and so on), the effect of which may be to make the student apathetic or even antagonistic toward these stimuli. Furthermore, apathy and antagonism in school is sometimes regarded as merely a symptom of a much more serious problem, for example, mental illness, requiring extensive psychotherapy—a procedure having little or no relationship to reading training. Staats and Butterfield (1965) report a case study that illustrates this:

The subject was a 14-year-old Mexican-American delinquent boy who came from a culturally deprived, uneducated family. He had a history of bad behavior, including running away, burglary, truancy, incorrigibility, and malicious mischief. He had been referred to the juvenile department nine times for these offenses. Although the training program was initiated while he was living at home, he finally ended up in an industrial school for juvenile delinquents. His IQ was 106 (full scale on the Wechsler-Bellevue Intelligence Scale), and he was described as having a short attention span and poorly integrated thought processes, lacking in intellectual ambitiousness, and having good conventional judgment. His school-work was failing. His teachers described him as incorrigible (he was disrespectful, a liar, a thief, and profane), and the school principal regarded him as a troublemaker and mentally retarded.

The training program designed for the boy started with the assumption that problem behaviors can arise because an individual's behavior repertoire does not include behavior appropriate in the society, and does include disruptive behavior, or because the training (school) situation is not sufficiently reinforcing. The essentials of the reading training program were as follows:

GENERAL PROCEDURES:

There were three essential elements in the training. First, the use of programmed reading materials that contained stories of high interest level, graded difficulty, and frequent testing (the Science Research Associates Programmed Reading Laboratory). Second, the use of reinforcements (tokens) that could be earned for appropriate behavior. Third, a "teacher," or "monitor," who assisted the student in performing the tasks required by the program and provided the reinforcing consequences.

SPECIFIC PROCEDURES:

1. Preparation of materials.
   A. A running test of new vocabulary words that appeared in the stories was prepared, and each word was placed on a flash card.
   B. Each paragraph of the SRA story materials was typed on a card.
   C. Each SRA story along with the reading comprehensive test items for that story was typed on 8½-by-13-inch sheets.

2. Training procedures.

   A. Vocabulary presentation.
   The initial phase of training on each story involved the presentation to S of the new words (on flash cards). S was then required to pronounce them. Correct R's were followed by the presentation of a white token of mid-value (⅕ cent). The word was then dropped from the list. S was instructed to indicate any difficulty he had with word meaning, and assistance was given when needed. Occasions of incorrect responses or no responses to the words were followed by the trainer's giving the response. S then repeated the response while looking at the card. The card was presented again (in the next series), and correct R's, without prompting, were followed by a blue token or low-valued token (1/10 cent).

   B. Oral reading.
   The next phase consisted of S's reading aloud the story paragraphs in the order in which they occurred in the story. When a paragraph was read in its entirety without error, a red token of high value was presented (½ cent). When errors occurred, the trainer corrected S while S looked at the word. When S erred in reading a paragraph, the paragraph was presented again at the end of the series, and each paragraph was presented over and over again until no errors were made. At that time S received a white token of mid-value.

   C. Silent Reading and the Reading Comprehension Test.
   S was then given the story work sheet with the comprehension test items on it and instructed to read the material silently for understanding and to answer all questions on it. Reinforcements consisting of blue low-valued tokens were given for the "attentive behavior" of "scanning" the work sheet on a VI schedule of 15 seconds. Any other behavior occurring during this phase was not reinforced, and reinforcements were given no sooner than 5 seconds after return to scanning. S then wrote his answers to the story

comprehension test. Correct R's were followed by a high-valued token (½ cent). A correct R with a spelling error self-corrected by the S was followed by a white mid-valued token. When incorrect R's occurred, S had to reread the appropriate paragraph and correct his answer, for which he received a white mid-value token.

3. Progress Testing Procedures.

A. A vocabulary review of the words learned to date was carried out after twenty stories had been read. During this test S was given a blue token of low value if he read the word presented correctly. S's attention faltered during this test, and so he was given a white token of mid-value for correct R's. When S emitted incorrect R's or no R to the word, the trainer prompted him, and S was required to read the word aloud while looking at it. Again, when these words were presented later (at the end of the series), correct R's were followed by the presentation of a blue token.

4. Session Duration.

Most of the sessions lasted an hour or less, although the range of session duration was from 30 minutes to 2 hours.

5. Other Features of the Procedure.

S's performances were recorded daily, as were the number of reinforcers earned, and a curve showing his earnings was plotted.

What is particularly significant about the program is the results. Over a 40-hour period, spread out over 4½ months, the boy learned and retained 430 new words. In reading achievement he improved from grade level 2 to grade level 4.3, and he received passing grades in all subjects he attempted. He also showed a decrease in school misbehavior from ten incidents during the first month of training to none during the fourth month of training and none during the remaining two weeks of the semester, at which time training was concluded. It was estimated that during the training program he emitted 64,307 single-word reading responses. Moreover, the trainer was not a classroom teacher but rather the boy's probation officer. The estimated cost was 70 hours of trainer time (and the training could have been carried out by subprofessional workers) and $20.31 for reinforcers. In short, this program of training was spectacularly successful, compared with the 8½ years of classroom training he had received in the past.

Among the reasons that underlie the relative difficulty of reading acquisition, as compared, for example, with the acquisition of speech, Staats and Staats (1963a) suggest the following:

1. Reading training normally begins much later in life than speech training.
2. Reading training often begins abruptly.
3. Reading-training procedures frequently use relatively weak reinforcers or stimuli (for example, teacher's approval) that do not function as reinforcing events for many students.

4. Typically, reading training involves delays in reinforcement and intermittent reinforcement.

5. Reading training usually occupies a small portion of the time in a "working day."

6. When it does occur, reading training tends to be intensive, and because most difficult or intensive work situations tend to become aversive, reading training may acquire aversive properties.

7. In order for the acquisition of knowledge through reading to become automatically reinforcing, children must have been exposed early in life to adequate training, presented by both teachers and parents, that stressed positive reinforcement for skill acquisition.

8. Much reading training is group-managed. Thus the time and opportunities available to the teacher to monitor and reinforce the *individual* child's performance are limited.

9. The basic skills that are essential in learning to read, such as looking at textual stimuli and responding to prompts, may be absent or weak in many children to begin with.

Recent developments in reading-training procedures have been extremely encouraging, particularly those procedures that utilize programmed instructional materials and token reinforcers. In programs using such procedures, token reinforcers (poker chips or points on a counter) can be earned for appropriate performances, and these are augmented with backup reinforcers (such as candy, toys, jewelry, films, and phonograph records), which can be obtained in exchange for the tokens.

SHIFTS IN THE STIMULUS CONTROL OF VERBAL STIMULI

An interesting problem encountered in reading training is the possibility that controlling stimuli may, in a sense, undergo a shift (say, from the printed material as a textual S^D to the trainer's vocal or written responses as intraverbal S^D's). The author observed just such a shift in the case of a 6-year-old boy, who appeared to be able to read a series of numbers (1, 2, 3, 4, 5, ... 10) printed on a piece of paper. As he read the numbers, however, the author noticed that from time to time the boy glanced around the room, which suggested that at least some of his responses were intraverbals rather than textuals. (That is, the verbal operant "four" was controlled by the preceding verbal operant, "three," as an intraverbal stimulus rather than by the printed, textual stimulus "4.")

The author tested this hypothesis by printing each number on a separate card and presenting the cards to the boy individually in random order. There was an immediate decrease in the frequency of the child's accurate responses, and he appeared to do considerable guessing. Interestingly, as the boy progressed in school, he tended to make similar errors while reading stories. He would juggle or insert prepositions that were frequently syntactically correct but were actually inaccurate. For the sentence "The boy played with the ball," he would read, "A boy played with a ball." It was believed that thoroughgoing drill, in which the trainer stressed accuracy and carefully monitored the student's performances and made certain that only correct responses were reinforced, would go a long way toward helping the boy overcome this type of behavior. It was, therefore, decided that he would receive chocolate chips for correct texts of the numbers, and when he erred or guessed incorrectly, a previously earned chocolate chip would be taken from him. This procedure brought about an immediate decrease in the frequency of guessing. As training progressed, his utterances came to be more and more under the control of the textual S^D's (the printed numbers, visual stimuli) and less and less under the control of the intraverbal S^D's (his own previous utterances, auditory stimuli).

Although one cannot be sure, it seems likely that somewhere in the boy's training history, he had been reinforced for emitting a series of numbers, probably as an intraverbal sequence. Often, children learn to count aloud first and then later learn to read numbers. Later, during reading training, the boy may have been reinforced for correctly emitting the intraverbal sequence (saying "one, two, three, four, five, six, seven, eight, nine, ten" merely in the presence of the numbers 1 to 10, but not necessarily under the control of each and every one of them) as visual (textual) stimuli. In the same way, during reading training, he may have been reinforced for emitting sequences of responses some of which were under appropriate textual stimulus control and others of which (especially prepositions and articles) where inserted as intraverbals. Because these insertions were plausible, they remained undetected by the teacher and were perhaps reinforced. The effect of such reinforcements following an emitted series of numbers or letters is to strengthen both correct and incorrect elements in the series, thereby aggravating the boy's reading problem.

STUDY QUESTIONS

1. Give a definition of language and indicate the minimal social unit involved in language.
2. With what kinds of raw data does the student of language concern himself? What are the possible payoffs of studying such data?
3. Contrast the approaches of those of a traditional persuasion with those of a behavior theorist regarding the role of the following in language:
   a. Private and public events.
   b. Abilities.
   c. Environmental stimuli.

4. What two types of stimuli acquire stimulus control functions over the verbal behavior of a speaker? Give an example of each from the episode involving the child who wants a carrot stick.
5. Give an example of each of the following responses, describing the characteristic prior stimuli (when applicable) and types of consequences.
   a. The mand.
   b. The echoic.
   c. The intraverbal.
   d. The tact.
   e. The textual response.
   f. The audience response.
   g. The transcription response.
   h. The dictation response.
6. Identify the following as types of verbal behavior. Suggest the type of situation in which they are most apt to occur and the most likely consequences strengthening them in that situation:
   a. The speech therapist said, "Ba," and the child said, "Ba."
   b. The doctor asked the patient about his past illnesses.
   c. The draftsman made an exact copy of the insignia on tracing paper.
   d. A nurse on the ward asked the disturbed child the question, "What is your name?" and he replied, "What is your name?"
   e. A college student was talking to his girl friend by the Commons when his Spanish professor walked by. His conversation with the girl broke off, and he said, "Buenos días, Señor Cardenas."
   f. As the family drove by the park, the mother turned to her 4-year-old son, pointed, and said, "What's that, Jimmy?" and Jimmy replied excitedly, "Merry-go-round merry-go-round."
7. What do extended mands and tacts have in common?
8. Under what conditions is one's speech described as echolalic?
9. Describe a matching-to-sample sequence for training a child to make an echoic response.
10. Distinguish between the stimulus and response dimensions of verbal behavior.
11. Distinguish between formal and point-to-point correspondence.
12. What is the autoclitic? What functions does it serve in a speaker's verbal behavior?
13. Describe some of the events that make verbal behavior a multiply caused phenomenon.
14. What is the verbal community?
15. A dog whines at the back door, and his master lets him in. It is very cold outside. Is this an example of an operant or a respondent? Discuss interpretations of this episode.
16. Describe how larger response units can be derived from smaller ones.
17. How can a speaker's verbal behavior be made to control his functional motor behavior?
18. Although intraverbal behavior can be usefully viewed as chained behavior, describe an alternative account for it. From the point of view of behavior theory, suggest one criticism of this account.
19. What implications does the case of Dee have for these accounts of chained behavior?
20. What two major conclusions are reached about this case?
21. Distinguish between expressive and receptive language.

22. In the training of Sarah, what communicative acts did she perform that were defined as language? Why were these acts regarded as verbal behavior? Contrast these acts with human vocalizations. Which of the two—Sarah's behavior or human vocalizations—is more difficult? Offer a plausible reason for your choice.
23. What were the stimulus dimensions and response products of Sarah's language?
24. In what way did Sarah's training arrange for generalization of her behavior once it was acquired?
25. In what two ways did Sarah's training for the use of sentences differ from the training required for the use of words?
26. In training Sarah, how did the trainer deal with incorrect responses?
27. Describe the effect on a speaker's verbal repertoire of minimal speaker–listener relationships. Why does this effect, rather than others, occur?
28. What is meant by skill variations in the different types of verbal behavior? What are some of the explanations often given for skill variations?
29. Cite two explanations commonly given for poor reading skills.
30. How does B. F. Skinner's description of reading differ from the more conventional views?
31. Give an example of how the formal properties of textual stimuli can be involved in a perceptual reading problem.
32. What unfortunate interpretation might be made of the behavior of an individual who shows serious problems in his reading behavior? Discuss how such an interpretation may actually worsen an individual's situation.
33. In what ways do speech-training and reading-training procedures differ?
34. Distinguish between a token reinforcer and a backup reinforcer.
35. What is meant by shifts in the stimulus control of verbal behavior?
36. Describe a remediation procedure for a child who shows shifts in stimulus control.
37. Explain how the acquisition of intraverbal responses may account for shifts in stimulus control. What events may serve to maintain such shifts?

REFERENCES

Chomsky, N. Review of B. F. Skinner, *Verbal behavior. Language*, 1959, **35**, 26–58.

Ferster, C. B. Positive reinforcement and behavioral defects in autistic children. *Child Development*, 1961, **32**, 437–456.

Guess, D. A functional analysis of receptive language and productive speech: Acquisition of the plural morpheme. *Journal of Applied Behavior Analysis*, 1969, **2**, 55–64.

Guess, D., Sailor, W., Rutherford, G., and Baer, D. M. An experimental analysis of linguistic development: The productive use of the plural morpheme. *Journal of Applied Behavior Analysis*, 1968, **1**, 297–306.

Holland, J. G., and Skinner, B. F. *The analysis of behavior*. New York: McGraw-Hill, 1961.

Holz, W. K., and Azrin, N. H. Conditioning human verbal behavior. In W. K. Honig (Ed.), *Operant behavior: Areas of research and application.* New York: Appleton-Century-Crofts, 1966.

Kellogg, W. N. Communication and language in the home-raised chimpanzee. *Science*, 1968, **162**, 423–427.

MacCorquodale, K. B. F. Skinner's *Verbal behavior:* A retrospective appreciation, *Journal of the Experimental Analysis of Behavior*, 1969, **12**, 831–841.

Premack, D. A functional analysis of language. *Journal of the Experimental Analysis of Behavior*, 1970, **14**, 107–125.

Skinner, B. F. *Verbal behavior.* New York: Appleton-Century-Crofts, 1957.

Staats, A. W., and Butterfield, W. H. Treatment of non-reading in a culturally deprived juvenile delinquent: An application of reinforcement principles. *Child Development*, 1965, **36**, 925–942.

Staats, A. W., Minke, K. A., Goodwin, W., and Landeen, J. Some effects of "back-up" reinforcers on reading behavior. *Journal of Experimental Child Psychology*, 1967, **5**, 50–57.

Staats, A. W., and Staats, C. K. A comparison of the development of speech and reading behavior with implications for research. *Child Development*, 1963, **33**, 831–846. (a)

Staats, A. W., and Staats, C. K. *Complex human behavior.* New York: Holt, Rinehart and Winston, 1963. (b)

CHAPTER 8

BEHAVIOR AND ECOLOGY

A persistent problem in psychology has been the relationship between an organism's behavior and its past and present environment. What is needed is a detailed account of the essential features of an organism's environment that are involved in the acquisition, maintenance, and elimination of behavior. To a degree, we have already discussed some of the important environmental antecedents to behavior. In this chapter the way in which differences in the organism's environment can produce differences in the organism's behavior will be examined in more detail.

THE ENVIRONMENT AND RESPONDENT AND OPERANT BEHAVIOR

Certain objects and events in the organism's environment can function as elicitors of respondent behavior. Unconditioned stimuli, such as food, water, noxious stimuli, and irritants, elicit various patterns of respondent behavior. Similarly, other objects and events in the organism's environment become conditioned stimuli through stimulus pairing and are also elicitors of patterns of respondent behavior. For example, before a baby is given cereal (an object, an unconditioned stimulus), which is an elicitor of the respondent pattern of behavior involved in digestion (that is, salivation, HCl secretion, and so on), a bib is placed around his neck. Subsequently, because of its temporal relationship (pairing) to the cereal, the bib becomes an elicitor of comparable respondents. Similarly, a sonic boom (an event, an unconditioned stimulus) is an elicitor of a respondent pattern of startle. This respondent pattern is often preceded by the visual simulus of a high-speed aircraft in the sky, and this visual stimulus becomes an elicitor of the startle pattern, because of its repeated pairings with the sonic boom.

Environments may, therefore, be characterized in terms of (1) their *stimulus properties* (objects or events functioning as unconditioned and conditioned stimuli), and (2) the *patterns of respondent behavior* elicited by these stimulus properties. Perhaps only in middle-class American society does the bib function as a conditioned stimulus. Only in societies or environments in which the aircraft can be found does it function as a conditioned stimulus. There are, no doubt, places inhabited by man in which neither aircraft nor sonic booms occur and so that such eliciting stimuli do not exist. It would seem, therefore, that the startle pattern of respondent behavior to these stimuli may not even occur in some individuals simply because these stimuli are absent from their environments. Thus both the objects and events that characterize the texture of a given organism's environment and the types of stimuli they produce, both conditioned or unconditioned, can vary widely from one environment to the next. Because of this, a wide range of respondent behavior patterns can also be expected.

As in the case of respondent behavior, the stimulus function of the objects and events in the organism's environment can also profoundly affect the organism's operant behavior. Environments may differ in *the nature and availability of objects and events functioning as consequences.* In poor, agrarian societies, such as India, chronic deprivation may be a characteristic of the environment, the effect of which is to intensify the strength of unconditioned reinforcers such as food while on the other hand, in wealthy, industrialized societies such as ours, stimulus change and novel stimuli may be the stronger reinforcers, at least for the majority of the population. The poverty or wealth of a society may also affect the *schedule with which the consequences are presented.*

The presence of certain implements or tools as manipulanda affects behavior both in terms of the response differentiation required for tool manipulation and in terms of the types of stimuli that acquire stimulus control over tool manipulation operants. For example, the Indian farmer's repertoire primarily involves the manipulation of hand tools and a plow, and his American counterpart needs only to manipulate levers, pedals, and a steering wheel to perform the same task of sowing crops.

Environments differ, too, in the *temporal relationship* that occurs between the organism's behavior and in the kinds of objects or events that serve as environmental mediators of consequences (in effect, as trainers). Again, the Indian mother as a mediator (provider) of reinforcements for her child may, because of her household duties, have less time to spend with her child. This may result in delayed reinforcements or even fewer occasions of reinforcement compared with her American middle-class counterpart, who because of automatic household equipment has more time to spend with her child.

Table 8-1 summarizes those aspects or features of the organism's environment that affect the organism's respondent and operant behavior. The manner in which these aspects or features of the organism's environment interact to affect the organism's behavior is complex. In the more general sense of behavior acquisition, maintenance, and elimination, the net effect of their

Table 8-1 Some Significant Features of the Organism's Environment, Their Functions in the Organism's Behavior, and the Effect of the Organism's Behavior on Its Environment.

ENVIRONMENTAL FEATURE	FUNCTION IN RESPONDENT BEHAVIOR	FUNCTION IN OPERANT BEHAVIOR
Objects, events	Unconditioned and conditioned stimuli	Discriminative and reinforcing stimuli
Temporal relationships between the organism's behavior and objects, events	Delayed or optimum interval of presentation of objects, events to give them appropriate stimulus functions	
Environmental mediators producing objects, events (trainers or instructors)	Accidental, natural, and contrived presentations from the physical and social environment of objects, events	
Manipulanda	Acquisition of conditioned emotional responses	Acquisition of differentiated and discriminated operant behavior
Response classes	Reflex activity, patterns of respondent behavior	Verbal and motor operants
Functions of response classes	Changes in the intraorganic environment	Acts or operates to produce changes in the environment (consequences)

interaction is to instruct or train the organism. Those objects or events functioning as environmental mediators–trainers are of particular interest. They typically have control over the amount, kind, and temporal characteristics of the consequation presented to the organism, and as a result they often possess discriminative and eliciting stimulus functions as well. (The manner in which this eliciting stimulus function is acquired will be discussed in Chapter 9.) Some of the environmental mediator–trainers are physical objects in the organism's environment. A candy-vending machine is, perhaps, a good example. In the typical sequence a coin is inserted, a lever is pulled, and candy is delivered. The candy itself is the reinforcer, and to the inveterate candy eater with a dime, the candy machine is a discriminative stimulus for approach, coin-inserting, lever-pulling, and candy-reaching operants and an elicitor of positive respondents. In the absence of a properly working candy machine, the candy is not available, and in the presence of such a machine, the candy is available. The candy machine is, then, an *environmental mediator–trainer* because it transacts with the individual—its behavior (of candy delivery) is determined by the individual's behavior (of proper coin insertion and lever pulling) and vice versa. There are also social objects in the organism's environment having comparable characteristics. Most commonly, they are other people with whom one transacts and without whom there would be no reinforcements. (This transactional process is discussed in more detail in Chapter 9.)

THE ACQUISITION OF BEHAVIOR AND THE ORGANISM'S ENVIRONMENT

One might say that "instruction" from the environment leads to the acquisition of two major kinds of repertoires: instrumental or purposive behavior and superstitious behavior. As we shall see, the instruction the organism receives from its environment varies in its efficiency. Some environments are more apt to strengthen instrumental behaviors, and others are more apt to strengthen superstitious behaviors.

The Development of Instrumental or Purposive Behavior

Instrumental or purposive behavior occurs when the organism's responses act or operate on the environment to produce certain consequences and when such consequences are not available in the absence of such behavior. In other words, instrumental or purposive behavior is behavior essential to the occurrence of certain consequences. For example, the bird that probes the lawn with its beak finds a worm and eats it. The worm is not available *unless* and *until* the bird probes for it (response-contingent consequences), and it can be said that the purpose of the bird's probing the lawn is to find the worm. It would seem, therefore, that instrumental behavior, or purposive behavior, refers to a situation involving a special relationship between the organism's reinforcements appropriate to these deprivation states, and behavior of the organism producing these reinforcements.

In our example the bird transacted with a mediator–trainer in its physical environment and received the kind of instruction that leads to the acquisition of an operant behavior chain consisting of looking, approaching, probing, and pulling up a worm. The effect of this instruction (because it involves positive reinforcement) is to make the probing behavior more likely on comparable future occasions. Furthermore, because the consequences maintaining the bird's behavior (the worm) are not explicitly arranged by the mediator–trainer, the situation can be described as involving *nonprearranged consequences.*

When the organism is part of a social group, others in that group may serve as mediator–trainers and may provide explicit instruction as the trainee and trainer engage in social transactions involving the use of *prearranged consequences.* For this to occur, the trainer must know thoroughly the response class(es) characteristics of a good final performance, and reinforcements must be presented contingent on the emission of approximations to it (the R^D's). The trainer may also extinguish irrelevant or devious response classes. Such training involves the trainer's continual surveillance over the trainee's performance and the systematic presentation of consequences. The use of such prearranged consequences requires that the trainer emit two distinct response classes: (1) the responses involved in observing the trainee and (2) the responses involved in the presentation of consequences.

On some occasions the trainer may also emit the response class(es) he wants the trainee to learn. He provides the trainee with a sample performance, and if this performance is matched by the trainee, it is then reinforced. In essence, the *trainee imitates the trainer.* Consider the following:

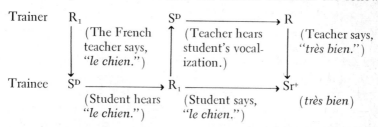

In this example the trainer provides a sample performance (R_1) that also functions as an S^D for the trainee and is to be matched by him. The performance is a good one and is reinforced. Had the trainee pronounced *le chien* incorrectly, his teacher would no doubt have corrected him, saying, *"non,*

non," thus punishing the student's matching-to-sample performance. In such a sequence, the trainer emits three distinct response classes consisting of (1) the sample performance, (2) observing the trainee's response, and (3) the responses involving the presentation of the consequences. In the first step the sample performance that functions as a prompt acquires discriminative properties because it is a stimulus event (presented by the trainer) in the presence of which appropriate responses have been reinforced. The trainer may also use his fingertips to shape, or mold, the trainee's mouth in order to restrict or even prevent the occurrence of poorer component responses (R^Δ's). This putting-through procedure makes use of an additional prompt, consisting of proprioceptive cues that arise from the positioning of the trainee's mouth.

This analysis also applies to the acquisition of motor behavior. For example, the author had the opportunity to observe a highly skilled and well-known ballet teacher work with her students. Because her Russian dialect interfered, at least in part, with the free use of verbal instructions, much of her instruction consisted of (1) showing the students the proper positions, (2) using manual and stick-tapping positioning of the students' limbs, trunk, and so on, and, (3) occasional verbal instructions. Constant surveillance of the students' behavior was maintained both when she watched them and when the students viewed their own performances by standing in front of a mirror. As the teacher moved up and down the line, she seldom reinforced the students verbally. Incorrect student posture and positioning appeared to be events that were correlated with positioning and stick tapping until the student assumed the proper position. Essentially positioning and stick tapping were teacher-presented nonverbal, or gestural, negative reinforcers, and correct posture and positioning by the student were events correlated with its absence. Thus the students knew if their performances were or were not satisfactory.

In these examples the *other* functions as trainer and engages *directly* in transactions with the trainee, the effect of which is the trainee's acquisition of behavior and receipt of reinforcements. There are also occasions when the other carries out comparable functions as a trainer but in the absence of extensive direct transactions with the trainee. This may occur when the other arranges or sets up an instructional environment for the trainee.

Both of these types of "instructive roles," those with and without direct transaction between the trainer and the trainee, can be studied in an instructing environment for pigeons designed by Herrnstein (1964) and shown in Figure 8-1. Two pigeons are magazine trained and put into the box shown in Figure 8-1. The behavior of one pigeon is shaped, so that he acts as the teacher. After the pigeons have spent a sufficient amount of time in the box, the following behavior emerges: The teacher (compartment B) watches the student (compartment A), and when the student steps on the switch plate, the teacher pecks at the disk. The peck on the disk by the teacher causes

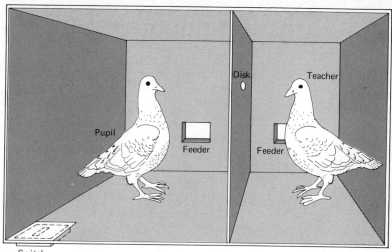

Switch

FIGURE 8-1 A "classroom," or instructing environment, for pigeons. From R. J. Herrnstein, "Will." *Proceedings of the American Philosophical Society,* 1964, **108,** 455–458. Copyright © 1964, American Philosophical Society, Inc., and reproduced by permission.

the food tray in compartment A to become illuminated and also activates the grain-feeding mechanism, which produces an audible click. Both the illuminated food tray and the audible click are S^D's for the pigeons to approach the food tray and eat grain. After a few seconds the food tray is removed, the disk light goes off, and the cycle repeats itself.

Although the teacher engages in direct transactions with the pupil, the training situation was arranged by someone else, namely a professor of psychology. (Who else?) The chart shown in Figure 8-2 illustrates the response classes emitted by all the parties to the situation in their roles as both trainees and trainers. Early in the game the professor plays a vital role by magazine training both birds and shaping and maintaining the behavior of the teacher. The professor is reinforced by the changes he observes in the birds' behavior, and the birds are reinforced by the grain presented by the professor. Moreover, the pigeon–teacher shapes the professor's behavior to the extent that changes in the pigeon's behavior are more rapid when the professor carefully observes the pigeon and promptly reinforces appropriate pecking responses. After initial training is completed, the professor steps out of the situation, and the birds mediate the reinforcements for each other. The teacher is reinforced only when the student stands on the switch plate, and the student is reinforced only when the teacher pecks at the disk.

There are two significant things about this example. First, it suggests that the distinction made earlier between a trainee and the trainer in the acquisition of behavior is questionable. All parties to this situation—the student,

		Response Classes Required As Mediator–Trainers		
		Professor (man)	Teacher (pigeon)	Student (pigeon)
Response Classes Required As Trainees	Professor		reinforces watching and pellet magazine switch depression	reinforces watching and pellet magazine switch depression
	Teacher	magazine training, shapes pecking, maintains pecking on VI schedule		reinforces watching and pecking at disk
	Student	magazine training	reinforces standing on switch plate	

FIGURE 8-2 Response classes emitted by those involved in the instructing environment for pigeons.

the teacher, and the professor, pigeon and man alike—were engaged in transactions that were instructive and in which, at one time or another, each was a trainee and each was a trainer. Second, each party to the transactions —the professor, the teacher, and even the student—had control over the behavior of the other parties in the situation. In a sense, each made the other do his bidding. (In everyday language one might say that one party exerted his will over the other party.)

Some Remarks About the Characteristics of a Good Trainer

What are the essential characteristics of a good trainer. Of course, the trainer must arrange in some way for the relatively prompt presentation of consequences. Must the trainer also be able to perform the behaviors (R_2^D's) that the trainee must learn? It seems clear that he need not. He must, however, be able to recognize or identify (1) the characteristics of the final performance and (2) earlier approximations to it (the R^D's). With this skill he is able to strengthen the R^D's through the systematic presentation of response-contingent consequences.

There are, however, certain benefits that arise when a trainer can make the performances required of the trainee. When such performances are presented to the trainee, they may function as prompts—discriminative stimuli for the trainee's behavior to be acquired (R^D's). This is because such trainer-presented performances may be stimulus events in the presence of which trainee behavior has been reinforced. When trainer performances do possess discriminative stimulus (prompt) functions, training time can be telescoped simply because the trainer can evoke at least some approximations (R^D's) to the final performance and consequate them without having to simply wait for them to occur. Of course, only some of the trainee behavior can be controlled by prompts in this manner. Most likely, the behavior would consist of unit response classes that have already been differentiated and discriminated but are being sequenced or chained into more complex performances. For example, the French teacher assisted the student (1) by providing repeated sample (prompting) performances in which *le chien* was broken down into each unit response (that is, *"le," "le"; "chi," "chi"; "en," "en"*), (2) by listening to the student's unit responses and consequating each unit response (that is, when the student said *"le"* the teacher said *"très bien,"* then *"chi"* and so on) until it matched her performance, and (3) by prompting the student to chain the unit responses (that is, first the teacher then the student said, *"le chi-en"*). In this way, the teacher's prompts came to control, more and more, the occurrence of the R^D's, which, in turn, were chained or sequenced into one or the other new, larger, and more complex response units.

The putting-through procedure can also telescope training time. It can be quite effective for the acquisition of behaviors (1) that can be easily observed by the trainer (especially skeletal muscle responses and, to a lesser extent, vocal responses) and (2) that the trainer can manually assist the trainee in making. A putting-through procedure makes the occurrence of the R^D more likely (because of the trainer's manual assistance) and at the same time makes the occurrence of the R^Δ less likely (because the trainer can block or prevent it from occurring).

When a trainer combines prearranged consequences, imitation (the procedure in which the trainer's sample performances function as prompts for the trainee), and when applicable, putting-through procedures, he is able to provide a highly efficient instructional environment. He is able to take advantage of existing behaviors in the trainee's repertoire under the stimulus control of prompts, restrict and constrain the trainee's responding, and present prompt, response-contingent reinforcements.[1]

---

[1] Several investigators (Mowrer, 1960; Bandura, 1962; and others) assert that sensory stimulation arising from the model's performance and observed by the trainee is *the* necessary and sufficient condition for response acquisition, and reinforcement operations are merely facilitative of response selection. Thus the trainee need not emit the R^D or be presented with strengthening consequences. Confirmation of this is by no means unequivocal, since an experimental demonstration requires that prior to his exposure to the model's performance, the trainee did not have, as part of his repertoire, either the component response classes or the total performance. Finding human subjects who meet this requirement is difficult, indeed. Perhaps exposure to a model's performance provides a basis for the sequential ordering or chaining of response classes already part of the trainee's repertoire rather than their acquisition. In a later paper Bandura (1965) acknowledges that sensory stimulation arising from a model's performance may not be the necessary and sufficient condition for acquisition.

The Development of Superstitious Behavior

We have seen that instrumental or purposive behavior is required in environments where there is a close temporal relationship between the operant and the consequences following it and where the consequences are response-contingent. It frequently happens, however, that (1) delays occur in the temporal relationship between the operant and the consequences that follow it or (2) the consequences that occur after an operant is emitted are not response-contingent. In a sense the consequences are gratis as if they simply occurred by accident. Either of these two situations will produce superstitious behavior. A number of different types of environmental events can produce different types of superstitions.

One type, *classical superstitious behavior*, occurs when an organism is the recipient of non-response-contingent reinforcement at regular intervals such as that presented on an FI schedule. For example, Skinner (1948) observed pigeons engaging in head thrusting, head tossing, or turning after they had been exposed to an FI 15-second schedule of reinforcement in which the reinforcer was presented regardless of what response class had preceded it. In other words, whichever response class had occurred (head tossing or turning) immediately prior to reinforcement was strengthened. Similar events occur in human situations, as when some peculiar mannerism or verbalization *happens* to be followed by a reinforcing event. Some tics, gestures, and affectations may have been followed by such accidental or adventitious reinforcements and are, therefore, examples of classical superstitious behaviors.

Concurrent superstitious behavior occurs when one element of a response class is followed by response-contingent reinforcement, and another concurrent or ongoing response element just happens to occur at the same time. The latter response element becomes part of the response class but is actually irrelevant or noninstrumental to the reinforcement. A student just happens to be scratching his head when he solves a tough problem. This strengthens both the relevant, instrumental problem-solving behavior and the irrelevant, noninstrumental superstitious behavior. One subject in a conditioning experiment was observed to raise one leg off the floor and lean forward in a bizarre position while she was reinforced momentarily for lever pulling.

When various stimuli are accidentally correlated with consequences, the result can be either *positive* or *negative sensory superstitious* behavior (Morse and Skinner, 1957). Infrequent reinforcement produces low rates of pecking, and frequent reinforcement produces higher rates. If a stimulus is presented, even for only a portion of the time, while either schedule is in force, say a blue light during infrequent reinforcement and an orange light during frequent reinforcement, that stimulus will come to control the pecking rate. Pecking will come to be emitted at a lower rate when the blue light is on and at a higher rate when the orange light is on, even though the actual schedule of reinforcement is unchanged. In human situations some objects are viewed as bad or good luck simply because of their accidental correlation with either aversive or positively reinforcing consequences. Many gamblers will carry a token, piece of cloth, or a ring, which they believe has brought them good luck, simply because they happened to have the item on their person during a winning streak. A related phenomenon is *generalized super-stitious behavior* in which an operant is controlled by a stimulus that happens to be similar to another previously encountered controlling stimulus. For example, Migler (1963) observed that rats would press a newly introduced lever, even though presses on the lever had never before been followed by consequences. It was, however, similar to a lever that had terminated shock when pressed. Similarly, people will often strike a vending machine to make it work, even though the machine is dissimilar in some ways from previously encountered machines, simply because a machine encountered earlier did work after it had been struck.

Finally, *superstitious chaining* can occur when one response class is im-mediately followed by another instrumental response class that produces response-contingent reinforcement (Catania and Cutts, 1963). The effect of the reinforcer at the end of the sequence is to strengthen both the final (instrumental) response class and the one that preceded it (the superstitious response class), thus forming an operant chain. Mannerisms and gestures may be parts of a superstitious behavior chain that were accidentally hooked to the reinforced response class. For example, the public speaker may always clear his throat before speaking, even when he doesn't actually need to. Con-ceivably, taking a puff on a cigarette before speaking, or eating while watch-ing television or while reading may involve similar chains. In the former if the puff is followed by reinforced speech, it will become more likely to occur. Similarly, if eating is followed by TV watching or reading (which may be automatically reinforcing), it may become more frequent.

The important thing to remember about superstitious behavior is that it is acquired in environments where reinforcements are independent of, or noncontingent on, the behavior preceding them and in situations where the reinforcements are poorly timed or delayed. Essentially, such situations are those where man has poor control over the reinforcement contingencies and where a few occasions of reinforcement have powerful effects on the be-havior preceding them, because reinforcements are scarce and deprivation states are high. Thus the mysterious incantations and rituals of the witch doctor are strengthened when followed by rain. Drought-produced water deprivation makes man particularly vulnerable to such superstitions. In con-trast, the inhabitant of the modern industrial society is not ordinarily water-deprived, and water as a reinforcer is available contingent on such obvious instrumental behavior as turning on a faucet. However, even the inhabitant of a modern industrial society may show superstitions, some of which are acquired through the occurrence of the same kinds of events as those de-scribed. Usually, however, human superstitions arise from complex forms of instruction involving many different procedures including verbal instructions, imitation, and prearranged consequences. A parent may train his child to toss salt over his shoulder for good luck by giving him verbal instructions, showing him how to do so, and praising him for a good performance. Such training may even involve the trainer's presentation of negative reinforce-ment. Unlike the kinds of superstitious behavior that is generated by ad-ventitious or non-response-contingent reinforcement, the superstitions arising from events such as these are, in actuality, a form of instrumental or pur-posive behavior.

It was observed that efficient instructing environments tend to strengthen instrumental rather than superstitious operant behavior. The effect of this is to promote the survival of the organism, because it is the organism's operant behavior that acts or operates on the environment to produce consequences. Stated another way, instrumental behavior gives the organism control over its environment. By contrast, superstitious behavior is maintained by chance events (adventitious contingencies) that are not affected by the organism's behavior and are thus independent of it. Behavior acquired under such cir-cumstances does not favor survival, simply because it has no effect on (control over) the organism's environment. (It does not act or operate on the en-vironment.)

Finally, while the environment acts to instruct the organism in the acquisi-tion of either instrumental or superstitious operant behavior, it also acts to instruct the organism in the acquisition of respondent behavior. The conse-quation involved in the acquisition of operant behavior may also have elicit-ing stimulus functions. Food, for example, is not only an unconditioned positive reinforcer, it is also an unconditioned eliciting stimulus. Thus the amounts and kinds of consequation available in an environment, besides affecting the operant behavior preceding the consequation, affect the respon-dent behavior following it.

OBJECTS AND EVENTS IN THE ENVIRONMENT AND THE ACQUISITION OF DISCRIMINATED OPERANT BEHAVIOR: SPECIFIC EXAMPLES OF THREE INSTRUCTING ENVIRONMENTS

In the preceding examples emphasis was placed on the importance of those features of the organism's environment that relate to the reinforcement con-tingency. These features included such things as the amount, kind, and fre-quency of reinforcement and its temporal relationship to the operant. Also important, however, are the objects and events in the organism's environ-ment that are present when the organism's behavior is followed by consequences. These objects or events (in the presence of which an organism's operant behavior is followed by consequences) acquire discriminative stimulus functions. It would seem then, that an operant followed by consequences is affected by these consequences in two ways. First, it is either weakened or strengthened by them; second, it is brought under their discriminative control.

Three human environments will be used to illustrate the importance of the objects and events in the organism's environment that possess discriminative stimulus functions. They are (1) the lower-class, disadvantaged residential and community environment, (2) the middle-class residential and community environment, and (3) the mental institution residential and community environment. The examples and descriptions of these environments will stress the differences in the numbers and kinds of *distinguishing objects* and in the number and kinds of *distinguishing events*. (In the context of the discussion to follow, a distinguishing object or event is one that possesses a particular function appropriate to the environment in which it occurs and that sets that environment off from other possible environments. For example, dishes and cooking a meal are distinguishing objects and events, respectively, for the kitchen.)

As the reader will observe, it is not always possible to differentiate between the discriminative stimulus functions and the consequating stimulus functions of the object or event studied. What is important, however, is that the reader get a feel for how differences in the number and kinds of distinguishing objects and events in the environment can, through their discriminative stimulus function, make for differences in the behavior of those inhabiting such environments.

Distinguishing Objects and Events Characteristic of the Lower-Class Disadvantaged, Middle-Class, and Mental Institution Residences

Figures 8-3, 8-4, and 8-5 show photographs of two "slices" of lower-class disadvantaged, middle-class, and mental institution residences. In particular, the family living areas (or dayroom in the institutional setting) and eating areas and the furnishings characteristic of them are shown. Each setting contains a number of distinguishing objects, which are related to the function of the room and provide a basis for comparing the environments.

Some objects are common to all of the environments. For example, all three living areas contain a television, a table, reading material, and chairs. More important, however, are the differences between the environments both in terms of the numbers of objects and in terms of the kinds of objects in them. These differences are summarized in Tables 8-2 and 8-3.

For example, Table 8-2 shows that the family or living area of the lower-

Blanket

Magazine

Couch

Milk carton

Wood floor

Room items
(5)

(a)

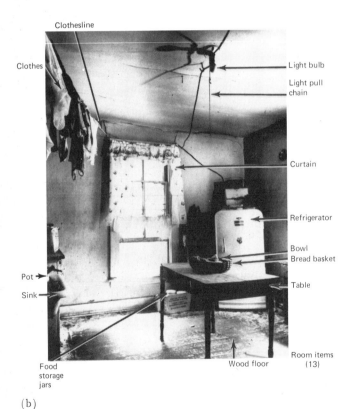

Clothesline

Clothes

Light bulb

Light pull
chain

Curtain

Refrigerator

Bowl
Bread basket

Pot

Table

Sink

Food
storage
jars

Wood floor

Room items
(13)

(b)

FIGURE 8-3(a) The family or living area and (b) the eating area of the lower-class, disadvantaged residence. Photo courtesy of the United States Office of Opportunity.

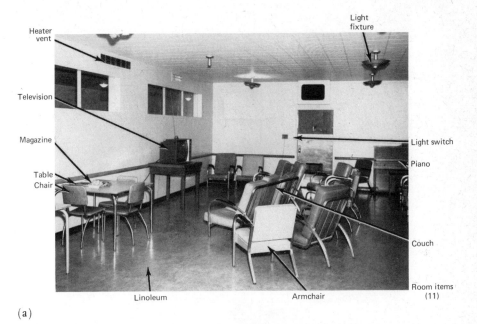

Heater
vent

Light
fixture

Television

Magazine

Table
Chair

Light switch

Piano

Couch

Room items
(11)

Linoleum

Armchair

(a)

Light fixture

Air duct

Thermostat
Light switch
Silverware
Knife
Fork
Spoon
Food tray

Table

Chair

Room items
(11)

Asphalt tile

(b)

FIGURE 8-4(a) The dayroom (family or living room) and (b) the eating area of a mental institutional residence. (Photo courtesy of Patton State Hospital.)

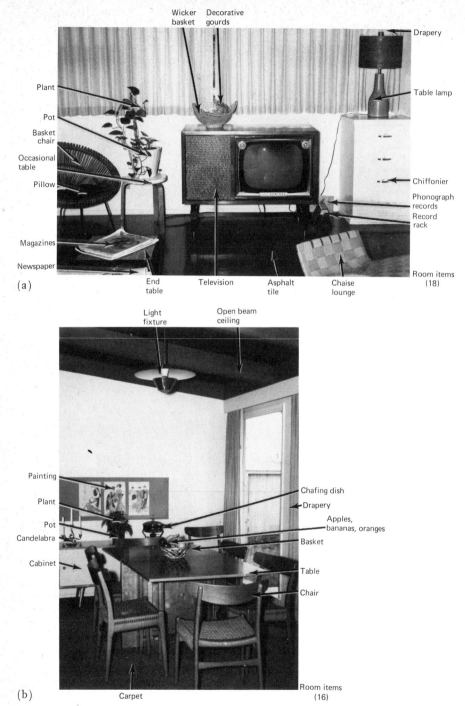

(a)

Wicker basket
Decorative gourds
Drapery
Plant
Table lamp
Pot
Basket chair
Occasional table
Pillow
Chiffonier
Phonograph records
Record rack
Magazines
Newspaper
End table
Television
Asphalt tile
Chaise lounge
Room items (18)

(b)

Light fixture
Open beam ceiling
Painting
Chafing dish
Plant
Drapery
Pot
Apples, bananas, oranges
Candelabra
Cabinet
Basket
Table
Chair
Carpet
Room items (16)

FIGURE 8-5(a) The family or living area and (b) the eating area of the middle-class residence. (Photo by author.)

Table 8-2 Distinguishing Objects Characteristic of the Family Area of Lower-Class, Middle-Class, and Mental Institution Environments

DISTINGUISHING OBJECTS	LOWER-CLASS, DISADVANTAGED RESIDENCE	MIDDLE-CLASS RESIDENCE	MENTAL INSTITUTION RESIDENCE
drapes		x	
potted plant		x	
occasional table		x	
pillow		x	
magazines	x	x	x
newspapers		x	
end table	x (not shown)	x	
TV	x (not shown)	x	x
chaise longue		x	
records		x	
record rack		x	
wicker basket		x	
decorative gourds		x	
table lamp		x	
floor lamp	x (not shown)	x	
chiffonier		x	
game table			x
piano		x (not shown)	x
chair(s)	x (not shown)	x (not shown)	x
Total number	5	18	5

class, disadvantaged residence contains about the same number of distinguishing objects as the mental institution dayroom area (about five objects). In contrast, the middle-class family or living area contains more than three times as many objects (eighteen objects). Some of the objects come in different forms. For example, the lower-class, disadvantaged living area contains only an end table; the middle-class living area contains both an end table and an occasional table; and the mental institution dayroom contains a game table.

Table 8-3 shows the number of distinguishing objects characteristic of the eating areas of these three residential environments. Notice that although both the lower-class, disadvantaged and the middle-class environments contain more objects than the institutional eating area, generally, the two do not contain the same objects. For example, the eating area of the lower-class, disadvantaged person contains objects ordinarily observed in the food preparation area of the middle-class residence, namely, the refrigerator, stove, sink, food storage jars and the like, suggesting the obvious fact that in the lower-class, disadvantaged residence there is a lack of room differentiation. (In some cases a single room may serve as a family, eating, and sleeping area.)

Table 8-3 Distinguishing Objects Characteristic of the Eating Area of Lower-Class, MiddleClass, and Mental Institution Environments

DISTINGUISHING OBJECTS	LOWER-CLASS, DISADVANTAGED RESIDENCE	MIDDLE-CLASS RESIDENCE	MENTAL INSTITUTION RESIDENCE
painting		x	
potted plant		x	
candellabrum		x	
cabinet	x (not shown)	x	x
chafing dish		x	
draperies, curtains	x	x	
carpet		x	
fruit basket		x	
clothesline	x		
light pull chain	x		
refrigerator	x		
table	x	x	
food storage jars	x		
sink	x		
stove	x		
chair(s)	x (not shown)	x	x
dishes	x	x	x
bread basket	x		
steam table			x
coffee urn			x
Total number	12	11	5

Each environment also possesses objects that are unique to it. For example, the lower-class, disadvantaged eating area contains a clothesline; the middle-class eating area contains a candelabrum and a chafing dish, and the institutional eating area contains a steam table and coffee urns. If one moves away from the specific characteristics of these rooms, as representative of the three environments, to a more generalized description, even larger differences between the three environments appear. Such is the case when one compares the head of the household in lower-class disadvantaged, middle-class, and institutional residences. (See the household family configurations in Table 8-4.) Notice that in the lower-class, disadvantaged residence a female (either mother or grandmother) is the head of the household. In the middle-class residence the head of the household is a male (the father), and in an institutional residence it may be either a male or a female, neither of whom is actually related to the hospital patient. Large differences also exist in the household membership and in the enriching objects (such as musical instruments, reading materials, and toys) characteristic of these environments.

Table 8-5 presents some of the distinguishing events that characterize the three environments. Again, large differences exist ranging from ambient noise and privacy as physical characteristics of the household, caretaker characteristics, to mealtime and verbal exchange as characteristic enriching events occurring in the residence.

Distinguishing Events Characteristic of the Lower-Class Disadvantaged, Middle-Class, and Mental Institution Communities

Not only are there large differences between the three residential environments, there are also large differences in the community environments, that

Table 8-4 Distinguishing Objects Characteristic of the Lower-Class Disadvantaged, Middle-Class, and Mental Institution Residential Environments

THE LOWER-CLASS, DISADVANTAGED RESIDENCE	THE MIDDLE-CLASS RESIDENCE	THE MENTAL INSTITUTION RESIDENCE
Household Family Configuration		
HEAD OF HOUSEHOLD		
Female (mother or grandmother)	Male (father)	Male or female (nursing staff)
HOUSEHOLD MEMBERS		
Mother, grandmother, children (less often father), cousins, other kin, sometimes boarders	Nuclear family (father, mother, children)	Nursing staff and patients serve as family; however, staff or patient reassignment to other units is frequent.
Enriching Objects		
Folk musical instruments, family radio frequently turned to foreign-language station, TV	Various musical instruments, stereo, personal radio for each family member, TV	Often piano, radio, TV
READING MATERIALS		
Papers, few magazines, few books (if any)	Papers, magazines, books, pictures, verbal games	Papers, magazines, books (from hospital library)
TOYS		
Few toys, often cheap or homemade	Many different kinds of toys, often store-bought and educational	Few if any toys, often broken

Table 8-5 Distinguishing Events Characteristic of the Lower-Class Disadvantaged, Middle-Class, and Mental Institution Residential Environments

THE LOWER-CLASS, DISADVANTAGED RESIDENCE	THE MIDDLE-CLASS RESIDENCE	THE MENTAL INSTITUTION RESIDENCE
Physical Characteristics of Household		
HOUSEHOLD AMBIENT NOISE		
Household interior noisy from outside noise sources (street, adjacent apartment noises)	Household interior insulated from outside noise, rooms insulated from inside noise	Household interior insulated from outside noise, but interior may be noisy
PRIVACY		
Child shares room, often bed, with others.	Child has own room and sleeping space.	Child has no private room, only private bed.
Caretaker Characteristics		
SUPERVISION		
Child often home without supervision (mother, grandmother work)	Usually one parent home for supervision (mother)	Nursing staff provides shared supervision.
MODE OF CONTROL		
Beatings common	Beatings infrequent	Beatings infrequent
Enriching Events		
MEALTIME		
Sandwiches common bill of fare	Multi-course meals common bill of fare	Menu simple, unchanging
Discussion usually consists of (1) parent giving out household task assignments and punishment and (2) is limited to immediate situation (for example, "Eat your dinner").	Discussion encouraged, extended to activities of that day (school, work, and so on) and past and future events	Discussion minimal
Father usually absent from meal or eats by himself	Family eats together	Only patients sit together, not joined by nursing staff during meals
Child may eat while moving around.	Child eats while seated at the table.	Child eats while seated at the table.
Meal times irregular	Set mealtime	Set mealtime
Acceptance of use of gestures, pointing, head-shaking, monosyllables, incomplete sentences	Acceptance of only correct use of grammar, vocabulary	

Table 8-5 *(Continued)*

THE LOWER-CLASS, DISADVANTAGED RESIDENCE	THE MIDDLE-CLASS RESIDENCE	THE MENTAL INSTITUTION RESIDENCE
Infrequent parent–child verbal exchanges	Frequent parent–child verbal exchanges	Infrequent nursing staff–patient verbal exchange
Parents seldom engage in language-training activities.	Parents frequently train child to read, memorize nursery rhymes, songs, poems, stories	Nursing staff do not train child in language skills; there may be minimal speech therapy training.
		Occasional group singing and games

is, in the objects and events occurring immediately outside the home. Some of these differences are shown in Table 8-6. For example, in the lower-class, disadvantaged family contact with the police seldom occurs when it is needed, and when it does occur, it is usually negative; whereas the middle-class family has immediate police contact when it is needed. The middle-class family also has more, and more positive, contacts with the school and the classroom. Particularly significant are the events occurring in the classroom for the disadvantaged child. It is not uncommon for the disadvantaged child's performance of classroom tasks to be followed by nonreinforcement or even punishment. The effect of this is to make the classroom situation (the teacher, the room, the books, and so on) a discriminative stimulus for extinction, punishment, or both. Finally, there are large differences in the means of travel and points of travel. Again, it is the middle-class child who is most often exposed to the diverse forms of stimulation (for example movies, plays, concerts, and zoo and museum trips).

Some Differences in the Behavior of Lower-Class Disadvantaged, Middle-Class, and Institutionalized Children

The objects and events described for the three environments and presented in Tables 8-2 to 8-6 have some interesting implications for behavior. Table 8-7 presents some specific examples of the verbal and motor discriminated operant behaviors descriptive of disadvantaged, middle-class, and institutionalized elementary-school-aged children.[2] Examination of this table clearly

[2] Most, but not all of the behaviors described in Table 8-7 have actually been observed in the children. For reviews, see Metfessel (1970), Deutsch, Katz, and Jensen (1968), Bronfenbrenner (1958), Keller (1966), and Robinson and Robinson (1965).

Table 8-6 Distinguishing Events Characteristic of the Lower-Class Disadvantaged, Middle-Class, and Mental Institution Community Environments

THE LOWER-CLASS, DISADVANTAGED COMMUNITY	THE MIDDLE-CLASS COMMUNITY	THE MENTAL INSTITUTION COMMUNITY
The School		
Parents seldom attend school affairs. Parents seldom check child's progress. Parents most often hears from school when child is in trouble.	Parents frequently attend school affairs. Parents frequently check child's progress. Parents support school, join PTA.	Nursing staff may have only minimal contact with school if patient attends school.
The Classroom		
Child seldom receives social reinforcers for success in classroom learning tasks. Approval and other intangible events are seldom presented, and when they are, they may not be reinforcing. Tangible reinforcers, though they may be reinforcing, are seldom presented. Task failure frequent	Child frequently receives social reinforcers for success in classroom learning tasks. Approval and other intangible events are often reinforcing to the child. Tangible reinforcers, though seldom presented, may not be reinforcing. Task failure not too frequent	Most often, institutional patients do not receive the formal education that the classroom situation provides.
The Police		
Family seldom has contact with police when help is needed. Parent contact with police, when it occurs, frequently negative (occasion for punishment)	Family has immediate contact with police when help is needed. Parent contact with police frequently positive (occasion for help and assistance)	Not applicable
Travel		
Trips often limited to visits with relatives living in comparable environments. Vacation trips rare, bus used as transportation	Trips to zoos, parks, museums, theaters, concerts, and so on. Vacation trips fairly frequent, family car used as transportation	Trips to hospital canteen or movies may occur frequently. Field trips to sites off the hospital compound are infrequent, bus used.

Table 8-7 Some Specific Examples of Some Differences in the Behavior of Lower-Class Disadvantaged, Middle-Class, and Institutionalized Children.

GENERAL BEHAVIOR CLASS	THE LOWER-CLASS, DISADVANTAGED CHILD	THE MIDDLE-CLASS CHILD	THE INSTITUTIONALIZED CHILD
Motor	Uses fingers for eating, seldom uses utensils	Seldom uses fingers for eating, uses all utensils properly	Uses fingers for eating or simple utensil (spoon)
	Can dress, bathe himself, often prepares own meals, which consist mainly of sandwiches	Can dress, bathe himself, seldom prepares own meals, makes occasional sandwiches	May be able to dress, bathe himself; no meal preparation skill whatever (kitchen neutral stimulus)
	Possesses limited skills in toy and tool manipulation	Possesses elaborate toy and tool manipulation skills	Minimal toy and tool manipulation skills
	Performs occasional errands and household tasks	Regularly performs chores and household tasks	May perform simple, ward housekeeping functions
	Frequently avoids teacher, school officials, police, civil authorities	Often approaches teachers, school officials, police, civil authorities	Has little or no behavior for teacher, school officials, has no behavior for police, civil authorities (They are neutral stimuli.)
	Possesses few hobbies or sports skills (such as model building, fishing, or swimming)	Possesses many hobbies and sports skills (such as model building, fishing, and swimming)	Possesses few, if any, hobby and sports skills (such as model building, fishing, or swimming)
Verbal	Calls sibs, parents: "Sister," "Junior," "Poppa" (doesn't know their given names)	Can call sibs, parents by given name or title	Can call only a few of the other patients and staff members by either their given name, title, or nickname
	Knows names of objects (foods, furnishings, and so on) and events (supper, and so on) in household	Knows names of many objects (foods, furnishings, and so forth) and events (dinner, and so on) in household	Knows few, if any, names of objects (foods, furnishings) in household

Table 8-7 *(Continued)*

GEN- ERAL BEHAV- IOR CLASS	THE LOWER-CLASS, DISADVANTAGED CHILD	THE MIDDLE-CLASS CHILD	THE INSTITUTIONALIZED CHILD
	Knows names of objects, places, events in immediate community but not in larger community	Knows names of objects, places, and events in immediate community and larger community	Knows few, if any, names of objects, places, or events in immediate or larger community
	Communicates by pointing, gestures, head-shaking, incomplete sentences, mono-syllables	Communicates by using complete, grammatically correct sentences	Communicates by monosyllabic sounds, pointing, gestures, incomplete sentences
	Seldom gives any accounts of daily events	Frequently gives extensive accounts of daily events	Seldom, if ever, gives accounts of daily events
	Seldom initiates conversation with adults	Frequently initiates conversation with adults	Seldom initiates conversation with adults
	Never argues with parents	Often argues with parents	Seldom, if ever, argues with staff
	Seldom challenges parental demands	Often challenges parental demands	Seldom, if ever, challenges staff demands
	Shows serious deficits in all basic skills	May show deficits in some specific basic skills	Shows severe deficits in basic skills
	Almost never reads in spare time	Occasionally reads in spare time	Has little or no behavior for books (They are neutral stimuli.)

reveals that there are distinct differences between the disadvantaged, middle-class, and institutionalized child across a rather wide range of behaviors. For example, a child's skill in naming or labeling objects or events in his environment is related to the objects and events present in that environment. The middle-class child, compared with the disadvantaged and institutionalized child, is most able to name the objects, places, and events both in his household, and in his immediate and larger community. (Compare the descriptions in Tables 8-2 to 8-6 with Table 8-7.) Similarly, it is the middle-class child who is best able to engage in a variety of verbal exchanges, including giving verbal reports, initiating conversation with an adult, and carrying out an argument with an adult. In fact, the middle-class child asserts his superiority over both the disadvantaged and the institutionalized child in all of the behaviors shown in Table 8-7.

The same is true of the motor behavior. The middle-class child is superior in such small-muscle skills as eating with various utensils, model building, and toy and tool manipulation, and such large-muscle skills as swimming.

It is also the middle-class child, not the disadvantaged or institutionalized child, who shows approach responses to school personnel and members of the community government. The disadvantaged child may actually avoid such personnel, because they may be discriminative for extinction, time-out, or even punishment. The institutionalized child simply has no behavior for such individuals. Rather, because these individuals do not possess any stimulus control over the institutionalized child's behavior, they are, in effect, neutral stimuli.

Then, too, there are important differences in who prepares the meals, what food is served, how one eats, who is present at the meal, and what else besides eating goes on during the meal. The disadvantaged child is most apt to prepare his own meal, a sandwich, to eat by himself or with his mother, grandmother, or a sibling (not his father), to carry on only a minimal conversation during meals, and even on occasion, to walk around while eating. The middle-class child is most apt to be served different foods by his mother, who prepares them, eat with certain utensils, eat with his entire family, and talk about his day while eating. Thus the middle-class child's verbal presentations are accompanied by both food and social reinforcers. Most deprived of all is the institutionalized child. He eats simple, staff-prepared foods with groups of other patients, most of whom are not particularly verbal. He is not, therefore, very apt to receive verbal stimulation during meals from those he eats with. Furthermore, the staff does not join the patient in eating at mealtime, thereby eliminating the one remaining source of verbal stimulation. Rather, the staff members supervise the patients during mealtime, talking with other staff members and only occasionally engaging in exchanges with the patient. Most of these exchanges are verbal instructions such as "Stop grabbing" and "Use your spoon." Such exchanges lead to the acquisition of receptive rather than expressive communication skills. It would seem, then, that both the disadvantaged and institutionalized child, through their solitary or nonsocial eating, may actually reinforce themselves with food for remaining silent.

Although the evidence presented for the relationship between the numbers and kinds of distinguishing objects and events in the individual's environment and behavior is correlational and somewhat speculative, it seems reasonable to assume that the middle-class child is the beneficiary of the most instructive environment. This is an environment in which procedures enhancing behavior are most often used. Such procedures are used the least often with the institutionalized child. The effect of this lack is to make the objects and events occurring in the environment into neutral events and to make the institutional environment a poor instructing environment. Although the objects and events going on in the disadvantaged child's environment may lead to some behavioral enhancement, not infrequently procedures that suppress behavior are used. This means that some behaviors are appropriately strengthened, others appropriately weakened, and still others, particularly escape and avoidance when strong suppression procedures are used, may be inappropriately strengthened. Thus the instructing environment of the disadvantaged child, although not as poor as that of the institutionalized child, is quite inadequate.

The preceding discussion has been primarily concerned with operant behavior and its antecedent stimulus events. Of no lesser significance, however, is the impact of instructing environments on the respondent behavior of the children living in them. As we shall see in the next chapter, a natural consequence of the extensive use of behavior enhancement procedures in an instructing environment, particularly procedures employing positive reinforcement, leads to the acquisition of conditioned positive emotional responses. Similarly, when extensive use is made of behavior suppression procedures in an instructing environment, particularly procedures employing punishment, extinction, or time-out, one can expect the acquisition of negative conditioned emotional responses. It is not surprising, therefore, that conditioned positive emotional responses are more frequently characteristic of the middle-class child than of the disadvantaged or institutionalized child. The conditioned emotional responses of the disadvantaged child are more apt to be negative. The institutionalized child, subjected to minimum behavior enhancement or suppression procedures, would be likely to show few positive or negative conditioned emotional responses.

STUDY QUESTIONS

1. Explain how a neutral stimulus event can acquire a stimulus function in a respondent behavior. Give an example of this as it might occur in nature.
2. Explain how differences in the environment can result in differences in the stimulus and response components of respondent behavior.
3. Describe and discuss six ways in which objects and events in the environment are significant in operant behavior.
4. What is meant by an environmental mediator–trainer? Give an example of an

environmental mediator–trainer in the physical environment. In the social environment.

5. What is the essential feature of instrumental or purposive behavior? Give an example of such behavior in situations involving (a) nonprearranged consequences and (b) prearranged consequences.

6. What kinds of responses are made by a trainer in a situation involving (a) prearranged consequences, (b) imitation, and (c) "putting through"?

7. Explain why social learning involving imitation is far more efficient than the learning acquired in a natural setting involving nonprearranged consequences.

8. What additional element may make the putting-through procedure particularly powerful?

9. In the classroom for pigeons
   a. what maintains the behavior of the professor, teacher, and student during acquisition?
   b. what maintains the behavior of the teacher and the pupil after training is completed?

10. From the descriptions in Figure 8-2 and the text, see if you can derive a formal definition of a transaction between a mediator–trainer and a trainer. Must a good trainer be able to make the performance he wants his trainee to learn? If yes, under what conditions? If no, what must he be able to do?

11. Must the trainee make the response to be learned in order to learn? What are some of the problems in finding an answer to this question?

12. If the trainee's exposure to a model's performance does not produce acquisition, what function may it have?

13. Superstitions may occur under what two general situations of environmental events?

14. Be able to (1) give an example, (2) describe precisely the environmental events involved in, and (3) describe a plan for eliminating each of the following:
    a. Classical superstitious behavior.
    b. Concurrent superstition.
    c. Positive or negative sensory superstition.
    d. Generalized superstitious behavior.
    e. Superstitious chaining.

15. Give an example of a human superstition arising from a situation in which reinforcements are either non-response-contingent or delayed. One arising from a complex transaction with someone else. Contrast the environmental events involved in each situation.

16. Explain why superstitious behavior is regarded as not favoring survival of the organism.

17. Contrast the efficiency of the instructing environment of an inhabitant of a primitive society with that of the inhabitant of the modern industrial state.

18. What are the two principal effect(s) of consequences on an operant given on page 203.

19. What particular stimulus function is attributed to the distinguishing objects and events of the different environments described on pages 203–211 and why is this important in the discussion?

20. Give a summary statement of the differences and similarities between lower-class disadvantaged, middle-class, and institutional environments regarding the following:
   a. Number and kinds of distinguishing objects in living and eating areas.
   b. Number and kinds of distinguishing objects characteristic of the three types of households.
   c. Number and kinds of distinguishing events characteristic of the three types of households.
   d. Number and kinds of distinguishing events characteristic of the three types of communities.
21. Look over Table 8-7 and identify a specific type of discriminated verbal or motor behavior characteristic of the lower-class disadvantaged, middle-class, and institutionalized child and relate this behavior to your summaries prepared for question 20. Be specific as to the distinguishing object and/or events and the related behavior.
22. What is meant by the observation that for the institutionalized child books are neutral stimuli?
23. Distinguish between a discriminative stimulus and a neutral stimulus.
24. In what sense is the environment regarded as instructive? In our society, who is the beneficiary of the most instructive environment? The least instructive? Explain and defend your answers.
25. What is the effect of behavior enhancement procedures on an individual's operant behavior? Respondent behavior? What event ties these two behaviors together?
26. Suggest an explanation for the minimal skills and the shallow emotion observed in institutionalized children.

REFERENCES

Anonymous. Compensating education in the Chicago Public Schools. Study Report #4. Chicago: Board of Education of Chicago, 1964.

Bandura, A. Social learning through imitation. In M. R. Jones (Ed.), *Nebraska Symposium on Motivation.* Vol. 10. Lincoln: University of Nebraska Press, 1962.

Bandura, A. Influence of the model's reinforcement contingencies on the acquisition of imitative responses. *Journal of Abnormal and Social Psychology*, 1965, 1, 589–595.

Bronfenbrenner, U. Socialization and social class through time and space. In E. Maccoby, T. M. Newcomb, and E. L. Hartley (Eds.), *Reading in social psychology.* (3rd ed.) New York: Holt, Rinehart and Winston, 1958.

Catania, A. C., and Cutts, D. Experimental control of superstitious responding in humans. *Journal of the Experimental Analysis of Behavior*, 1963, 6, 203–208.

Dennis, W. Causes of retardation among institutional children: Iran. *Journal of Genetic Psychology*, 1960, **96**, 47–59.

Deutsch, M., Katz, I., and Jensen, A. R. *Social class, race and psychological development.* New York: Holt, Rinehart, and Winston, 1968.

Hermstein, R. J. "Will." *Proceedings of the American Philosophical Society,* 1964, **108,** 455–458.

Hermstein, R. J. Superstition: A corollary of the principles of operant conditioning. In W. K. Honig (Ed.), *Operant behavior: Areas of research and application.* New York: Appleton-Century-Crofts, 1966.

Holland, J. G., and Skinner, B. F. *The analysis of behavior.* New York: McGraw-Hill, 1961.

Hunt, R. G. Socio-cultural factors in mental disorder. *Behavioral Science,* 1959, **4,** 96–107.

Keller, S. *The American lower class family.* Albany: New York State Division for Youth, 1966.

Metfessel, N. S. Conclusions from previous research findings which were validated by the Research and Evaluation by the staff of the Project Potential. Center for the Educationally (culturally) Disadvantaged Youth. Los Angeles: University of Southern California, 1965.

Metfessel, N. S. Individual correlates of reading success and disability with children and youth from the culture of poverty. In T. Horn (Ed.), *Readings for the disadvantaged.* New York: Harcourt Brace Jovanovich, 1970.

Migler, B. Experimental self-punishment and superstitious escape behavior. *Journal of the Experimental Analysis of Behavior,* 1963, **6,** 371–385.

Morse, W. H., and Skinner, B. F. A second type of superstition in the pigeon. *American Journal of Psychology,* 1957, **70,** 308–311.

Mowrer, O. H. *Learning theory and the symbolic processes.* New York: Wiley, 1960.

Raph, J. B. Language development of socially disadvantaged children. *Review of Educational Research,* 1965, **35,** 389–397.

Riessman, F. *Culturally deprived child.* New York: Harper and Row, 1962.

Robinson, H. B., and Robinson, M. *The mentally retarded child.* New York: McGraw-Hill, 1965.

Skinner, B. F. Superstition in the pigeon. *Journal of Experimental Psychology,* 1948, **38,** 168–172.

Skinner, B. F. *Science and human behavior.* New York: Macmillan, 1953.

Skinner, B. F. *Verbal behavior.* New York: Appleton-Century-Crofts, 1957.

Stewart, D. D., and Austin, M. *Pockets of poverty.* San Diego, Calif: San Diego Community Welfare Council, 1964.

Taba, H. Cultural deprivation as a factor in school learning. A lecture at the Merrill-Palmer Institute, March, 1963.

CHAPTER 9

SOCIAL TRANSACTIONS AND BEHAVIOR

Essential to the development of behavior of most individuals is membership in various social groups. Through the influence of the members or agents of the group, the social control of the individual's behavior emerges. This influencing process is mediated by (1) the highly complex and intricate stimulation that arises from the responses of the group members as they interact with one another, and (2) the physical-environmental settings in which these interactions occur.

THE GROUP AND BEHAVIOR CONTROL

Most of us are engaged in social transactions throughout our lives. In the course of our development, however, there are marked changes in the stimulus and response complexes that make up the transactions, in those with whom we transact, and in the physical-environmental setting in which the transactions occur. Within any given period of an individual's life, however, similar transactions with the same individuals are common.

Consider a mother's changing her baby's diaper. If she changes it only six times a day, at the end of the first year she will have changed it more than two thousand times. Moreover, if each time she changes the diaper only three social transactions occur, at the end of the year there will have been more than six thousand transactions. If the number of transactions occurring during feeding, bathing, dressing, and playing is also three (a minimal number at that), the total number of all social transactions will be in excess of ten thousand. Situations such as this, in which the individual repeatedly engages in social transactions with others, may lead to response class acquisition, response class maintenance, or both.

If a given response class occurs more often in the presence of certain individuals or members of a group than in their absence, the individual's behavior is said to be under the *social control* of the group. (This is essentially the same as audience control, a type of verbal behavior described in Chapter 7.) A white bigot, for example, is more apt to make anti-Negro remarks around his Southern friends than in the presence of Yankee carpetbaggers. *Behavior control* occurs when, in addition to the greater likelihood of the behavior occurring in the presence of certain individuals than in their absence, these behaviors are valued by the group. (Behavior control as defined here is quite similar to the notion of social control in sociology.) In such a case there is correspondence or congruence between the behavior valued by the group and the behavior of the individual. Thus if the white bigot belongs to the K.K.K., his behavior (anti-Negro remarks) is more likely to occur around other K.K.K. members than with nonmembers (social control), and in addition, it is valued and reinforced by this group (behavior control). The behavior occurring in groups may have been acquired during social transactions among members in a given group or may have been acquired earlier. In the latter case the social transactions currently going on within the group serve to maintain the behavior. Such maintenance may be due to stimulus control (discriminative stimuli occurring during social transactions), schedule control (consequating stimuli occurring during social transactions in the group), or both.

The acquisition or maintenance of certain behaviors in individuals, as they engage in social transactions, is complex and involves one or more of the following events:[1]

ESSENTIAL FACTORS IN RESPONDENT CONDITIONING

1. r (response class) factors   Nature and number of respondents
2. e (eliciting stimuli) factors   Nature of prepotent and neutral stimuli
3. k (contingency) factors   Schedule of stimulus pairing, schedule of

---

[1] For a detailed description of how this analysis can be used in observing and treating retarded behavior, see an excellent paper by O. R. Lindsley (1964).

presentation of eliciting stimuli, temporal relationship between prepotent and neutral stimuli

4. s (state of the organism) factors — Deprivation conditions

ESSENTIAL PROCEDURES IN RESPONDENT CONDITIONING

1. Nonprearranged stimulus pairing — Individual in a social transaction adventitiously, or accidentally, makes paired presentations of a prepotent and a neutral stimulus, thus making the neutral or non-group-valued (irrelevant) stimulus the elicitor

2. Prearranged stimulus pairing — Individual in a social transaction makes paired presentations of a prepotent and a neutral stimulus, thus making the neutral or group-valued (relevant) stimulus the elicitor

ESSENTIAL FACTORS IN OPERANT CONDITIONING

1. R (operant response class) factors — Nature and number of operants
2. C (consequation) factors — Nature and amount of consequation
3. K (contingency) factors — Schedule of consequation, temporal relationship between the operant and the consequation
4. s (state of the organism) factors — Deprivation conditions

ESSENTIAL PROCEDURES IN OPERANT CONDITIONING

1. Nonprearranged (adventitious) consequences — Individual in a social transaction accidentally, or inadvertently, consequates the behavior of another, thus strengthening or weakening irrelevant behavior of the other individual in the transaction

2. Prearranged consequences — Individual in a social transaction presents response-contingent consequation of another's behavior, thus strengthening of weakening relevant behavior of that individual

3. Imitation — Individual in a social transaction presents a sample performance to another person and, when the latter makes a comparable performance, presents response-contingent strengthening consequation

4. Putting through — Individual in a social transaction manually assists another individual in a performance and then provides response-contingent strengthening consequation.

ESSENTIAL FACTORS AND PROCEDURES IN OPERANT DISCRIMINATION

1. S (discriminative stimuli) factors   Nature of physical and social stimuli in the presence of which the operant behavior of an individual is adventitiously (in superstition) or purposely (in relevant behavior) consequated by others in the course of social transaction

When a social transaction leads to the acquisition or maintenance of behavior, the transaction can be analyzed in terms of the essential factors and procedures of respondent or operant conditioning or operant discrimination. In any given social transaction, compared with other social transactions, the extent to which certain response classes are acquired or maintained, as well as the extent to which all or part of these procedures occur, is quite variable.

In the large, highly structured, task-oriented infantry company, for example, classes of behavior essential to military tactics and weapon manipulation are valued, and the officers and men of the training staff seek control over the behavior of the recruits in the sense that these are the final performances sought by the staff. Inherent in the social transactions between the recruit and the staff are procedures that may possess elements of respondent and operant conditioning and operant discrimination training. For example, recruits may acquire skill in firing weapons by exposure to prearranged consequences (as when points are given for accurate shots), imitation (as when the drill instructor (D.I.) shows the recruit proper form in holding a weapon), putting-through procedures (as when the D.I. positions the recruit's head and arms so he holds the rifle correctly), or verbal instructions (as when the D.I. instructs his recruits to slowly "sque-e-ze" the trigger). Such procedures are used in characteristic physical-environmental settings (that is, on the firing range or on maneuvers) similar to, if not identical with, those required in natural settings, so that the final performances acquired during such training are apt to generalize to real combat situations. Other procedures are aimed at the acquisition of respondent behavior. For example, recruits are exposed to stimulus pairing in which the stimuli characteristic of the enemy (insignia, uniforms, weapons, the names or photographs of military and political leaders) are paired with prepotent negative eliciting stimuli (pictorial, printed, and verbal descriptions of enemy atrocities and acts of repression), which makes the stimuli characteristic of the enemy elicit negative respondents. Such respondent conditioning may involve the use of posters, films, pamphlets, and lectures about the enemy.

In contrast, a loosely structured, small expressive-behavior-oriented psychotherapy group values classes of behavior essential to interpersonal relationships. Again, elements of operant conditioning and operant discrimination training procedures may be used, including prearranged consequences (as when the shy patient is reinforced for assertive remarks), imitation (as when the patient watches others describe their feelings and then describes his own feelings), and most extensively, verbal instructions (as when one patient asks another in the group, "How do *you* feel about it?"). Moreover, because of the positive reinforcements occurring during social transactions in the group, being in the group and expressing oneself may, through pairing with these reinforcements, elicit positive respondents. Behavior acquired or maintained in a group, like the transactions that may occur between caretakers (that is, parents, teachers, probation officers, counselors, and those who possess the legal or moral right and obligation to control behavior) and their charges, can include any of the following:

1. Those behaviors that are valued by the group, over which behavior control is sought, and that *are* relevant and essential to the individual performances occurring in the group. An example of this is the behavior of a bank teller who cashes a customer's check.

2. Those behaviors that are valued by the group and over which behavior control is sought, but that *are not* relevant or essential to the performances of individuals in the group. The bank teller must be able to cash the customer's check; it would be desirable if the teller were also friendly and possessed an attractive smile, rather than being businesslike in his manner.

3. Those behaviors that are *neither* valued by the group *nor* relevant to the performances of individuals in the group, but nevertheless appear to be under the social control of the group. Such behaviors may be viewed, in a sense, as social superstitions, because they arise accidentally out of the social transactions occurring in the group and are not essential to those transactions. Before the teller says to the customer, "Sign here," he may scratch his chin, or before giving the customer his cash, the teller may sit down on his stool.

THE ANALYSIS OF SOCIAL BEHAVIOR

Although the essential events involved in the acquisition or maintenance of behavior have been discussed in preceding chapters (See Chapters 2–8) and are summarized on pages 221–223, understanding these processes as they occur in social settings requires a detailed examination of the nature of social transactions.

The Nature of Social Transactions

The behavior of the individual as he interacts with others in a group on any given occasion is called a *response complex*. Typically, this response complex consists of concurrent operant and respondent behavior. The behavior of the individual, in turn, combines with the physical-environmental setting in which the behavior occurs to form a *stimulus complex* that has relevance for the behavior of others engaging in the transaction. The behavior does this because it has one or more of the following functions:

1. It may be an eliciting stimulus for the behavior of others.
2. It may be a discriminative stimulus for the behavior of others.
3. It may be a consequating stimulus, having a strengthening or weakening effect on the behavior of others.

This characteristic dual function of the individual's behavior in a group (as a response and stimulus complex) is called an *interaction process unit*. It is illustrated as follows:

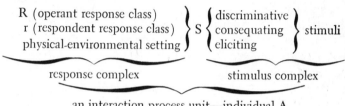

an interaction process unit—individual A

In this illustration the interaction process unit derived from the behavior of individual A is made up of two essential elements: (1) the response complex, consisting of individual A's operant (R) and respondent (r) response classes, and (2) the discriminative, consequating, and eliciting stimuli. These stimuli combine with the physical-environmental setting in which the response complex occurs to form the stimulus complex (S).

When two interaction process units are *causally* related to one another, the result is a social transaction:

Individual A   Individual B

$\left\{ \begin{array}{c} R_1 \\ S_1 \\ r_1 \end{array} \right.$ ————————→ $\left\{ \begin{array}{c} R_1 \\ S_1 \\ r_1 \end{array} \right.$

interaction   interaction
process unit   process unit

A_1 B_1

In this illustration a single social transaction has occurred between individual A and individual B, consisting of two interaction process units (A_1 and B_1). Each interaction process unit contains elements of operant (R) and respondent (r) behavior, and response-produced stimulation (S), consisting of eliciting, discriminative, or consequating stimuli or any combination of these. The arrow connecting the two interaction process units reveals that the interaction process unit of individual B would not have occurred in the absence of the interaction process unit of individual A. There is, therefore, a causal link between interaction process units A_1 and B_1. This causal linkage is an essential feature of a social transaction. Derived from this is the social group, which consists of at least one social transaction between two or more individuals occurring in a physical-environmental setting.

As was illustrated earlier (See Chapter 7), this interactive process occurring during social transactions can be seen in the verbal behavior that occurs between a speaker and a listener. For example, individual A sees individual B in the hall and says, "Hello, how are you?" to which individual B replies, "I'm fine, thank you." This sequence is diagrammed on page 227.

In this illustration the response complex characteristic of individual A (his greeting), combined with the physical-environmental setting in which it occurred (the hall), functioned as a stimulus complex for individual B. That complex consisted of a component of auditory (A's greeting) and visual (A's presence in the hall) stimulation functioning as a discriminative stimulus in the interaction process unit. Similarly, the response complex characteristic of individual B (her reply), combined with the same physical-environmental setting in which it occurred (the hall), functioned as a stimulus complex having reinforcing properties, thereby strengthening individual A's behavior (his greeting). If we assume that individual B is an attractive girl, long admired by individual A, it would be reasonable to assume that her reply would be especially reinforcing and would, perhaps, also elicit a pattern of positive respondents in individual A. (This process whereby this occurs will be described shortly.) Her reply, therefore, is a response complex possessing both consequating and eliciting stimulus functions.

The number of social transactions in a given situation depends, among other things, on the number of individuals involved and the duration of the situation. However, the occurrence of a single social transaction in human societies is rare. Tables 9-1 and 9-2 illustrate the complexity of the stimulus and response complexes occurring during social transactions between characters in familiar social situations.

For example, in situations 1–3 (Table 9-1), the response complexes consist of at least two operant or respondent component responses (or both). Situation 2 is especially interesting because it illustrates an apparent contradiction (the freshman saying "I love you" to his girl while winking at someone else), a problem in the analysis of behavior to be dealt with in Chapter 10.

In situation 1 in Table 9-2, for example, the doctor's behaviors of filling a hypodermic syringe, sterilizing an area on the patient's arm, making a verbal entreaty ("This is going to hurt me more than it hurts you"), and smiling were immediately followed by the jab of the hypodermic needle, all of which combines to make an eliciting stimulus complex for a pattern of negative respondents in the patient. Similarly, the patient seated before the physician

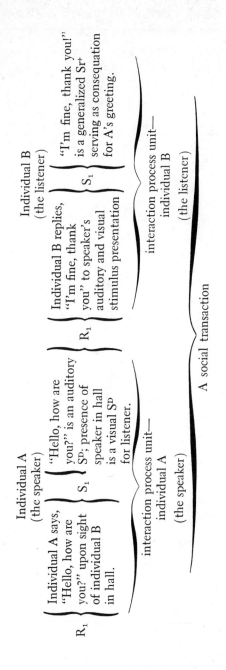

Individual A
(the speaker)

Individual B
(the listener)

R_1 { Individual A says, "Hello, how are you?" upon sight of individual B in hall. }

S_1 { "Hello, how are you?" is an auditory S^D; presence of speaker in hall is a visual S^D for listener. }

R_1 { Individual B replies, "I'm fine, thank you" to speaker's auditory and visual stimulus presentation }

S_1 { "I'm fine, thank you!" is a generalized Sr^+ serving as consequation for A's greeting. }

interaction process unit—
individual A
(the speaker)

interaction process unit—
individual B
(the listener)

A social transaction

Table 9-1 Response Complexes Occurring During Social Transactions.

	CHARACTER	ANALYSIS OF RESPONSE COMPLEX
Situation 1		*Concurrent Operants*
The company commander enters the inspection area swinging his swagger stick. The staff sergeant comes to attention and shouts, "Attention!" Corporal Jones stands at attention fixing his gaze straight ahead.	company commander	walking into inspection area (motor) swinging swagger stick (motor)
		Concurrent Operants
	staff sergeant	standing at attention (motor) shouting "Attention!" (verbal)
		Concurrent Operants
	Corporal Jones	standing at attention (motor) gaze fixed straight ahead (motor)
Situation 2		*Concurrent Operants*
While dancing with his girl, a college freshman whispers into her ear, "I love you." At the same time he winks at another girl, who happens to face him while dancing with her partner.	college freshman	dancing with partner (motor) whispering "I love you" (verbal) winking (motor)
Situation 3		*Concurrent Operants*
A man is seated in the waiting room of his doctor's office, awaiting the evaluation of his physical eamination. He is seated next to a lady, who is telling him about her operation. He occasionally nods, smiles, and says, "Uh huh." However, he appears pale, and he can feel his heart pounding lightly.	the man	being seated (motor) smiling (motor) nodding (motor) saying "Uh huh" (verbal) *Concurrent Respondents* constriction of the blood vessels in the skin increased pulse rate increased blood pressure
		Concurrent Operants
	the lady	being seated (motor) recounting her operation (verbal)

Table 9-2 Stimulus Complexes Occurring During Social Transactions

	CHARACTER	ANALYSIS OF STIMULUS COMPLEX
Situation 1		*Eliciting Stimuli:*
A doctor fills a hypodermic syringe with vaccine, turns to his patient, and sterilizes an area on his arm with alcohol. At the same time, the doctor smiles faintly and says, "This is going to hurt me more than it hurts you." He then jabs the patient with the needle.	the patient	the doctor's office the doctor the hypodermic syringe the alcohol the doctor's smile the jab of the needle the expression: "This is going to hurt me more than it hurts you."
		Discriminative Stimuli:
	the doctor	the patient with his sleeve rolled up the syringe the vaccine the alcohol
Situation 2		*Discriminative Stimuli:*
A patient is reclining on the couch in his psychiatrist's darkened consultation room. The psychiatrist, seated nearby, says, "Tell me. How did you feel about your father when he did that?"	the patient	the psychiatrist's office the psychiatrist seated nearby the verbal instructions: "Tell me. How did you feel about your father when he did that?"
		Discriminative Stimuli:
	the psychiatrist	the darkened consultation room the patient reclining on the couch
Situation 3		*Discriminative Stimuli:*
An 11-year-old boy stands before a table in a mental hospital's "quiet room." A psychiatric technician looks through a window in the door, and the boy commences to bang his head repeatedly against the table. The technician leaves, and the boy stops banging his head against the table.	the boy	the room with the table the technician peering through the window
		Discriminative Stimuli:
	the technician	the window in the door of the "quiet room" containing the boy banging his head on the table

Table 9-2 *(Continued)*

CHARACTER	ANALYSIS OF STIMULUS COMPLEX
Situation 4	*Eliciting Stimuli:*
At the request of his swinging girl friend, an obviously middle-class young executive of the gray-flannel-suit set visits a one-man art show. The artist, a way-out hippie type, is seated on a large pillow with his legs crossed. The young man in the gray flannel suit inspects one of the paintings, turns his head away, and remarks "Gee, this is good!" Although the artist is gazing straight ahead, apparently transfixed, he is badly shaken when he hears the young man's remark. the artist	the young man inspecting the painting the young man's remark: "Gee, this is good!"
	Consequating Stimuli:
	the young man inspecting the painting the young man's remark: "Gee, this is good!"
	Eliciting Stimuli:
the young executive	the art show the painting
	Discriminative Stimuli:
	the art show the painting
Situation 5	*Eliciting Stimuli:*
A college freshman has brought his girl friend home for dinner for the first time. They are seated in the living room, talking and waiting to be called for dinner. The young man's mother enters and says to her son, "Dinner's ready. Wash your hands, John, and we'll eat." John blushes, but he gets up slowly and heads for the bathroom. the college freshman	his girl friend seated in the room his mother's verbal instruction: "Wash your hands, John, and we'll eat."
	Discriminative Stimuli:
	waiting for dinner to be announced situation the mother's expression: "Dinner's ready. Wash your hands, John, and we'll eat."
	Consequating Stimuli:
	his girl friend seated in the room his mother's verbal instructions: "Wash your hands, John, and we'll eat."
	Discriminative Stimuli:
the mother	the food on the table her son seated in the living room, waiting for dinner

with his bare arm exposed, the hypodermic syringe and vaccine, and the alcohol and cotton all combine to make a stimulus complex for the doctor's response complex consisting of the administration of the hypodermic injection and the verbal entreaty.

In situations 2 and 3 of Table 9-2 discriminative stimuli characterize the stimulus complexes in the social transactions. In situations 4 and 5 consequating stimulus functions are added to the stimulus complexes occurring in the social transactions. What is particularly interesting is that the consequation that emerges from these transactions is somewhat unexpected. In situation 4, for example, the young executive's expression "Gee, this is good!" seems to evoke a negative emotional response and even avoidance in the artist. The same behavioral effect is evident in situation 5, where a mother gives her son the verbal instruction to wash his hands in front of his girl friend. In these two examples, as in many human social transactions, it is important to emphasize that *eliciting, discriminative, or consequating stimulus functions arise out of the total social situation. The stimulus function of an event in a social setting depends on its relationship to other stimulus events going on at the same time.* Had the swinging girl friend described in situation 4 said of the artist's painting, "Gee, this is good," the artist might have responded more positively. Likewise, had the boy's girl friend not been present in situation 5, the boy might have responded differently also. All of this seems to illustrate that social transactions, as they occur in nature, are complex events. It is often difficult to specify precisely the eliciting, discriminative, or consequating stimuli that occur in a single transaction, and most social situations involve sequences of rapidly occurring social transactions. For those trying to provide an account of variation in behavior, it is frequently easier to attribute the source of variation to other factors, such as genetics. The reader would do well to keep this in mind, since most individuals encounter few situations that are devoid of the social stimulation that arises from the responses of others.

In conclusion, the behavior of individuals in social groups consists of response complexes, which, in turn, often possess eliciting, discriminative, or consequating stimulus functions for others in the group. An individual's given unitary act in a group possessing such response complex and stimulus complex functions is called an interaction process unit. When the occurrence of a given interaction process unit could have happened only as the result of the response complex and stimulus complex of another individual, a social transaction has taken place. The eliciting, discriminative, or consequating function of a stimulus event occurring in the course of a social transaction depends on the event's relationship to other ongoing events that are part of the total social situation. It is this characteristic that makes for the complexity of social stimulation and for the variability of behavior in social settings.

The Efficiency of the Group in Behavior Control

The efficiency of a social group in controlling the behavior of an individual can be characterized in three ways. First, efficient groups tend to produce and maintain performances in the individual that are valued by those in the group. Second, at any given moment efficient groups are able to control the total behavior (concurrent operant and respondent behavior components) that make up the response complexes of the individual in the group. A group that both values and possesses control over the individual's verbal and motor operant behavior is viewed as more efficient than a group that values both but has control over only one. For example, utterances against drug use and the avoidance of drugs are behaviors valued both by Synanon (a rehabilitation group for drug addicts) and by the drug addict's caretaker. During therapeutic interviews the caretaker may eventually control the addict's verbal behavior, so that its content consists of remarks against drug use. Unlike Synanon, the caretaker may not be able to extend that control to the motor avoidance of drugs.[2] Third, in efficient groups the acquisition of valued behaviors is fast. Conversely, in an inefficient group (1) there may be little or no control of all or some of the components that make up the group-valued response complexes of the individual, (2) there may be some or considerable control over nonvalued behaviors, and (3) acquisition may be slow rather than fast.

The efficiency of a group in controlling the acquisition or maintenance of behavior in the individual depends on the following:

1. *The ease with which the individuals in the group can identify an acceptable performance.* Before the individuals in a group can consequate the behavior of others, they must first be able to observe it. Some behaviors are more readily observable than others and are therefore more likely to be consequated. This is especially true of vocal and locomotor (operant) behavior. On the other hand, difficulty may be encountered in identifying acceptable emotional (respondent) responses, because they tend to be covert and they require the use of special instrumentation, which may not be available to the group. For example, a supervisor may wish to obtain behavior control over his employees so they will have (a) appropriate task-related behaviors and (b) positive feelings about the company. Task-related behavior may be observed directly as it occurs, or it may be observed indirectly through the finished product that the employee produces. Without special observation

---

[2] This singular control over the verbal but not motor behavior of an individual in therapeutic groups has been called the *therapeutic contract*. For example, during therapeutic interviews convicts will tell the therapists evaluating them for parole, what they think the therapists want to hear (for example, "I'm going straight. That's the only way you can make it, man."). See L. Yablonsky (1965).

techniques, however, the supervisor must rely on other evidence—most probably the employee's verbal behavior—to determine the employee's feelings. The employee's response of "You bet I like working here" when the supervisor queries him may or may not accurately describe the employee's feelings toward the company. Thus the employer may have to rely on other sources of evidence in addition to the employee's verbal reports.

In some cases the group members may not be able to identify acceptable performance because the group seeks control over classes of behavior that are too broad or over intrapsychic states or events that are going on in other dimensional systems. Such might be the case in a therapy situation in which the therapist seeks to increase the patient's "awareness of reality" by giving him "insight"—that is, by bringing his unconscious needs into the realm of awareness. In this situation the therapist aims to control a broadly defined behavior class (awareness of reality) and aims at manipulating hypothetical states in other *dimensional systems* of the organism (insight, unconsciousness needs). Social transactions between the therapist and the patient under such circumstances may also, on occasion, produce superstitions in the patient, because the therapist-presented consequences are imprecise. They follow a shifting or grossly changing response class, which the therapist himself may have difficulty monitoring. For example, some therapists, asserting that their interest is only in the here and now of the patient's problem, may nevertheless from time to time be attentive when the patient verbalizes about his dependence on his mother as a child and because of this, strengthen such remarks. In the same way, the presence of the cronies, the bartender, the furnishings, and the signs in the bar will acquire eliciting stimulus functions for positive emotional responses through (adventitious) stimulus pairing with the eliciting stimuli occurring during the social transactions among the cronies in the bar (the beer and the jokes).

2. *The nature and frequency with which eliciting stimuli are paired in the course of social transactions in the group.* Not only may different types of positive or negative eliciting stimuli occur in the course of social transactions, but they may be paired with a wide range of neutral stimuli, and at varying times as well. Social transactions in which a patient is treated by a doctor are apt to involve occasional presentations of prepotent painful stimuli. These, in turn, are paired with the kinds of stimuli often present during treatment—the smell of alcohol, surgical instruments, and so on. In contrast to this are the positive prepotent stimulus presentations of the waitress who brings her customers food and drink. These presentations are paired with other stimuli characteristic of the dining room setting.

3. *The nature and frequency of the consequences occurring in social transactions in the group.* A wide range of consequences occurs in groups, and they are most frequently presented on a concurrent schedule. Group-valued

behaviors are followed by strengthening events such as positive or negative reinforcement and high probability behavior (the Premack principle), and other behaviors are followed by weakening events such as extinction, aversive stimulation, and the removal of positive reinforcement. Often, too, behavior in a group situation is not followed by consequences every time it occurs, so that the predominant schedules of reinforcement are intermittent schedules.[3] This is because there may be other stimuli controlling behavior in the individual that is incompatible with the behavior that is essential to sustained social transactions. For example, a mother may say to her child, "Make your bed" without thanking him as she normally does because the telephone is ringing and she has to leave the room to answer it. Or the child may make the bed and then, hearing a playmate call, run out to play without hearing his mother's words of thanks.

4. *The nature and frequency of the discriminative simuli occurring during social transactions in the group.* The number and kinds of events that possess discriminative stimulus functions in groups also vary. Certain behavior of an individual may be followed by strengthening consequences in the presence of certain stimuli, and other behaviors, occurring in the presence of other stimuli, may be followed by weakening consequences. A classroom teacher will probably provide positive reinforcements to those pupils who seat themselves promptly after being instructed to do so, whereas pupils who talk out of turn in class are likely to be reprimanded. Moreover, groups in which social transactions are minimal exert little stimulus control over the behavior of the individual member and when such stimulus control over the behavior of the individuals in a group does develop, abrupt changes either in the individuals who constitute the group or in the physical-environmental settings in which the social transactions in the group occur will produce an abrupt disruption of the performance normally occurring in the group. The taxi driver who is suddenly assigned to provide service to transient clientele rather than to the regular customers with whom he frequently had conversation and repartee will probably show a deterioration in behavior (most probably in his conversation, not in his driving skills), due to the removal from his environment of important controlling stimuli, his regular customers.

5. *The temporal relationship between the stimulus events and the response events occurring during social transactions in the group.* There are variations in groups with respect to the promptness with which neutral stimuli can be paired with prepotent eliciting stimuli in the acquisition or maintenance of respondent behavior and the promptness of the consequences in the ac-

---

[3] The behavior of some individuals cannot be maintained under conditions of intermittent or delayed reinforcement because they have not had, in the past, gradual exposure to intermittent schedules of reinforcement or they have deficiencies in the acquisition of chained performances.

quisition or maintenance of operant behavior. Prompt stimulus pairing and prompt consequences lead to rapid acquisition or maintenance of group-valued behavior. On the other hand, delayed stimulus pairing or consequences, as we have seen, lead to the development of many irrelevant behaviors, or social superstitions.

6. *The degree of similarity between the stimulus complexes during response class acquisition, response class maintenance, and at other times.* The degree to which the group can arrange for similarity in the stimulus complexes subsequent to acquisition of behavior is crucial to the maintenance of behavior in that group. Gross changes in the stimulus complex (in the eliciting, discriminative, and consequating stimuli) will produce disruptions in behavior. When gradual changes can be accomplished, however, the characteristic stimulus complex maintaining behavior can be quite dissimilar from that during acquisition without any loss in behavior. Finally, response complexes acquired during social transactions in the group may, on occasion, generalize to other situations. Such *transituational generality* occurs when the stimulus complex occurring in the group is similar to the one occurring outside the group. Such is the case when a pupil's appropriate classroom behavior remains in full strength as he moves from the elementary school classroom to the junior high school classroom, despite changes in teachers, classmates, scheduling, and to a degree, physical surroundings.

In the absence of extensive environmental control of these factors, groups or caretakers must perforce be inefficient in behavior control. Moreover, environments differ widely in the degree to which they contain potential eliciting, discriminative, or consequating stimuli. Nevertheless, despite large differences in the types of stimuli available in different environments, behavior control through the same behavioral processes is a universal phenomenon.

In conclusion, social control emerges when as a result of repeated social transactions between the same individuals, an individual's behavior in the presence of another individual is different from his behavior in the absence of that individual. Often such behaviors are not valued by the group or caretaker or relevant to the social transactions between the group or caretaker and the individual. They are, in a sense, social superstitions. Behavior control refers to a situation in which the characteristic behavior of an individual is under the social control of a group or caretaker and is valued by them. Such behavior has been acquired, maintained, or both through a number of different environmental events occurring in the group and during social transactions between individuals in the group. Efficient groups or caretakers can arrange for more rapid behavior control than inefficient groups. However, all groups or caretakers are somewhat inefficient because of the difficulties encountered in arranging precise control over the stimulation going on during social transactions.

The Role of Consequating Stimuli in Social Behavior

In any given social transaction speech and movement responses (operants) are more apt to possess stimulus functions for the response complexes of others than reflex activity (respondents). This is because of the manner in which operants affect the organism's environment. The classroom teacher is more apt to respond to the child's reading utterances as he continues to falter than to the changes that take place in the blood vessels of his skin (the vasomotor response) as he blushes lightly. Moreover, the consequences that occur as the individual transacts with the other person arise from the operant component of the other's response complex. Such is the case when the teacher vocally responds to John's attempt to self-correct his utterances with "That's right, John."

As we have already seen, other-presented consequences arising from a social transaction may strengthen or weaken the individual's operant behavior immediately preceding such presentations. Furthermore, other *incidental behavioral and physical events* occurring before and during such presentations, and the *physical-environmental settings* in which they occur, are either paired with, or become discriminative for, the primary forms of consequences occurring during social transactions.[4] This means that these incidental events (behavioral and physical events and the physical-environmental setting in which the social transactions occur) acquire stimulus properties as consequences somewhat comparable to those possessed by the primary form of consequences occurring during the social transaction. For example, in a classroom where the teacher makes extensive use of positive reinforcement, not only is it highly reinforcing to make correct recitations in class, but the teacher's presence and one's being in class are also reinforcing. Similarly, when extensive punishment is used (especially in the form of the presentation of aversive stimuli), the teacher and classroom become conditioned aversive stimuli. When so conditioned, these incidental events are paired with, or are discriminative for, positive reinforcement or punishment. Either way, once such a historical relationship exists, these incidental events may be used for the purposes of behavior enhancement (or strengthening) or behavior suppression (or weakening). All that is required is that these incidental events immediately follow the behavior of concern. Thus through their historical relationship to the consequating stimuli occurring during social transactions, these incidental events may also elicit positive or negative conditioned emotional responses.[5]

---

[4] The reader may find a review of the section on conditioned reinforcement in Chapter 6 helpful.

[5] Neutral stimuli may, of course, acquire eliciting stimulus functions independent of the primary consequences occurring during a social transaction. A political propagandist may pair the name of an adversary with other prepotent, eliciting stimuli in order to elicit

Table 9-3 illustrates the relationship between the primary forms of consequences occurring in somewhat commonplace social transactions, incidental behavioral or physical events occurring before or during the presentation of such consequences, and the characteristic physical-environmental settings for these transactions. For example, when the individual is presented with positive sexual reinforcers as the primary form of consequences in a social transaction, these reinforcers are apt to be preceded by instances of prolonged eye contact with another person (incidental behavioral event), to occur in the presence of certain music or perfume (incidental physical events), and to involve a car, discotheque, or bedroom (characteristic physical-environmental settings). Or when an individual is presented with the generalized positive reinforcers of approval or a smile as the primary form of consequences in the social transaction, the reinforcer may be preceded by an instance of agreement on some idea (incidental behavioral event), occur in the presence of certain persons, some of whom may possess certain physiognomic characteristics (incidental physical events), and occur in a dining area or classroom (characteristic physical-environmental setting). These illustrations are merely suggestive of the possibility that many incidental events may acquire both eliciting and consequating stimulus functions beyond those presented by others during social transactions. Of course, the individual's reinforcement history must always be taken into account, for as the reader will observe, such events may be reinforcing for some individuals and not for others, depending on whether or not (1) the individual has been presented with primary forms of consequences, such as those given in Table 9-3, and (2) such events have been paired with, or are discriminative for, consequating stimuli.

The reader will also observe that some of these events possess intrinsic consequating stimulus functions over and above those that are acquired through the processes involved in social transactions. For example, music may not only be reinforcing for an individual because in the past it has occurred before or during social transactions in which the consequences consisted of positive reinforcement, but also because it possesses properties of stimulus change.

In conclusion, it is important to emphasize that the consequences presented by others during social transactions (1) possess behavioral enhancement or suppression functions over the individual's operant behavior, (2) make the individual's behavior sensitive to a very large number of incidental behavioral and physical stimuli and physical-environmental settings, and (3) provide the basis for the characteristic conditioned emotional responses elicited by groups.

---

negative respondents in the voter. He may assert that "John Doe is a comsymp (Communist sympathizer)" so that the negative respondent elicited by the expression "comsymp" will be elicited by the name John Doe.

Table 9-3 Primary Forms of Consequences, Incidental Behavioral Events and Incidental Physical Events Apt to Occur Before or During Social Transactions and the Characteristic Physical-Environmental Settings for these Transactions.

PRIMARY FORM OF CONSEQUENCES	INCIDENTAL BEHAVIORAL EVENTS	INCIDENTAL PHYSICAL EVENTS	PHYSICAL-ENVIRONMENTAL SETTING
Positive Reinforcers			
edibles	instances of food presentation from others	clothes-dress-insignia cigarettes presence of certain people	dining area
sexual reinforcers	instances of prolonged eye contact with others	clothes-dress-insignia music perfume physiognomic characteristics of others presence of certain people	car discotheque bedroom
Generalized Positive Reinforcers			
praise	instances of attention–listening responses from others instances of prolonged eye contact with another instances of agreement on issues or ideas with another	clothes-dress-insignia cigarettes physiognomic characteristics of others presence of certain people	bedroom dining area discotheque
approval	instances of agreement on issues or ideas with another instances of shared beliefs, interests with others	physiognomic characteristics of others presence of certain people	car dining area classroom
smile(s)	instances of consensual validation	presence of certain people	dining area classroom

hug(s)	instances of task performance with others that is reinforcing or is reinforced	presence of certain people finished product of work	classroom playground work area
Aversive Stimuli			
slap(s), scowl(s), threat(s)	instances of inattention from others instances of avoidance of eye contact	presence of certain people	closet room
verbal disapproval	instances of disagreement on issues or ideas with another	presence of certain people	dining area classroom playground work area
exclusion or isolation (time-out)	instances of inattention from others instances of avoidance of eye contact instances of disagreement with another about issues or ideas instances of differences in beliefs, interests with another instances of consensual negation	physiognomic characteristics of others presence of certain people	bedroom dining area classroom playground work area
engaging in low-probability behavior (LPB)	instances of performance of tasks that have aversive stimulus properties	clothes-dress-insignia presence of certain people finished product of work	work area

The Other as a Behavior Innovator

In the course of social transactions with an individual, the other may function as a behavior innovator through the presentation of stimulation that affects the acquisition and maintenance of behavior by the individual. Such stimulation may consist of the following:

1. The other may elicit respondent behavior from the individual through the presentation of unconditioned and conditioned eliciting stimuli.

2. The other may, through prearranged positive consequation and the use of differential reinforcement and successive approximations, shape the individual's behavior or maintain satisfactory behavior through the use of contingent reinforcement.

3. The other may weaken an individual's behavior through the presentation of punishment, extinction, or time-out procedures.

4. The other may control the individual's behavior through the presentation or removal of discriminative stimuli. Such discriminative stimuli may consist of other-presented verbal instructions directed toward the individual, or other-presented vocal or motor sample performances (modeling). In the latter case, comparable performances by the individual in the presence of the discriminative stimulus are reinforced.

5. The other may engage in contingency contracts with the individual. Through the presentation of verbal instructions and response-contingent reinforcement, those engaging in such contracts specify clearly the behaviors that each person must emit as well as the form of consequation following each of these behaviors.

There are also occasions when the other significantly influences the individual's behavior in the *absence* of any *social transactions* between the individual and the other. This influence occurs in both imprinting and modeling.

IMPRINTING

The mere presence of the other during certain critical periods of development has been observed to provide that other with releasing or cue functions, in a behavioral phenomenon known as *imprinting*. If between the thirteenth and sixteenth hour of life a young duckling is exposed to a moving, clucking decoy, the duckling will, for some time thereafter, follow the decoy about whenever the decoy is in the duckling's presence (Remsay and Hess, 1963). The likelihood of such behavior is significantly decreased when exposure occurs prior to or after this period. Furthermore, the *imprinting stimulus*, whether it be an animate or inanimate object, also functions as a reinforcer. The young duckling will not only peck at a disk to bring the imprinting stimulus closer, but in its presence the duckling will emit fewer distress cries, even when confronted with a fear stimulus (Hoffman, Searle, Toffey, and Kozma, 1966). Comparable phenomena have been observed in dogs, the critical period with dogs being between 6 and 8 weeks of age (Scott, 1968).

Many observers feel that such approach behavior is quite significant in that it is a precursor for later-developing social responses. Because such imprinted approach responses seem to be so clearly associated with critical periods of development, and because they appear to occur in such a large variety of species, they have come to be regarded by many as a form of species-specific behavior, having antecedents in the phylogenetic programming of various organisms. It has not been clearly shown that such released behavior occurs in humans, although there is some evidence with respect to the occurrence of certain related social behaviors, an example of which would be fear of strangers.

Whether or not one chooses to regard such locomotor responses as walking or following after another to be phylogenetically programmed behavior, the notion that such responses are released by an imprinting stimulus would seem to be open to question. Animals who maintain a certain spatial proximity to other members of their species are more likely to receive food and remain safe from (avoid) predators, and both consequences are reinforcing. In any case two questions remain: How does any stimulus, presented during a critical period in an organism's development, become an imprinting stimulus? And why is this effect so peculiarly dependent on the age of the organism at the time the stimulus is presented? Skinner (1966) suggests that what is programmed is actually a critical period in the development of the organism, during which time the mere proximity to an imprinting stimulus is a reinforcing event. Or, perhaps, imprinted approach behaviors, such as pecking responses, are shaped by natural contingencies of reinforcement, which later serve to keep the imprinting stimulus proximal.

MODELING

The individual's behavior may also be influenced by the other when (1) the other engages in a performance as he transacts with his physical or social environment, (2) these performances are followed by consequences, and (3) the entire sequence, whether it be in real life or a filmed portrayal, is observed by the individual.[6]

Following are some situations in the natural environment in which modeling could occur. In these situations the other functions as a model, even though the other does not engage in social transactions with the individual.

[6] For additional information on the experimental procedures and findings in the study of modeling, see the classic works of Miller and Dollard (1941) and Bandura (1962, 1965).

SITUATION 1

Mother stealthily entered the kitchen and walked over to the pantry. She opened the pantry door and reached for a can of coffee. She lifted the plastic lid and took out four gum drops. As he watched his mother from a partially opened door, a smile crept across Junior's face. In the past he had searched high and low for the candy, but without success. As soon as his mother left the room, he ran over to the pantry and got a mouthful of candy for himself.

Thus Junior secretly watched his mother (the model) as she entered the kitchen, opened the pantry, then opened the can (her performance), and took some candy (self-presented strengthening consequences). All of this was discriminative for a comparable performance by Junior.

SITUATION 2

Tim Smith was waiting his turn for a job interview. He sat talking to another young man, who was also waiting for an interview. During the course of their conversation it was revealed that neither had worked before. Then the other young man was called into a nearby interview room, and Tim overheard the personnel man ask about the young man's prior work experience. Tim heard the young man reply, "Why yes, I've had several part-time jobs." A short while later the young man came out of the room smiling, indicating that he had gotten a job. When Tim was called for his interview, he gave the same answer to the personnel man's question and got himself a job also.

This situation is similar to situation 1, except that the model engages in a social rather than a physical transaction with his environment.

SITUATION 3

A college student waited politely while another student inserted a dime in an ice cream vending machine. Following the coin insertion, the student pulled the delivery lever, and nothing happened. He pulled the lever vigorously again and again, but still nothing happened. Finally, he pushed the coin return lever, but this too was out of order. Following repeated attempts to get his money back, he finally gave up and walked away. The college student who had been waiting also walked away.

In this situation the student's behavior with the ice cream vending machine was punished (through the loss of the coin, which in this case would have functioned as a positive reinforcer), and this suppressed comparable behavior in the student who was watching.

SITUATION 4

While his classmates looked on, Jimmy, a fifth-grade student, threw a spitball at the teacher. The teacher had seen him, however, and she took him firmly by the arm and led him to a corner of the room. As Jimmy crouched there before her, she shook him vigorously and said, "Never, never do that again!" Jimmy started crying. Michael, a classmate of Jimmy's, who sat next to him, had seen the whole thing. Michael began to tremble, and when the teacher wasn't looking, he hurriedly took his spitball out of his mouth and put it into his pocket.

In this situation not only was Michael's spitball throwing suppressed by his observation of the punishment his friend received, but in addition, he also showed a pattern of fear respondents.[7]

SITUATION 5

During recess Jerry, an 8-year-old boy, watched a movie on TV in which an older boy went to the teacher's desk and took a dollar from her purse. Jerry had seen his teacher's purse on the desk many times. During recess the next day Jerry did the same thing he had observed the older boy do in the TV movie.

In this situation Jerry made a comparable performance after observing a filmed presentation of a classroom theft, even though in the past, he had not committed a theft when the opportunity had presented itself.

It seems, then, that a model's performance and the consequences following it may have the following behavioral effects:

1. It may elicit in the observer a pattern of respondents comparable to those elicited in the model. Such a pattern may consist of positive or negative emotional responses.

2. It may be discriminative for a pattern of operants in the observer that are comparable to those emitted by the model. Such a pattern may consist of approach, avoidance, or escape. In some cases, it may even consist of complex chained performances not previously emitted.[8]

Whether or not observation of a model's performance and the consequences following it will have such effects depends on several factors, including:

[7] In situations such as this one a pattern of fear respondents may be elicited by the commotion going on—the cries, loud threatening remarks, foot shuffling, and so on—not simply by the model's performance and the consequences following them.

[8] As was noted in Chapter 8, there is some question as to whether or not exposure to a model's performance can lead to the acquisition in the observer of completely novel performances. It is reasonable to assume, however, that some minimal response differentiation must have preceded more complicated performances acquired in this manner.

1. The degree of response differentiation that characterizes the repertoire of the individual.

2. The degree of response differentiation characteristic of the model's performance.

3. Whether or not the individual has been reinforced in the past for emitting the same response classes as those emitted by the models—essentially discriminated operant behavior under the control of the model's performance.

4. The degree of stimulus similarity between (1) prior stimulus situations containing a reinforced model and a physical-environmental setting (in the presence of which the individual emitted performances comparable to the model that were reinforced) and (2) the present stimulus situation.

5. The deprivation state of the individual.

In conclusion, the other may function as a behavior innovator and model in the course of social transactions with the individual and in the absence of such social transactions. In the former case other- or model-presented eliciting, discriminative, or consequating stimuli may result in the individual's acquisition or maintenance of operant and respondent behavior. In the latter case, following the observation of a model's reinforced performance, the individual may show comparable respondent or operant patterns and, in some cases, relatively novel performances. Prerequisite to these modeling effects is the individual's history of response differentiation, the individual's reinforcement history for imitating a model's performance, the response differentiation characteristic of the model's performance, the stimulus similarity between past and present modeling situations, and the deprivation state of the individual. The possibility that all of these events can continuously and frequently occur in the environment of the individual makes others rather powerful agents of behavior control. This is especially true when the others consist of several persons engaging in social transactions with the individual over relatively long periods of time.

STUDY QUESTIONS

1. What are the possible behavioral effects on the individual of the stimulation arising from social transactions with others?
2. Distinguish between social control and behavior control.
3. What are the essential factors in respondent conditioning? In operant conditioning?
4. What is meant by nonprearranged pairings of stimuli? Nonprearranged consequences? What is the behavioral effect of these procedures?
5. What types of behavior may be acquired or maintained in a group?
6. Describe an interaction process unit and its function in social transactions.
7. What situation defines a social group?

8. Identify the type(s) of behavior and/or stimulus functions described in the following examples:
   a. Assisting a lady by taking her arm while one is crossing the street and conversing with her.
   b. A novocaine dental injection for killing pain.
   c. A baby cries as he smells alcohol and sees a nurse with a hypodermic syringe for an injection.
   d. As John appears at the door, he is greeted by "Hi!"
9. Describe some commonly occurring situations in which the other is paired with positive or negative eliciting stimuli.
10. Create an example of a social transaction involving one individual's verbal communication to another in which the communication contains both discriminative and consequating functions. Analyze the communicative act for both functions.
11. Why is the *total* social setting important in the analysis of social behavior?
12. What are the three criteria of the efficiency of a group in behavior control?
13. Look over the several factors affecting the efficiency of a group in behavior control. Then estimate the relative efficiency of the following groups and defend your estimates:
    a. An encounter group aimed at providing "gut level" insights into one's emotional needs.
    b. A small-parts-sorting work group paid on a piecework basis.
14. What essential condition must prevail for one's behavior to be consequated by another?
15. Describe the problems encountered in seeking control over an individual's respondent behavior and give some solutions.
16. When gross changes occur in the stimulus complex, what is the effect on behavior that has been acquired in the course of social transactions?
17. Define transituational generality.
18. Is the other more likely to respond to an individual's operant or respondent behavior? Why?
19. How may incidental behavioral and physical events, and the settings in which they occur, acquire reinforcing or aversive stimulus functions? Eliciting stimulus functions?
20. Give an example of (1) an incidental behavioral event, (2) an incidental physical event, and (3) an incidental physical setting that probably functions as
    a. a positive eliciting stimulus.   c. a positive reinforcer.
    b. a negative eliciting stimulus.   d. an aversive stimulus.
    Describe in detail how each event and setting probably acquires its stimulus functions.
21. Define a behavioral enhancement or a behavioral suppression event.
22. What kind of consequences are the following incidental behavioral events apt to be paired with or to be discriminative for:
    a. smile.   b. scowling expression.
23. What additional forms does the stimulation arising from others take that leads to the acquisition or maintenance of behavior?
24. What two conditions must prevail in order for imprinting to occur?

25. One attempts to make a doll into an imprinting stimulus by presenting it to a young dog for a 2-week period from the sixth to the eighth week of the dog's life. Describe a test to determine if the doll
   a. has become an imprinted stimulus.
   b. possesses reinforcing stimulus functions.
   c. possesses a positive eliciting stimulus function.
26. Compare modeling during social transactions aimed at acquisition of behavior in the trainee with modeling in the absence of such social transactions in terms of
   a. types of ongoing stimulus events.
   b. the recipient of the consequation.
   c. the essential role of the trainer.
27. What kind of history must one have in order for the other to serve as a model?

REFERENCES

Adams, J. S., and Romney, A. K. A functional analysis of authority. *Psychological Review*, 1959, 66, 234–251.

Azrin, N. H., and Holz, W. C. Punishment. In W. K. Honig (Ed.), *Operant behavior: Areas of research and application.* New York: Appleton-Century-Crofts, 1966.

Bales, R. F. *Interaction process analysis: A method for the study of small groups.* Reading, Mass.: Addison-Wesley, 1950.

Bandura, A. Social learning through imitation. In M. R. Jones (Ed.), *Nebraska Symposium on Motivation.* Vol. 10. Lincoln: University of Nebraska Press, 1962.

Bandura, A. Influence of model's reinforcement contingencies on the acquisition of imitative responses. *Journal of Personality and Social Psychology*, 1965, 1, 589–595.

Bandura, A., and Walters, R. H. *Social learning and personality development.* New York: Holt, Rinehart and Winston, 1963.

Berg, I. A., and Bass, B. E. *Conformity and deviation.* New York: Harper and Row, 1961.

Hoffman, H. S., Searle, J. L., Toffey, S., and Kozma, F., Jr. Behavioral control by an imprinted stimulus. *Journal of the Experimental Analysis of Behavior*, 1966, 9, 177–199.

Homans, G. C. *Social behavior: Its elementary forms.* New York: Harcourt Brace Jovanovich, 1961.

Karen, R. L., and Bower, R. C. A behavioral analysis of a social control agency: Synanon. *Journal of Research in Crime and Delinquency*, 1968, 5, 18–34.

Lindsley, O. R. Direct measurement and prosthesis of retarded behavior. *Journal of Education*, 1964, 147, 62–81.

Miller, N. E., and Dollard, J. *Social learning and imitation.* New Haven, Conn.: Yale University Press, 1941.

Remsay, A. O., and Hess, E. H. A study in imprinting. In D. E. Dulany, Jr., R. L. DeValois, D. C. Beardslee, and M. R. Winterbottom (Eds.), *Contributions to modern psychology.* (2nd ed.) New York: Oxford University Press, 1963.

Schacter, S. Deviation, rejection and communication. *Journal of Abnormal and Social Psychology,* 1951, 46, 190–207.

Scott, J. P. *Early experience and the organization of behavior.* Belmont, Calif.: Brooks/Cole, 1968.

Secord, P. F., and Backman, C. W. *Social psychology.* New York: McGraw-Hill, 1964.

Sidowski, J. B. Reward and punishment in a minimal social situation. *Journal of Experimental Psychology,* 1957, 54, 318–326.

Skinner, B. F. *Science and human behavior.* New York: Macmillan, 1953.

Skinner, B. F. The ontogeny and phylogeny of behavior. *Science,* 1966, 153, 1205–1213.

Staats, A. W., and Staats, C. K. *Complex human behavior.* New York: Holt, Rinehart and Winston, 1963.

Yablonsky, L. *The tunnel back.* New York: Macmillan, 1965.

APPLICATIONS

CHAPTER 10

SOME PROBLEM
SOCIAL BEHAVIORS

In the discussions to follow an analysis will be made of some of the behaviors that are often related to the social problems in our society. Whenever possible, the analysis will stress the importance of environmental events as antecedents to the behavior of concern, and suggestions will be made about the possibilities of finding solutions to the problem behavior through the manipulation of environmental events in what might be called *social engineering*.

COOPERATION AND COMPETITION

There are sharp differences of opinion among both laymen and specialists on the relative importance of *cooperation* and *competition* to man's survival. This problem is especially significant because it has profound implications for the design of social and political systems. As forms of operant behavior, cooperation and competition emerge from the social transactions that occur between two or more individuals. Cooperation occurs when the behavior of one individual makes a reinforcer available to another individual in the transaction and vice versa. Without this appropriate behavior, the reinforcers would not be available to either party. Such cooperative behavior is, by its nature, *other-response dependent*. Competitive behavior occurs when the behavior of only one individual is reinforced, regardless of the behavior of the others with whom the individual transacts. The availability of the reinforcer is not other-response dependent, but *individual-response dependent*.

Following are some examples of social situations in which cooperation, competition, or neither is apt to occur:

SITUATION 1

Two boys, Bill and Jim, both 5 years old, are taken to the park for the first time. They run over to the playground area and approach a teeter-totter. Each end of the teeter-totter has a seat on it, so that it controls the response class of operants of sitting down. Bill sits down at the low end of the teeter-totter and does not get a ride. Jim sits down at the high end a fraction of a second after Bill has sat down, so that on the impact of his weight with the seat, Jim starts his ride down, and Bill starts his ride up. Bill screams with delight because the ride up is very reinforcing. As the teeter-totter reaches the top of its excursion, the ride stops. Bill's weight at the top end of the teeter-totter combined with the slight upward movement produced when Jim pushes off the ground starts Jim's ascent, and he too screams with delight. In this manner the ride continues.

In this situation the reinforcing event that maintains both Bill's and Jim's behavior on the teeter-totter is the ride. Neither boy is reinforced without the cooperative behavior of the other (remaining seated on the teeter-totter), and the reinforcer is simultaneously presented to each boy. The reinforcement of riding is, in effect, cooperative-response contingent, and acquisition of this behavior is rapid.

SITUATION 2

Two boys, Joe and John, both aged seven, set up a "bicycle garage" on the corner. They charge one cent to put air in the bicycle tires of the kids in the neighborhood. Joe pushes the pump handle up and down, while John holds the pump hose nozzle against the tube valve in the tire. They take turns collecting the pennies.

In this situation both Joe and John are alternately reinforced for their cooperative behavior, in which one handles the air pump while the other holds down the pump nozzle. A brief disruption of such cooperative behavior may occur early in acquisition if one of the boys, after being paid, refuses to continue working. However, such a situation will tend, in the long run, to produce a stable pattern of cooperation.

SITUATION 3

Two 3-year-old girls, Mary and Jane, enter a playroom at a nursery school for the first time. Two large panda dolls are seated on a toy chest. As the girls run around the room, Mary notices the dolls. She screams out "Dolly! Dolly!" and runs over to grab them. Jane quickly follows suit. Mary gets there first and attempts to grab both dolls, but because of their size she is only able to grab one. Jane arrives at the toy chest and grabs the other doll. Now, each with her own dolly in hand, the girls skip around the room shouting, "Dolly! Dolly!"

This situation presents an interesting contrast. By its nature the situation is not very likely to strengthen cooperative behavior nor is it very apt to reinforce competitive behavior either. This is because both Mary and Jane were reinforced by doll possession after engaging in behavior that was not competitive in the sense that neither child had to be faster or stronger, for example, than the other to be reinforced. Nor was it necessary for the other to respond in some way *first* for either girl to be reinforced.

SITUATION 4

At a kindergarten the teacher dismisses the class for recess in the play area. All six of the boys in the class run for the swing. Johnny is the tallest and is able to run fastest, so he gets to the swing first. For the remainder of the recess period no one else is able to use the swing. The same thing happens the next day, so after Johnny has ridden on the swing for 5 minutes, the teacher goes over and eases Johnny out of the swing, saying "Okay, Johnny, now it's someone else's turn. Get off and let Jim ride. Good boy!" In this way, each child is able to get a ride on the swing during recess.

In this situation Johnny's behavior is maintained by rides on the swing, which he alone is able to enjoy. The availability of the reinforcer is not other-response dependent. Furthermore, because only one individual can ride on the swing, Johnny's competitive behavior of running to the swing first would most likely have occurred on every occasion of recess had the teacher not intervened. This is because the reinforcer of riding on the swing was initially available to only one child, then only after such behavior had occurred.

The development of cooperative or competitive behavior depends on a number of factors, including (1) the degree of deprivation of the individuals in the situation, (2) the extent to which the individuals in the situations have engaged in social transactions in the past, (3) the degree of instruction in the situation (discriminative properties of the situation, such as verbal instructions and the physical-environmental setting, that have stimulus control over previously acquired cooperative or competitive behavior), (4) the presence of a leader in the situation, who initiates the cooperative or competitive behavior, (5) the nature of the reinforcement contingency, (6) the nature of the consequences, and (7) the amount of consequences available. Some environments will strengthen cooperative behavior by their very nature and without further consequation, as when the individuals are either simultaneously or alternately reinforced for cooperation and not reinforced in the absence of it (situations 1 and 2). Some situations will strengthen competition without further consequation, as when only one occasion of reinforcement is available following the occurrence of an individual's behavior, regardless of the behavior of others (situation 4). Moreover, there may be occasions when further consequation is required (by the intervention of an individual in a superordinate position) to attenuate the effects of a history involving excessive reinforcement of competitive behavior, as when, in situation 4, the teacher, through instructions and consequation, eased Johnny out of the swing so that others could use it. Finally, when the reinforcers that are contingent on either cooperative or competitive behavior are repeatedly paired with or repeatedly discriminative for the cooperative situation (each individual is reinforced) or the competitive situation (only the one individual is reinforced, irrespective of the behavior of others), these stimulus complexes, too, will become reinforcing. The skilled athlete receives a medal not only for the fastest 100-yard dash, but also for being the only individual in first place. The winning situation consists of the medal, one winner, and a bunch of losers. After some training in such a situation, just being the winner with a bunch of losers may become reinforcing in its own right.

The enhancement or suppression of either cooperative or competitive behavior seems clearly dependent on the availability of sufficient reinforcers and the nature of the reinforcement contingency. When deprivation is high, when there is an insufficient number of reinforcers to go around (a perennial problem in society), or when the reinforcement contingency does not require cooperative behavior, competitive behavior is most likely. Even though competitive behavior is less likely when the opposite of the first two conditions prevails, cooperative behavior is not. Cooperative behavior is a special case and is especially social. It requires than an individual *not* be reinforced *except* after the occurrence of some behavior by the other and vice versa. A person planning a program of social engineering aiming at the enhancement of cooperative behavior must, therefore, take this into consideration.

AGGRESSION

To many observers, man's aggressive behavior qualifies him as the most dangerous animal "with but a thin veneer of society" controlling his aggression. Violence in the streets, wife beating, assassination, and war are but a few examples of man's aggressive nature and of society's failure to control it.

Although there has been a great deal of study of aggression, there still remains considerable confusion about its nature, because workers have included a wide range of different behaviors in their definitions of aggression and because these behaviors occur in a wide range of stimulus situations. In general, however, any behavior that results in injury to another organism or the destruction of an inanimate object is viewed as aggressive behavior.

Behaviors described as aggressive show a great deal of intraspecies generality. A classical aggressive attack pattern, called *elicited, reflexive,* or *respondent aggression,* has been reported in rats (Ulrich and Azrin, 1962). It consists of the rat's standing on its hind legs and striking and biting its victim, regardless of whether the victim is another animal or an inanimate object. This pattern of behavior, which is illustrated in Figure 10-1, is characteristically elicited by a wide range of stimuli, which may or may not have occurred during a social transaction. For example, it may be elicited by

FIGURE 10-1 Two rats showing the shock-elicited, reflexive, or respondent, aggressive pattern. From R. E. Ulrich, R. R. Hutchinson, and N. H. Azrin, Pain-elicited aggression. *Psychological Record*, 1965, **15**, 116–126. Copyright © 1965 by the Psychological Record Inc. and reproduced with permission.

strongly noxious stimuli (such as an electric shock, an air blast, heat, or tail pinching), food or morphine withdrawal, intracranial stimulation in the hypothalamus, heavy work requirements, or extinction. Comparable attack patterns have also been reported in mice, rabbits, squirrel monkeys, cats, and pigeons, to mention but a few other species. It appears that there is more interspecies variation in the response patterns than in the stimulus situations eliciting them.

Interestingly, such respondent aggression occurs more often when animals are confined to small spaces or to social situations with other animals. Respondent aggression may even displace the lever-pressing behavior that normally terminates the shock that induces the respondent aggression. Moreover, through respondent conditioning (stimulus pairing) in which, for example, the CS is a tone and the US a strong shock capable of eliciting the attack pattern, the tone itself will come to elicit the attack pattern as did the shock. In essence, the attack pattern, which is normally elicited by a variety of different stimulus events functioning as unconditioned elicitors, may also be elicited by other conditioned elicitors. This elicited, reflexive, or respondent aggression is a momentary, stereotyped pattern occurring only when the eliciting stimulus is presented.

Another type of aggression has been observed, which (1) often involves complex chains of behavior, (2) shows more intraspecies and interspecies variability than respondent aggression, and (3) is sensitive to consequences (such as food, water, or intracranial stimulation) that follow it whether or not the consequences occur in a social transaction. Such aggression is *operant aggression*. It is strengthened by positive and negative reinforcers and high-probability behavior, and weakened by extinction, punishment, time-out, and low-probability behavior. Moreover, such aggression may be controlled by stimuli that are discriminative for reinforcing events. For example, a child will punish another child who knocks down his pile of blocks, the effect of which is to terminate the other child's disruptive acts by following them with aversive consequences. The disrupted block pile, then, becomes a discriminative stimulus for punishing the other child, because the punishment terminates the other child-presented disruptive acts (knocking down the block pile when building such piles is reinforced) (Ulrich and Favell, 1969).

In rats the opportunity to kill a mouse is a reinforcer that serves to strengthen the key pressing that produces the mice (Von Hemel, 1972). What is more, the opportunity to engage in an elicited aggressive attack, following the presentation of a painful stimulus, may itself be a reinforcer. For example, when monkeys are shocked through their tails, they will bite a ball (respondent component), and when access to the ball requires pulling a chain (operant component), they will do so. Such an operant-respondent behavior chain has been reported by Azrin, Hutchinson, and McLaughlin (1965) and is illustrated in Figure 10-2.

(a)   (b)

FIGURE 10-2 An operant–respondent aggressive behavior chain. After its tail is shocked, the monkey will (a) pull the chain (the operant component), then (b) bite the ball (the respondent component). From N. H. Azrin, R. R. Hutchinson, and R. McLaughlin, The opportunity for aggression as an operant reinforcer during aversive stimulation. *Journal of the Experimental Analysis of Behavior*, 1965, 8, 171–180. Copyright © 1965 by the Society for the Experimental Analysis of Behavior, Inc., and reproduced with permission.

This distinction between respondent and operant aggression once again stresses the importance of environmental (stimulus) events in behavior. There are many observers, however, who believe that because aggression (in a more general sense) tends to be universal and to lead to the survival of a species, it must perforce have its origins in organismic states such as instinctive needs or phylogenetic programming. Frequently cited in defense of this view is the aggressive attack pattern that occurs in many species when an intruder enters an animal's territory. Tinbergen (1967) reports such an attack pattern in *The Herring Gull's World*:

> As soon as we are able to distinguish between individual gulls, we see that each pair has its own station. The birds are present there for only part of the time, and as the daily rhythm of different pairs does not exactly coincide, there appears to be less regularity in the occupation of territories than is actually the case. Also, a territory may be temporarily invaded by strangers in

the absence of the owners. As soon as the latter return, however, there is trouble. Usually the resident male (males can be distinguished from females by their larger size) walks up to the strangers in a remarkably rigid attitude. Instead of having the neck drawn in, as when at rest, he stretches it upwards and forwards, while at the same time he points his head downward. In this attitude, the tension in his neck-muscles can often be seen quite clearly, despite the thick layer of feathers covering the skin. In the highest intensity of this pose his wings are lifted a little, so that they are no longer half concealed in the supporting contour-feathers, but stand out at a little distance from his body. As we shall presently see, this is the first preparation that the gull makes for actual fighting, i.e. for delivering a blow with the wing. In this posture, the male walks with stiff steps either straight towards the intruder, or, in other cases, by a detour which seems determined by the local situation. This posture I will call the "upright threat posture"; it functions as a threat against other gulls. The human observer is so little impressed by it that he has difficulty in noticing it at all when he sees it for the first time, and he has to learn what it means; but for all herring gulls it is full of meaning and their reaction to it seems to be entirely innate. As a rule the intruders react immediately. Until then, they may have been quietly resting, but as soon as the attacker assumes the threat posture, they begin to sidle away. Usually the attacker is not satisfied by their slow preparations and he then increases the speed of his approach, lifts the wings more and more, and finally charges, half running and half flying. Once such a charge begins, it continues with increasing speed, because the avoiding movements of the intruders act as an extra stimulus to the attacking bird, and the latter's threatening approach induces increased anxiety in the intruders. Few intruders stand up to such a charge; usually they fly away, taking care not to be overtaken. Sometimes, when the intruders are familiar with the local situation, they merely run a few paces, until they are just beyond the territorial boundary, and then stop at a sufficiently safe distance. Both pursuer and pursued may then stand still for some seconds, with their powerful wings raised aloft and their necks still in the rigid threat posture, and this is one of the most wonderful sights to be seen in these fine birds.[1]

This attack pattern in defense of territory is particularly interesting because of the stimulus events that both precede and follow it. For example, an animal can recover positive reinforcers (such as his mate or food) by attacking an intruder, or he can lose them to the intruder by failure to attack. Moreover, attack of the intruder is more likely when the intruder is in the middle of the animal's territory than when the intruder is in its peri-

---

[1] Excerpted from Chapter 6, "Fighting and Threat" in *The Herring Gull's World*, by Niko Tinbergen. Garden City: Anchor Books, 1961. Revised edition copyright © 1961 by Niko Tinbergen and reproduced by permission.

meter. The presence of the intruder in the middle of an animal's territory becomes an S^D for the loss of reinforcement, and the escape or presence of the intruder on the perimeter of the territory becomes an S^D for the recovery of reinforcement. All of this seems to suggest that the attack of an intruder in the defense of territory may be affected by the events that follow the attack (positive reinforcement) and may, therefore, involve an operant behavior component. The stimulus events preceding such behavior may also have an important elicitation function. For example, the presence of an intruder may be a conditioned stimulus for food removal and, during the attack encounter, for the presentation of unconditioned eliciting stimuli of a painful or noxious sort as the intruder strikes back.

It would appear, therefore, that such attack patterns may be regarded as having both an operant and a respondent component and that the stimulus events following and preceding such attack are highly significant events. Moreover, although the respondent component of the attack pattern seems to be more reflexive in character, more stereotyped, perhaps having its base in the genetics or phylogenetic programming of the organism, there is also a significant operant component involved. What is suggested, therefore, is an alternative interpretation of the attack pattern—one that stresses the importance of environmental, rather than innate, antecedents to aggressive behavior.[2]

In man both the range of behavior characterized as aggression and the kinds of situations in which this behavior occurs are quite variable and involve complex transactions between the individual and his physical and social environment. Following are some examples of human aggression occurring both during social transactions and in their absence. As the reader will see, some forms of human aggression do not involve motor attack or injury to a victim in the physical sense of the word.[3] Also, even though the examples illustrate human analogues of *either* respondent or operant aggression, it should be remembered that the responses occurring in these situations most probably contain both respondent and operant components.

SITUATION 1

John and Mike, two nursery playmates, are playing in a sandbox. Mike strikes John with a shovel, causing him to cry. John immediately strikes

[2] Some observers go so far as to state that the expression of "instinctive aggressive needs" is essential to the well-being of the organism. A recent advocate of this view is Konrad Lorenz, who asserts that "in prehistoric times intra-specific selection bred into man a measure of aggressive drive for which in the social order of today he finds no adequate outlet." (See Lorenz, 1963, p. 243.)

[3] The earlier definition of aggression included acts that result in physical injury to a victim and excluded verbal attack. In psychological literature, however, verbal attack is most often viewed as a form of human aggression, and an example of it is presented in situation 2. The reader may wish to determine for himself the prudence of this decision, as he may find good reasons for not viewing such attack patterns as aggression.

Mike back with his fist. A few seconds later both boys quiet down and resume play.

In this situation John's attack of Mike seems to have been elicited by Mike's blow to him with the shovel.

SITUATION 2

At a party a young and pretty girl is dancing very, very close with a good-looking young man, who happens not to be her husband. As others just stare on, her husband comes out of the kitchen, and sees the couple dancing. Just then he overhears another young man say: "Man, look at her go! She's really great! I get her next before her old man comes back. He's in the kitchen boozing it up. A real clod." Suddenly, the husband begins yelling at his wife: "You no good tramp. You're a bitch in heat!" Even before she breaks contact with her dance partner, her husband grabs and forcibly pulls her away, causing her to scream out in pain.

In this situation the husband's verbal attack on his wife followed by his motor attack causes her to stop dancing in a manner that is embarrassing not only to him, but perhaps to some of the onlookers as well. Her behavior has caused others to berate him, the termination of which, is more likely following his attack. On future comparable occasions, he is more likely to control her behavior by such attacks.

SITUATION 3

A young man hides in an alley, waiting for a drunk, who he knows is carrying a large amount of money, to pass. When the drunk finally appears, the young man comes up behind him and strikes him with a karate chop to the back of the neck. The drunk falls down and moans. The young man quickly goes through his pockets, finds the money, takes it, and flees.

In this situation the aggressive attack seems to be reinforced by the money the mugger obtains from the drunk.

SITUATION 4

A young police rookie is firing a pistol at a manlike target at the Police Academy pistol range. He scores six consecutive hits on the target earning thirty points. His instructor remarks, "Good work, Jones!"

In this situation the police rookie's aiming and trigger squeezing are followed by points and praise presented by the Police Academy instructor. Of course, such behavior within the context of the Police Academy firing range does not injure a person. However, generalization of this behavior to the environment of the patrolman's beat, where a person could be injured, seems likely.

SITUATION 5

An ICBM combat team sits at their controls, waiting for the final order to launch the fourteen Polaris missiles that are carried aboard their submarine. Finally, they hear the captain's voice: "..5 ..4 ..3 ..2 ..1 .. Fire!" Given the command to fire, Chief Petty Officer Roberts pushes the red button on his console, thereby launching all fourteen missiles against the enemy.

This situation illustrates nicely how human aggressive behavior in modern technological society seems to be quite different from the classical elicited aggression or the operant aggression in which an attack is made on a victim with whom the individual transacts socially. Petty Officer Roberts' red-button-pushing response is the result of a social transaction between himself and his captain. The victims of his attack are not directly involved in the social transaction, nor are they even nearby.

From these examples it seems clear that, from the point of view of the response events involved, human aggression is seldom similar to the pattern of elicited or respondent aggression observed in lower animals. The one example in which the response complex was similar to that observed in respondent aggression was that described in situation 1, and this pattern of direct, retaliatory physical attack is more likely in children than in adults. Perhaps the reason for this is that adults seldom present such strong eliciting stimuli to each other. Furthermore through social training and training by the physical environment, the attack pattern takes the form, either motor or verbal, that is characteristic of the class and culture of the verbal community.[4] The other illustrations seem to involve protean response classes, some of which are chained complex performances with a history of shaping. From the point of view of the stimulus events involved, the possibility exists that noxious or painful stimuli, extinction, or food removal may elicit respondent aggression in naïve humans, possibly young children or perhaps teen-agers.[5] Moreover, the stimulus events or consequences (positive or negative reinforcers, aversive stimuli, and the like) occurring after the emission of

---

[4] In middle-class society parents who wish their children to learn to "turn the other cheek" may, by various means, suppress the sort of retaliatory attack behavior described in situation 1.

[5] Kelly and Hake (1970) report that human Ss from 14 to 18 years of age struck (forcibly punched) a rubber pad far more often when the monetary payoff for lever pressing ceased (extinction) and when the punching response, an alternate response to button pressing, turned off a noise.

operant aggression appear to affect it. Then, too, aggression may be more frequent when, during a transaction, stimuli are presented that are discriminative for it. There are four major classes of such discriminative stimuli.

First, there are *weapons* that have stimulus control over attack operants. Young (preschool) children are often given toy weapons, such as cap guns and rifles (which often possess remarkable authenticity), knives, and the like, and often receive instruction in their use. Furthermore, a lively game of cops and robbers or cowboys and Indians in which a child is able to shoot down his adversary first is an occasion for considerable social reinforcement. The presence and handling of the weapon thus becomes a discriminative stimulus for this reinforcement.

Second, there are *victims* of prior aggressive transactions who are "safe" (nonpunishing or nonretaliatory) and against whom aggression is reinforced, thus making the presence of such a victim a discriminative stimulus for attack.

Third, there is exposure to the aggressive performances of others, as real-life or filmed *models*, who are themselves reinforced for aggression. The stimulus functions of such models were described earlier.

Fourth, there is the *verbal attack behavior* of the individual himself that often precedes the motor attack of a victim. When such verbal then motor attack sequences are reinforced, the verbal attack becomes a discriminative stimulus for the motor attack. For example, just before a child strikes another child (motor aggression), he may say, "You're a rat" (verbal aggression).

Aggression in either form, respondent or operant, may *generalize* to other stimulus situations involving social or nonsocial transactions with the environment.

As in the case of cooperation and competition, environments differ with respect to the likelihood of their producing aggression. One would expect that in environments where there is chronic food deprivation and numerous painful stimuli there would be a greater incidence of elicited aggression. Similarly, one would also expect that when environments in which there is chronic food deprivation provide positive reinforcements for aggressive attack, there would be greater incidence of operant aggression, perhaps even among large numbers of individuals, as a form of violent revolution. Although such a revolution is a complex event with complex causes, it is often marked by individual acts of aggression (injury of others) and does, therefore, involve social transactions between an aggressor and a victim. It has even been suggested that "systemic frustration," in which the magnitude of various deprivation states exceeded the availability of reinforcers appropriate to them, was an important factor, among others, in the French Revolution of 1789, the American Civil War of 1861, the Nazi Revolution of 1933, the black revolution in America in the 1960s, and even the student rebellions of the 1950s and 1960s (Davies, 1969).

It has also been observed that there is an increase in violence and aggression following a decline in political or socioeconomic "satisfactions" (a decrease in the availability of reinforcers) when this decline was preceded by an improving situation. This has led some observers, particularly those favoring the S-O-R, or three-stage, model, to introduce another set of causes of behavior in the form of intrapsychic states or events—for example, to postulate that expectation is an important factor in the occurrence of riots, assassinations, wars, and other large-scale forms of aggression (Davies, 1969; Feierabend, Feierabend, and Nesvold, 1969). From the point of view of behavior theory, however, such expectations may be the result of any one or more of the following environmental events, which are apt to precede mass aggression.

First, significant numbers of individuals may engage in aggression because they receive verbal instructions in real or canned (TV or filmed) presentations from others, usually leaders of various political, social, or religious groups. For example, such a presentation could take the form of "The only way to bring about a change in the Establishment is through revolution and, mark my words, as long as the military is in power, blood must be and will be shed! Their blood, not ours! Shoot them! Bomb them! Attack them! Now!"

Second, the presentations of others may be discriminative stimuli when the others, as models, are reinforced. For example, an individual may see a looter knock down a storekeeper and successfully walk off with the merchandise, and then the individual may follow suit.

Third, through reinforcer sampling the individual may be briefly exposed to reinforcers not ordinarily available, so that when his behavior is subsequently reinforced, he shows increased sensitivity to them. Thus the peasant revolutionary who, because of a successful counterattack by the Federales, spends only one night in the plantation owner's sumptuous house later fights desperately to gain it back.

Fourth, a loss of satisfaction may be somewhat analogous to being placed on an extinction schedule in the sense that an individual's behavior normally producing reinforcements no longer does so to the same degree that it did before. This, as we have already seen, induces increased variability in behavior, intensification of behavior, emotional behavior, and in the extreme, aggression.

Fifth, although loss of satisfaction may undoubtedly occur and be related to the occurrence of violence, many individuals may have never shared in the satisfactions intended for them (because of the manner in which they are distributed), and thus when violence occurs, it may be more the result of systemic frustration (chronic deprivation) than of expectation (being on extinction).

Sixth, some governments may be more likely to engage in retaliatory, provocative acts during times of social change, even though such times may be, because of increased availability of reinforcers, "good times." Thus although in the United States desegregation policies and the war on poverty may actually give black Americans a better life, in individual cases black leaders and even ordinary black citizens may be subject to greater harassment from the government (that is, the police, FBI, and so on), the effect of which is to stimulate counter-aggression.

Finally, the physical and social events marking a period of decline can induce aggression because they may be discriminative for even more deprivation in the future, because this has been the case in the past. For example, a food shortage now (following a period of greater abundance) may mark an even greater food shortage later on, perhaps because of a widespread and continuing crop failure—something that the individual has gone through before.

It would seem, then, that deprivation states may interact in a complex way with other environmental events. Although one can perhaps predict greater aggression under various conditions of deprivation, such a conclusion only seems reasonable under the assumption that the organism is being subjected to deprivation levels that are not incapacitating and contingencies that are relatively simple—for example, a single schedule. As we have already seen, the stimulation that ordinarily goes on during social transactions involves concurrent contingencies. This means that although aggression is often preceded by noxious stimulation or followed by positive reinforcements, it may also be followed by aversive consequences or nonreinforcement, both of which tend to have weakening effects on aggressive behavior.

The control of aggression is a formidable problem, since it requires arranging an environment in which eliciting stimuli occur infrequently and are of minimal magnitude. This is, perhaps, easier to arrange in the physical than the social environment. However, even though many of the deprivations and formerly noxious stimuli have been reduced in the modern industrial states, many are still with us. However, there is some evidence that the frequency of elicited (shock-induced) aggression can be decreased by following the attack pattern with weakening consequences (for example, electric shock) (Azrin, 1970).

Although operant aggression may not be reinforced by unconditioned reinforcers as it was formerly, it is still often followed by powerful reinforcing social consequences. Training programs such as those in the armed forces make extensive use of various procedures for the acquisition and maintenance of operant behaviors characteristic of modern warfare. (See Chapter 9 for a review of these procedures.) Trainees in such programs who are unwilling to submit to the procedures of acquisition are often dealt with harshly through the presentation of punishment, both in the service and out of it. Many of the performances essential to the development of the necessary repertoires are acquired early in the trainee's life. Toy guns, grenades, rocket launchers, and the like all possess such similarity to the actual weapons that the skills acquired in their manipulation easily generalize to many of the skills required in training and combat situations. Moreover, it is not uncommon for some parents to reinforce operant aggression when a child "stands up for his rights" and to punish him when he fails to do so.

Still others assume that man possesses aggressive energy that must be drained off through aggressive acts that serve as a catharsis. This catharsis may take any one of several forms. It may merely involve a verbal attack involving name calling, such as "I hate you, you bastard!" It may involve a motor attack of the victim or of a victim surrogate, as when, for example, a child in the course of play therapy is given a doll to strike. It may and often does involve both verbal and motor components, and the verbal attack (which typically begins before or precedes the motor attack) becomes discriminative for the motor attack.

Attempts to achieve a catharsis are sometimes made by exposing a child to the aggressive performances of a model. What is unfortunate about this is that when parents condone aggression as a form of catharsis, they are, at the very least, following aggression with nonreinforcement (thereby allowing it to be maintained, at least occasionally, by other possible natural contingencies) or, at the very most, encouraging it (as when they give the child verbal instructions to "get it off his chest" and, when he does, reinforce his behavior with the remark: "Yes, Yes, dear. I understand how you feel"). Although such training may have as its primary focus the child's verbal attack behavior, it may strengthen a child's motor aggression under certain conditions. It may do so when the child's verbal aggression is discriminative for his motor aggression or when a child's verbal and motor attack behavior are both members of the same response class (at one time or another they were concurrent and were followed by the same reinforcing consequences) (Lovaas, 1961). All this suggests that parents who arrange for a cartharsis to reduce a child's aggressive energy may actually intensify it.[6]

The only way to control aggression is to make sure it is followed by weakening rather than strengthening consequences and that, whenever possible, discriminative stimuli controlling aggressive operants are eliminated from the environment. These include weapons, safe victims, and the individual's own verbal attack behavior.[7]

---

[6] Mallick and McCandless (1966) found that giving third graders an opportunity for a catharsis following exposure to either frustration or nonfrustration, which was ostensibly presented by another child, intensified aggressive speech and did not significantly reduce motor attack of the frustrater. Interestingly, what did reduce the child's aggression was a "social interpretative talk" (verbal instruction) between the investigator and the child, which gave a reasonable explanation for the behavior of the other child, the frustrater.

[7] This has interesting implications for a therapy program. Unlike traditional therapeutic approaches, in such a program someone whose problem is engaging in the verbal attack of others would not be encouraged to do so.

PREJUDICE

Many observers believe that the social phenomenon known as prejudice underlies the interpersonal conflict that occurs between members of various religious and ethnic groups, social classes, and even age groupings (the so-called generation gap). Then, too, prejudice often interferes with the adoption of a social invention. Ironically, the prejudiced person may be prevented from enjoying the benefits of such inventions because of his own prejudice. For example, a farmer may not adopt new techniques of agriculture because he refuses to associate with the "foreigner" agricultural agent from whom such knowledge is available.

Broadly stated, prejudice occurs when an individual shows positive or negative behavior toward a person, an object, or an event with which he has had little or no direct experience. Prejudice may be viewed from two aspects: (1) from the standpoint of the *stimulus properties or functions* of the *things* or *entities* involved and (2) from the standpoint of the *types of response complexes* that characterize the behavior of the prejudiced person.

Stimulus Characteristics and Stimulus Functions of the Objects of Prejudice

It will be recalled that the consequating stimuli occurring during social transactions between an individual and other persons give the others either eliciting or discriminative stimulus functions or both. The objects or events present or occurring during the transaction also acquire such stimulus functions. (See Chapter 9.) The particular characteristics of a person, object, or event that acquire these stimulus functions are variable and depend on two factors: (1) the nature of the entities themselves and (2) the cultural and social class characteristics of the verbal community.

Even though one may be prejudiced for or against something, this discussion will primarily deal with prejudice directed at others who are members of racial or ethnic minorities. This emphasis seems reasonable, since the majority of behavioral scientists regard prejudice against racial and ethnic minorities as a chronic social problem. The analysis to follow applies equally to the obverse of the situation. For example, black militants who exclude white students from their dormitories or from black studies classes have acquired their behavior through the same basic behavioral processes as prejudiced whites.

The following characteristics of a person acquire stimulus functions in prejudiced behavior:

1. The person's physiognomy—his hair color, texture, and style; nose shape; head shape; body build; skin color; and so on.

2. The person's behavior—his speech content and dialect, gestural mannerisms, ritualized behavior, and practices.

3. Symbols—insignia, ornaments, and names.

Certain of these characteristics may be combined to form a stimulus class that is an exaggeration or caricature called a stereotype. For example, one stereotype of the black American is that of the militant revolutionary and includes kinky, and long hair, worn in an Afro haircut, dark skin (physiognomic characteristics); non-Southern dialect, speech content showing hatred for whitey (behavioral characteristic); and displaying the black nationalist flag (symbolic characteristic). Still another stereotype of the black American may consist of physiognomic, behavioral, and symbolic characteristics of the Uncle Tom, including kinky, close-cut hair, dark skin, broad nose; Southern dialect, speech content showing deference to whites, ambling gait; the name "boy" or surnames like Washington, Jones, or Lincoln. Any of these characteristics or combinations of them can possess stimulus functions in prejudice. A comparable analysis could be made of the stimulus characteristic of other stereotypes such as that of the Chicano, the hippie, or the Catholic.[8]

Two features of the preceding analysis constitute the defining characteristics of prejudice. First, the persons, objects, or events that belong to a stimulus class which form a stereotype, *need not* and *frequently do not* possess all of the characteristics of that stimulus class. For example, not all black Americans speak with a Southern dialect or have dark skin. Second the stimulus functions may be acquired in the *absence of or under conditions of minimal social transactions between the prejudiced individual and those forming the stimulus class.* For example, many white Americans have never actually engaged in social transactions with black Americans, and even those who have may have had only a few transactions.

Stated behaviorally, then, prejudice occurs when an entity belongs to a stimulus class of persons, objects, or events having eliciting or discriminative stimulus functions for positive or negative behaviors, when such behaviors were acquired in the absence of or with minimal transactions between the individual and the entity.

Attitudes, Beliefs, and Actions as Forms of Prejudice

Like other forms of behavior, the response complexes of which prejudice consists contain respondent and operant components. Traditionally, however, investigators have chosen to observe prejudice primarily through the study

---

[8] A similar analysis could be made for other entities such as rock concerts and welfare programs, since they, too, acquire important stimulus functions over the behavior of the prejudiced.

of the individual's attitudes and beliefs, as they are revealed by his verbal reports. Secondarily, investigators have studied the individual's actions as revealed by his locomotor behavior in the presence of the persons, objects, or events against which he is prejudiced.

When an individual makes positive or negative evaluative remarks about something, these remarks are often regarded as the *overt manifestation* of an underlying causal (antecedent) intrapsychic state or event called an attitude.

This attitude, as a mental state or event, possesses three essential components: (1) an *affective* component, which is a pattern of positive or negative respondents elicited by the entity, (2) a *cognitive* component, which consists of the individual's *ideas* about the entity, and (3) a *motivational,* or *action tendency,* component, which is said to *direct* the individual's behavior toward the entity.

Evidence for the presence of attitudes is generally *inferred* from the verbal behavior of the individual. For example, when asked the question "How do you feel about the Jews?" an individual may assert: "I hate the damn Jews and 'Commies'! They're one and the same. I'd like to put them all in jail before they ruin the country." Such a statement provides us with an operational definition of that individual's attitude toward Jews and Communists, and presumably it contains elements (the form and intensity of the words used and the syntactical relationships between those words) from which the characteristics of the attitudes can be inferred. The expression "I hate the damn Jews and 'Commies'!" suggests that the remark was made with a certain degree of intensity, reflecting the negative affective (respondent) component; "They're one and the same" and "before they ruin the country" reflect the cognitive component; and "I'd like to put them all in jail" describes the motivational or action tendency component.

For many psychologists who adopt the S-O-R, or three-stage, model, the attitude is a key explanatory organismic concept. They believe that a person's attitudes direct his behavior toward entities in a consistent manner. Such *attitude-directed consistency* would consist of showing verbal and motor behaviors of comparable content and intensity. For example, the statement "I hate the Jews and 'Commies'! . . . I'd like to put them all in jail before they ruin the country" not only expresses the individual's negative attitude toward Jews, but would, it is assumed, also be accompanied by motor operants consistent with such remarks. For example, a person with a strongly negative attitude would be expected during a social revolution to join a group that would go out and actually round up Jews and Communists and put them in jail. He would also be expected to vote for legislation that would authorize such behavior. It is also believed by those who employ the concept of attitudes, that attitudes possess extensive *transituational generality.* That is, a person's attitude would direct his verbal and motor behavior toward an entity in a similar manner in all kinds of different situations relating to the entity. Not only would the individual make such remarks about Jews and Communists to the pollster, but he would also make them to his wife, his minister, and his employer.

From the point of view of behavior theory, however, whether or not one would show such consistency in his verbal and motor behavior toward something is a matter of his reinforcement history. As we saw in the discussion of aggression, if the individual's verbal behavior is discriminative for his motor behavior or if his verbal behavior and his motor behavior are members of the same response class, he will show consistency. However, individuals are frequently trained to be inconsistent. For example, if a boy who is a member of a minority group arrives in the neighborhood, a child living in the neighborhood may receive intensive training, in which he is berated (punished) for publicly saying, "I hate him," praised (reinforced) for saying nice things about him, and punished for actually playing with him. Such training cannot help but lead to the acquisition of verbal behaviors that are publicly acceptable but essentially inconsistent with the child's motor behavior.

Of course, there are occasions when an individual's verbal and motor behaviors *are* consistent, as when, for example, a Caucasian who is asked to make a donation to the Black Panthers replies, "I am sympathetic with their aims," and at the same time gives the Black Panther representative five dollars. The verbal and motor components of the man's behavior are members of the same response class, are consistent, and have comparable content and intensity. It is quite possible, also, that if a white person had solicited funds from him, his response would be of comparable content and intensity and, therefore, show transituational generality. Whether or not one would wish to describe him as having a positive attitude toward the Black Panthers would depend entirely on the utility of doing so. Such descriptions, however, should describe *all* of his behavior toward the Black Panthers both at any given time and over time, and in different situations.

A classic study conducted from 1930 to 1932 nicely illustrates the problem:

Over a 2-year period a well-known sociologist, R. T. La Piere, traveled extensively across the United States, east and west, north and south, covering over 10,000 miles. He was accompanied by a young, foreign-born, Chinese couple, who were students. They stopped at 66 hotels, auto camps, and tourist homes and 184 restaurants. At each stop the Chinese couple made the initial contact with the staff of these establishments, while the sociologist busied himself with the luggage outside. A record was kept of the reception the Chinese couple received at each place, and it revealed the following:

1. Out of the 184 eating establishments, there were only 5 "hesitant receptions" and 1 "definitely though temporarily embarrassing" reception. In all others contacts were judged to involve ordinary or more than ordinary consideration.

2. Out of 66 housing establishments, there was only 1 refusal, 4 "hesitant receptions," and 1 "definitely though temporarily embarrassing reception." All others were judged to involve ordinary consideration.

Six months later a letter, containing one of two forms of a questionnaire, was sent to these establishments. In one form the question "Will you accept members of the Chinese race as guests in your establishment?" was asked (a measure of management's attitude toward the Chinese). In the other form the same question was asked repeatedly and included in addition to the Chinese, Germans, French, Japanese, Russians, Armenians, Jews, Negroes, Italians, and Indians. As a control, 32 hotels and 96 restaurants that had *not* been visited but were in areas comparable to those that had been were also polled.

Ninety-one percent of the housing establishments and 92 percent of the eating establishments answered No to the question of whether or not they would give service to the Chinese race. Refusals were just as frequent among those establishments receiving the alternative form of the questionnaire, and they were as frequent among those that had been visited as they were among those that had not been visited.

La Piere concluded that the behavior of others toward the Chinese was primarily determined by such things as the quality and condition of the clothing worn by the Chinese, the quality of their luggage, their cleanliness and neatness, their unaccented English, and their genial smile.

There are two things that seem particularly significant about this study. First, it showed that there was a significant disparity between the attitudinal measure (the stated refusal in the questionnaire to provide service to members of the Chinese race) and the action measure (the acceptance of the Chinese as guests in both the eating and housing establishments). Second, the social transactions taking place between the Chinese couple and those serving them seemed to have a powerful effect on the behavior of those who may have been prejudiced. Another way to state the problem of the relationship between attitude and action is this: Is it possible, by means of verbal instructions given to the individual (the questionnaire or interview presentaton), to distill and summarize the stimulus presentations that can *actually* occur *during* transactions between the individual and the entity toward which prejudice exists? Or can we assume that the question "Will you accept members of the Chinese race as guests in your establishment?" possesses the same discriminative properties as the Chinese couple in person does (for example, their Oriental but neat appearance, their unaccented English, their quality luggage, and their friendly, smiling manner). The answer seems to be No. Moreover, even if the question did possess the same discriminative properties as the in-person presentations, the evidence suggests that the consequating stimuli—the apparently friendly response-contingent reinforcement (smiles) presented by the Chinese couple during their social transactions with hesistant (prejudiced?) individuals—changed the couple's discriminative properties.[9]

What this suggests is that attitudinal measures of prejudice, through the use of questionnaires and interview investigative techniques, deal with the individual's verbal behavior and are, therefore, most likely affected by audience control. (See Chapter 7.) Although it is probably less expensive and more convenient to prepare, administer, and score questionnaires than it is to study intensively the individual's day-to-day verbal *and* motor behavior toward things in various natural settings, there is the possibility that even though an observer has a knowledge of an individual's attitude, he will still not be able to predict the individual's actions.[10, 11]

The question seems to be whether or not it is possible to reduce complex social situations to a form that would be appropriate for questionnaire and interview investigative procedures. One need also ask whether an individual having *no previous experience* with an entity and *no special training* in reporting or predicting *his own behavior* toward that entity in *various situations* is capable of predicting his behavior.[12] In short, the usefulness and reliability of attitudes as an explanatory concept in psychology would seem to be questionable.

Finally, when an individual makes remarks with content that is descriptive of the characteristics of a person, an object, or an event, such verbal behavior is generally referred to as the expression (overt manifestation) of beliefs. Such beliefs are generally considered to be devoid of any affective or emotional content and, according to one popular view, are said to reflect the cognitive component of an individual's attitude. Beliefs are regarded by many as also having a *directive* function over behavior, and for this reason their study and analysis involves problems that are comparable to those encountered in the study of attitudes.

[9] It can be argued, of course, that the individuals refusing service to the Chinese race in the questionnaire measure may not have been the people with whom the couple engaged in transactions. This may certainly have been true of some of the contacts. It's unlikely, however, that the couple would have missed contact with large numbers of those who later replied to the mailed questionnaire or that the couple contacted individuals who were not aware of management's policies concerning service to members of the Chinese race.

[10] In order to make such predictions, observers using the three-stage model would assert that behavior is also a function of certain other antecedents (that is, they would use "if . . . then" statements), including such intrapsychic states as the individual's perception of the situation and his needs.

[11] For interesting reviews on attitudes and action, see Festinger (1964) and Wicker (1969).

[12] Such training would consist of providing the individual with positive reinforcement for accurate reports of his behavior in the presence of the entity.

The Acquisition of Prejudice

Some of the essential elements and procedures involved in the acquisition and maintenance of prejudice behaviors have already been presented on pages 221–223. However, there are some additional considerations.

Any number of individuals acquire their prejudices through limited or minimal, but often intense, social interactions with others who are members of racial or ethnic minorities. Such transactions seem typically to consist of other-presented stimulus complexes consisting of predominantly negative-eliciting or -consequating stimuli, as when, for example, a child is physically attacked and made to suffer injuries at the hands of another child who belongs to a minority group. The following account illustrates such a situation:

A young Jewish boy, who later became a successful writer and passionate advocate of desegregation and assimilation, was born and raised in the 1930s in Brooklyn in a community made up mostly of Jews, Italians, and Negroes. In school the teachers regarded the Jewish children as the most intelligent and the best students. Physical conflict seldom occurred between the Jewish and Italian children, although it was common between the Jewish and Negro children. The Negro children almost always won such encounters, and as the writer matured, he came to dread even the sight of a group of Negroes on the streets. Although he presents a number of accounts of these encounters, the following narrative seems to best illustrate how unpleasant they must have been:

The athletic meet takes place in a city-owned stadium far from the school. It is an important event to which a whole day is given over. The winners are to get those precious little medallions stamped with the New York City emblem that can be screwed into a belt and that prove the wearer to be a distinguished personage. I am a fast runner, and so I am assigned the position of anchor man on my class's team in the relay race. There are three other seventh-grade teams in the race, two of them all Negro, as ours is all white. One of the all-Negro teams is very tall—their anchor man waiting silently next to me on the line looks years older than I am, and I do not recognize him. He is the first to get the baton and crosses the finishing line in a walk. Our team comes in second, but a few minutes later we are declared the winners, for it has been discovered that the anchor man on the first-place team is not a member of the class. We are awarded the medallions, and the following day our home-room teacher makes a speech about how proud she is of us for being superior athletes as well as superior students. We want to believe that we deserve the praise, but we know that we could not have won even if the other class had not cheated.

That afternoon, walking home, I am waylaid and surrounded by five Negroes, among whom is the anchor man of the disqualified team. "Gimme my medal, mo'f———r," he grunts. I do not have it with me and I tell him so. "Anyway, it ain't yours," I say foolishly. He calls me a liar on both counts and pushes me up against the wall on which we sometimes play handball. "Gimme my mo'f——n' medal," he says again. I repeat that I have left it home. "Le's search the li'l mo'f——r," one of them suggests, "he prolly got it hid in his mo'f——n' *pants.*" My panic is now unmanageable. (How many times had I been surrounded like this and asked in soft tones, "len' me a nickel, boy." How many times had I been called a liar for pleading poverty and pushed around, or searched, or beaten up, unless there happened to be someone in the marauding gang like Carl [a Negro school chum] who liked me across that enormous divide of hatred and who would therefore say, "Aaah, c'mon, le's git someone else, this boy ain't got no money on 'im.") I scream at them through tears of rage and self-contempt, "Keep your f——n' filthy lousy black hands offa me! I swear I'll get the cops." This is all they need to hear, and the five of them set upon me. They bang me around, mostly in the stomach and on the arms and shoulders, and when several adults loitering near the candy store down the block notice what is going on and begin to shout, they run off and away.

I do not tell my parents about the incident. My teammates, who have also been waylaid, each by a gang led by his opposite number from the disqualified team, have had their medallions taken from them, and they never squeal either. For days, I walk home in terror, expecting to be caught again, but nothing happens. The medallion is put away into a drawer, never to be worn by anyone.[13]

There are, of course, a large number of individuals who acquire their prejudices *without* having engaged in social transactions with members of racial or ethnic minorities. In this case the acquisition and maintenance of prejudiced behavior may be seen to emerge from the social transactions that occur between the individual and those persons who function as behavior models and behavior innovators: his immediate peers, his caretakers, and their symbolic representations in films, television, and other communications media.

Individuals may also be exposed to printed or graphic communications media in which racial and ethnic stimuli, such as names, linguistic habits, gestures, and physiognomic characteristics, are paired with prepotent elicitors of negative respondents, such as certain words (*dirty, dishonest, violent*) or pictorial representation (of, for example, individuals engaged in tabooed acts or atrocities). Following the individual's exposure to such presentations, racial and ethnic stimuli may come to elicit negative conditioned emotional responses. Such acquisition occurs in the absence of social transactions between the individual and others belonging to racial and ethnic minorities.

Finally, the acquisition of prejudice as a form of discriminated operant

[13] Reprinted with the permission of Farrar, Straus and Giroux, Inc., from *Doings and Undoings* by Norman Podhoretz, pp. 359–360, copyright © 1963 by Norman Podhoretz.

behavior is a two-stage process. First, avoidance, escape, or attack behavior is differentiated early in life through transactions with one's physical and social environment. Such transactions normally involve punishment or aversive stimulation usually unrelated to the stimulation arising from persons in the racial and ethnic minorities. Second, these differentiated operants are hooked to the stimuli characteristic of persons from minority groups, through the behavioral processes of (1) operant discrimination or (2) generalization of discriminated operant behavior. In this situation, avoidance, escape, or attack behavior in the presence of stimuli characteristic of racial or ethnic minorities are followed by other-presented strengthening consequences. Such stimuli may be the object itself (a person from a minority group) or its symbolic representation. For example, a child may be praised for adding his verbal attack to a conversation in which his parents are discussing Negroes, or he may be punished for similar remarks at another time, say, when his parents are discussing whites. In the second case the discriminated operant behavior is already part of the individual's repertoire, but comes under the control of new stimuli, characteristic of racial or ethnic minorities, that control the escape or avoidance behavior, as when a child not only avoids playing with Negroes, but also avoids playing with Mexican-Americans because of the relative darkness of their skin.

Although there is a widely held belief among both laymen and some professionals that prejudice arises out of some innate tendency to like and be conscious of one's own kind and to dislike those of another kind,[14] prejudice will not occur in the absence of appropriate training. The response complexes characteristic of an individual's prejudiced behavior depend on the peculiarities of his verbal community. Some individuals may have repertoires consisting of discriminated avoidance behavior, feelings of dislike, and extensive verbal expressions with content that is descriptive of the characteristics of persons in minority groups. Other individuals may show more positive behaviors and still others may possess repertoires that consist of a combination of positive and negative behaviors.

Following are some examples of situations involving prejudice:

[14] One psychologist who is an advocate of this view is D. O. Hebb (1966), who asserts that

prejudice can spring up where there has been no occasion for learning, and the learning, when the prejudice is taught, occurs with extraordinary ease. An essential component in prejudice is the emotional reaction of human beings to the strange, to what is the same and yet different, to the thing that can cause a conflict of ideals [A textbook of psychology. (2nd ed.) Philadelphia: Saunders, p. 245.]

There is, of course, considerable evidence of fear of strangers in young children. However, the child may fear anyone who is physiognomically different from the child's caretaker as well as any novel or rapidly approaching stimulus. Moreover, such fear may not occur when the child is exposed early in life to strangers, all of which seems to make this view questionable.

SITUATION 1

In a lower middle-class white neighborhood, a pollster asked the owner of an apartment house the following question: "Do you believe that blacks are less desirable as tenants than whites?" The owner replied: "Why, of course not. Some of my best friends are Negroes. They're my kind of people." A moment later a black man, responding to the FOR RENT sign on the building, asked if he could see the vacancy. The landlord pointed to the pollster, who was driving off, and said; "I'm sorry, but I've just rented the apartment to that gentleman."

This situation provides a good illustration of an individual whose repertoire consists of both positive and negative behaviors. The landlord's behavior in front of the pollster would seem to indicate a positive attitude toward black Americans ("Some of my best friends are Negroes"), but a moment later his behavior in a social transaction with the black apartment hunter suggests just the opposite ("I'm sorry, but I've just rented the apartment to that gentleman"). This disparity in the landlord's behavior reflects a history of training, especially with respect to the verbal operant described earlier as the audience control response.

SITUATION 2

In a small Southern town the local board of education refused for the third time to comply with federal directives for racial integration in the public schools. When asked to comment on the board's decision during a TV news interview, the mayor stated: "I'm glad they did that. Everybody's happy about it, especially the Nigras. Anybody with common sense knows that people—and especially the Nigras—are happier with their own kind."

This situation is illustrative of a belief, or verbal behavior, that describes the characteristics of the Negro. The mayor's remarks are entirely suppositional in character. Nevertheless, because of his position in the body politic of the town, his statements become particularly significant, because they may function as verbal instructions for many of the townspeople hearing them.

SITUATION 3

Once again each member of the executive committee of an exclusive country club raised his hand in support of a resolution that would exclude Jews, Italians, Mexican-Americans, blacks, Orientals, and Indians from membership in the club.

SITUATION 4

A husband gave his wife the guest list for their New Year's Eve party. Among the names on his list was that of Jim McNeil, a black colleague of his. Some time later the husband noticed that McNeil's name had been deleted from the list. When he questioned his wife regarding this matter, she replied: "It wouldn't bother *me* if he came, but the other guests might be offended." The husband replied: "You're full of baloney. Invite him!" She did.

Situation 3 and situation 4 are quite similar in that both illustrate avoidance of individuals in minority groups. (Raising one's hand is essentially the same type of response as crossing a name from a guest list.) However, the two situations differ significantly in other respects. In situation 3, when each member of the executive committee showed avoidance behavior by raising his hand in support of the resolution, he also reinforced the other members of the group, who were showing the same behavior (by agreeing with them). In situation 4 the husband and wife disagreed, causing him to change her behavior. He did this in two ways. First he followed her remark ("It wouldn't bother *me*, but the other guests might be offended") with aversive stimulation ("You're full of baloney"). Second, he modified her motor behavior (crossing McNeil's name from the guest list) through the use of verbal instructions ("Invite him!").

In conclusion, an interesting comment can be made about the explanations individuals give following the emission of an act for which they receive other-presented punishment (for example, the wife's explanation for not inviting her husband's black friend to the party). Often, the other will attempt to modify the behavior of those in his charge through a combination of verbal instructions and aversive stimulation. For example, a mother, in the course of scolding her child, may yell or threaten the child and instruct him to give a reason for his bad conduct. Frequently, giving a reason—whether it is the real reason or not—may terminate the parent's aversive display and strengthen the reason-giving behavior. Under such conditions it does not matter whether or not the child can actually verbalize the contingencies that maintain his behavior; it is his reason-giving behavior that controls the behavior of the caretaker. Often, too, the caretaker may assert that if her charge comes clean, he will be less apt to engage in the bad behavior again.

A Program for the Elimination of Prejudice

Ideally a program for the elimination of prejudice in a society would include the following:

1. Other-presented behavior suppression procedures (that is, extinction, punishment, time-out, engaging in low-probability behavior) would be used when the individual transacts with others and whenever he verbalizes expressions of dislike or erroneous, unsupported statements concerning the nature of minority groups or displays avoidance, escape, or attack behavior in their

presence. Preferably, the others presenting such consequences would be the individual's caretakers, rather than members of racial or ethnic minorities.

2. Other-presented behavior enhancement procedures (that is, positive reinforcement and engaging in high-probability behavior) would be used when the individual transacts with persons from minority groups, whenever he verbalizes expressions of like and relatively valid statements concerning the nature of racial and ethnic minorities, and when he displays approach or embracing behavior. Such consequences could be presented by both the individual's caretakers and persons who are members of the minority groups.

3. Stimulus pairing of both textual and pictorial materials, in which positive-eliciting stimuli are paired with racial-ethnic stimuli, would be presented in the communications media, and presentations of the opposite type of pairings would be systematically eliminated.

4. Caretakers and peers who engage in frequent social transactions with the individual would, as models, show positive emotional responses toward minority groups and verbalize expressions of liking for them. It would be essential that these others make relatively valid statements about the nature of people in minority groups and show approach or embracing behavior toward them.

5. Whenever possible, modifications would be made in the environment that would increase the frequency of cooperation between individuals and members of racial and ethnic minorities and decrease the frequency of competition between them.

In a great many respects the intensification of competitive behavior between people, and the subsequent and unavoidable loss of reinforcers to those who lose in such competitive enterprises, may as we have already seen, be one of the most significant antecedents to aggressive behavior toward minority group members. There is considerable evidence to show that during the 1930s in the deep South the persons most likely to engage in the lynching of Negroes were those individuals involved in the most intense economic competition with them, namely the red-necks. More recently it has been the white, blue-collar workers (hard-hats) who are in direct competition with the blacks, and it is from them that attacks can be anticipated as black Americans successfully win jobs in the labor market.

Inasmuch as the ultimate goal of the listed procedures is the modification of response complexes of individuals displaying prejudiced behavior, the author contends that the main thrust of behavior change should be directed at prejudiced individuals. It will no doubt occur to some, however, that alternative programs could be directed at the modification of the stimulus complexes of persons from racial and ethnic minority groups, thus reducing the frequency of acts of prejudice through the removal of the stimuli eliciting and/or controlling prejudiced behavior. Such a program would require that both the behavior and the physiognomic characteristics of those in the minorities be made similar to the members of the majority classes and groups. It is obvious that even if the behavior of minority persons could be modified sufficiently, modification of physiognomic characteristics would present insurmountable difficulties. From the standpoint of social engineering, however, programs requiring a change in the stimulus properties of minorities must be considered impractical for two reasons: As we have already observed, we must learn to make social approach or avoidance responses to those having certain physiognomic characteristics or behavioral stimuli of other persons by being reinforced for having done so. Second, much can be said for training individuals to approach others having diverse physiognomic, and particularly behavioral, stimulus properties such as those presented by persons in the racial and ethnic minorities. A program of this type would provide for the public well-being through the acquisition of minimum socially acceptable behaviors by everyone, yet would also provide for other-presented stimulation. Thus, while everyone—Jews, blacks, Chicanos, Anglos, Poles, Italians, and white Southern Baptists—observed the law, Jews would enjoy cheese blintzes, Chicanos would enjoy enchiladas, Anglos would enjoy Yankee pot roast, and so on. The obvious advantage of reinforcing social approach responses in the presence of racial or ethnic stimuli is that a wide variety of individuals might come to like and appreciate more diverse forms of stimulation. Such a program could readily be implemented in homes, schools, or playground areas as individuals engaged others in social transactions. Occasionally, superordinate sources of consequation would be necessary. For example, an elementary school teacher who expressed dislike for or engaged in verbal attack of the minority children in her class would become subject to appropriate consequation by the school administration.

DELINQUENT AND CRIMINAL BEHAVIOR

Delinquency, unlawful behavior committed by minors, and crime, unlawful behavior committed by adults, have long been problems in society defying solution. Unlawful behavior may be directed at other persons (as in assault or homicide), property (as in arson or bombing), or both. Suggestions for the management of such behavior will be made in Chapter 13. The present discussion will examine the possible causes of such behavior. Our analysis must begin with the obvious statement that what constitutes unlawful behavior is a matter of group definition and group reaction, particularly the reaction of the dominant groups in society. The process of labeling individuals as delinquents or criminals, whether or not they have actually committed delinquent acts, does two things. First, it serves to specify the types of behavior that are tabooed by the dominant groups in society. Second, it gives people who are labeled as delinquents or criminals discriminative properties that profoundly affect the ways others respond to them.

Unlawful behavior, like other forms of behavior, arises out of the transactions that occur between the individual and his physical and social environment. The nature of these transactions is indicated by the following summary of the differential association-reinforcement theory of deviant behavior.[15]

1. *Unlawful behavior is learned according to the principles of operant conditioning.* Thus unlawful behavior, like other forms of behavior, is sensitive to the consequences that follow it. The skilled hand movements of the safecracker and the skillful gab of the con artist are reinforced by the valuables (jewels, money, and so on) they produce.

2. *Unlawful behavior is learned both in physical (environment) situations that are reinforcing or discriminative and in social (environment) situations that are reinforcing or discriminative for such behavior.* The transactions between the individual and his physical and social environment, and the reinforcers and discriminative stimuli arising out of these transactions, provide the essential basis for the acquisition of such behavior. In the simplest case the child who easily reaches for and grabs a candy bar when the store clerk is in the storeroom is engaging in a transaction with his physical environment, and the behavior occurring in this transaction (the theft) is automatically reinforced. Similarly, the leadership of a gang may plan a rumble (attack of another gang) by giving the members verbal instructions on who the victims will be, where they will be, when to attack, and how to attack. The latter may involve a number of instructional procedures, such as differential reinforcement and successive approximations of appropriate attack operants, verbal instructions, putting through, and even modeling. Subsequently, defeat of the rival gang may establish a safe territory for members of the gang participating in the rumble and may even provide a source of income, both of which may be highly reinforcing. Moreover, individuals or members of the gang will be attracted to (make approach responses), and find quite reinforcing, those physical or social situations (or both) in which reinforcements have been available. This is because these situations are discriminative for, or have been paired with, reinforcement.

[15] Although in the original discussion of this theory, the term *criminal behavior* was used (see Burgess and Akers, 1966), the author prefers the term *unlawful behavior*. There are several reasons for this. First, the term avoids specifying the age of the offender, a factor that ordinarily determines whether or not the behavior was defined by the authorities as a delinquent or criminal act. Second, it tends to stress that unlawful behavior is behavior that is not consistent with standards set by others. Third, it implies that the processes involved in the development of unlawful behavior, regardless of whether it is delinquent or criminal behavior, are essentially the same as those involved in the development of lawful behavior. However, *unlawful behavior*, as used here, does refer to the more serious acts—acts against persons or property.

3. *The principal part of the learning of unlawful behavior occurs in those groups (social situations) that comprise the individual's major source of reinforcements.* Early in life the primary group (the family) is typically the primary source of reinforcements, some of which are particularly powerful (that is, unconditioned and generalized positive reinforcements). Should unlawful behavior occur at that time, it is most likely to occur through social transactions between the individual and members of his family. Later on the teen-age peer group assumes this powerful position, particularly because the peer group has access to positive reinforcers (especially generalized positive reinforcers), punishers (especially verbal or gestural aversive stimuli such as snubbing), and even time-out (in the form of exclusion or rejection from a group).

4. *The learning of unlawful behavior, including specific techniques or procedures, positive emotional responses toward unlawful acts and the situations in which they occur, the verbal repertoire about such acts, and the avoidance of law enforcement, is a function of the effective and available reinforcers and the existing reinforcement contingencies.* A skillful unlawful performance, such as a theft, is more apt to be reinforced and is more apt to avoid the kinds of consequences law enforcement makes available for such behavior than an unskillful performance. Furthermore, the kinds of reinforcers occurring during and following such behavior, along with the situation in which the behavior occurs, become, through stimulus pairing, a reinforcer which elicits positive emotional responses and strengthens both the motor and verbal behaviors preceding them.

5. *The specific class of behaviors that are learned and their frequency of occurrence are a function of the reinforcers that are effective and available and the rules by which these reinforcers are applied (the reinforcement contingency).* For example, some members of a juvenile gang might acquire skills in operating a midnight auto supply (car parts theft), while others might become muggers. Of course, the reinforcers made directly available by such acts are important (salable car parts, or cash or jewelry). Also important, however, is the approval the individual receives from the group (that is, verbal expressions of praise or agreement, such as "Yeah, man! That's good" when the individual successfully jimmys a door). The more loot brought in while the individual successfully avoids the authorities, the more apt the individual is to receive group approval. The less skillful the performance is, either because less loot is obtained or because difficulty is encountered with the authorities, the greater is the likelihood of disapproval (through verbal aversive stimulation or even banishment from the group). It is, therefore, the skillful unlawful performance occurring during a transaction with the physical or social environment that is most apt to produce reinforcers, the effect of which is to strengthen some behaviors, for example, theft, and not others. In addition, the rules specifying the reinforcement con-

tingency, besides taking the form of the actual consequation used by the group (for example, "Yeah, that's it man. Like that!" contingent on properly jimmying a door), may also take the form of verbal or written instructions or directions that proscribe or prescribe behaviors. As members of the group transact with one another, such directions or instructions function as discriminative stimuli, because they are stimuli correlated with certain consequences. For example, a gang leader may say, "Listen Sam, the next time you blow it, we're gonna give it to you." Later on, when Sam does blow it, he is beaten up, as he was on previous occasions when similar threats were made and he blew it. In this example, both the rules by which the reinforcers (or punishers) are applied (the reinforcement contingency) and the discriminative stimuli preceding them (the verbal instructions) serve to specify both appropriate and unappropriate behaviors.[16]

6. *Unlawful behavior is a function of stimuli that are discriminative for such behavior, the learning of which takes place when such behavior is more highly reinforced than lawful behavior.* Verbal instructions, criminal talk, making responses characteristic of an unlawful act (that is motor responses), being in situations in which unlawful acts are reinforced, and being in the presence of the reinforcers themselves—all of these acquire discriminative properties for unlawful behavior when followed by reinforcers. The thief who is told where a job is, who discusses its execution, who perhaps manipulates the tools needed for the job, who is in the actual job situation, who sees the jewels, and who has been reinforced for theft before is more likely to steal again when these stimuli are present. Moreover, when such acts are more highly reinforced than lawful acts, such behavior is more apt to be acquired. This may be stated more simply as follows: First, unlawful acts are more apt to be acquired when they are more highly reinforced than lawful behavior; second, unlawful acts are more apt to occur when the individual is presented with stimuli that are discriminative for these acts. Finally, when environments seldom provide a legitimate means for obtaining reinforcers and when the reinforcers that can be obtained by illegitimate (unlawful) means occur infrequently, such environments can be expected to have two effects on the individual's behavior. First, because individuals living in such environments are on a deprivation schedule, the reinforcers will be extraordinarily reinforcing. Second, because reinforcers are more likely to occur after unlawful than after lawful behavior, the former will be strengthened. It is not surprising, therefore, that when individuals are denied employment because of race,

---

[16] In one sense verbal instructions that proscribe or prescribe behaviors, like the reinforcement contingency, can be regarded as norms. Individuals whose behavior falls within the limits specified by these instructions or the reinforcement contingency can be said to conform to these norms. Furthermore, in the example above Sam's successful door-jimmying behavior conforms to the norms set by the gang. It does not, however, conform to the norms set by law-abiding citizens.

ethnic background, lack of skills, age, or their delinquent or criminal records, they will engage in unlawful behavior. Such unemployment denies the individual a legitimate means for securing reinforcers and at the same time deprives him. It is no wonder that such environments as the ghetto have the highest delinquency and crime rates. Such environments are inhabited by blacks, Puerto Ricans, the uneducated, the ex-con and the aged, most of whom are denied legitimate means of securing reinforcers whether deserved or not.

7. *The strength of unlawful behavior as measured by its rate (frequency over unit time) is a direct function of the amount, frequency, and probability of reinforcement.* Thus increased frequency of purse snatching can be expected following an occasion when the snatcher grabs a purse with a large amount of money in it, when a great number of purses with money in them are grabbed (high reinforcement rate), or when snatched purses very often have something in them (a higher probability of reinforcement).

All of these, as single-schedule phenomena, interact in a complex way with the kinds of reinforcements available and the nature of other concurrent contingencies. For example, on some occasions peer group approval may be more reinforcing than money. On still other occasions a shoplifter may get some merchandise, be interrogated by a house detective (an aversive event), only to be let go following surrender of the merchandise. On still other occasions a small "take" may be followed by interrogation, arrest, and booking at the city jail—a relatively aversive consequence. Because the reinforcing and punishing events are on an intermittent schedule, once unlawful behavior has been acquired, it is more apt to be maintained than eliminated.

Although there are numerous studies in support of the differential-association reinforcement theory of deviant behavior, the study by Buehler, Patterson, and Furniss (1966) is, in the author's opinion, a classic. It is based on observations of the social transactions occurring in a correctional institution for teen-age delinquent girls. The investigation consisted of three different studies summarized as follows:

In the first study an observer sampled the transactions occurring between inmates during fifteen 2-hour periods. A record was kept of two essential events: (1) the occurrence of pro-delinquent remarks by the inmates (for example, "I think she's [a staff member] sickening") and of pro-societal remarks (for example, "I'm sorry I didn't go to college"), and (2) the nature of the social events following such remarks, that is, whether they were regarded as positively reinforcing (as when another inmate agreed, smiled, nodded, or attended to the remark) or punishing (as when another inmate disagreed, threatened, frowned, ignored, or sneered at the remark). Following each observation period the observer wrote descriptive accounts of the transactions. The results revealed that delinquent behaviors, such as rule breaking, criticism of the staff and staff rules, and aggressive behavior, were reinforced 70 percent of the time.

In the second study an observer made a detailed observation of the transactions by sampling "communicative acts" between inmates of 2.5 seconds duration. These acts were categorized as delinquent or socially appropriate behavior (as defined by reference to the girl's handbook of the institution), and the social events following these acts were described as verbal or gestural (nonverbal) reinforcing or punishing events. The transactions of six inmates from each of two "open" (less restricted) and two "closed" (more restricted) cottages were observed for 50 minutes. No significant differences between the transactions occurring in open and closed cottages were observed. However, positive reinforcement of delinquent behavior occurred significantly more often than did punishment for this behavior. Similarly, punishment for socially appropriate behavior occurred more often than did reinforcement for this behavior. Finally, for both types of behavior, peer-presented positive reinforcement was more nonverbal or gestural than verbal. For delinquent behavior, 82 percent of the positive reinforcement was nonverbal, and 18 percent was verbal; for socially appropriate behavior, 64 percent of the reinforcement was nonverbal, and 36 percent was verbal.

In the third study the frequency of reinforcement the inmates received from others (peers and staff) and gave to others (also peers and staff) for social, hostile, coercive, delinquent, and socially appropriate behaviors (see preceding study for the definition of this) was observed over a 5-day period for 5 hours a day. Six subjects were studied. Detailed data presented for one subject revealed that the peer group punished her about three times as often as they reinforced her for socially appropriate behavior, and the staff reinforced her for such behavior nine times more often than they punished her. However, the data also revealed that she transacted with her peers with this behavior about twice as often as with the staff. For hostile behavior, her peers reinforced her about twice as often as they punished her. The staff did not reinforce her once for hostile behavior, and they did punish her five times. Again, however, such transactions occurred with her peer group about four times as often as with the staff. Results also revealed that the peer group reinforced hostile behavior and punished socially appropriate behaviors more consistently than the staff's reinforcement or punishment of behavior.

There are several things about this study that must be emphasized. First, although this is not an experimental study, the data do suggest that there are significant social transactions going on in a correctional institution which may result in the acquisition and maintenance of delinquent behavior. Second, the effects of these transactions were probably overestimated, because the authors adopted a priori definitions of the reinforcing and punishing events they studied rather than using strict behavioral definitions. (That is, they did not define these events by their effects on behavior.) Finally, although observers have long observed the recidivism of inmates of correctional institutions, this study is particularly significant because it illuminates some of the salient features of human social transactions that are most likely to be involved in the behavior control that criminal and delinquent groups possess over their members.

STUDY QUESTIONS

1. Define the term *competition* in terms of the
   a. number of individuals involved.
   b. relationship of an individual's response to his reinforcement.
   c. number of reinforcers available.
2. With respect to each of the factors listed in question 1, describe the conditions under which intervention would be required.
3. What conditions affect the development of
   a. cooperation?   b. competition?
4. From your knowledge of toys and games suitable for a preschool population, describe a play situation designed to enhance children's skills in
   a. competition.   b. cooperation.
5. Must competitive behavior always be reinforced by the reinforcing events made available during the acquisition of the behavior? Explain your answer.
6. Define aggression. Suggest some reasons why the definition probably should *not* include verbal attack of the victim. Suggest some reasons why the definition should include verbal attack.
7. Distinguish between respondent and operant aggression in terms of
   a. the stimulus events functioning as antecedents.
   b. stereotypy and the variability of the response complex as it occurs in the infrahuman and the human animal.
8. Human aggression is said by many to have unique properties that distinguish it from animal aggression. Describe them.
9. Respondent aggression is most likely to occur in what human population?
10. What types of stimuli most likely maintain adult aggression in
    a. the modern industrial state?
    b. primitive societies?
11. Describe some of the events that maintain an animal's defense of its territory.
12. Many observers regard aggression as essential to the survival of the organism. Some even maintain that aggression is part of the phylogenetic programming of the organism. Suggest some reasons why these observers take this point of view, and offer an alternative account for aggression.
13. Describe in detail the training that makes each of the following events into S^D's for aggression:
    a. Weapons.   c. Models.
    b. Victims.   d. Verbal attack.

14. A 4-year-old boy receives a cap pistol (a six-shooter) and a holster for Christmas. His father loads the pistol, straps the pistol and holster on him, and sends him out to play. From your knowledge of behavior theory, describe the possible salient events that will lead to the acquisition and maintenance of "gun-slinging" operants. (Assume that at first he plays alone, then later engages in a game of cowboys and Indians.)

15. Suggest a behavioral account of the relationship between aggression and systemic frustration.

16. One observes an increase in aggression and violence in society even though things have been worse in the past. Suggest some reasons why this might be the case.

17. From your knowledge of behavior theory, suggest a plausible account of the notion of expectancy—as an explanatory intrapsychic state or event.

18. Design a small communal living situation consisting of twenty families that is aimed at the elimination of aggression in its members. Assume that you have one generation to work on the problem and ample money for the project.

19. Why is it perhaps unwise to encourage an aggressive catharsis?

20. How would you define prejudice?

21. What are some of the stimulus characteristics of specific groups toward whom prejudice occurs?

22. Give a behavioral definition of the notion of a stereotype in racial or ethnic prejudice.

23. What are the two defining characteristics of prejudice?

24. The author describes an attitude as a mental state or event. What does he posit as the three essential components of an attitude? Why are attitudes regarded as important by those psychologists who choose to study them? (Hint: What are attitude-directed consistency and transituational generality?)

25. Under what assumptions and conditions of an individual's history would the concept of attitude be as useful as it is purported to be?

26. To many observers, the concept of attitude as an intrapsychic state or event, like the concept of trait or faculty of the mind, is a static concept, leading to research and theory that ignore the nature of the group process and its importance in behavior. Read the La Piere study carefully and find evidence in it in support of this criticism.

27. Why does the author take the point of view that an attitude is essentially a form of verbal behavior?

28. The author states that the acquisition of prejudice is a two-stage process. Do you agree? Explain your position.

29. The author describes a program for the elimination of prejudice. Cite an alternative program, or be able to discuss the pros and cons of the one in the text.

30. Does the author view prejudice as innate or acquired (learned)?

31. From the point of view of behavior theory and enlightened social policy, discuss the implications of the "When in Rome, do as the Romans do" solution to prejudice.

32. What functions are attributed to the labeling of certain behaviors as delinquent or criminal?

33. According to the differential association-reinforcement theory of deviant behavior, what group is the most powerful early in life? Later on? Why?
34. In what ways do the consequences of an unlawful act affect the behavior of the person engaging in it?
35. Parents of youth from upper middle-class families are often able to provide ample clothes, toys, cars, and so on as reinforcers. Yet, their children may get busted for theft, drug possession, and the like. Assuming that the latter offense does not involve addictive drugs, offer an account of this behavior in the context of the differential association-reinforcement theory.
36. Suggest two important consequences of a situation in which unlawful behavior is more highly reinforced than lawful behavior.
37. What kinds of personal conditions favor the development of unlawful behavior?
38. From the point of view of the control of unlawful behavior, analyze the relationships between the following:
   a. Single and concurrent contingencies affecting unlawful behavior.
   b. Deprivation state of the individual engaging in unlawful behavior.
39. Recidivism is a chronic problem in law enforcement and can perhaps be attributed to two sets of events: those occurring during incarceration and those when the individual is released to society following incarceration. From what you know about the possible causes of unlawful behavior, describe and discuss the significant events occurring in both situations that may cause recidivism.
40. Outline the main features of your ideal program for the rehabilitation of delinquents or criminals.

REFERENCES

Akers, R. Thoughts on the sociology of deviance: Social definitions and behavior. Unpublished manuscript, University of Washington, 1967.

Azrin, N. H. Punishment of elicited aggression. *Journal of the Experimental Analysis of Behavior*, 1970, **14**, 7–10.

Azrin, N. H., and Holz, W. C. Punishment. In W. K. Honig (Ed.), *Operant behavior: Areas of research and application*. New York: Appleton-Century-Crofts, 1966.

Azrin, N. H., Hutchinson, R. R., and McLaughlin, R. The opportunity for aggression as an operant reinforcer during aversive stimulation. *Journal of the Experimental Analysis of Behavior*, 1965, 8, 171–180.

Azrin, N. H., and Lindsley, O. R. The reinforcement of cooperation between children. *Journal of Abnormal and Social Psychology*, 1956, **52**, 100–102.

Bandura, A. Social learning through imitation. In M. R. Jones (Ed.), *Nebraska Symposium on Motivation*. Vol. 10. Lincoln: University of Nebraska Press, 1962.

Bandura, A. Influence of model's reinforcement contingencies on the acquisition of imitative responses. *Journal of Personality and Social Psychology*, 1965, **1**, 589–595.

Bandura, A., and Walters, R. H. *Social learning and personality development.* New York: Holt, Rinehart and Winston, 1963.

Berkowitz, L. *Aggression: A social psychological analysis.* New York: McGraw-Hill, 1962.

Bronson, G. W. The fear of novelty. *Psychological Bulletin*, 1968, **69**, 350–359.

Buehler, R. E., Patterson, G. R., and Furniss, J. M. The reinforcement of behavior in institutional settings. *Behavior Research and Therapy*, 1966, **4**, 157–167.

Burgess, R. L., and Akers, R. L. A differential association-reinforcement theory of criminal behavior. *Social Problems*, 1966, **14**, 128–147.

Byrne, D. Interpersonal attraction and attitude similarity. *Journal of Abnormal and Social Psychology*, 1961, **62**, 713–715.

Byrne, D., and Griffitt, N. A developmental study of the law of attraction. *Journal of Personality and Social Psychology*, 1966, **4**, 699–702.

Cloward, R. A. Illegitimate means, anomie and deviant behavior. *American Sociological Review*, 1959, **24**, 164–176.

Davies, J. C. The J-curve of rising and declining satisfaction as a cause of some great revolutions and a contained rebellion. In H. D. Graham and T. R. Gurr (Eds.), *Violence in America.* New York: New American Library, 1969.

Feierabend, I. K., Feierabend, R. L., and Nesvold, B. A. Social change and political violence: Cross national patterns. In H. D. Graham and T. R Gurr (Eds), *Violence in America.* New York: New American Library, 1969.

Feierabend, R. L., and Feierabend, I. K. Aggressive behaviors within polities, 1948–1962: A cross national study. *The Journal of Conflict Resolution*, 1966, **10**, 249–271.

Festinger, L. Behavioral support for opinion change. *Public Opinion Quarterly*, 1964, **28**, 404–417.

Kelly, J. F., and Hake, D. F. An extinction-induced increase in an aggressive response with humans. *Journal of the Experimental Analysis of Behavior*, 1970, **14**, 153–166.

La Piere, R. T. Attitudes vs. actions. *Social Forces*, 1934, **13**, 230–237.

Lindsley, O. R. Experimental analysis of cooperation and competition. In T. Verhave (Ed.), *The experimental analysis of behavior.* New York: Appleton-Century-Crofts, 1966.

Lorenz, K. *On aggression.* New York: Harcourt Brace Jovanovich, 1963.

Lovaas, O. I. Interaction between verbal and non-verbal behavior. *Child Development*, 1961, **32**, 329–336.

Mallick, S. K., and McCandless, B. R. A study of catharsis of aggression. *Journal of Personality and Social Psychology*, 1966, **4**, 591–596.

National Advisory Commission, Report of the National Advisory Commission on Civil Disorders. New York: New York Times Company, 1968.

Osgood, C. E., Suci, C. J., and Tannenbaum, P. H. *The measurement of meaning.* Urbana: University of Illinois Press, 1957.

Podhoretz, N. *Doings and undoings.* New York: Farrar, Straus and Giroux, 1963.

Secord, P. F., and Backman, C. W. *Social psychology*. New York: McGraw-Hill, 1964.

Staats, A. W. and Staats, C. K. *Complex human behavior*. New York: Holt, Rinehart and Winston, 1963.

Tinbergen, N. *The herring gull's world*. Garden City: Anchor Books, 1967.

Ulrich, R. E. *The experimental analysis of aggression*. Unpublished manuscript, 1969.

Ulrich, R. E., and Azrin, N. H. Reflexive fighting in response to aversive stimulation. *Journal of the Experimental Analysis of Behavior*, 1962, 5, 511–520.

Ulrich, R. E., and Favell, J. E. Human aggression. In C. Neuringer and J. L. Michael (Eds.), *Behavior modification in clinical psychology*. New York: Appelton-Century-Crofts, 1969.

Ulrich, R. E., Hutchinson, R. R., and Azrin, N. H. Pain-elicited aggression. *Psychological Record*, 1965, 15, 111–126.

Ulrich, R. E., Wolfe, M., and Dulaney, S. Punishment of shock-induced aggression. *Journal of the Experimental Analysis of Behavior*, 1969, 12, 1009–1016.

Von Hemel, P. E. Aggression as a reinforcer: Operant behavior in the mouse killing rat. *Journal of the Experimental Analysis of Behavior*, 1972, 17, 238–245.

Wicker, A. W. Attitudes versus actions: The relationship of verbal and overt behavioral responses to attitude objects. *Journal of Social Issues*, 1969, 25, 41–78.

CHAPTER 11

BEHAVIOR DISORDERS

Occasionally, an individual may have behavior problems that bring him into contact with those persons in society whose area of specialty is behavior management. In our society it is the psychiatrist or clinical psychologist who performs such service functions, whereas in primitive societies it is the tribal shaman or witch doctor. Typically, these specialists engage in social transactions with individuals for the express purpose of obtaining behavior control so that the individual's problem(s) will be remedied. Professionals providing such service must address themselves to two basic questions: (1) What is the nature of the behavior disorders? and (2) how can they be managed? The present chapter will deal with the first of these problems, namely, the nature of behavior disorders; problems in management will be dealt with in later chapters.

SOME EXAMPLES OF BEHAVIOR DISORDERS

Following are several examples of behavior disorders. These examples are presented in the form of summary verbal descriptions of the individual's behavior (response complexes), and the individual's physical condition (anatomic-physiological characteristics).

EXAMPLE 1

Jimmy is a 10-year-old who lives in a residential school. Although he is pleasant and assists the teacher in school activities, his test performance is low (IQ 58). His speech is often garbled and unintelligible because of his somewhat protruding tongue. He understands instructions and communicates his needs to others well. His self-help skills are good, and he does simple clean-up tasks without direction. However, he can neither read nor write.

Physical: Trisomy 21 (an extra number 21 chromosome); Brushfield's spots; muscular hypotonia; palmar simian line; fissured, protruding tongue; epicanthus; brachycephaly; and strabismus, left eye (Down's syndrome).

EXAMPLE 2

Greg is a 5-year-old arrested hydrocephalic. He possesses some speech, blurts out TV commercial slogans, and follows simple instructions. Most often he is hyperactive and easily distracted. Although he shows some self-help skills and, to a degree, social skills, he cannot read or write or even color with crayons. He must be watched or he gets into dangerous situations.

Physical: Some dilation of the cerebral ventricles with thinning of the corpus callosum. Otherwise, normal.

EXAMPLE 3

Joey is 10 years old and big for his age. He has been in a state institution for the retarded since he was five. He seldom, if ever, gets into trouble on the ward. He has little speech, although when spoken to he shows eye contact and will occasionally smile. He spends a good part of his day sitting against the wall, rocking back and forth. He shows some self-help skills, such as feeding, dressing, and toilet training.

Physical: Essentially normal.

EXAMPLE 4

Mary is 12 years old and has been described as autistic. Although she follows instructions reasonably well, she has little speech. Her self-help skills are strong, but most of her day is spent playing on the swing, waving her hand in front of her eyes, or swaying back and forth in a standing position.

Physical: Congenital cataracts removed at 3 years. Wears corrective lenses. When she walks, it is on her toes. Otherwise, normal.

EXAMPLE 5

Terry is an 11-year-old-boy who has been in an institution since he was nine. He is currently in a state institution for the retarded, living on a ward for boys between the ages of eight and eighteen. He possesses strong speech, self-help, and motor skills, but is capable of terribly disruptive temper tantrums, which are sometimes accompanied by vicious, aggressive attacks on others. He can neither read nor write. He has an IQ of about 50.

Physical: Essentially normal.

EXAMPLE 6

David is 39 years old and has spent 21 of these years in a state hospital for the mentally ill. Before that he was an average student who had completed his high school education. Now he shows little speech, but will occasionally smile when spoken to. The smile is sometimes accompanied by nonsense vocalizations. He always looks dirty, and over the years has lost all but one tooth, an incisor, which, when exposed during a smile, seems to give him a silly look. He can dress himself, bathe himself, and feed himself. He works two hours a day in the hospital laundry.

Physical: Essentially normal except for dentition.

EXAMPLE 7

Susan is a college student who, from time to time, shows a lack of concentration in her studies and is depressed and withdrawn from social contacts. She cries easily, and frequently seems on edge. Three times last semester she walked out of her midterm examinations and received Fs. At present she is worried and depressed about her future, and finds it difficult to leave the dormitory to attend classes.

Physical: Essentially normal.

EXAMPLE 8

Sarah is a 58-year-old, overweight woman (she is 5 feet 7 inches tall and weighs about 240 pounds), with curious speech and mannerisms. When a person meets her for the first time, she will go up to that person and tell him about her career as a movie star. She will also tell him of her new contract with MGM studios. Of course, all this is untrue. When she talks to someone, she always tips her head back, so that the person can look up her nostrils. She has a funny habit of bursting into song at the most inopportune times.

Physical: Excessive obesity, heart enlargement, and hypertension. Otherwise, normal.

EXAMPLE 9

Steve is 15 years old and has been in juvenile hall three times in the past 3 years. On each occasion he had been arrested for possession of drugs. He has taken heroin, speed, and pot. On the last occasion he was arrested he was on LSD and was picked up for "trying to walk to the moon" by climbing the side of a building. He is a brilliant musician and student. He has an IQ of 148.

Physical: Essentially normal.

After studying each of these examples carefully, the reader should ask himself the following questions:[1]

1. Who first reported the individual's behavior problem(s)? What is his relationship to the individual?

2. What are the significant features of the individual's behavior problem(s)? Of his physical condition?

3. Of what response complexes do his behavior problem(s) consist? Are they vocal operants, motor operants, or both? Are they respondents?

4. How are the significant features of the behavior problem(s) assessed? By whom?

5. How long has the individual had the behavior problem(s)? How long has he had his assessed physical condition?

6. What, if any, is the relationship between the individual's behavior problem(s) and his physical condition? Is it one of correlation or causation?

7. At what point does the individual's behavior problem become a behavior disorder?

The examples reveal that the descriptive term *behavior disorder* covers a rather wide range of (1) response complexes, (2) age groups, (3) physical-environmental settings, and (4) physical conditions of the organism. All of this suggests that the study and management of behavior disorders is a formidable task. Much of the language and many of the procedures used in this study are the same as those used by workers in the related fields of biology and medicine. Workers in all of these fields typically began their studies by obtaining a careful description of the phenomena of concern. This is the first step in one of the primary methods of investigation in the biological sciences —taxonomy. We shall begin our analysis of the problem of behavior disorders by examining this method.

---

[1] The reader is not expected to be able to answer all of these questions. First, the examples do not present sufficient information, and second, because of the present state of our knowledge, many questions cannot be answered, even when a great deal more information concerning the individual cases is available.

TAXONOMY AND THE BEHAVIOR DISORDERS

Taxonomy is the classification of entities (flora and fauna, for example) according to their characteristics and is a widely used method of study in the biological sciences. The aim of taxonomy is a logical and orderly description of nature. Thus we have vertebrates (animals with backbones) and invertebrates (animals without backbones), protozoa (single-celled animals) and metazoa (multicellular animals), and so on. In each case a precise description and identification of the class to which the organism studied belongs is obtained by the taxonomic method. This description and identification is based on a careful examination of the entity's characteristics. Moreover, as the investigation of the entity progresses, more and more descriptive information is obtained about its many characteristics (*contiguous relationships*) and the characteristics of other entities like it (*similarity relationships*). For example, an amoeba is described as a single-celled animal possessing a nucleus (contiguous relationship between one structural characteristic and another structural characteristic), which reproduces by simple cell division (contiguous relationship between structural characteristic(s) and behavior in reproduction). Furthermore, an amoeba is like a paramecium in that both are single-celled animals (similarity relationship based on structural characteristics of both entities), and they both reproduce by simple cell division (similarity relationship based on behavior). Finally, because of their similarities each may be identified as a member of the same class: protozoa.

Other animals identified as members of the class protozoa would also be described as single-celled and possessing a nucleus (among other structural features), and, it could be predicted that they would also have the behavioral characteristic of reproduction through simple cell division. *Taxonomy, then, not only gives us a description and classification of entities, but in addition allows us to make predictions about other structural and/or behavioral characteristics or correlates of the individual entities and between entities. It does not, however, allow us to deal with the matter of causation of these behavioral or anatomic-physiological characteristics. It is a descriptive and logical process, not a manipulative or experimental one.*

The currently used psychiatric (that is, medical) classification systems are based on a taxonomic approach to behavior disorders. As in the case of the biological application of taxonomy, certain aspects of the entity are observed. These include: (1) the individual's behavioral characteristics or response complexes, (2) the correlates of or relationships contiguous (anatomic-physiological or environmental) to these behavioral characteristics, and (3) the nature of the antecedents or causes of the behavior disorder (again, anatomic-physiological or environmental events), when these are known.

Typically, the application of taxonomy to the study of behavior disorders involves the following steps:

1. Someone in the individual's environment observes his behavior and finds it in some way deviant or deficient. The observer may be a parent, a teacher, a neighbor, a physician, or a law enforcement official. For example, Steve in example 9 was first observed (busted) by the police for illegal drug use.

2. A psychological examination is made of the individual to obtain a description of his behavior. This observation process typically involves psychological tests, interviews with the individual himself and with the individuals who are responsible for him (his caretakers), and direct observation of the individual in other forms of social interaction. When the individual's behavior is under direct observation, the examiner will typically study the patient's gestures and especially his speech, from which inferences are often made about the patient's feelings—his respondent behavior.[2] Subsequently, an evaluation is prepared, consisting of summary verbal descriptions of the individual's salient behavioral characteristics—his symptoms and their possible antecedents or causes. This evaluation is based on the particular theory of disease held by the psychiatrist or clinical psychologist examining the individual.

3. A comparable observation process occurs in the medical examination, in which neurological, biochemical, and bacteriological tests are administered to find out if there are any physical correlates (contiguous relationships) to the behavior in question. Summary verbal descriptions of the individual's salient anatomic and physiological features are prepared by the neurologists, the endocrinologists, the internists, and so on. Again these descriptions reflect the viewpoint or theory of disease possessed by the person preparing the report.

4. These observations and descriptions of the individual's behavioral and medical characteristics are collated and followed by a final evaluative process called a diagnosis, in which the behavior disorder class to which the individual belongs is identified.[3] The evaluator, usually a psychiatrist, studies the behavioral and anatomic-physiological contiguous relationships characteristic of the individual in question and compares them with the characteristics or contiguous relationships of known behavior disorders or syndromes specified in the classification system he uses.

When congruence exists between the psychological and medical contiguous relationships of the patient and the psychological and medical contiguous

---

[2] This process of evaluating the patient's verbal behavior is not unlike that described in Chapter 9 in which management wished to assess the employee's feelings about the company. Assessment of the individual's feelings is important to many psychological workers, because historically many behavior disorders without physical antecedents have been viewed as emotional disorders—the latter being a correlate if not a cause of the former.

[3] Not all individuals possessing deviant or deficient behavior receive such an evaluation. Many such individuals go unnoticed by their caretakers, and others may be noticed but not examined. Still others may be noticed and examined, but never receive therapy. Middle-class caretakers are perhaps most apt to notice the behavior of their kin and are most able financially to provide for diagnostic services.

relationships of a known behavior disorder, the individual is described as hav-ing that behavior disorder. Thus in example 1 Jimmy was described as having subaverage measured intelligence, a speech problem, and minimal social and verbal learning skills, and all of these behavioral characteristics are contiguous with his structural (physical) characteristics, that is, an extra number 21 chromosome pigmentation on the pupil (Brushfield's spots), the palmar sim-ian line, muscular hypotonia (flacidity), a protruding tongue, and an epi-canthal fold (an extra fold of skin covering the corner of the eye). Moreover, previous knowledge about these behavioral and structural contiguous relation-ships indicates that they often occur together and may thus form the same behavior disorder class—Down's syndrome (Mongolism). Furthermore, when adequate prior knowledge about a behavior disorder is available, accurate de-scriptions (predictions) can be made about the causes, or *etiology* of the dis-order, its outcome, or *prognosis*, and its appropriate treatment, or *therapy.*

Although the behavioral characteristics of Jimmy in example 1 and Greg in example 2 are similar in some ways, their anatomic-physiological character-istics are not. They are viewed, therefore, as possessing different behavior dis-orders, Down's syndrome and hydrocephaly, respectively. There are occasions, too, when the individual is diagnosed as possessing more than one behavior disorder, because he possesses contiguous relationships that are characteristic of those observed in two or more types of behavior disorder. For example, Terry (example 5) possesses some behavioral characteristics in common with Jimmy and Greg (none of them can read or write); in addition, Terry has temper tantrums and aggressive outbursts, but his physical examination was negative. He would most likely be described as having a mixed behavior dis-order (mental retardation with psychotic coloring).

The taxonomic method has led to two major problems. First, there is a tendency among psychological workers to assume that the taxonomic method reveals the causes of behavior disorders. Actually, all that it reveals is a de-scription of psychological and medical contiguous relationships and the class to which they belong in the individual case. When sufficient prior knowledge is available, this method does allow us to make many relevant predictions about the characteristics of behavior disorders. However, the study of causa-tion, as we shall see, is a matter of experimentation, not simply a matter of description and classification. Second, there is also a tendency among workers to use a kind of circular reasoning in which they fallaciously assume that the antecedents to the behavior disorder are the same as the behavior itself. Although the deviant behavior of a paranoid schizophrenic individual may identify him as having a behavior disorder characteristic of the class of dis-orders referred to as paranoid schizophrenia, it cannot legitimately be assumed that the reason for (causes of) his behavior is that he is a paranoid schizo-phrenic. (Another example of this kind of fallacious reasoning occurs in the case of Sam on pages 314-319.) Of course, when there is a complete and thorough understanding of the nature and limitations of taxonomy, these problems can be avoided.

In summary, the study and management of deviant behavior or behavior deficits involves both psychological and medical evaluation, consisting of the observation of the individual and the preparation of a summary verbal description of (1) salient behavioral and medical characteristics (symptoms) or contiguous relationships and (2) their antecedents when known. The description of the contiguous relationships prepared from the observations of an individual is then compared with descriptions characteristic of known behavior disorders. The aim of this procedure is the identification of the behavior disorder class or classes to which an individual does or does not belong. When adequate prior knowledge exists about the characteristics of the class to which the individual belongs, predictions can then be made about the etiology, prognosis, and therapy of the behavior disorder forming that class. The classification system and the behavioral and medical symptoms from which it is derived depend on the viewpoint or theory of disease possessed by the person making the evaluation.

PSYCHOLOGICAL AND MEDICAL EVALUATION

Although the adequacy of a psychiatric classification system can be viewed from any one of a number of viewpoints, our greatest concern is with *the degree of accuracy of predictions of behavioral and medical characteristics of individuals within the various classes of which the system is made.* For example, if a child is identified as a member of the behavioral disorder class Down's syndrome, or Mongolism, because of the presence of an epicanthal fold and a protruding, fissured tongue (two anatomic contiguous characteristics), then accurate predictions can be made about his other anatomic-physiological (his chromosome count, his skull shape, and so on) and behavioral characteristics (his IQ).

There are two major factors that determine the adequacy of a given classification system. First is the relevance of the anatomic-physiological and behavioral characteristics (contiguous relationships) embodied in the various classes of behavior disorders described in the psychiatric classification system. These characteristics are chosen by the evaluator over other possible characteristics, because *from the evaluator's point of view or his theory of disease, they are the essential and significant indicators of disease and are characteristic of it.* For example, the psychoanalyst may, among other things, be particularly concerned with a patient's oral habits (eating, biting, chewing, speaking, and so on), whereas a Rogerian psychologist may be particularly concerned with the frequency with which the patient makes positive or negative statements about himself. In either case these behavioral events, as characteristics of a behavior disorder, are presumed to be important because they are significantly related to intrapsychic events in the patient. Second, once the characteristics that make up the classification system are chosen,[4] suitable procedures must be available, so that individuals can be examined and those possessing these characteristics be identified. Table 11-1 shows some representative psychological and medical tests used in evaluation, some of the contiguous characteristics revealed by these tests, the status of these contiguous characteristics, and some of the behavior disorder classes identifiable in such evaluations.

There appears to be an interesting contrast between the psychological and medical tests. Although in both tests the characteristics may be verified through their contiguous relationship to other behavior and/or structural characteristics, medical tests are viewed as useful because they reveal directly observed characteristics—the individual's test performance. For example, a medical evaluation in which the skull x ray or EEG is used may directly reveal areas of the brain possessing certain shapes and shadows or voltage or frequency characteristics (anatomic and physiological contiguous characteristics). By contrast, a psychological evaluation in which the Stanford-Binet Intelligence Scale is used may directly reveal the individual's performance on a variety of paper-and-pencil tests (a behavioral contiguous characteristic summarized by the IQ), and in addition, it is presumed to reveal indirectly (inferentially) his intelligence. Furthermore, because individuals may make comparable performances on tests having somewhat comparable content (for example, obtain comparable IQ's on different tests of verbal intelligence), workers believe that what they are really measuring is a trait or faculty of mind, which has extensive transituational generality. Thus workers find psychological tests useful and significant in the study of behavior because such tests have meaning over and above that which is revealed by the test performance itself. The tests reveal such things as intelligence, social maturity, and personality traits (see Table 11-1), which are viewed as faculties of the mind or intrapsychic states, not just the test performance per se.[5]

---

[4] These characteristics are not "chosen" in the sense that they are completely arbitrary selections. Rather they are based on prior clinical experience (observed similarities between individuals who have a behavior disorder and their differences from "normal" individuals).

[5] The reader may recall from his reading of Chapters 1 and 10 that the analysis of behavior may deal with at least two different levels or dimensions. First, behavior may be analyzed in terms of a measurement, or procedural, dimension—the actual operations performed by the investigator as he studies the organism. This is sometimes called the formal, operational, or procedural dimension. It is the notation for what the investigator does in the way of procedures and how the organism responds to them. Second, behavior may be analyzed in terms of a theoretical, inferential, or hypothetical dimension—the organism's inferred intrapsychic or neurophysiological states that function in behavior. An example is intelligence. Thus IQ is representative of the measurement, or procedural, dimension of analysis, and intelligence is representative of the theoretical, or inferential, dimension of analysis.

Table 11-1 Contiguous Characteristics, Their Status, and Some of the Behavior Disorder Classes That Can Be Identified by Some Representative Psychological and Medical Tests

PSYCHOLOGICAL TEST	CONTIGUOUS CHARACTERISTIC	STATUS OF CONTIGUOUS CHARACTERISTIC	BEHAVIOR DISORDER CLASSES IDENTIFIABLE WITH TEST
Stanford-Binet Intelligence Scale	intelligence	Never directly observed. Verified by other structural or behavioral contiguous relationships (These characteristics are constructs.)	various classes of mental retardation
Wechsler Intelligence Scale for Children	verbal intelligence performance intelligence		
Vineland Social Maturity Scale	social maturity		various classes of mental illness
Minnesota Multiphasic Personality Inventory	personality traits: hypochondriasis, depression, hysteria, psychopathic deviate, masculine-feminine interests, paranoia, psychasthenia, schizophrenia, hypomania		

MEDICAL TEST	CONTIGUOUS CHARACTERISTIC	STATUS OF CONTIGUOUS CHARACTERISTIC	BEHAVIOR DISORDER CLASSES IDENTIFIABLE WITH TEST
electroencephalogram	nature and location of alpha, beta, delta, lambda, mu, theta, vertex, spike, and sharp waves; response to photic stimulation; sleep patterns; flat records	Directly observed. Verified by other structural or behavioral contiguous relationships and in some cases by a postmortem.	various classes of mental retardation
pneumoencephalogram	type amount of locus of shadow(s) on x ray		
tests for phenlypyruvic acid	amount of phenylpyruvic acid in urine		

The presentation and scoring of these tests must be standardized so that an obtained performance can be attributed to the individual examined rather than to variations in the manner of test presentation and scoring. Table 11-2 shows some sample test items and acceptable and unacceptable responses.[6] In the matter of psychological tests, the relevant discriminative stimulus complex consists of the following:

1. The verbal instructions presented to the individual by the examiner.

2. When required, the apparatus used in the test situation that is relevant to the test item verbal instructions.

3. The stimulus properties of the examiner—his physical appearance, gestures, mannerisms, and so on.

4. The stimulus properties of the test situation or surroundings—the room, other test materials, recording blanks, and so forth.

It is assumed that when an individual is presented a test item consisting of all four of these elements, it functions as a discriminative stimulus complex possessing stimulus control over appropriate verbal and motor operant behavior. However, *such an assumption is justified only when the individual has had adequate training from the verbal community.* Such training, as we have seen, consists of contingent positive reinforcement for the emission of the appropriate operant in the presence of the socially appropriate stimulus complex. (The reader may find a review of Chapter 5 helpful.)

For example, on the Picture Vocabulary item of the Stanford-Binet Intelligence Scale (see Table 11-2), the subject is shown a line drawing of a cow and asked, "What is this?" The situation is illustrated as follows:

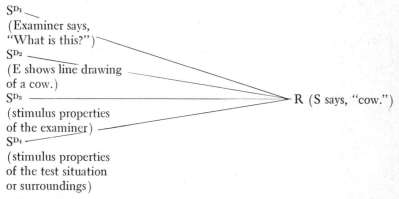

Each time the test is given, the examiner reads the test question from the Examiner's Manual (S^{D_1}, "What is this?") and he uses the same apparatus (S^{D_2}, a printed card with a line drawing of a cow on it) so that these ele-

[6] Acceptable responses are those that are usually characterized as the responses emitted by "normal" individuals—those not identified as being members of any behavior disorder class.

Table 11-2 Sample Items that Are Similar, if Not Identical, to Those Used in Standardized Psychological Tests

TEST	SUBTEST	AGE LEVEL	ITEM	ACCEPTABLE RESPONSES	UNACCEPTABLE RESPONSES
Stanford-Binet Intelligence Test Form L-M*	Picture Vocabulary	2	The question "What's this?" or "What do you call it?" is asked.		
			cow	cow	animal, mule, horse, moo-moo
			apple	apple	ball, baseball, round thing, toy
			fork	fork	toy, eating thing, food, spoon, knife
			cane	cane, walking stick	stick, wood, bat, tree, candy

Table 11-2 (*Continued*)

Opposite Analogies	4	"The turtle is slow; the fox is . . .?"	fast, faster, swift, quick, rapid, speedy	running faster
Materials	5–6	"What is a building made of?"	wood, boards, brick, adobe, cement, tile, lumber, stone, blocks	walls, sticks, nails, to go in
		"What is a door made of?"	wood, boards, glass, lumber, steel	sticks, nails, walls, to go in
Picture Absurdities	7	"What's funny (foolish) about that picture?"	Hammer is upside down. He's hammering the wrong way. He's holding it backwards. He has the hammer wrong. He ain't hammering right.	He's hammering a nail. He's hitting (going to hit) the wood. His arm is up (raised). He's holding a hammer.
Opposite Analogies	7	"Foxes are wild; cats are . . .?"	tame, very tame, tamed, tamed or civilized, domestic	tameful, gentle, pets, calm, playful, friendly, timid, quiet, mild
Wechsler-Bellevue Intelligence Scale for Children*	General Information***	"Who wrote *The Taming of the Shrew?*"	Shakespeare	

Table 11-2 (*Continued*)

TEST	SUBTEST	AGE LEVEL	ITEM	ACCEPTABLE RESPONSES	RESPONSES SCORED ON A GRADUATED SCALE
	General Comprehension ***		What would you do if you happened to lose one of your friend's toys?		*General:* Make good the loss. *2 points:* Try to find it or return it. Give him (her) one of my toys. *1 point:* Look for it. Tell my parents; they'd help me look. Advertise in the papers. *0 points:* I suppose I would cry. I'd say I'm sorry.
			Why is it better to save money at a bank than to keep money at home?		*General:* It's safer. You always have a record of how much you have. It earns interest. *2 points:* A response that includes or approximates two or more of the above ideas. *1 point:* A response that recognizes only one of the above. *0 points:* It makes you rich. So nobody can steal it. So you can get it when you need it.

Table 11-2 (*Continued*)

Similarities***

"In what ways are whiskey and champagne alike?"

2 *points:* A response indicating they are alcoholic beverages or intoxicants.
1 *point:* Both are beverages.
You drink both.
Both make you dizzy.
Both are liquid.
0 *points:* Both come in bottles.
They are made out of grain and grapes.
1 point for each correct response within 15 seconds

Picture Completion***

What's missing in this picture?

(one of the) legs missing.

The minute hand is missing.
No minute hand.
One of the hands is missing.

Table 11-2 *(Continued)*

TEST	SUBTEST	AGE LEVEL	ITEM	ACCEPTABLE RESPONSES	RESPONSES SCORED ON A GRADUATED SCALE
	Object Assembly***		Say: "If you put these pieces together properly, they will make a girl. Now, put them together properly." Time called after 120 seconds.		If all pieces in correct position: 4 *points*: 21–120 seconds 5 *points*: 16–20 seconds 6 *points*: 11–15 seconds 7 *points*: 1–10 seconds Partial credit: 1 *point*: 2 pieces in correct position 2 *points*: 3 pieces in correct position 3 *points*: 4 pieces in correct position

Table 11-2 (Continued)

TEST	SUBTEST	AGE LEVEL	ITEM NUMBER	ACCEPTABLE RESPONSES
Vineland Social Maturity Scale**	Communication	11.58	84	*Enjoys books, newspapers, magazines*—Reads for practical information or personal enjoyment, such as story or news columns in papers, magazine stories, library books, stories of adventure or romance
	Self-Direction	21.5+	102	*Uses money providently*—Lives within income, meets proper financial obligations promptly, avoids waste and extravagances, lives within a standard of living prudently related to income, resources, and obligations. Expenditures are for serious rather than frivolous purposes.
	Socialization	25+	104	*Contributes to social welfare*—Participates in local social work or activities of altruistic nature, and does so on own initiative; gives personal or financial support to such social groups as church, school, welfare organizations. Is a member of semi-professional clubs or social groups such as P.T.A., church guild, occupational or political organizations.
	Self-Direction	25+	105	*Provides for future*—Retains economic independence (allowance being made for emergencies outside own control), anticipates future needs or advantages by setting aside significant part of income or resources in savings, insurance, investment, etc., credit purchase of own home, special home furnishings, provision for higher education of children, and such investment expenditures as have cash value or which anticipate future welfare as opposed to immediate needs or pleasures. Defers immediate satisfaction for remote benefits. Scale of living allows surplus for emergencies.

Table 11-2 *(Continued)*

TEST	SUBTEST	AGE LEVEL	ITEM NUMBER	ACCEPTABLE RESPONSES
	Occupation	25+	107	*Engages in beneficial recreation*—Makes profitable use of leisure time for safeguarding or improving mental or physical welfare through reading, games and sports, and hobbies, gardening, music, art, theaters. Mere passive recreation, "low-brow" amusements, or time-killing pursuits not be credited.
	Socialization	25+	110	*Promotes civic progress*—Takes active part in advancing commercial, industrial, civic, educational, social movements beyond immediate occupational routine. Is a prominent member of professional, occupational, fraternal, religious, civic, or other group contributing to public welfare.
	Socialization	25+	115	*Shows community responsibility*—Participates in general management of large affairs, e.g., as a member of board of directors of important business, social, educational, institutional, civic organization. Holds major position of public trust.
	Socialization	25+	117	*Advances general welfare*—Has attained wide recognition as one who promotes public progress in philanthropic, religious, educational, cultural, scientific, industrial, patriotic fields.

* Although these items may appear to resemble comparable items from the Stanford-Binet Intelligence Test and the Wechsler-Bellevue Intelligence Scale for Children, care has been taken not to reproduce, in whole or in part, any specific items because of the effect such reproduction could have on the validity of the tests.
** From E. A. Doll, Vineland social maturity scale, *Condensed manual of instructions.* 1965 ed., pp. 4–7. Minneapolis: American Guidance Service, Inc. Copyright © 1965 and reproduced by permission.
*** There are no specific item-age equivalences. However, this test is designed for children from 5 to 15 years of age.

ments of the discriminative stimulus complex are standardized and controlled. Examiners are also trained in the importance of standardized test presentation, which is assumed to eliminate S^{D3} (the stimulus properties of the examiner) and S^{D4} (the stimulus properties of the test situation or surround) as uncontrolled discriminative stimulus elements of the discriminative stimulus complex affecting S's operant behavior. At the response end, the examiner is given a list of acceptable response classes against which S's performance can be compared and when it matches those on the list, he "passes" that test item.

There are three major sources of variability that contribute to the S's performance on a given psychological test. First, at the stimulus end of the test situation, verbal instructions may, on occasion, be so vague or ambiguous that performance will vary from one subject to the next. For example, on the actual Wechsler-Bellevue Intelligence Scale for Children, Object Assembly subtest, subjects may earn three extra points for rapid assembly of the manikin, even though they are not instructed to work rapidly. (See Table 11-2.) No doubt some subjects could earn more points if they were told initially to work as fast as they can. Second, at the response end, scoring standards are also vague or ambiguous on occasion. For example, on the Vineland Social Maturity Scale, Self-Direction subtest, item 102, the definition of "avoids waste and extravagance" may be difficult to determine and may reflect the characteristics of the examiner more than the characteristics of the subject. (Again, see Table 11-2.) Finally, and perhaps most important, is the assumption that all of the individuals who are tested have had the same history of reinforcement, that all have had the same opportunities to acquire differentiated and discriminated operant repertoires, in short that the individuals examined are from the same verbal community as those individuals identified in the norm group. A careful examination of these representative test items, as well as others not shown in Table 11-2, suggests, however, that the acceptable responses are more representative of the middle-class verbal community than of other verbal communities.

Poor performance on these tests, or more specifically, deficits in the types of discriminated operant behavior of which test performance consists, may be the result of any one of the following:

1. *The appropriate stimulus was never presented in discrimination training of the individual.* For example, on the Stanford-Binet Intelligence Scale, the Picture Vocabulary subtest contains a drawing of a cow, which could be a completely novel stimulus for a slum child.

2. *The subject has never emitted the appropriate response class in the presence of the appropriate stimulus.* For example, on the Wechsler-Bellevue Intelligence Scale for Children, Object Assembly subtest, the subject is told to put the manikin together, but some individuals may never have manipulated a jigsaw puzzle.

3. *The individual has emitted the appropriate response class in the presence of the appropriate stimulus, but was infrequently reinforced or perhaps punished for emitting the correct response, or delays in reinforcement strengthened some other response class.* For example, a child's correct recitation response to the Wechsler-Bellevue Intelligence Scale General Information subtest item—"Who wrote *The Taming of the Shrew?*"—may have gone unnoticed by the teacher and thus been extinguished.

4. *The subject may have been presented with both the appropriate stimulus and the appropriate consequence but emitted some inappropriate response class, which was strengthened.* For example, to the Stanford-Binet Intelligence Scale Opposite Analogies III, subtest item: "Foxes are wild, cats are ...?" a child may have been reinforced for saying "mild" (being poetic!) rather than saying "tame."

To sum up, variations in psychological test performances appear to be influenced by three factors: (1) ambiguity in the stimulus properties of the test item presentation, (2) ambiguity in scoring standards, and (3) perhaps most important, test item selection that ignores important historical differences in operant differentiation and discrimination and that favors the individual coming from the middle-class verbal community.

Table 11-3 shows some of the tests used in medical evaluation, along with acceptable and unacceptable responses. For example, on the quantitative test for phenylpyruvic acid, the individual's urine sample is treated with reagents and then compared under standard conditions with known amounts of phenylpyruvic acid. Similarly, in the electroencephalogram electrical activity of the brain is observed under standardized conditions. These standardized conditions include electrode type and placement of the electrodes on the scalp, amplification and recording apparatus characteristics, and environmental stimulation during the observation. The individual's record is then compared with records of individuals having known diseases.

As in the case of psychological tests, standardized test administration and scoring procedures are assumed to prevent variations in the individual's performance attributable to the characteristics of the examiner. It is also assumed, as in the case of psychological tests, that the norms against which the individual is compared, when norms are available, are representative of the population at large.[7]

Both psychological and medical evaluation procedures yield crude descriptions of the individual's contiguous characteristics. However, medical evaluation procedures are capable of yielding more precise descriptions for the following reasons:

[7] However, on some tests (EEG, for example) large intersubject variation occurs, making the development of norms based on the similarity of characteristics among individuals difficult to obtain (Glaser, 1963).

Table 11-3 Some of the Tests Used in Medical Evaluation and Acceptable and Unacceptable Responses to Them.

TEST	ITEM	ACCEPTABLE RESPONSES	UNACCEPTABLE RESPONSES
Test for Phenylketonuria	quantitative test for presence of phenylpyruvic acid Reagents: 10 percent ferric citrate 10 percent citric acid Procedure: A 1:10 dilution is made of urine. To 5 ml. of the diluted urine, 0.5 ml. of 10 percent ferric citrate and 0.5 ml. of 10 percent citric acid are added. The color reaction is read in 3 minutes in a photoelectric colorimeter at 630. The unknowns are compared with standard solutions of phenylpyruvic acid treated in the same manner.	0.0 mg. phenylpyruvic acid/24 hrs.	in phenylketonuria 500–1,000 mg. phenylpyruvic acid/24 hrs.
Electro-encephalogram	Procedure: Electrodes are placed bilaterally as follows: right and left motor-temporal, temporal-parietal, and parietal-motor areas.	 l. motor - temp. l. temp. - pariet. l. pariet. - motor normal waves	 r. motor - temp. r. temp. - pariet. r. pariet. - motor abnormal activity—slow waves in phase reversal indicative of either a tumor or trauma

Table 11-3 (*Continued*)

TEST	ITEM	ACCEPTABLE RESPONSES	UNACCEPTABLE RESPONSES
Skull X-Ray	left lateral view of skull	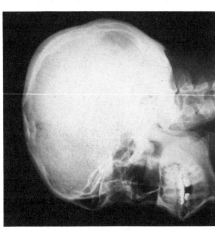Absence of localized calcification in the x-ray	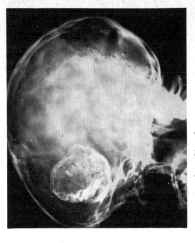extensive localized calcification of the olfactory groove—indicative of a tumor

Table 11-3 (*Continued*)

TEST	ITEM	ACCEPTABLE RESPONSES	UNACCEPTABLE RESPONSES
Pneumo-encephalogram	dorsal-ventral view of skull following introduction of air into the cerebral ventricles	normal configuration and positioning of the cerebellopontine recess of the cisterna pontis and the fourth cerebral ventricle	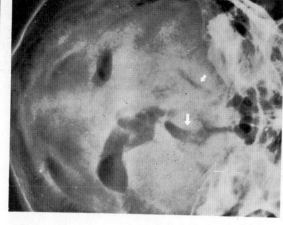 elevation and medial displacement of the cerebellopontine recess (small arrow) of the cisterna pontis, rotation of the fourth ventricle (large arrow) assuming a banana configuration

1. Precise specification of the test administration and scoring is possible, as illustrated by the procedures used in the quantitative test for phenylpyruvic acid. Test administration and scoring procedures are precisely stated, and machine scoring with the photoelectric colorimeter makes the test objective, with examiner bias having little influence.

2. Norms obtained in medical tests are probably more representative of the populations studied than those used in psychological evaluation.

3. Most important of all, medical tests are often administered to the same individuals repeatedly over a period of time, so that some idea of the individual's base-line performance can be determined. Urine analysis, blood counts, electroencephalograms, and the like may be repeatedly administered to an individual as part of a clinical treatment program, whereas psychological testing, especially intelligence testing, may occur only two or three times in an individual's lifetime and may, even at that, involve different tests having different procedures.

In both psychological and medical evaluation different tests may be administered, so that the evaluation is based on several different performances, or a pattern of the individual's characteristics or contiguous relationships. Furthermore, observed behavioral-behavioral contiguous relationships (for example, an individual having both low intelligence and low social maturity) or structural-behavioral contiguous relationships (for example, the presence of an extra chromosome in the individual's somatoplasm and low intelligence) are not descriptions of antecedent-consequence relationships. Rather, they are correlations between contiguous relationships observed in a clinical setting. For although clinical studies of human behavior may lead to the discovery of laws of behavior and the application of these laws to solve human problems, the verification of these laws in the laboratory under controlled conditions is essential.[8]

THE PSYCHIATRIC CLASSIFICATION SYSTEM

Table 11-4 shows sample descriptions illustrating the taxonomy of behavior disorders for a disease entity viewed as a form of mental illness (schizophrenia) and one viewed as a form of mental retardation (amaurotic familial idiocy). Notice that the characteristics and the symptoms described under

[8] Because of the moral questions involved, human subjects are not likely to be used in certain types of experiments. This means that some laws may never be verified by laboratory study. Nevertheless, animal studies may provide the verification of a lawful relationship in a given species that is applicable to human subjects, and subsequent clinical practice may provide a kind of further verification. The uncontrolled nature of clinical observation, however, bars the verification of lawful relationships if the observations are made only in the clinical setting and nowhere else. This is perhaps more true of the $R_1 = f(S_1)$ type of law than of the $R_1 = f(R_2)$ type of law, described in Chapter 1.

Table 11-4 Sample Descriptions Illustrating the Taxonomy of Behavior Disorders for a Disease Entity Viewed As a Form of Mental Illness (Schizophrenia) and One Viewed As a Form of Mental Retardation (Amaurotic Familial Idiocy)

	MENTAL ILLNESS	MENTAL RETARDATION
Class Symptoms	functional psychosis personality disintegration with disorientation for time, place, and/or person; hospitalization required	organic mental retardation subaverage general intellectual functioning and impaired adaptive behavior originating in the developmental period
Subclass Symptoms	schizophrenia withdrawal from reality, disturbed thought processes, emotional blunting, panic, breakdown of perceptual filtering, delusions, hallucinations	amaurotic familial idiocy blindness, impaired balance and coordination, apathy, muscular weakness, paralysis, convulsions, mental deterioration, death
Type Symptoms	paranoid schizophrenia poorly systematized delusions, often hostility and aggression, homosexual conflict	infantile type retinal cell degeneration, hypersensitivity to sound and light, swollen brain ganglion cells, muscular weakness, convulsions, paralysis, cranial enlargement, progressive retardation
Antecedents	no known physical causes; psychological stress?	Transmitted by a rare recessive gene. The antecedents to the disposition of lipids on the nervous-system ganglion cells is unknown.

the former are suggestive of deviant behaviors, whereas the characteristics and the symptoms described under the latter are suggestive of behavior deficits. In addition, a distinction is made between entities having known anatomic-physiological antecedents—*organic disorders*—and those for which there are no known anatomic-physiological antecedents—*functional disorders*. Besides the gross classes characterized by certain symptoms, there are subclasses, each containing descriptions of the characteristic patterns of symptoms for the syndrome. For example, schizophrenia is a subclass of functional psychosis characterized by withdrawal from reality, emotional blunting, panic, breakdown of perceptual filtering, disturbances in thought processes, and delusions and hallucinations. Within the subclass schizophrenia are various types, such as paranoid schizophrenia and simple schizophrenia, and each type has additional symptoms, each of which is broad and covers a wide range of contiguous relationships. For example, disturbances in thought processes would include, among other things, unusual word combinations (word salad), newly coined words (neologisms), and speech with good syntax but unusual content (that is, delusions like "The Lord chose me to avenge him"). Similarly, amaurotic familial idiocy is a subclass of organic mental retardation, characterized by subaverage intellectual functioning, originating in the developmental period and associated with impaired adaptive behavior, hypersensitivity to sound and light, muscular weakness, apathy, impaired balance and coordination, paralysis, convulsions, and death. Also within this subclass are various types, such as late infantile and juvenile, with each type possessing additional symptoms. In both cases it is the psychological and medical evaluation that reveals the symptoms consisting of the contiguous relationships characteristic of the given behavior disorder.

As we have seen, the utility of the diagnostic procedure that permits the identification of the behavior disorder class to which the individual belongs is twofold. First, as in biology, taxonomy, as a logical descriptive process, provides a basis for the systematic study of disease entities (behavior disorders) through a careful analysis of the similarities and differences in their characteristics. Second, when sufficient information is available, it provides a basis for the control of behavior disorders through their prevention, therapy, or both.[9] The psychiatric classification system, then, consists of descriptive classes or syndromes made up of patterns of behavioral and anatomic-physiological symptoms (contiguous relationships) and their causes, when known.

The following example gives an actual case study, including the patient's background, the time and place of the events described, and summary verbatim verbal descriptions given by the various professionals who, as part of their obligation to the patient, were required to prepare them. These professionals were either the patient's caretakers or specialists in behavior management. The reader should carefully study these reports, keeping in mind that *they represent what the person writing the summary regarded as the salient behavior and/or anatomic-physiological characteristics of the patient:*

Sam is the youngest of four children of upper middle-class parents. He is 12 years old. His sibs are normal. His prenatal development and birth were normal. However, a postnatal examination revealed that, like his sib predecessor, he was born jaundiced. Tests revealed the presence of bilirubin (red pigment) in the urine due to Rh factor incompatibility. Despite this condition at birth, no exchange blood transfusions were required, and his condition, again like his sib predecessor, quickly improved. Later on

---

[9] The psychiatric classification system encompassing diagnosis, etiology, prognosis, and therapy of behavior disorders is analogous to Mendeleev's periodic table in chemistry. This table describes the elements, their properties (that is, their weight, valence, and so on), and their behavior (for example, metals, when combined with the halogens, form salts), all of which is useful in the prediction, control, and understanding of nature. The psychiatric classification system purports to function in a similar manner.

his parents observed some behavioral retardation, and in 1963, when Sam was 5 years and 9 months old, a neurologist's report disclosed the following:

> The child began to walk at about the age of 17 months, and put two or three words together until about the age of 3, and then had what his parents call a "regression." At present he has severe nightmares, occasional bruxism [grinding teeth], is afraid of heights and stairs and is uncooperative at school. This consists of not hanging up his coat or attending to instruction. He is hyperactive and resistant to correction for such things as standing in the middle of the street or playing with knives. His favorite words seem to be "red" and "dirty poo-poo." For saying the latter in a group he has been remonstrated frequently "for swearing." From May to June 1962 he went to nursery school. Beginning this month he has been going to kindergarten, but due to his lack of progress and his behavior, his teacher suggested that he be evaluated on his ability to learn. About the time of his "regression," he had several flu-like illnesses, measles, and chicken pox. None were unduly severe.
>
> On examination, he would more or less repeat verbatim everything that was said to him or call colors and pictures and everything he was asked to name "red" or just aimlessly repeat "dirty poo-poo." His attempts with a pencil resulted in repetitive scribbling. He used the pencil and threw a ball with his right hand. The discs, maculae, and other cranial nerve functions were normal. His coordination, strength, deep tendon reflexes, and perception of vibration were normal. Auscultation of the head and neck was normal. The skin was tan-olive.
>
> Impression: Retardation, the degree and etiology of which is not clear. His learning ability will probably be severely impaired. Psychometrics are scheduled on 1 October 1963.

Two months later a psychological evaluation revealed the following:

> Sam, an attractive-looking little boy, was hyperactive, distractible, and impulsively autonomous during much of his visit here. The amount of attention he paid to instructions was sometimes nil, and he tended to echo what was said, or to clown silliness, or to cover his face with his hands if he didn't immediately grasp the nature of a given task. However, with those items that were within his range, especially if they involved doing rather than talking, he sobered down and showed sustained interest, as well as pleasure about his success with them. On the Stanford-Binet, Form L-M, he passes most of the two, two-and-one-half, three-year-old tests, but his few successes at the three-and-a-half-year level of difficulty are of marginal quality, and might be due to chance, while for the most part he just doesn't understand what is expected. Thus, his developmental status compares, roughly, with that expected of the average child of just three. The quotient, or ratio between his so-called mental and his chronological age, is about 47.
>
> Impression: Retardation, mental and social, in a boy whose limitations call for specialized teaching, preferably in a small group of children.

In 1964 the Stanford-Binet was again administered, and the following summary was given:

> Sam was brought in for testing by his parents for consideration for placement in a special program. He was fearful and quite reticent at first but related satisfactorily to the examiner as the session continued. His speech is quite limited and is characterized by echolalia [the meaningless repetition by the patient of the words spoken by the examiner]. A basal mental level was established at the Year II level and testing continued through Year IV–VI, at which level no credits were accrued. Sam was successful at Year IV in performing the memory subtest. Sam's muscular coordination appears good and he seems to be a tractable child. His IQ is 46.

Later that year he was declared ineligible for public school bus transportation because of boisterousness, insubordination, having his arms exposed outside the bus, requiring constant correction, and not remaining seated in the bus. The next year the following report was written by his teacher and sent to an examining psychiatrist:

> When Sam entered my room last year, he literally climbed the walls. When mother would put his hand in mine, he would scream, stamp his feet, and jump up and down. At first mother would "freeze" until I could get Sam quiet. After she left, he would go to the back of the room, put his face against the wall with one arm over his face, and refuse to be coaxed out. As this behavior improved, he would pace restlessly. He never did learn last year to sit for any long period of time. He would kick or hit other children if not carefully supervised. At play time he had to be carefully watched or he would wander around the school. June finally rolled around and Sam was still with us.
>
> This year he was advanced to the next grade. He sat all day and made a noise like a little animal. After a week of this, he started laughing and would continue this for an hour at a time. Finally, I agreed to take him back. I'm glad I did because it has been fascinating to watch the change.
>
> He will sit quietly now attempting the work. He is trying to read—has done well on chart stories—little on formal reading. He has at times counted five —sometimes does not know one to two. He is beginning to play and, in general, is becoming a *person*.
>
> I feel there is a "learning ability" if you can help it come through his shell of behavior. As this is improving, his learning is improving.

At the end of the school year (June 1965) Sam was promoted to the second grade special education class. He was described by his teacher as having shown the best improvement of any of the children in his group, and he showed an interest in chart reading and telling time. The examining psychiatrist sent this report to Sam's father in June of that year:

> This is a report of my impressions of your son, Sam, whom I saw recently on two occasions, May 6 and May 19, 1965.
>
> At the first interview, Sam's behavior was so immature and disorganized

that I was unable to perform an adequate psychiatric examination but gained the impression of a severe degree of physical and emotional handicap. The best estimate that could be made at that time would place his IQ somewhere between 40 and 60.

When I examined Sam the second time, on May 19, he was seen with his mother, and was well controlled, subdued, and tractable. He responded to simple commands, was eager to please, and displayed considerable self-control as well as charm. Throughout the examination, he showed constant repetitive behavior and verbal echoing of his own and other's comments. These latter signs are very characteristic of brain-injured, retarded children. It was very apparent that Sam's intellectual range is a limited one and I would concur with the earlier diagnosis of mental retardation due to brain injury as a result of blood type incompatibility.

It is obvious, too, that Sam has a significant behavior disorder, and this is consistent with the degree of developmental retardation and organic central nervous system pathology. This kind of behavioral difficulty often improves with firm and consistent management by parents, and with the use of medication to control hyperactivity and impulsivity. It does not usually respond to psychotherapy, and I feel that there is little reason to believe that his basic disorder is a reversible one. At best, I feel we can hope for a reasonably well adjusted, moderately retarded, pleasant youngster who will require supervision and professional care throughout his life.

Toward the end of the year (1965), the family moved East, and psychological and psychiatric evaluations were performed. The psychological evaluation, which was requested by the psychiatrist, consisted of the Wechsler-Bellevue Intelligence Scale for Children and Figure Drawing. The following summary was given:

Sam R., age 7, was seen for psychological evaluation at the request of Dr. C. Sam is a very cute looking little youngster with brown hair and eyes, who at the time of testing was hospitalized at ——— Hospital.

When we arrived at Sam's room he seemed quite friendly and accepting of the fact that we were going to talk with him. However, after sitting down for approximately one minute, Sam decided that he was going to walk around the room. We told him to return to the table where we were attempting to administer the Wechsler and Sam complied, but with any question that was asked there was an echolalia on Sam's part and this continued throughout the time I remained with him. He was unable to answer any question on the Wechsler or to perform any of the tasks required of him. We finally got him to take a pencil and attempt to draw a person; however, this resulted in mere scribbling on the page. All during the time of the testing Sam not only repeated what we would say to him, but he would get up, do various things like pulling on the cord which rang for the nurse and talking in the third person in regard to himself.

Although it is noted in medical records that there is a possibility of organic brain damage, clinical observation would lean heavily toward a childhood schizophrenia. This is not necessarily in contradiction to former diagnosis, but it is felt that there is definitely a superimposition of a psychotic process. It is felt that this youngster would profit from the kind of treatment institutionalization would provide. Little apparently can be done on an outpatient basis and a more skilled, professional treatment, which the parents aren't able to provide, is considered essential.

Although the parents didn't receive the psychiatric evaluation, the examining psychiatrist, Dr. C., did send a summary of his observation to a home for retarded children, where placement of Sam was being considered. He reported that:

> This child has been treated by me for a Schizophrenic Reaction, Childhood Type, with secondary mental retardation. In addition to psychotherapy and a period of hospitalization, he has been maintained on Thorazine 50 mg. four times a day.
> Sam was found to be at times rather belligerent, hyperactive, and perseverative. Hallucinations were not documented; however, he does voice his own superego as he states the action he is prohibited to do and then goes ahead and does it. He responds to internal impulses and acts upon them regularly without any censorship. This may be slapping a nurse or masturbating in front of an audience. However, he is a very likable, nice-looking young boy, and when he is quiet, he can relate some, but only partly and not deeply. There is occasional word salad, echolalia, and echopraxia [the meaningless repetition by the patient of motions started by the examiner]. There was a question of organic brain syndrome, which was not documented by the EEG, or by psychological testing.
> Routine lab work: Urine for PKU and porphyrin was negative. Skull x-ray is also negative.
> The parents are not in agreement as to how to handle this child, as well as future plans for him. Institutionalization for long-term therapy is also recommended.

In June of 1966 Sam concluded another year in a public school special education class. The pupil's progress and teacher's report revealed that Sam should be excluded from the fall enrollment. His teacher reported that "Sam would profit from a residential situation. Sam has frequent tantrums which disturb the class and other classes on the hall. The sudden outbursts are numerous and the cause not usually known by the teacher."

In August of that year another medical exam revealed that Sam was an "alert hyperactive fearful child who looks his age physically—talks well."

In September, upon the family's return to the West coast, another psychiatric evaluation was made to implement Sam's institutionalization. In addition, he was enrolled in a special education class, which soon resulted in Sam's exclusion from school because he wouldn't remain seated in class, was disruptive, and threatened violence. In December of 1966 Sam was arraigned in juvenile court for aggressiveness and throwing rocks at children in the neighborhood. Finally, Sam spent almost 24 months in the children's psychiatric unit of the County General Hospital without behavior change and was then institutionalized.

In addition to the reports of the initial postpartum examination, of routine medical examinations, and of the special education teachers, Sam's parents were able to provide for additional comprehensive medical and psychological evaluations from a neurologist, two psychiatrists, and two psychologists. It would seem, therefore, that there was ample opportunity to study his case, identify the behavior disorder class to which he belonged, and to generate from this, accurate descriptions (predictions) about the etiology, prognosis, and therapy. However, a careful study of the predictions made in the reports reveals the following:

1. In the matter of *diagnosis*, there appears to be some disagreement. Although all agree that Sam is retarded, only in his later years were psychotic features reported.

2. In the matter of *etiology*, there is also disagreement. Although the postpartum examination revealed the presence of bilirubin in the urine, due to an Rh factor, rapid improvement without complications was reported, and the neurological report more than 5 years later was negative. An examination by a psychiatrist 2 years later, however, reported irreversible brain damage due to the Rh factor, and a psychologist reported a functional psychosis (childhood schizophrenia). Still later, the report of another psychiatrist did not confirm irreversible brain damage, but did report childhood schizophrenia.

3. In the matter of *prognosis*, there is, perhaps, *less* disagreement between the specialists (the neurologist, psychiatrists, and psychologists) and the caretakers (special education teachers). The former reported continued severe impairment of learning ability, some possible behavioral improvement, but with continued moderate retardation, requiring care and supervision. In 1964 the latter reported considerable improvement, although in 1966 Sam was excluded from public school.

4. In the matter of *therapy*, there is also little disagreement except within the line functions of the specialists involved (only the physicians could prescribe drugs). Initially, special education and firm and consistent management by the parents was recommended, but later on institutionalization.[10]

There are several points that should be made about this case. First, despite the extensiveness of the psychological and medical evaluation Sam received, there was significant disagreement among evaluators, especially in the matter

---

[10] It should be clear that institutionalization is by no means synonymous with therapy, except in the medical-custodial sense that a patient with a behavior disorder may receive therapy for his physical ailments.

of diagnosis and etiology, the effect of which was to also produce some disagreement on prognosis. Moreover, the assertions that were made regarding diagnosis, etiology, and prognosis were broadly stated. Second, each evaluator had access to the reports of his predecessors, so that his evaluation was not blind (that is, uninfluenced by previous evaluators). Finally, the reports did not give any specific recommendations for treatment (aside from the drug prescriptions), although special education programs and institutionalization were recommended.

In many respects, the evaluation and management procedures in this case are typical. Occasionally, these evaluation and management procedures have grave implications for the welfare of the patient. This is revealed by the following example, which includes excerpts from a brief prepared by Judge Richard Heller (1966) of the New York State Court:

On October 6, 1925, 16-year-old Stephen Dennison, "a maladjusted youth from a broken family, the product of an atmosphere of cultural poverty," pled guilty to an indictment of third-degree burglary, which specified "that he had broken into a roadside stand and stolen about $5.00 worth of candy." He was given a suspended sentence, but violated his terms of probation by "failing to report monthly to a minister in his hometown," and on August 14, 1926, he was confined at the New York State Reformatory at Elmira, New York, pursuant to Section 384 of the Correction law.

Through a tragic error in psychological testing and evaluation, Dennison was classified as a low grade moron, and on September 15, 1927, he was transferred to the Institution for Male Defective Delinquents at Napanoch, New York. Except for a brief but unsuccessful release on parole, he was confined at Napanoch until March, 1936, at which time, on the basis of a "Certificate of Lunacy," he was transferred to Dannemora State Hospital, where he was retained until December 16, 1960. It is significant that, although his criminal sentence would have expired on September 17, 1936, shortly after his arrival at Dannemora, Dennison was at that time still regarded as insane by the prison authorities, an evaluation that seems to have been based on nothing more than (1) observation and psychological tests administered while he was at Elmira Reformatory, (2) a period of time during his stay at Napanoch during which he exhibited "psychotic tendencies," and (3) his "dull" appearance, which it was later determined was caused by a "purely physical condition which caused his eyelids to droop and which was related in no way to his mental capacity."

An action for false imprisonment was eventually brought before Judge Richard S. Heller in the Court of Claims at Elmira, New York. Ruling in favor of Dennison, compensatory damages based on the Claimant's earning capacity as a production worker had he not been wrongfully incarcerated (a decision later reversed by the New York State Appellate Court) in the amount of $115,000.00 was awarded the Claimant. Judge Heller felt this to be *minimum* damages considering the years of degradation, humiliation, and frustration endured by the Claimant. Judge Heller stated that "the illegality of the Claimant's confinement for the period indicated . . . is unquestionable." He went on to state that "damages . . . would be minimal if he [Dennison] were, in fact, dangerously insane and a fit subject for retention at or commitment to Dannemora," but that "at the time his criminal sentence expired, he had recovered from his insanity in the sense that overtly psychotic behavior had ceased."

Subsequent to his release, secured by his half brother through a habeas corpus proceeding in 1960, tests administered to Dennison not only established that he had "average intelligence," but also gave rise to a consideration of how much better he might have performed on those tests had he not been "subjected to the *deadening atmosphere* of Napanoch and Dannemora for a period of more than thirty years." The Court depicted the institution at Napanoch—at least during Dennison's years there—as "a repository for unfortunates of varying degrees of imbecility, idiocy and moronity," and regarded it as obvious that a person's "fundamental rights would be infringed . . . were he to be confined with mental defectives whose appearance, speech, and personal habits were abhorrent, as clearly as if he were required to live in a madhouse[,] . . . were constantly subjected to offensive odors, or [were] confined for long periods to a dungeon or solitary confinement!"

As for the records from Dannemora State Hospital, which repeatedly described Dennison's behavior as paranoid, Judge Heller had this to say: "If a person is, in fact, being treated unjustly or unfairly, the fact that he perceives, resents and reacts to the inequity could hardly be regarded as competent and conclusive evidence of paranoia or paranoid tendencies." The Judge concluded that the appearance of psychotic symptoms was caused by the nature of his confinement, and that, in a sense, "society labeled him as sub-human, placed him in a cage with genuine sub-humans, drove him insane, and then used the insanity as an excuse for holding him indefinitely in an institution with few, if any, facilities for genuine treatment and rehabilitation of the mentally ill."

Judge Heller's remarks concerning the psychiatric evaluation process and the compensable damages due the Claimant for more than 30 years incarceration are interesting:

> Although relatively easy to state, the issues are extremely difficult to resolve. A considerable amount of speculation is necessarily involved in at-

tempting to reach a satisfactory conclusion with respect to a person's potentialities or capacities. That psychiatry and psychology are not exact sciences becomes painfully clear to anyone charged with a fact finder's responsibility in cases such as that before the Court.

It is easy for laymen to simply throw up their arms when confronted with the semantic jungle of psychiatric and psychological concepts and terminology. One psychiatrist testifies that stress may give rise to certain types of psychotic disorders. Another states that stress doesn't "cause" but merely triggers or fosters the appearance of symptoms in an individual with latent psychotic tendencies or psychoses. What then do we mean by the "causes" or by "psychosis"? What appear to be different diagnoses turn out to be semantic disputes, the existence of which are the clearest indication that in the field of psychiatry there are many hypotheses but distressingly few answers.

Ultimately a decision must be based upon which hypothesis or proposed analysis appears most reasonable in the light of a commonsense appraisal of all relevant facts. To this must be added that, when we are concerned with personality traits or mental condition, almost every fact seems to be relevant to one expert or another.

The cases of Sam and Stephen Dennison possess interesting similarities and differences. In both cases psychological tests were used; the behavior disorder class to which the boys belonged was identified, and the information was passed on to the evaluators;[11] both boys broke the law, and both were institutionalized. Moreover, the physical appearance (physiognomies) of both boys, though not explicitly stated as significant, was mentioned and may have figured in their dispositions. However, the two boys possessed different behavior problems and came from different socioeconomic strata, and there were large differences in the integrity of their families. These differences contributed to the large differences in the evaluation and management procedures they received.[12]

Underlying the evaluation and final description of both boys was the assumption that because of their anatomic-physiological and behavioral con-

---

[11] Although completely a matter of speculation, it is possible that both were victims of a self-fulfilling prophecy. Once they had been labeled in the diagnostic process and the prognosis specified, their caretakers may have "scaled down" their performance demands to accommodate the patient. In so doing, the caretakers would have been merely following "doctor's orders" (instructions). There is evidence of such an effect in the classroom (see Rosenthal and Jacobson, 1968) and in the mental hospital (see D. L. Rosenhan, 1973).

[12] This is not an uncommon observation. For example, Hollingshead and Redlich (1958) report that individuals from the lower classes are more apt to be diagnosed as schizophrenic, more apt to be placed in a state rather than a private institution, and more apt to be given custodial care or physical-chemical therapy, rather than psychotherapy, than individuals from the middle and upper classes, while Szasz (1970) eloquently argues that such evaluative and management practices have in fact, become instruments of social rejection and social control.

tiguous characteristics, they both had behavior disorders. The *presumption* that Sam had sustained brain damage was only one of several other anatomic-physiological characteristics (bilirubin in the urine and jaundice) along with numerous behavioral characteristics (low IQ, aggressiveness, echolalia). These characteristics were contiguous and identified Sam as being in the behavior disorder classes of mental retardation and childhood schizophrenia. Similarly, Stephen's behavioral contiguous characteristics (low IQ, feelings of persecution) identified him as being in the behavior disorder classes mental retardation and paranoia or paranoid tendencies. It was further assumed that each of these disorders was a real, specifiable disease entity, having specific antecedents, predictable outcomes, and appropriate therapies. It was as if the anatomic-physiological and behavioral contiguous characteristics making up these behavior disorder classes were regarded as merely representative of something else more fundamental and basic, namely mental illness. Such mental illness, it was assumed, involved root causes having predictable effects over time and requiring specific procedures for their removal. This viewpoint is widely held in psychiatry and is sometimes called the *mental illness, or medical, model.*[13] It plays a fundamental role in the study and management of behavior disorders.

There are a number of objections to psychological and medical evaluations and the psychiatric classification system as they are used in the study and management of behavior disorders:

1. *The language of the systems (that is, "mental illness," "mental retardation" and on so) implies that the antecedents to the behavior deviation(s) or deficit(s) are, at least in part, in the mind or psyche of the patient.* For example, the peculiar speech of the patient is viewed as being due to cognitive disorganization, or the retardate's lack of skills is regarded as being due to a lack of mentality.

2. *The language of the systems (that is, "paranoid schizophrenia," "catatonia," and so on) possesses "surplus meaning" through the presumed generality to the patient's other behaviors in other situations (transituational generality) and to other patients grouped in the class.* Actually, it is the patient's specific acts in specific situations, not all of his acts, that provide the basis for his diagnosis. Furthermore, it is not uncommon for patients who are members of the same class to show great variability in behavior. For example, a psychotic may emit only neologisms in some situations and not in others. The behavior of such a patient does not show transituational generality, even though such generality is implied by the behavior disorder class psychotic. Furthermore, many of the patients identified as psychotics may not emit any neologisms.

---

[13] The reader should not confuse these notions with "medical prejudice"—the view that one day it will be observed that all behavior disorders are perforce caused by some organic or physical pathology, even though present evidence is to the contrary.

3. *The classification system stresses the peculiarities of the patient—what is offensive about him or what he cannot do—rather than how adequate his behavior is.* Thus despite the schizophrenic's highly adequate speech and self-help skills, great emphasis is placed on his deviant behavior (opposite speech, for example).[14]

4. *Following diagnosis, the labeling of the patient (as paranoid schizophrenic or having Down's syndrome, for example) gives him stimulus properties that often result in differential treatment by his caretakers and may intensify his deviant behavior or behavior deficits, resulting in a self-fulfilling prophesy.* Thus, because the form or content of the psychotic's peculiar speech and mannerisms is viewed as theoretically significant, they may be especially attended to by the psychiatric staff and thus strengthened.[15] Or the retardate may fail to develop appropriate skills because he is viewed by his caretakers as incapable of learning them and thus is not trained in them.

5. *Trivial acts may provide a basis for psychiatric evaluation because of*

[14] In opposite speech, there is a lack of congruence between the patient's verbal report and his motor behavior. For example, Laffal, Lenkoski, and Ameen (1956) report a case of a schizophrenic patient who was unaware of the fact that his language was frequently the opposite of his thought and action. For example, when asked if he wanted a cigarette, he would reply No (verbal report), yet take one from the person offering it and smoke it (motor behavior).

[15] The author once attended a clinic on mental retardation at a large hospital for the retarded. There were about two hundred students in the audience, and the psychiatrist in charge introduced a female patient, about 40 years old, as a schizophrenic. He suggested that the students be especially watchful of her speech, as she would describe herself as being younger than she actually was, married (which she was not), and as having seven children (which she did not have). Evidence of her condition was to be revealed by her responses to the following questions, which were asked in an interview before the entire group:

Psychiatrist: "What's your name?"
Patient: "Rosie."
Psychiatrist: "How old are you?"
Patient: "Twenty-two."
Psychiatrist (smiling and turning to the audience): "How old?"
Patient: "Twenty-two."
Psychiatrist: "Are you married?"
Patient: "Yes."
Psychiatrist: "Any children?"
Patient: "Yes, seven."
Psychiatrist (now laughing and turning to the audience): "Tell us their names."
Patient: "Well, there's Sarah, Timmy, John, Tony, and...."
Psychiatrist (again laughing and turning to the audience, some members of which are now smiling): "Who else?"
Patient (now laughing also): "Well there's Stanley and Hazel ... (laugh) ... and ..."

It seemed to the author that this performance, as well as the performances of some of the other patients at the clinic, were maintained, at least in part, by the verbal instructions presented by the psychiatrist (discriminative stimuli) and the attention, interest, smiling, and laughter presented by both the psychiatrist and the audience (reinforcing stimuli).

their symbolic-theoretical significance. Thus an individual may be viewed as possessing severe conflicts simply because he washes his hands an inordinate number of times a day.

6. *When behavior that is not consistent with middle-class notions of propriety is under the scrutiny of middle-class psychologists and psychiatrists, it may be viewed as symptomatic of mental illness.* For example, excessive use of profanity, lack of ability in verbal expression, absence of a stable employment history, and lack of ambition with respect to middle-class goals may be viewed as evidence of simple schizophrenia.

7. *The crudeness of the evaluation methods (especially psychological evaluation) and the broadness of the descriptions of the symptoms of which the syndromes or behavior disorders consist yield at best only limited agreement among evaluators on diagnosis, etiology, and prognosis.*[16]

8. *When the classification system is not backed up by adequate knowledge regarding appropriate therapeutic procedures, it loses much of its usefulness.* Therapeutic goals for a given patient will depend on the theory held by the psychiatrist or clinical psychologist responsible for the patient, and in some cases the goals are very difficult to define. And even when some definition is possible, procedures for reaching the goals are often ineffective or may even make the patient worse.

To sum up, although the psychiatric classification systems represent extensions of the taxonomic method of the biological sciences to behavior problems, their value in actual practice leaves much to be desired and may be outweighed by their shortcomings.

AN ALTERNATIVE TO TRADITIONAL PSYCHIATRIC CLASSIFICATION SYSTEMS

In contrast to the traditional classification system and the psychological and medical evaluation processes underlying it, the behavior theory view stresses the following:

1. Concern with the individual's specific respondent or operant behaviors rather than possible intrapsychic or neurophysiological events or states representing other dimensional systems.

2. The absence of traditional methods of psychological evaluation and especially psychological tests that by their nature refer to other dimensional systems—that is, intelligence tests, personality tests, and the like—the results

---

[16] Professional inter-judge agreement on the diagnosis of mental deficiency ranges from 42 to 73 percent and on schizophrenia from 53 to 80 percent. Sources of disagreement are inconsistency of the patient's behavior (5 percent), inconsistency of the diagnostician (32.5 percent), and inadequacy of the classification system (62.5 percent) (Zubin, 1967).

of which are presumed to have generality extending beyond that of the test situation (transituational generality).

3. Descriptions of the individual's current behavior repertoire, in terms of behavior deficits (for example, the absence of self-help, speech, social, motor, or verbal learning skills) or behavior deviations (for example, the presence of objectionable verbal and/or motor interpersonal behaviors), the specific nature of which is deemed significant or important by the individual or his caretakers, rather than because of the relationship of the individual's behavior to a group norm.[17]

4. Precise, objective descriptions of the individual's behavior repertoire through the use of repeated observations of base-line performances and a functional definition of the environmental events under which they occur.

5. Medical evaluations, although anatomic-physiological contiguous relationships in behavior disorders are generally viewed as descriptions of correlation rather than causation.[18]

6. The rejection of the *similia similibus curantur fallacy*, which asserts that "only like can be cured by like." According to this fallacy, a patient with a behavior disorder having verified organic (anatomic-physiological) antecedents can only be cured by medical (physical-chemical) therapies, or a patient with a behavior deficit having verified behavioral-environmental antecedents can only be cured by psychological (behavioral) therapies.

7. The recognition that although it is the patient's operant behavior deficits or deviations that are most apt to get the attention of the caretaker because of the changes they produce in the patient's physical and social environment, any behavior deficit or deviation consists of both operant and respondent behaviors.

8. The assumption that except in cases where a behavior disorder has verified organic antecedents,[19] the same laws of behavior that apply to the development of normal behavior apply to the development of abnormal behavior.

[17] Although workers have tried to specify what *normal* behavior is without cultural bias, one encounters many difficulties. Normal behavior has been defined variously as behavior that is (1) socially acceptable (to whom?), (2) frequent or widely practiced (in what group?), (3) normal in terms of a theory of healthy psychic functioning (whose?), and (4) adaptive, or leading to survival (in what context and over the short or long term?). Despite the obvious appeal of the latter, confusion is apt to occur between behavior leading to survival and behavior that benefits the caretaker. For example, a child who eats with his hands and not silverware may be described as possessing a deficit in adaptive behavior (Nihara, Foster, and Spencer, 1968).

[18] For example, individuals described as having Down's syndrome have, among other things, forty-seven instead of forty-six chromosomes (a structural contiguous relationship) and, as a group, show varying degrees of behavior deficits (a behavioral contiguous relationship). This is, however, a correlation, not a description of causation.

[19] The question of verification of an antecedent-consequence relationship in clinical studies has been dealt with earlier both on moral and on methodological grounds. However, clinical studies may yield a kind of verification when (1) the psychological evaluation *consistently* reveals that the patient has definite behavior deficits and/or behavior deviations, (2) the medical evaluation *consistently* reveals the presence of an anatomic-

9. The recognition that the behavioral contiguous relationships or the symptoms possessed by an individual identified having a behavior deficit or behavior deviation are always protean and reflect that individual's history.

As we have seen, individuals identified as showing a behavior deficit or deviation are so designated because *their behavior repertoires contain specific, observable acts or response classes that are in some way regarded, by themselves or their caretakers, as inadequate.* These repertoires consist of respondent behaviors, which, for the purpose of analysis, have been described in terms of r (response class) functions, e (eliciting stimulus) functions, and k (contingency) functions, or operant behaviors, which have been described by Lindsley (1964) in terms of R (response class) functions, S (discriminative stimulus) functions, C (consequation) functions, and K (contingency) functions.

An additional factor, s (state of the organism), is relevant to both types of behavior. (See Tables 11-5 and 11-6.) From these key elements descriptions of the behavioral contiguous relationships and the possible antecedent environmental events characteristic of behavior deficits and behavior deviations can be generated. Such descriptions are shown in the examples given at the beginning of the chapter. Thus Greg, described in example 2, possessed certain behavioral and anatomic-physiological contiguous characteristics—absence of reading and writing, limited speech and self-help skills, hyperactivity and distractibility, and evidence of some dilation of the cerebral ventricles and thinning of the corpus callosum. Under the traditional behavior disorder classification system, these characteristics would *identify* him as belonging to the class of organic mental retardation; subclass, hydrocephaly; type, noncommunicating. Under the alternative system proposed here, he would *only be described* as possessing behavior deficits in reading, writing, speech, and self-help skills (the specific nature of which was not mentioned).[20] Similarly,

---

physiological contiguous relationship, and (3) there is sufficient knowledge in the field supporting the conclusion that these anatomic-physiological contiguous relationships are antecedents to the observed behavior. In terms of these criteria, Sam, the boy described earlier, would not be correctly described as brain-damaged, simply because such an inference is based on his behavior and is not confirmed by several other medical tests (such as, a test of reflexes, EEG, and x rays). Had any of these medical tests been consistently positive, perhaps a kind of verification of the anatomic-physiological contiguous relationship as antecedent to Sam's behavior would have occurred. Even then, such an antecedent-consequence relationship could have been presumed to exist only during and immediately after its occurrence.

[20] Although the etiology of Greg's behavior deficits seems straightforward (brain damage—the thinning of the corpus callosum due to dilation of the cerebral ventricles), this may be more apparent than real. Recovery from brain damage is not uncommon, and current deficits may have been due to inadequate training history rather than irreversible brain damage. From the sketchy information available, the etiology cannot be determined. What is needed is information on when his symptoms first appeared, their nature, the diagnosis made, when the corrective surgery was performed, the quality of his postoperative environment, and any progress observed.

Table 11-5 Some Behavioral Contiguous Relationships Characteristic of Behavior Deficits and Their Possible Antecedent Environmental Events

BEHAVIORAL CONTIGUOUS RELATIONSHIPS	POSSIBLE ANTECEDENT ENVIRONMENTAL EVENTS
Operant Behavior	
R (RESPONSE CLASS) FUNCTIONS	
undifferentiated or poorly differentiated self-help, social, speech, motor, and verbal learning skills, atavistic behavior	extinction, infrequent reinforcement, delayed reinforcement, non-response-contingent reinforcement, punishment, absence of or infrequent availability of manipulanda, absence of or infrequent presentation of behavior-shaping procedures
rocking, self-stimulatory motor behavior, low activity level	behavior in the absence of other discriminated incompatible operant behavior*, **
low activity level, tantrums	extinction, tantrum-response-contingent reinforcement
s (DISCRIMINATIVE STIMULUS) FUNCTIONS	
caretaker-presented verbal instructions, gestures, and other physical stimuli not discriminated or infrequently discriminated	absence of or infrequent exposure to environmental social and physical stimuli, absence of or infrequent reinforcement following appropriate responses emitted in the presence of appropriate social and physical stimuli
c (CONSEQUATION) FUNCTIONS	
lack of behavioral effect of SR+	satiation*, **
lack of behavioral effect of SR−	presentation of SR− historically discriminative for SR+ and Sr+
lack of behavioral effect of Sr+, Sr−, lack of behavioral effect of generalized Sr+, token Sr+	absence of or infrequently paired and/or discriminated conditioned, generalized, or token reinforcing stimuli, delayed pairing and/or discriminated conditioned, generalized, or token reinforcing stimuli*, **
k (CONTINGENCY) FUNCTION	
lack of behavioral effect of delayed consequences	absence of or weakly formed operant behavior chains
lack of behavioral effect of intermittent consequences	absence of, abrupt, or too rapid a change in reinforcement schedule
lack of behavioral effect of episodic reinforcement	absence of or weakly formed operant behavior chains

* Heavy dosages of sedatives or tranquilizing drugs may also have these effects.
** Nervous system trauma or disease may also have these effects.

Table 11-6 Some Behavioral Contiguous Relationships Characteristic of Behavior Deviations and Their possible Antecedent Environmental Events

BEHAVIORAL CONTIGUOUS RELATIONSHIPS	POSSIBLE ANTECEDENT ENVIRONMENTAL EVENTS
Operant Behavior	
R (RESPONSE CLASS FUNCTIONS)	
gradual deterioration of self-help, speech, social, motor, or verbal learning skills	extinction, weak reinforcers, infrequent reinforcement, delayed reinforcement
repetitive, stereotyped, rhythmic, "small" motor behavior (playing with shoelaces, excessive handling small objects), twirling	behavior in the absence of other discriminated incompatible responses, small-behavior-contingent reinforcement
tantrums, atavisms	extinction, contingent reinforcement
low activity level	contingent reinforcement, punishment*
postural-gestural acts, walking on toes	adventitious reinforcement
aggressiveness	presentation of strongly noxious or irritating stimuli, abrupt introduction of extinction or intermittent schedule of reinforcement, aggressive-response-contingent reinforcement
lack of congruence of verbal and motor operants (opposite speech)	contingent reinforcement for either verbal or motor operant component with the other component adventitiously reinforced, contingent reinforcement for both components of concurrent behavior even though they are not congruent
tics	adventitiously reinforced concurrent operant**
S (DISCRIMINATIVE STIMULUS) FUNCTIONS	
self-destructive behavior, smearing	contingent reinforcement
imitative vocal or motor acts (echolalia and echopraxia)	contingent reinforcement of imitative behavior in the presence of a trainer-presented sample performance
abrupt deterioration of discriminated self-help, speech, social, motor, or verbal learning skills, abrupt decline in activity level	sudden removal of controlling stimuli (such as caretaker, physical environment) when repertoire is under limited or narrow range of stimulus control**
neologisms, speech with bizarre content	contingent reinforcement of this speech in the presence of a trainer
C (CONSEQUATION) FUNCTIONS	
lack of behavioral effect of SR+, Sr-, lack of behavioral effect of generalized Sr+, lack of behavioral effect of token Sr+	delayed pairing and/or discriminated conditioned reinforcing stimuli, satiation,*

Table 11-6 *(Continued)*

BEHAVIORAL CONTIGUOUS RELATIONSHIPS	POSSIBLE ANTECEDENT ENVIRONMENTAL EVENTS
K (CONTINGENCY) FUNCTIONS	
lack of behavioral effect of delayed consequences	extinction of operant behavior chains, satiation
lack of behavioral effect of intermittent consequences	weak reinforcers, satiation

Respondent Behavior

BEHAVIORAL CONTIGUOUS RELATIONSHIPS	POSSIBLE ANTECEDENT ENVIRONMENTAL EVENTS
R (RESPONSE CLASS) FUNCTIONS	
restricted or limited patterns of respondent behavior (shallowness of affect)	absence of presentation of positive or negative US
E (ELICITING STIMULUS) FUNCTIONS	
restricted or limited patterns of respondent behavior (shallowness of affect)	infrequent pairings of positive or negative US with CS, positive or negative respondent behavior patterns elicited by narrow range of CS's
chronic activation syndrome	prolonged presentation of events having US functions like sustained physical exertion, painful or noxious stimuli extinction, or a CS eliciting comparable respondents that is not necessarily known, stimulus generalization
acute activation syndrome	brief presentation of events having US functions like sustained physical exertion, painful or noxious stimuli extinction, or a CS eliciting comparable respondents that is not necessarily known, stimulus generalization
strong negative respondents to neutral stimuli (phobia)	repeated stimulus pairing of mildly painful or noxious stimuli with CS or a few stimulus pairings of strongly painful or noxious stimuli with CS, stimulus generalization
respondent depression pattern	absence or infrequent presentation of either US or CS eliciting positive respondent patterns
K (CONTINGENCY) FUNCTIONS	
lack of behavioral effect of stimulus pairing (US with CS)	infrequent stimulus pairing, weak US paired with CS, absence of deprivation, long delay between US and CS

---

* Heavy dosages of sedatives or tranquilizing drugs may also have these effects.
** Nervous system trauma or disease may also have these effects.

under the traditional behavior disorder classification systems, Sarah (example 8), because of her behavioral and anatomic-physiological contiguous characteristics (the unusual content of her speech, her posture, her tactless bursting into song, and her basically negative physical exam), would probably be *identified* as belonging to the behavior disorder class of functional psychosis; subclass, schizophrenia; type, mixed. Again, under the system proposed here, she would only be described as possessing deviant behavior consisting of speech with bizarre content, unusual posture and speech (her songs) under inappropriate stimulus control.[21] The other examples would be dealt with in the same manner. In each case the individual or caretaker would define the specific behavior deficits or deviations characterizing the behavior problem.[22]

An examination of Tables 11-5 and 11-6 reveals several interesting conclusions about behavior deficits and behavior deviations. First, *behavioral contiguous relationships characteristic of either behavior deficits or behavior deviations may have different antecedents.* For example, the antecedents to low activity level may be either heavy dosages of sedatives or tranquilizing drugs or the absence of other discriminated operant behavior that is incompatible with low activity level.

Second, *the behavioral contiguous relationships and their possible antecedents, in either behavior deficits or behavior deviations, are overlapping, thus making it difficult to distinguish between the two types of disorders.* For example, a patient with either a behavior deficit or behavior deviation may show the behavioral contiguous relationship of tantrums with the same possible antecedents: extinction or tantrum-response-contingent reinforcement.

Third, *the severity of a behavior deficit or behavior deviation can be described in terms of the number and quality of the behavioral contiguous relationships of which it consists.* For example, a patient with a behavior deviation in which he shows opposite speech has a less severe disorder than one who shows an abrupt deterioration of discriminated self-help, speech, social, motor, and verbal learning skills.

[21] As in the case of Greg, the nature of the etiology of her deviant behavior is indeterminate.

[22] Many professionals in the study and management of behavior disorders would argue that the patient or his caretakers are not necessarily the best judges of the patient's "real problem." Probably, they would assert that the patient's real problem has its root causes in the patient's unconscious, his self-image, and the like, events occurring in another dimensional system over and above the actual behavioral contiguous relationships observed in that patient. On this question, time and study will, in the long run, provide the answer. To date, both study and behavior management without entities from other dimensional systems appear to be increasingly useful. It might be added that describing behavior disorders in terms of the individual's or his caretakers' definition in no way precludes the necessity of a physical evaluation. Whenever a behavior disorder is suspected, a physical examination is imperative, both from the point of view expressed here and for the patient's best interests, and he should be encouraged to take the physical examinations needed, even though he may not be required to do so legally.

Fourth, *behavior deficits tend to involve behavioral contiguous relationships that consisted from the onset of inadequate repertoires, whereas in behavior deviations once-adequate repertoires may have deteriorated.* For example, a patient with a behavior deficit in which the behavioral contiguous relationship is the absence of self-help skills may never have acquired these skills, whereas a patient with a behavior deviation involving a somewhat comparable behavioral contiguous relationship may have acquired these skills, but they deteriorated.

Fifth, *any of the behavior deficits or deviations described in Tables 11-5 and 11-6 may involve several antecedents, including environmental events critical in the development of operant and respondent behavior, drugs, and impairment of the organism's nervous system due to trauma or organic disease.*

Finally, *because the behavioral contiguous relationships and their possible antecedent environmental events observed in behavior deficits and behavior deviations are specifiable, objective events, descriptions of them may be useful in the development of programs of therapy and prevention of behavior disorders.*

In summary, the terms *behavior deficit* and *behavior deviation* have been used to describe instances where the repertoire of the individual is either inadequate or in some way offensive to himself or to others. Behavior deficits or deviations can be described in terms of the number and quality of their behavioral contiguous relationships and the possible antecedents of these relationships. From the point of view of behavior management, however, it is perhaps more important to stress the specific behavioral contiguous relationships that characterize the patient rather than their possible antecedents for two reasons. First, establishing the antecedents to a behavior disorder in the individual case is precarious, and second, a program of successful behavior therapy may eliminate the behavioral contiguous relationships characteristic of a given patient, regardless of their antecedents.

In conclusion, the analysis presented in this chapter should not be regarded as comprehensive or exhaustive of the types of behavioral contiguous relationships in behavior disorders or their possible antecedents. Rather, the analysis is to be regarded as illustrative of some of the problems encountered in this area and the possible contributions behavior theory can make to their solution.

STUDY QUESTIONS

1. With whom do the behavior management specialists socially transact and for what purpose?
2. From what science do the language and procedures used in the study and management of behavior disorders historically derive?

3. What is obtained from the use of the taxonomic method in the biological sciences?
4. Distinguish between a contiguous relationship and a similarity relationship.
5. Distinguish between a behavioral and a structural contiguous relationship.
6. In addition to their description and classification, what else does the taxonomic method reveal about entities? What is *not* revealed by the method?
7. What are the typical steps in the implementation of the taxonomic method in the study and management of behavior disorders?
8. Identify each of the following as behavioral characteristics and structural characteristics of organisms and/or similarity and contiguous characteristics of organisms:
   a. A child frequently has terrible tantrums.
   b. Single-celled.
   c. Presence of the simian line on the palm of the hand.
   d. The patient has trisomy 21 and an IQ of 51.
   e. The patient's x ray shows some brain damage in the motor cortex, and he has spasticity in his left hand and arm.
9. What three elements are involved in psychological or medical evaluation processes?
10. What condition must prevail in order for an individual to be identified as a member of a behavior disorder class?
11. Define diagnosis, etiology, prognosis, and therapy.
12. Distinguish between the mental illness, or medical, model and medical prejudice.
13. What does the author regard as the most critical feature of an adequate psychiatric classification system?
14. What two factors determine the adequacy of a given classification system? What are the essential characteristics of each?
15. In what ways are psychological and medical tests similar? In what ways do they differ?
16. What meanings can be attributed to psychological test performances?
17. Why must psychological and medical tests be standardized?
18. What discriminative stimuli function in a psychological test situation? What kind of behavior is controlled by such a stimulus complex?
19. What behavioral processes are presumed to have occurred in the history of an individual who is being given a psychological test?
20. What elements in the discriminative stimulus complex of a test situation are assumed to be controlled by standardized test presentations?
21. What defines a subject's passing a psychological test item?
22. Describe and give an example of the three sources of variability that contribute to an individual's performance on a psychological test. Which source is viewed as the *most critical?* Why?
23. From the point of view that psychological test performance is a form of discriminated operant behavior, describe four reasons for poor test performance.
24. Compare the representativeness of the populations used in the evaluation of an individual's performance on psychological and medical tests.

25. Give three reasons why medical tests may yield more precise descriptions than psychological tests.
26. Give examples of the kinds of behavioral-behavioral contiguous relationships and of the kinds of structural-behavioral contiguous relationships revealed by medical and psychological tests.
27. What kind of law may be revealed by behavioral-behavioral contiguous relationships? By structural-behavioral contiguous relationships?
28. What kind of law may be *discovered* in a clinical setting?
29. Discuss two reasons why some laws can never be *verified* in clinical settings.
30. Distinguish between organic and functional disorders. Between symptom and syndrome.
31. Describe two advantages of the diagnostic process that identifies the behavior disorder class to which an individual belongs.
32. In which areas did the professionals evaluating Sam's case agree the most? In which areas did they agree the least?
33. What were the concluding critical remarks made about Sam's case?
34. Describe and account for the similarities and differences between the case histories of Sam and Stephen.
35. What is a self-fulfilling prophesy?
36. What objections are made to the traditional psychiatric classification system as it is currently implemented?
37. How much agreement is there among professional judges on diagnoses involving mental deficiency? Involving schizophrenia?
38. What is the major source of disagreement among professional judges with respect to the classification of behavior disorders?
39. What is the general conclusion the author reaches about the value of traditional psychiatric classification systems?
40. Which classes of events, described as objectionable to the behavior theory view, are referred to as other dimensional systems?
41. What is the *similia similibus curantur* fallacy?
42. Characterize the following as either directly observed or inferred:
    a. A verbal report of one's being followed.
    b. The trait psychasthenia.
    c. A flat EEG record.
43. Contrast the traditional method of psychological evaluation and that proposed by behavior theory in terms of
    a. dimensional systems.
    b. transituational generality.
    c. setting criteria for deficits or deviant behaviors.
    d. the nature of base-line observations.
44. Behavior deficits and deviations are concurrent operant–respondent behavior patterns. Which is most likely to get the attention of caretakers—the operant or the respondent component? Why?
45. Does the behavior theory view assert that special laws are necessary to account for behavior disorders?
46. What is meant by the statement that an individual's behavior deficits or behavior deviations are always *protean?* Why is this so?

47. Review Tables 11-5 and 11-6, and be able to give examples of behavioral contiguous relationships and possible antecedents for the following:
   a. A severe or a mild behavior deficit.
   b. A severe or a mild behavior deviation.
   c. A behavior deficit involving R, S, C, K, and s functions.
   d. A behavior deviation involving R, S, C, K, r, e, k, and s functions.
48. Identify some of the possible antecedents to the following behavioral characteristics:
   a. Low activity level.
   b. Opposite speech.
   c. Organ neurosis (essential hypertension).
   d. Shallowness of affect (minimal emotional response to an emotional situation).
49. Give an example of behavioral contiguous relationships having different antecedents.
50. Describe how an individual may be identified as having both a behavior deficit and a behavior deviation.
51. What defines the severity of a behavior deficit or behavior deviation?
52. Describe one possible difference between a behavior deficit and a behavior deviation.
53. What kinds of antecedents may interact to produce a behavior deficit or behavior deviation?
54. Under what conditions may behavioral contiguous relationships and their possible environmental antecedents, as shown in Tables 11-5 and 11-6, be useful?
55. Cite two reasons why, from the standpoint of behavior management, it is more important to describe behavioral contiguous relationships than to describe their antecedents.

REFERENCES

Bergin, A. E. Some implications of psychotherapy research for therapeutic practice. *Journal of Abnormal Psychology*, 1966, 71, 235–246.

Coleman, J. G. *Abnormal psychology and modern life.* (4th ed.) Glenview, Ill.: Scott, Foresman, 1972.

Doll, E. A. *Vineland Social Maturity Scale: Condensed manual of instructions.* (1965 ed.) Circle Pines, Minn.: American Guidance Service, Inc., 1965.

Ferster, C. B. Positive reinforcement and behavioral deficits in autistic children. *Child Development*, 1961, **32**, 437–456.

Ferster, C. B. Animal behavior and mental illness. *Psychological Record*, 1966, **16**, 345–346.

Gibbs, E. I., Rich, C. L., Fois, A., and Gibbs, F. A. Electroencephalographic study of mentally retarded persons. *American Journal of Mental Deficiency*, 1960, **65**, 236–247.

Glaser, G. H. The normal E.E.G. and its reactivity. In G. H. Glaser (Ed.), *EEG and behavior.* New York: Basic Books, 1963.

Hathaway, S. R., and McKinley, J. C. *Manual for the Minnesota Multiphasic Personality Inventory.* (Rev. ed.) New York: Psychological Corporation, 1951.

Hollingshead, A. B., and Redlich, F. C. *Social class and mental illness.* New York: Wiley, 1958.

Heller, R. B. Legal decision in the case of Stephen Dennison vs. Court of Claims, State of New York (Claim No. 38868), March 15, 1966.

Hsia, I-jung, *Inborn errors in metabolism.* Chicago: Yearbook Publishers, 1959.

Koegler, R. R., Colbert, E. G., and Walter, R. D. Problems in the correlation of psychopathology with electroencephalographic abnormalities. *American Journal of Psychiatry*, 1961, 117, 822–824.

Laffal, J., Lenkoski, L. D., and Ameen, L. Opposite speech in a schizophrenic patient. *Journal of Abnormal and Social Psychology*, 1956, 52, 409–413.

Lindsley, O. R. Direct measurement and prosthesis of retarded behavior. *Journal of Education*, 1964, 147, 62–81.

Merritt, H. H. A *textbook of neurology.* (4th ed.) Philadelphia: Lea and Febiger, 1967.

Nihara, K., Foster, R., and Spencer, C. Measurement of adaptive behavior: A descriptive system for mental retardates. *American Journal of Orthopsychiatry*, 1968, 38, 622–634.

Phillips, L., and Draguns, J. G. Classification of the behavior disorders. In P. H. Mussen and M. R. Rosenzweig (Eds.), *Annual Review of Psychology.* Palo Alto, Calif.: Annual Reviews, 1971.

Pintner, R., Dragostiz, A., and Kushner, R. *Supplementary guide for the revised Stanford-Binet Scale, Form L.* Stanford, Calif.: Stanford University Press, 1949.

Robinson, H. B., and Robinson, N. M., *The mentally retarded child.* New York: McGraw-Hill, 1965.

Rosenhan, D. L. On being sane in insane places. *Science*, 1973, 179, 250–258.

Rosenthal, R., and Jacobson, L. F. *Pygmalion in the classroom.* New York: Holt, Rinehart and Winston, 1968.

Sattler, J. M., Hillix, W. A., and Neher, L. The halo effect in examiner scoring of intelligence responses. *Journal of Consulting and Clinical Psychology*, 1970, 34, 172–176.

Sattler, J. M., and Theye, F. Procedural, situational and interpersonal variables in individual intelligence testing. *Psychological Bulletin*, 1967, 68, 347–360.

Simpson, G. G. *Principles of animal taxonomy.* New York: Columbia University Press, 1961.

Strauss, H., Ostow, M., and Greenstein, C. *Diagnostic electroencephalography.* New York: Grune and Stratton, 1952.

Szasz, T. *The myth of mental illness: Foundations of a theory of personal conduct.* New York: Harper and Row, 1961.

Szasz, T. *Ideology and insanity.* Garden City, N. Y.: Anchor Books, Doubleday, 1970.

Terman, L. M., and Merrill, M. A. *Stanford-Binet Intelligence Scale.* Boston: Houghton-Mifflin, 1960.

Ullmann, L. P., and Krasner, L. A *psychological approach to abnormal behavior.* Englewood Cliffs, N. J.: Prentice-Hall, 1969.

Wechsler, D. *Wechsler Intelligence Scale for Children.* New York: Psychological Corporation, 1949.

Zubin, J., Classification of behavior disorders. In P. R. Farnsworth (Ed.), *Annual review of psychology.* Palo Alto, Calif.: Annual Reviews, 1967.

CHAPTER 12

SOME PROBLEMS IN BEHAVIOR MANAGEMENT

In the last chapter behavior problems were viewed in terms of (1) the respondent and operant behaviors that make up the response complexes of which the behavior problems consist, and (2) their possible environmental antecedents, whether they are the stimulus complexes in which the behavior occurs, drugs, or trauma or disease of the nervous system. It was observed that behavior problems cover a wide range of response complexes. The nature of these complexes may initially bring the individual into contact with his caretakers, and later may bring him into contact with various specialists in behavior management. These specialists may include psychiatrists, clinical psychologists, teachers, counselors, psychiatric technicians, and the like, each of whom specializes in the management of some aspect of the individual's behavior deficits or his behavior deviations. In every case, the specialist's professional obligation requires that he deliberately engage in social transactions with the individual for the express purpose of securing behavior control over the individual's behavior problem. In fulfilling his professional obligation, the specialist must make two essential decisions.

First, he must determine the nature of the individual's problem—the response classes requiring remediation (R^D's, r's in operant and respondent behavior, respectively). The reader will recall from Chapter 11 that the individual himself, or his caretakers, should decide what behaviors are of such significance or importance that they require remediation. Once, however, such a decision has been made, the specialist in behavior management may assist in the further specification of the problem. For example, once Johnny's parents decide that Johnny has a reading deficit, the reading specialist may find that Johnny's deficit is specifically in reading comprehension, and this is what requires remediation. Second, the specialist must choose a procedure that will have the desired effect on the individual's behavior.

Both decisions necessarily involve ethical considerations, although such considerations are far more obvious in the first decision. This decision, dealing as it does with the specification of the response classes requiring remediation, involves the deliberation of all parties concerned and yet rests singularly with the behavior manager on whose judgment everyone else relies. There are ethical considerations, too, in the consideration of the appropriate procedure to achieve behavior control. Should the behavior manager decide that some behavior should be suppressed, he may choose from an array of procedures— some positive (such as strengthening through contingent positive reinforcement other behavior that is incompatible with the behavior he wishes to suppress) and some negative (such as punishment). He may decide against the latter, even though it works, simply because he values eliciting positive respondents from the trainee rather than negative ones—also an ethical decision.

THE ETHICS OF BEHAVIOR CONTROL

Any program of behavior management whose goal is behavior control must necessarily deal with two vital issues. First, to what extent is the behavior of the individual a matter of choice or volition (will)? Second, to what extent is the individual responsible for his behavior?

Choice Behavior and Behavior Theory

The decisions required of those involved in behavior management, whether they are caretakers or specialists, may be viewed essentially as forms of *choice behavior*. The professional who engages in social transactions with the individual must choose the response classes requiring remediation, and he must choose appropriate procedures to achieve this remediation. The same is true of the child's parent, who (as the behavior manager of the child) must make comparable choices, and incidentally, so must the child.

These choices, because they seem to be related to changes in the individual's behavior, are regarded by both laymen and some psychologists in a very special way. They are viewed as evidence and confirmation of other antecedents to behavior occurring in other dimensional systems, especially those in the psyche of the individual. In reaching such a conclusion, both laymen and some professionals rely heavily on the following characteristics of choice behavior:

First, individuals often give good reasons or explanations for their choices. For example, "I smoke because I'm nervous."

Second, these verbal accounts frequently seem reasonable and consistent. They fit our cultural values and expectations about the "why" of behavior, and this adds to their credibility.

Third, individuals are often held responsible by others for their choices. The expression "She made her bed, let her sleep in it" reflects this.

Moreover, those who regard choice behavior as having its antecedents in the psyche of the individual are apt to make the following additional assumptions:

1. That the individual can, as a matter of choice, make two or more alternative responses to the same stimulus situation or stimulus complex. On a given occasion, an individual may choose to quit smoking, smoke only a few cigarettes, or continue to smoke at maximum consumption.

2. That because choice behavior consists of alternative responses to the same stimulus situation, it is caused by, and evidence of, a switching mechanism—the free will. Thus those who are able to quit smoking are regarded as having a stronger will than those who are not.

Although the manner in which the characteristics of choice behavior are consistent with behavior theory will be discussed shortly, these two assumptions are not. An obvious weakness in the analysis of choice behavior, under these assumptions, is that it makes an appeal to antecedents occurring in another dimensional system—namely, that choices are the result of some sort of intrapsychic mechanism. By contrast, behavior theory asserts that:

1. *All* behavior is lawful, and its antecedents are in the past and present environmental (S) events—events that are accessible to direct or indirect observation.

2. It is fallacious to assume that choice situations involve a single stimulus complex that controls several response alternatives. This is not to say that several responses cannot occur at the same time to form a response class. Indeed, they can and do in what has been described as concurrent behavior. What is inconsistent with behavior theory is the notion that a single stimulus complex can control two or more alternative response classes at the same time, each of which is incompatible with the others.

3. Whether or not an individual can correctly verbalize the contingencies affecting his behavior depends on his reinforcement history. Even when he

can, it is not clear that such verbalizations necessarily control (are the antecedents to) his choice behavior.

4. The individual, as we shall observe in more detail shortly, is not responsible for his choices in a traditional sense of the word.

Under these assumptions and from the point of view of behavior theory, the key to understanding choice behavior lies in the individual's reinforcement history and the stimuli in the presence of which reinforcements have occurred.

When a teacher makes a "correct decision" regarding the response classes of a particular pupil that require remediation, choosing response classes that are appropriate to the course of study or curriculum and an appropriate remediation procedure, that teacher's choice behavior reflects the social consequences that arise out of his social transactions with that pupil, with other pupils possessing comparable stimulus properties with whom he has transacted in the past, and the contingencies of reinforcement occurring during his training as a teacher.

The same is true of the choice behavior of the mother. Her choice of response classes and procedures for their acquisition, as she manages the behavior of her child, also reflects her own reinforcement history. In addition, her choice is related to her ethnic, religious, economic, and educational backgrounds.

Furthermore, from the point of view of behavior theory, the expression *choice behavior* is unfortunate. When a mother attempts to modify her child's behaviors, she has no more choice in selecting the behaviors for modification and the procedures for their modification than her parents did when they modified her behavior. The behavior of all parties to social transactions (parents and children) is determined by the social consequences arising out of that behavior. A mother who chooses to give the baby candy to quiet his tantrum (positive consequences following the tantrum response class) is actually being reinforced by the baby (for giving him candy) through the termination of an aversive stimulus (the tantrum display, which the baby "chooses" to stop when he gets the candy). Each party to the social transaction, then, may, in a sense, "choose" to behave in a manner such that more and more of the behavior of the parties to the transaction is controlled by that situation. Furthermore, transactions between the individual and his physical environment have the same effect. This is not to say, however, that a mother is not able to show different behaviors toward her child than her parents showed toward her. For one thing, others (such as her husband) may modify her behavior by following it with certain consequences, giving verbal instructions, and the like. All that is suggested here is that the *stimulus control that the social and physical environment has over the behavior of the individual is, in fact, the basis for his choices.*

Individual Responsibility and Behavior Theory

In many respects the notion of responsibility, like the notion of choice behavior, involves social and ethical considerations that are beyond the scope of behavior theory. Because programs of behavior management necessarily involve ethical considerations, however, the notion of responsibility requires some discussion. In view of the many types of social transactions that take place between the individual, his caretakers, and specialists in behavior management, there are at least two different types of responsibility.

The first might be called *behavioral responsibility* and arises out of repeated social transactions between the individual and others. It takes the form of the stimulus and schedule control the individual has over those with whom he often transacts (and vice versa). Again, the mother who reinforces her baby's tantrums (to terminate them) is no less and no more responsible for the tantrum than the baby who reinforces the mother for giving him candy is responsible for her giving him candy. The mother, then, is a stimulus in the presence of which a tantrum is reinforced (she is an S^D for a tantrum), and the baby is a stimulus in the presence of which giving candy is reinforced (the baby is an S^D for giving candy). In the sense that the behavior of one individual is the controlling stimulus for the behavior of the other, both are behaviorally responsible.[1] The nature of social transactions is such that they involve social consequences, the effect of which is to *necessarily* influence the behavior of each party to the transactions and to involve social control of the behavior of the individual. It is this control that is, in essence, behavioral responsibility.

From the point of view of society, parties to repeated transactions with others also possess an *ethical responsibility* for their behavior. This is true of the parent, the spouse, the teacher, the psychologist, and the like, all of whom are required by society to provide special essential services (behave in an appropriate manner in the presence of those to whom they are responsible). If the behavior of a parent, a spouse, a teacher, or a psychologist is grossly inadequate or inappropriate as defined by religious, ethical, legal, or professional standards, then such individuals are subject to social or legal penalties administered by superordinate agents in the society. A parent, for example, might give his teen-age son verbal instructions and reinforcements for stealing. Not

---

[1] Many professionals in psychiatry and clinical psychology who use the interview as their main therapeutic strategy feel that a skillful therapist will not use procedures that deliberately direct or instruct the patient. Rather, a skillful therapist responds passively to the patient in such a manner that the patient is able, on his own, to gain insight into his own needs, feelings, and the like. There is, of course, a real question as to whether or not either the patient or the therapist would engage in sustained social transactions with each other in the absence of some sort of social (or perhaps even monetary) consequation. Furthermore, there is increasing evidence that even mere passive agreement in the form of the vocalization "Um-humm" or gestural-attentional social responses from a listener may function as strengthening consequences (Williams, 1964).

only would such a parent be *behaviorally responsible* (through the behavior control produced by his verbal instructions and reinforcements for stealing), but he would also be regarded by society as *ethically responsible*. This would be true of any behaviors that are deleterious, injurious, or destructive of others or the possessions of others—behaviors that are incompatible with Judeo-Christian ethics and their codified manifestations in the law. Such responsibility deals with ethical considerations that *cannot* be ignored or avoided in any program of behavior management—the strengthening of behaviors that are, in the larger view, necessary to give society continuity and order.

Furthermore, this distinction between behavioral and ethical responsibility has important implications for the social practice of behavior principles. A person who has committed a capital crime is *not* assumed to have had a choice as to whether or not to commit the crime. Rather, it is assumed that there were highly significant past and present environmental (stimulus) events that led to the acquisition or maintenance of the criminal act. Such a person would *not* be held responsible for this behavior in a behavioral sense, although he would most certainly be responsible for his behavior in an ethical-legal sense.

In summary, a program of behavior management must necessarily be concerned with questions that transcend the substance of behavior theory and are essentially ethical. Most obviously, these deal with the question of the response classes that are of interest to the caretaker and the specialist and are the focus of behavior control. Less obvious, but also of ethical concern, are the procedures used by the caretaker or specialist to secure behavior control, since these procedures may have side effects beyond the effects on the response classes of concern.

An individual act described as choice behavior may be regarded in terms of

1. Its antecedents, either from the point of view of traditional psychodynamic or cognitive theories of behavior-intrapsychic states or from the point of view of behavior theory, or environmental (stimulus) events.

2. Its stimulus functions for the behavior of others (behavioral responsibility) and its effect on the stability and continuity of society (ethical responsibility).

Both of these effects are of serious consequence and must be given serious concern by the behavior manager.

THE QUESTION OF PUNISHMENT

When the problem presented by the client requires that certain behaviors be suppressed rather than enhanced, a serious question arises regarding the use of punishment procedures, especially those involving aversive control. Although the presentation of aversive stimuli may suppress the behavior more rapidly than alternative procedures (that is, extinction, strengthening incompatible responses, and the like), its choice in a given situation depends on a number of considerations:

1. The immediate risks that the individual's behavior presents to either himself or others.

2. The availability of sufficient social and physical-environmental controls and supervision at least to prevent self-injury or injury to others when the behavior does occur.

3. The nature of the long-term effects of allowing the "bad" behavior to occur (even if it is infrequent and does not injure anyone) compared with the short-term effects of using more powerful behavior suppression procedures. Even though the use of punishment procedures is repugnant to most of us, without them exceptional surveillance and environmental control is often required to suppress "bad" behavior, especially when such behavior has an elaborate reinforcement history. The following cases illustrate this point:

CASE 1

Jimmy, age eleven, a patient in a state hospital ward for the retarded, is a physically attractive boy with minimal speech and self-help skills. Despite his good looks, he seldom gains attention from his caretakers except for the wrong reasons, and even then he receives the wrong kind of attention. This is because he possesses a number of objectionable behaviors. For example, he has a funny habit of sticking his right little finger all the way up his right nostril and then taking it out, putting it all the way into his open mouth, and removing it with his lips tightly around it. Another favorite trick is to jab a person's arm with his hand clenched downward in a scraping manner. If his fingernails come in contact with the person's skin, he can "strip" off half an inch of skin with each one. Often, this happens before the victim is aware of it, and not uncommonly the wound becomes infected with staphylococcus.

CASE 2

Jenny, age fifteen, is the ward nose biter. In the past year she has eight attacks to her credit and three noses. Although the behavior occurs relatively infrequently, it poses a particular risk to the other patients on the ward. Besides the possible disfigurement of the victim, the risk of infection following an attack is quite high.

CASE 3

Mike, twelve, has strong speech and self-help skills, and he follows instructions well. Unfortunately, these positive characteristics are not strong enough to control patterns of approach in his caretakers. Most often they avoid him. The reason for this is that on some days he may have tantrums lasting as long as 3 hours. During these episodes he'll spit, scream, kick, bite, or strike anyone within reaching distance.

CASE 4

Steve, age seven, like Jimmy, seldom gets attention from the staff. He is one of the ward's "smearers," and to avoid having to clean him up, his caretakers will frequently pretend to not see what he is doing.

CASE 5

Jimmy, age nine, is ambulatory, can feed himself with a spoon, will play but not bathe himself in the shower, and can follow simple instructions such as "Come here" and "Sit down." What is striking about him is his dead-pan or poker face, which remains completely immobile and expressionless regardless of what kind of stimulation he receives from a caretaker. He does show eye contact, but he does not show speech. Except for the novelty of his dead-pan appearance, his caretakers seldom pay attention to him.

These examples, of course, are extreme and cover a wide range of behavior deviations and deficits. There are two things about them that should be emphasized. First, some of these cases possess behaviors that are either harmful or socially offensive to others, so that the behavior of those with whom they transact is apt to be maintained by negative reinforcements. Under such circumstances, others, even professional behavior managers, can be expected to show escape or avoidance in their presence (as in case 4, for example). Second, some of these cases show such weak social behavior that they are unable to provide others with sufficient social reinforcement to maintain repeated social transactions (as in case 5, for example). Even when there are enough caretakers available, individuals who are unable to maintain social transactions with them will become victims of social deprivation and either show behavioral deterioration (in those having some behavior) or little or no improvement in behavior (in those with minimum repertoires).

Almost always there are limitations in the time and personnel available for behavior management. Somehow, therefore, some means is required to guarantee that this type of less fortunate patient frequently receives positive transactions from his caretakers. This might be accomplished by the following:

1. A situation could be arranged such that the behavior managers themselves receive frequent and powerful reinforcements for engaging in positive (reinforcing) transactions with their patients. Such reinforcements might come from co-workers or preferably from superordinate sources and would be made contingent on the occurrence of such transactions.[2]

[2] Ironically, it is not uncommon for a psychiatric technician or classroom teacher to receive more acclaim for keeping a clean house than for his achievements in behavior modification. This would, of course, weaken the effectiveness of any behavior management program.

2. On occasion, when it has been established that (1) other procedures have failed and (2) the patient runs the risk of social deprivation because of a lack of positive contact with his caretakers, the behavior manager could use punishment for the suppression of destructive, injurious, or especially offensive acts. Initially this would take the form of the removal of positive reinforcers rather than the presentation of aversive stimuli.

The two forms of intervention, in combination, are particularly powerful, since they guarantee the presentation of strengthening consequences to both the patient and the behavior manager for appropriate behaviors and the presentation of weakening consequences to the patient for inappropriate behaviors—a concurrent schedule that will shorten training time.

THE BASE-LINE OBSERVATION AND
THE BEHAVIORAL PRESCRIPTION

The initial contacts between the specialist in behavior management and his client set in motion a complex process of evaluation and prescription.

In the first stage, *preliminary observation*, the specialist secures information about the nature of the client's problem. This information is gleaned from various sources including interviews with the client, his caretakers, and in some cases preliminary questionnaires, checklists, rating scales, and the like.

Arising from this is the second stage, consisting of first, the *base-line observation*—a precise, objective description of the individual's problem—and second, the *behavioral prescription*, the procedures for the remediation of the individual's problem.

Although both the preliminary and base-line observations are important in developing a successful program of behavior management, the base-line observation is particularly important for the following reasons:

1. It is the careful study and analysis of the base-line observation that is used to define and specify precisely the response classes requiring remediation, whether they are deficits or deviations in respondent or operant behavior. The definition will include specifications of the response class and the response class dimension whether the definition is in terms of response topography, rate, frequency, duration, or magnitude.

2. It is the base-line observation that provides the basis for the evaluation of the remediation procedure after it has been introduced. If, indeed, the procedure is effective, then observation of the behavior (the response class and the response class dimension) during training and a comparison of that behavior with the base-line behavior will reveal changes in the direction sought by the behavior manager. If, on the other hand, the anticipated behavior change does not occur, this will also be revealed by a comparison with the base-line behavior. Then the procedure will be regarded as ineffective, and a new one will be selected.

To get some idea of this sequence, the reader should examine the following outline, which shows the procedure for the analysis and remediation of an operant behavior deficit in reading.

I. *Setting the Final Performance:*

When the trainer presents the verbal instructions: "Read the sentence on this card aloud. Do what the sentence says," the individual reads the sentence aloud and then correctly performs the instructions contained therein. The card and three colored boxes (red, green, and yellow) are placed before the child. The card contains the following direction: "Open the red box."

II. *Base-line Performance—Acquisition of Sight-reading Task:*[3]

The card is placed before the child and he is given the following instructions: "Read the sentence on this card aloud. Do what the sentence says."

The child looks at the card but fails to respond. A second test is carried out in which the child is presented with the words on individual flash cards. Each word is presented five times for a total of twenty trials, the order of which is randomized. The number he gets correct out of 5 trials is as follows:

Open	*the*	*red*	*box*
0	5	5	0

A. Analysis of the sight-reading task by links in an operant behavior chain.

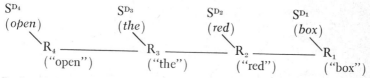

S^{D_4} (*open*) S^{D_3} (*the*) S^{D_2} (*red*) S^{D_1} (*box*)

R_4 ("open") ——— R_3 ("the") ——— R_2 ("red") ——— R_1 ("box")

B. Strengthening the individual links requiring remediation (the words *open* and *box*) from the base-line test—increasing the response class dimension of frequency of appropriate vocal operants (the response classes) until they are reliably controlled by the textual and instructional stimuli. A reliable performance is one in which the child correctly responds five times out of five opportunities to respond.

Trainer says, "Read this":

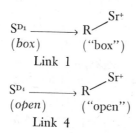

S^{D_1} (*box*) $\longrightarrow$ R ("box") $\nearrow Sr^+$

Link 1

S^{D_4} (*open*) $\longrightarrow$ R ("open") $\nearrow Sr^+$

Link 4

---

[3] It should be remembered that reading responses are differentiated operants under the control of textual stimuli. This base-line analysis assumes that the child can already say the words, but that they are not yet texts.

remediation procedure
The word is presented on a card. If the child fails to respond in 3 seconds, he is prompted (trainer says the word), and the child is instructed to repeat the word. Correct responses without a prompt are reinforced, and incorrect responses are not. Training continues until child says the word following presentations of the cards in random order.

C. Chaining the links in the sentence with the controlling stimuli (words) still on cards, but with a sequential arrangement of cards.
Trainer says, "Read this":

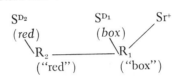

remediation procedure
The cards containing the words are presented side-by-side, and the child is reinforced for a correct performance of the chain.

"Read this sentence":

$$S^{D_3} \qquad S^{D_2} \qquad S^{D_1}$$
$$(the) \qquad (red) \qquad (box)$$
$$\diagdown R_3 \text{------} \diagdown R_2 \text{------} \diagdown R_1 \text{------} Sr^+$$
$$(\text{"the"}) \qquad (\text{"red"}) \qquad (\text{"box"})$$

"Read this sentence":

$$S^{D_4} \qquad S^{D_3} \qquad S^{D_2} \qquad S^{D_1}$$
$$(open) \qquad (the) \qquad (red) \qquad (box)$$
$$\diagdown R_4 \text{------} \diagdown R_3 \text{------} \diagdown R_2 \text{------} \diagdown R_1 \text{------} Sr^+$$
$$(\text{"open"}) \qquad (\text{"the"}) \qquad (\text{"red"}) \qquad (\text{"box"})$$

D. Sight-reading test—child reads sentence on a *single card* under the control of the verbal instructions: "First, read this sentence aloud."

III. *Base-line Performance—Acquisition of the Functional Reading Task:*
When presented with the verbal instruction: "First, read this sentence aloud. Do what the sentence says" and then with the card, the child now correctly reads aloud the text on the card. However, in five trials, he opens the red box once and the green and yellow boxes twice each. The operant behavior chain of looking at, reaching for, and opening a box are part of his repertoire. However, the self-presented verbal instructions of "Open the red box" merely controls reaching for and opening *any* box.

A. Analysis of the functional reading task as a discriminated operant behavior.

S^D ─────────────────→ R

(Child reads text on card aloud: (Child reaches for and
"Open the red box.")   opens the red box.)

B. Strengthening the discriminated behavior—increasing the frequency (response class dimension) of appropriate motor operants (response class) under the control of a verbal S^D (child's own vocalizations).

S^D ─────────────→ R ───────────→ Sr^+

(Child reads text   (Child reaches
on card aloud: for and opens
"Open the red box.")   the red box.)

remediation procedure
Child is presented with the card and in-structed to read it. Then, he is given 3 sec-onds to respond. Only the red box contains the candy. The others are empty. The child continues on the task until he makes five cor-rect choices in a row.[4]

Notice that the base-line observation reveals that the child possesses both a sight-reading deficit (he is unable to correctly read the sentence "Open the red box" and to read the words *open* and *box* presented separately) and a functional reading deficit (under the control of the sentence "Open the red box," the child opens the red box only once in five trials). Notice, too, that the behavioral prescription involves a two-stage remediation procedure.

First, the sight-reading skill is strengthened through the presentation of prompts and reinforcements. Second, the self-produced utterance is made the controlling stimulus (an S^D) for an appropriate movement. This is accom-plished by reinforcing only those responses that are consistent with the self-produced verbal instructions. It should also be mentioned that the task is essentially a problem in operant discrimination and not one of operant differ-entiation. Had the child been unable, for example, to reach for and open the box, then a remediation procedure for the acquisition of a three-link chain would have been required (R_3, looking at the red box; R_2, reaching for the red box; and R_1, opening the red box). This would have necessitated modify-ing separately the response class dimension of form or topography appropriate to each link in the chain until each was strong, and then putting the links into a chained sequence.

Figure 12-1 shows the performance (percentage of correct R's) of four dif-ferent individuals (S1–S4) during two base-line and nine training periods and

---

[4] Such a procedure involves a certain risk in that the child may make enough errors to extinguish both reaching for a box and reading the card as well. The reader should con-sider a solution to this problem.

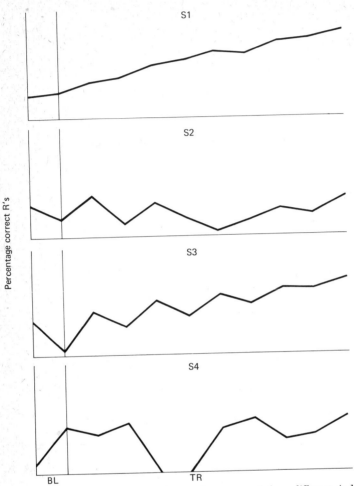

FIGURE 12-1 Base-line and training performances of four different individuals (S1–S4).

reveals some of the problems encountered in evaluating the adequacy of a training procedure (behavioral prescription).

During the base line, S1 and S2 show less variability in performance from base-line 1 to base-line 2 (about 4 percent and 12 percent, respectively) than S3 and S4 (both of whom show about 32 percent). The problem arises when one is trying to evaluate the effectiveness of the training procedure. When the initial variability is small, as in the case of S1 and S2, the effectiveness of the training procedure seems more obvious. For example, S1 showed a relatively consistent improvement, with all of the points plotted for training sessions exceeding the range of base-line performances. By contrast, S2 showed only slight improvement on two occasions (days 1 and 9 of training), and points plotted for the remaining training days fell within or below the base-line performances. Clearly, S1 benefited from the training procedure, and S2 did not.

When the initial variability is large, as in the case of S3 and S4, the effectiveness of the training procedure is not as obvious as in the case of S1 and S2, since it takes a larger improvement in performance to exceed base-line performances. Thus although the training procedure seems to be working for both S1 and S3, its effectiveness seems more obvious in S1's case than in S3's case, at least until the third training session or even beyond.

Thus several obvious conclusions can be drawn from these examples. First, when the base-line performances are quite variable, a large difference between base-line and training performances must occur before one can assume that the training procedure is effective.

Second, when base-line performances are quite variable, more training sessions may be required before the procedure's effectiveness can be determined.

Third, when base-line performances show little variation, a small difference between base-line and training performances permits one to assume that the training procedure is effective.

Finally, when the base-line performances are quite variable, the effect of the training procedure may initially be simply to reduce the variability in behavior.

When variability does occur during base-line performances (as in S3 and S4), it may indicate the presence of uncontrolled or extraneous sources of stimulation. Rather than introduce the training procedure, perhaps the behavior manager should examine the conditions under which the base line is obtained, so that in the event such uncontrolled sources of stimulation are found, they can be controlled. There is an obvious economy to this procedure, since it makes the early detection of a successful procedure more likely.

In the interests of a completely successful behavior management program, base-line observations of the client's behavior should be obtained in the client's natural environment as well. Furthermore, there should be periodic follow-up base lines, 6 months, 1 year, or even 2 years later. The use of repeated base-line observations provides the strongest means of evaluating the effectiveness of a treatment procedure. Of course, other evidence may be used, such as the therapeutic clinical impressions of the patient's behavior change and the verbal reports from the patient or his caretakers. However, these sources of evidence of the effectiveness of a treatment procedure must be considered only as *secondary* and corroborative sources.

SOME ESSENTIAL CHARACTERISTICS OF THE APPLICATION OF BEHAVIOR THEORY TO PROBLEMS OF BEHAVIOR MANAGEMENT

Although almost everyone at one time or another is called on to engage in behavior management, those described here as behavior managers, pursuant to their obligations to their clients, will stress the following:

1. The necessity of analysis of the individual's problem in terms of objective and observable response events (response complexes consisting of respondent and operant behavior) and objective and observable stimulus events (stimulus complexes consisting of eliciting, discriminative, and consequating stimuli).

2. The exclusion from the analysis of behavior, with the exceptions to be noted later, of dreams, images, thoughts, reveries, and feelings (as private events experienced by the individual, occurring within the skin of the organism, and accessible to observation only by those individuals experiencing them, not others), although the reality of such events is not denied.

3. The focus is on the individual's present and future environments, in which the behavior problem occurs, although the past history of the individual is important in obtaining an understanding of the antecedents to his behavior.

4. The use of base-line observations, consisting of the specific individual- or caretaker-defined response classes and response class dimensions (the performances), to assess the severity of the behavior problem and to assess the effectiveness of the procedures used in the remediation of the problem.

5. The manipulation of the stimulus events occurring in the individual's environment and the manipulation of the individual's own behavior (the Premack principle) in order to achieve behavior control.

6. When required, additional prosthetic modifications of the individual's physical environment and the use of aids and devices that accommodate for the individual's sensory or motor defects when they cannot be accommodated by ordinary behavior management procedures.

7. The modification of the procedures for behavior management as soon as it becomes apparent from an examination of both base-line and "treated" or "managed" performances that behavior control has not been obtained, rather than the invocation of intrapsychic states or events in the individual that are in other dimensional systems (such as stubbornness or lack of mentality).

8. The use of behavior management practices in stimulus complexes that are sufficiently comparable to the stimulus complexes occurring in the individual's natural environment for the individual's behavior to be maintained through generalization.

9. The recognition that even though successful behavior management may occur in the individual case because of the application of behavior theory

principles, the social practice of these principles often involves complex events, making the *precise* specification of antecedent-consequence relationships in the management of the individual's behavior problems hazardous. In short, the avoidance of the *post hoc ergo propter hoc* fallacy, which asserts that because or on account of a particular treatment a cure is effected.

In the chapters to follow two major areas of application of behavior theory principles to the problems of behavior management will be explored: (1) behavior modification and behavior therapy and (2) behavior management in the classroom.

STUDY QUESTIONS

1. What is the purpose of the social transactions between the behavior management specialist and the individual?

2. When one develops a program of behavior management, what two essential decisions must be made? In what way do these involve ethical issues? Who should make decisions on these issues? Why?

3. What are the assumptions about and characteristics of choice behavior from a traditional view? A behavior theory view?

4. A sixth-grade teacher has one boy in her class, John, who is a troublemaker. John talks, sasses her, and generally disrupts class, all to the amusement of his classmates. It's too bad, because John is very bright. One day the teacher took John aside in the hall and said, "John, why do you mess around in class?" John replied, "I guess I'm just a rotten egg." Later that day the teacher was heard to remark to another teacher, "Oh, John? Yes, he's such a problem. He's bright, but if he really wanted to stop, he would. He's chosen his bed. Let him sleep in it."

   a. What features of this situation seem to involve choice behavior?
   b. Is the teacher's analysis of the problem from the traditional or the behavior theory point of view? Explain why.
   c. What remark(s) did she make that leads you to the conclusion that she believes the antecedents to John's behavior are in his psyche?
   d. What events in the example suggest that the antecedents are in John's environment?

5. What antecedents necessarily affect the choices of
   a. parents?
   b. teachers?
   c. children?
   d. professional behavior managers?

6. A young mother, like her own mother, is a child beater. Suggest two different historical events occurring in the young mother's environment that may have produced such familiar trends or patterns of behavior management.

7. Distinguish between the behavioral responsibility and the ethical responsibility involved in social transactions between the individual and his caretakers or specialists.

8. Discuss some of the questions that arise in a decision to use aversive control in the suppression of behavior.

9. Give an example in which aversive control seems justified. One in which it is not.

10. What two major characteristics of the cases described on pages 344–345 are regarded as significant?

11. Under what conditions may punishment be the "lesser of two evils"?

12. Why is it suggested that the behavior of the caretaker as well as that of the patient must be maintained? Suggest two sources of stimulation that may serve this function.

13. Distinguish between preliminary observation, base-line observation, and behavioral prescription.

14. Cite two reasons for the importance of securing stable base-line observations prior to the introduction of remediation procedures.

15. Explain how variability in behavior observed during the base-line observation can interfere with an evaluation of the treatment procedure.

16. Describe two ways one can control for the variability in behavior observed during the base-line observation.

17. In the problem involving a behavior deficit in reading, described on pages 347–349, *why* is the remediation task one of operant discrimination rather than one of operant differentiation?

18. Identify each of the following as either preliminary observation, base-line observation, or behavioral prescription:
    a. John got twenty out of twenty-five problems correct on his diagnostic spelling test.
    b. A teacher tutored a child with a sight-reading problem. Positive reinforcements were given each time the child read correctly from a flash card, and incorrect responses were followed by No and a prompt that the child then repeated.
    c. A nurse reported that a certain patient on her ward was able to follow the verbal instructions "Go potty" only twice during three daily attempts made over a 1-week period.

19. Describe two characteristics of a successful program in behavior management. What other sources may be used as evidence that a program is successful and why must they be regarded as secondary sources?

20. Describe and evaluate four different sources of evidence that some progress is being made during a therapy program.

21. Study carefully the essential characteristics of the application of behavior theory to problems of behavior management and be able to discuss briefly each of the following:
    a. Analysis and behavior management based on objective and observable events rather than private events.
    b. The role of historical factors in behavior management.
    c. The value of individual- or caretaker-defined behavior problems.
    d. The type of manipulation used by the behavior manager.
    e. The interpretation and management of cases that do not respond to the management procedures.

f. The importance of behavior management in natural settings.

g. The significance, as evidence of an antecedent-consequence relationship, of successful behavior management.

REFERENCES

Ferster, C. B. Arbitrary and natural reinforcement. *Psychological Record*, 1967, 17, 341–348.

Karen, R. L. Observations on behavior management practices and facilities on Unit 343, Fairview State Hospital. Unpublished manuscript, 1968.

Keutzer, C. S., Lichtenstein, E., and Mees, H. L. Modification of smoking behavior: A review. *Psychological Bulletin*, 1968, 70, 520–533.

Krasner, L. The behavioral scientist and social responsibility: No place to hide. *Journal of Social Issues*, 1965, 21, 9–30.

Krasner, L., and Ullmann, L. P. *Research in behavior modification*. New York: Holt, Rinehart and Winston, 1965.

Skinner, B. F. *Science and human behavior*. New York: Macmillan, 1953.

Sussholtz, M. D. Staff interaction with hospitalized retardates. Unpublished master's thesis, San Diego State College, 1971.

Ulrich, R., Stachnik, T., and Mabry, J. (Eds.) *Control of human behavior*. Vol. 2. *From cure to prevention*. Glenview, Ill.: Scott, Foresman, 1970.

Williams, J. H. Conditioning of verbalization: A review. *Psychological Bulletin*, 1964, 62, 383–393.

CHAPTER 13

BEHAVIOR MODIFICATION AND BEHAVIOR THERAPY

Behavior therapy and behavior modification refer to procedures used by a group of specialists in behavior management (behavior therapists or behavior modifiers) who (1) approach the individual's behavior problems stressing the points presented at the end of Chapter 12, (2) regard the remediation of a behavior problem as essentially a training problem, and (3) use remediation procedures derived from modern behavior theory, especially the principles of respondent and operant behavior. Since these principles provide the basis for the procedures and practices of both behavior therapy and behavior modification, the two terms are often used interchangeably. Generally, in behavior therapy, however, the principles of behavior modification are applied to the remediation of behavior deviations (problems in interpersonal relationships) or behavior deficits (the absence or infrequent occurrence of behavior). The management of the former tends to involve the application of principles of both respondent and operant behavior, and the management of the latter tends to involve the application of the principles of operant behavior. However, many individuals possessing more severe behavior problems have both behavior deviations and behavior deficits. In such cases, remediation involves the use of procedures derived from the principles of both operant and respondent behavior, along with certain other procedures to be described later.

In general, respondent behavior problems are problems in the management of eliciting stimuli. However, because eliciting stimuli are by-products of the consequation that has occurred during the individual's prior transactions with his physical and social environment, these problems also possess components of operant behavior, which can be managed through the manipulation of consequences. In practice, it is often difficult to distinguish between behavior modification based on the manipulation of eliciting stimuli and behavior modification based on consequating stimuli.

Both types of manipulation may be carried out effectively by a specialist in behavior therapy in the context of visits to the office, clinic, or hospital. These visits are, in effect, training sessions. Such manipulations may also be carried out by the individual himself as a matter of "self-control." That is, the individual's own responses may produce stimulation that alters the probability of his emitting other (problem) behaviors at some future time, as when, for example, a smoker gives away his last pack of cigarettes (an event that decreases the likelihood of his smoking). In other cases the individual may manipulate his immediate environment under the direction of the specialist, and in still other cases the caretaker may have acquired the skills necessary to assist in the manipulation of the individual's environment. Thus the social practice of behavior theory principles in the modification of behavior can be carried out by caretakers as well as specialists. Effective behavior management is not the exclusive domain of the specialist.

The social practice of behavior theory principles to accomplish appropriate behavior control is rarely limited to the use of a single procedure. More often, several different procedures are brought to bear on a behavior problem, and these procedures may be used concurrently. For example, the behavior therapist who uses shock as a smoking behavior suppression technique is engaging in both respondent conditioning (in which smoking stimuli are paired with electric shocks) and operant conditioning (in which smoking operants are followed by aversive stimuli). Moreover, the behavior therapist may also use supplementary procedures such as drug administration or prosthetic modification of the individual's environment. For example, brain-damaged patients may be given Thorazine to reduce their hyperactivity, operant conditioning to increase their self-help skills, and prosthetic devices (for example, hearing aids or braces) to accommodate their sensory or motor defects.

MANAGEMENT OF RESPONDENT BEHAVIOR PROBLEMS

The management of respondent behavior problems requires the manipulation of eliciting stimuli in the individual's environment, in accordance with the principles of respondent behavior. Common examples of such respondent behavior problems, along with some procedures for their management, are shown in Table 13-1. Several manipulations are possible, including control over the eliciting stimuli in the individual's environment, respondent extinction, respondent conditioning, and respondent counter-conditioning.

Control Over Eliciting Stimuli

Not uncommonly, individuals may be especially sensitive to eliciting stimuli in their environment, the effects of which may be similar to the behavioral characteristics described in Chapter 11 (see Table 11-6), such as the acute or chronic activation syndrome, or strong, negative emotional responses to ordinary or common stimuli, such as those listed in Table 13-1. Once a disturbing eliciting stimulus has been "isolated," control (that is, reduction or elimination) of the pattern of respondents that it elicits can be accomplished by *completely removing the stimulus from the individual's environment.* Thus when the investor in the stock market who shows signs of the activation syndrome (high blood pressure, gastrointestinal motility, and so on) avoids visiting his broker, reading the newspapers, listening to the radio, and watching TV (all of which may contain stock quotations), he shows a reduction in the activation syndrome. Protracted exposure to disturbing unconditioned stimuli (painful or irritating stimuli, excessive work, and so on) may also produce the activation syndrome, and such stimuli can be dealt with in the same manner. Or the parents of a child who shows excessive fear of dogs, cats, and other furry animals may be able to remove all such stimuli from the child's environment, thereby eliminating the child's phobia.

The success of such a procedure depends on the degree of control the behavior manager is able to maintain over the individual's environment (the degree to which such stimuli can actually be removed). Moreover, when such disturbing eliciting stimulus complexes are seldom encountered by the individual, he may not really have a behavior problem, and so remediation may not be necessary. For example, the individual who has stage fright and panics when talking to groups of individuals does not really have a problem so long as his obligations to his family or his job do not require him to engage in public speaking.

On occasion the repeated presentations of positive eliciting stimuli, such as those shown in Table 13-1, can be used to eliminate *respondent depression.* Such depression might occur following separation, divorce, or the death of a spouse, and remediation would consist of massive doses of tender loving care—other-presented attentional behavior, consisting of verbal expressions of love and affection, and tactual stroking or contact, from an other possessing physical stimulus properties comparable to the lost spouse.

Table 13-1 Common Examples of Respondent Behavior Problems and Some Procedures for Their Management

PROCEDURE	SOME EXAMPLES OF ELICITING STIMULI
Control of Eliciting Stimuli	
REMOVAL OF THE AUTHENTIC OR ATTENUATED ELICITING STIMULUS	
complete removal of the CS from the individual's environment	being confronted by a snake being in a high place being in a crowd being in a confining space
INTRODUCTION OF A POSITIVE ELICITING STIMULUS	
repeated presentation to the individual of positive eliciting stimuli	other-presented verbal expressions of love or affection, other-presented tactual stroking or contact
Respondent Extinction (repeated presentations of the authentic or an attenuated version of the CS without the US)	
PRESENTED IN AUTHENTIC FORM	
repeated presentation of the disturbing eliciting stimulus in authentic form	tachycardia (racing heartbeat) being alone, away from others being confined in a classroom situation
PRESENTED IN ATTENUATED OR SYMBOLIC FORM	
repeated presentation of the disturbing eliciting stimulus in attenuated or symbolic form	killing a dental patient by performing dental (novacaine) injection failing an exam being in a high place being alone vomiting while eating in a restaurant

Respondent Conditioning (repeated pairings of prepotent unconditioned or conditioned eliciting stimuli or both with a neutral stimulus until the latter elicits a CEr)

Stage 1   CS $\longrightarrow$ CEr (crying)

stimulus pairing — US — (a painful or irritating stimulus—a slap)

(situation in which individual verbally admits to misdeeds)

Stage 2   CS $\longrightarrow$ CEr (crying)

(situation in which individual verbally admits to misdeeds)

or

Table 13-1 *(Continued)*

PROCEDURE	SOME EXAMPLES OF ELICITING STIMULI

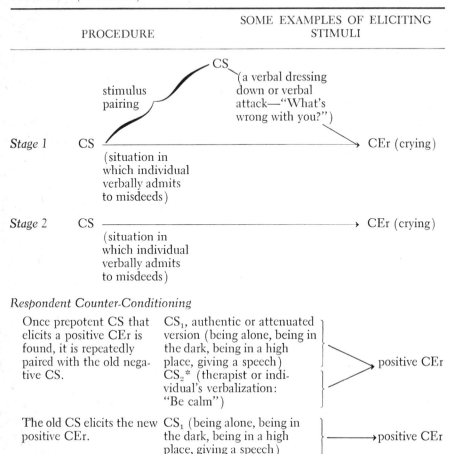

Respondent Counter-Conditioning

| Once prepotent CS that elicits a positive CEr is found, it is repeatedly paired with the old negative CS. | CS_1, authentic or attenuated version (being alone, being in the dark, being in a high place, giving a speech) CS_2* (therapist or individual's verbalization: "Be calm") | positive CEr |
| The old CS elicits the new positive CEr. | CS_1 (being alone, being in the dark, being in a high place, giving a speech) | positive CEr |

---

* CS_2 may have acquired its positive elicitation function through respondent conditioning in one of two ways. The verbalization "Be calm" may have been paired with other relaxation-inducing stimuli, such as tactual stroking or muscular relaxation stimuli, or it may have been paired with the termination of a painful or noxious stimulus, such as a shock.

Respondent Extinction When the CS Is Presented in Unattenuated Form

When the individual's sensitivity to eliciting stimuli is limited to conditioned stimuli, the problem may be remedied through a *respondent extinction procedure*. As indicated in Table 13-1, such a procedure involves the repeated presentation of the CS in the absence of the US with which it had formerly been paired. These presentations are continued until there is significant reduction in the strength of the negative CEr. When the CS is presented at full strength (that is, when the manner of presentation is similar to the stimulus situation with which the CS was paired in the natural environment), the procedure is called *flooding*. In flooding, the child who is afraid of dogs, cats, and furry animals would be confronted repeatedly with them but in such a way that they could not harm him. Such a procedure is risky for two reasons.

First, the presentation of conditioned stimuli in the complete absence of the unconditioned stimulus with which it has been paired requires exceptional control over the stimulus complex of which the CS is a part. For example, although the unattenuated presentation of the dog, as a CS eliciting a negative CEr, may be a reasonable remediation procedure for the elimination of the fear of dogs, the dog might bark or make sudden movements, which would amount to additional CS–US pairings, defeating the program of therapy.

Second, presentations requiring such exceptional control over the individual's environment may be hazardous because *new* negative respondents might emerge from the remediation procedure. For example, even though restraint and control over the presentation of the dog as a CS might be accomplished, the child's attempts to escape as the dog is presented and elicits the characteristic negative CEr might be blocked with physical restraint, which could possibly become a new elicitor of a negative pattern of respondents.

Furthermore, it may be physically impossible to arrange a therapy situation involving the original CS to which the individual is particularly sensitive. Under these circumstances, other stimuli that are members of the same stimulus class may be used.

Such problems make repeated but controlled presentations of the CS, in an unattenuated form without the US, a somewhat risky procedure. It is most useful when the magnitude of the negative CEr elicited by the CS is relatively weak.

Respondent Extinction When the CS
Is Presented in Attenuated Form

One alternative to the previous procedure is the repeated presentation of the CS in a weaker, or more *attenuated*, form *minus* the US component with which it was originally paired.

The CS may be attenuated by modifying its intensity, magnitude, or duration, its physical distance from the individual, or its authenticity. It may, then, be presented at low magnitude, for brief periods, and at a great distance from the individual. Or it may be presented in symbolic form. That is, a picture or photograph of the CS may be presented, or as in *implosion therapy*, the therapist may give the patient verbal instructions to imagine or visualize the CS situation (Stampfl and Levis, 1967).[1] All of these modifications have a weakening effect on the CS as an elicitor of a negative CEr. Initially, CS presentations tend to confront the patient with a version of the CS that is a relatively weak elicitor of the negative CEr. Subsequently, graduated presentations of the CS are made. Consider the following treatment program for a man with stage fright:

STAGE	LOCALE	PROCEDURES
early in training	therapist's office	Therapist presents the following verbal instructions to patient: "Imagine that from the stage of a theater you say, 'Hello,' to one person [audience size, or CS magnitude, minimal], who is seated in the back row [CS at a maximum distance], and then you walk off [CS exposure interval, brief; CS authenticity, minimal]."
later in training	therapist's office	Therapist presents the following verbal instructions to patient: "Imagine that from the stage of the theater, you say, 'Hello,' to two persons [CS magnitude increased], who are seated in the back row [CS at maximum distance], and then you walk off [CS exposure interval, brief]."
still later in training	therapist's office	Therapist presents the following verbal instructions to patient: "Imagine that from the stage of the theater, you say, 'Hello,' to two persons [CS magnitude the same], who are seated in the middle of the theater [CS physically closer], and then you walk off [CS exposure interval unchanged]."
still later in training	therapist's office	Therapist presents the following verbal instructions to patient: "Imagine that from the stage of a theater, you say, "Hello, my name is John Doe" [CS exposure interval longer] to two

[1] The patient's compliance with this procedure and the subsequent reduction in negative CEr elicited by the CS may be viewed in two ways. First, it may be viewed as a complex social situation in which the patient is the recipient of stimulation in the form of therapist-presented verbal instructions. This view is entirely consistent with behavior theory. Second, it may be regarded as indicative of the presence of a psychic faculty or state—namely, imagination, which is a private event. This view is not consistent with behavior theory. Many psychologists regard successful use of this procedure to be evidence that the patient has good imagination and failure in the use of this procedure to be evidence that he has a poor one.

		persons [CS magnitude the same], who are seated in the middle of the theater [and then you walk off]."
even later	theater	Therapist takes the individual to a theater, has him mount stage, and say "Hello" to one person (CS authenticity maximal; CS magnitude reduced), who is seated in the middle of the theater (CS physical distance unchanged), and then walk off (CS exposure interval reduced).
still later in training	theater	Therapist takes the patient to a theater, has him mount the stage and say, "Hello" to two persons (CS magnitude increased), who are seated in the front row (CS maximal physical closeness; CS authenticity maximal) and then walk off (CS exposure interval unchanged).

As training progresses, there is more and more similarity between the CS presentations in the therapeutic environment (the office situation) and the CS presentation as it occurs in the natural environment (the public-speaking situation).[2] For example, initial training involved a CS presentation of minimal authenticity (therapist-presented verbal instructions containing the symbolic form of the CS) at low magnitude (one person in the audience), maximal physical distance (audience seated in the back row), and brief exposure interval (the patient remained on stage only long enough to say, "Hello"). It is presumed that the CS presented in this manner (in attenuated form and without the US) will elicit a negative CEr of low magnitude. Ultimately, the therapist may wish to include terminal training with a large audience that is seated in the front rows of the theater and to require the patient to give a long speech. Even further, he may wish to vary the other characteristics of the situation: the audience composition, the theater, speech presentations, and so on in order to maximize generalization of the behavior, to eliminate stage fright completely from all possible public-speaking situations. Of course, there are a number of reasons why this procedure might not work. First, the symbolic presentations of the CS may be so dissimilar from the original CS occurring in the patient's natural environment that the symbolic CS fails to elicit the negative CEr. In short, the symbolic CS may not, in any way, be a member of the same stimulus class as the CS, and training (presentations of the symbolic CS without the US) will not extinguish the

[2] A combination of attenuated and authentic CS presentations may shorten treatment time (Wolpe, 1969).

negative CEr elicited by the CS. Then, too, with such CS presentations there is no control over the magnitude of the negative CEr elicited by the CS, so that on occasion it may be an excessively strong eliciting stimulus, whose effect is comparable to the original CS presentations. On such occasions the symbolic CS is antithetical to the goals of therapy. For example, even though a photograph is reduced in size and two-dimensional, viewing a photograph of an injury, as a CS, may be almost as strong as viewing the injury in real life. Moreover, repeated presentations of such stimuli, even though the stimuli are in attenuated form, may, in a sense, "spill over" affecting the patient's operant behavior, so that the termination of such a stimulus, through escape, is reinforcing. Such presentations, however, may be especially useful in remedying a patient's sensitivity to strong conditioned stimuli, particularly when the CS is authentic although attenuated through reduction in stimulus magnitude, physical distance, and exposure duration.

Respondent Conditioning

An individual may occasionally be regarded by himself or others as grossly insensitive to the social events or situations in his natural environment that possess conditioned eliciting stimulus functions for others. Because of the relative absence of positive or negative CEr's in his behavior, such an individual would probably be described as having a behavior characteristic referred to as shallowness of affect.[3] Remediation of such a behavior problem involves a two-stage process in which the individual is presented with repeated pairings of the CS—the conventional social event or situation—with a suitably conventional stimulus. For example, the child who fails to show remorse for his admitted misdeeds or for the suffering of others may be presented with either painful or irritating unconditioned stimuli (a slap), conditioned stimuli ("What's wrong with you?"), or both by his father until he does show the appropriate behavior (crying). (See Table 13-1.) Thus the remorseful social situation is paired with a strong eliciting stimulus.[4] Or in the Synanon program the drug addict showing withdrawal symptoms (muscular cramps, sweating, nausea, and so on) becomes the recipient of words of praise and encouragement (CS), and tactile stimulation from muscular

---

[3] Such shallowness of affect may have several antecedents, including a history of (1) insufficient or inadequate stimulus pairing between the social events or situations in the natural environment as potential CS's and the various types of US's with which they are usually paired or (2) pairings in which the forms of unconditioned or potential conditioned stimuli are limited. Either type of history may constrain the range of respondent patterns characteristic of such an individual. Long-term institutionalization early in life may have similar effects. (See Chapter 8.)

[4] In addition to the respondent conditioning component of the therapy in this example, there is also a component of operant conditioning—the presentation of remorse-response-contingent consequences (negative reinforcement).

rubdowns (US) administered to him by other Synanon members. Such presentations extend the individual's range of sensitivity to other physical or social stimuli in his environment.

Respondent Counter-Conditioning

A procedure that is useful in the remediation of excessive sensitivity to disturbing eliciting stimuli is *counter-conditioning*, the goal of which is to make the disturbing CS elicit a pattern of respondents that is incompatible with those it normally elicits. The implementation of this procedure requires (1) finding a suitable elicitor (CS_2 in Table 13-1) of a strong pattern of respondents that is incompatible with the CEr normally elicited by the CS (CS_1 in Table 13-1) and (2) repeatedly pairing the CS with the new elicitor until the former CEr no longer occurs. CS_1 comes to elicit a positive rather than a negative CEr. This procedure contains two essential processes: respondent extinction, in which presentations of the CS are *not* followed by the US with which it was formerly paired, and respondent conditioning in which the CS is paired with a new eliciting stimulus. Thus a baby's respondent crying following a hypodermic injection may be immediately reduced through the presentation of a strong stimulus eliciting a pattern of respondents incompatible with crying, such as the insertion of a pacifier in his mouth. This elicits a pattern of sucking, which because of its response characteristics, precludes crying. When the baby himself sticks his thumb in his mouth, he is using a self-control technique.

A similar procedure can be used on alcoholics. When alcohol, normally an elicitor of positive respondents, is repeatedly paired with an elicitor of negative respondents, such as the drugs tartar emetic, emetine, apomorphine, or gold chloride, all of which induce a pattern of nausea, alcohol will also induce nausea. In practice, treatment lasts from 7 to 10 days and consists of the following procedures: First, the patient drinks two 10-ounce glasses containing a warm acqueous solution of 1 g. of sodium chloride and .1 g. emetine; second, he is given a hypodermic injection of 30 mg. of emetine hydrochloride (to induce vomiting), 15 mg. of pilocarpine hydrochloride (to induce sweating), and 15 mg. of ephedrine sulphate (for "support"); third, the patient is given a glass of whiskey, which he smells deeply, tastes, and swishes about his mouth before swallowing. Another drink is poured, and this procedure is repeated. When the second drink is finished, nausea, hopefully, will occur.

Such procedures are useful for modifying respondent behavior when suitable and strong elicitors are available for pairing with the CS. However, counter-conditioning, like respondent conditioning, involves critical temporal relationships between the CS and US, so that when delays occur, the effect of counter-conditioning may be weak. In the preceding case, for example, counter-conditioning is most effective when the drugs are strong elicitors of nausea and the elicited pattern of nausea (through the ingestion of the drugs) occurs at the same time the patient smells, tastes, and swallows the alcoholic beverage. Inasmuch as counter-conditioning lends itself to several procedural modifications (that is, variation in the nature of the CS and US presentations), it is highly useful in contrived settings.

In conclusion, it should be stressed that if the procedure that the behavior manager chooses initially fails to work within a reasonable time, other procedures should be tried. An assessment of procedural effectiveness is based on a test at the end of treatment. In this test the individual is confronted with the significant eliciting stimuli as they occur in natural settings. This means he must confront the CS in unattenuated form. To rely on other tests of effectiveness would be a matter of risky business. Not uncommonly, the individual, or his caretaker, may report improvement in his condition. Such reporting consists of verbal behavior, and its control may arise out of the social transactions between the specialist and the individual. For example, unpleasant treatments may be avoided if the alcoholic reports that he no longer wants to drink. The alcoholic's verbal report might be: "Yeah, I'm really dried out. I couldn't even look a drink in the face" to which the caretaker might unfortunately reply: "Then I won't take you for a treatment today. I'll call the doctor and tell him you're well."

THE MANAGEMENT OF OPERANT BEHAVIOR PROBLEMS

There are two general classes of operant behavior problems that commonly require remediation. First, there are behavior deficits, in which certain behaviors are absent from the individual's repertoire or are part of the individual's repertoire but occur too infrequently. In such cases operant acquisition or maintenance procedures are required. Second, there are behavior deviations—behaviors that are disturbing or offensive to the individual or his caretakers. In this case operant elimination procedures are required.

Some examples of commonly encountered response classes that characterize operant behavior problems and some of the procedures for their management are shown in Table 13-2. Aside from certain auxiliary procedures to be discussed later, this table illustrates procedures derived from the principles of operant behavior that can be used in either operant behavior enhancement (strengthening procedures for the remediation of behavior deficits) or operant behavior suppression (weakening procedures for the elimination of behavior deviations). When the essential procedure involves making changes in the stimulus events that occur immediately *after* the operant, the procedure may be described as a *consequation* or *consequation schedule pro-*

Table 13-2 Some Examples of Operant Behavior Problems and Some Procedures for Their Management Consequation and Consequation Schedule Procedures

EXAMPLES OF RESPONSE CLASSES	EXAMPLES OF STRENGTHENING CONSEQUENCES	PROCEDURES	EXAMPLES OF PROCEDURES
Operant acquisition			
eye contact, gesticulating, observing, smiling, grasping, rocking, walking, eating with utensils, not eating (losing weight), bussing food tray, dressing, grooming, making a bed, writing and printing, information seeking, dancing, singing, conversing	Positive reinforcers: edibles, cigarettes, praise, vibration, eye contact with the other who agrees with individual, attending to the individual, nodding, token reinforcers (grades, money, chips, marks), free time, novel stimuli, backup reinforcers, applause from peers, Premack principle (high-probability behavior): running and screaming, watching TV, listening to records, talking to others, manual arts and crafts activities, playing ball, roughhousing, playing musical instrument Negative reinforcers: termination of yelling and screaming, termination of moderate physical restraint, termination of TV distortion	Differential reinforcement and successive approximation: R^D followed by response-contingent reinforcement. R^D's increasingly approximate the final performance. R^Δ's extinguished. When the R^D is a link in a chained performance, other links are comparably treated, and the links are put together. Putting-through procedures: The trainer manually positions the trainee's response system in the R^D position. Prompting: Trainer makes the response. Modeling: Trainer makes the response; trainee observes the response and is then reinforced for emitting an approximation of it.	Psychiatric technician reinforces patient with praise for first putting his left foot into pant leg, then for putting his right leg in his pant leg, then for reaching over and pulling his pants up, then finally only for doing all three. Coach grasps trainee from behind and puts trainee through follow-through of golf-club swing. Drama coach whispers line from behind curtain to actor whose speech is faltering. The tennis pro shows the onlooking pupil the proper way to grasp the tennis racket. When the grasp is matched by the pupil, it is an occasion for a smile.

Table 13-2 (Continued)

EXAMPLES OF RESPONSE CLASSES	EXAMPLES OF STRENGTHENING CONSEQUENCES	PROCEDURES	EXAMPLES OF PROCEDURES
		Specialized prosthetic training: Various procedures are used to induce the R^D	The speech therapist puts peanut butter against the roof of the child's mouth to produce tongue thrust responses.
		Drug administration	The child is given meprobamate to suppress his activity level and to increase the chances of an emission of an R^D.
Operant Maintenance	Positive reinforcers: edibles, cigarettes, praise, vibration, eye contact with the other who agrees with individual, nodding, token reinforcers (grades, money, chips, marks), free time, novel stimuli, backup reinforcers, applause from peers, Premack principle (high-probability behavior): running and screaming, watching TV, listening to records, talking to others, manual arts and crafts activities, playing ball, roughhousing, playing musical instrument Negative reinforcers: termina-	Present response-contingent strengthening consequences on a high-density schedule (CRF or small-ratio FR schedule)	About every second or every third time the child approaches the psychiatric technician when called, the technician hugs and praises the child.
eye contact, gesticulating, observing, smiling, grasping, rocking, walking, eating with utensils, not eating (losing weight), bussing food tray, dressing, grooming, making a bed, writing and printing, information seeking, dancing, singing, conversing		Gradually thin schedule until it is a long VI	

Table 13-2 (*Continued*)

tion of yelling and screaming, termination of moderate physical restraint, termination of TV distortion			

Operant Suppression

| spilling food, not eating, talking, defecating or urinating at inappropriate times, stroking others, hoarding, starting fires, stealing, lying, being late, being lazy, possessing dope, engaging in homosexual behavior, hiccoughing, horseplay, not studying, eating too much, drinking too much, swearing, not dressing, not grooming, not conforming to group-valued behaviors | Punishment: Removal of positive reinforcers such as edibles, consumables, praise, novel stimuli, tokens, backup reinforcers. Presentation of aversive stimuli such as yelling and screaming, slaps, shocks, breaking eye contact, ridicule, spilling food on individual, squirting individual. Premack principle (low-probability behavior): sitting Time-out: Immediate removal of individual from setting in which behavior occurs. | Present response-contingent weaking consequences on a high-density schedule | Each time the child grabs another child's food, he is immediately taken to the time-out area. |

cedure. When the essential procedure involves making changes in the stimulation that occurs immediately *before* the operant, it is a *stimulus control procedure.*

Consequation and Consequation Schedule Procedures

When an operant is absent from an individual's repertoire or occurs too infrequently, operant acquisition or maintenance procedures may be in order. Such procedures, along with some examples of response classes and strengthening consequences, are illustrated in Table 13-2.

Although the essential procedures for operant acquisition involve (1) precisely specifying the final performance, (2) finding suitable strengthening consequences, and (3) using differential reinforcement and successive approximation, additional procedures may be used to speed the acquisition processes, including putting through, prompting, modeling, specialized prosthetic training, drug administration. Some examples of these are also given in Table 13-2.

The following are examples of the operant behavior acquisition process:

EXAMPLE 1

Dickie is a 3½-year-old autistic child, who because of possible irreversible damage to his vision, was trained by Wolf, Risley, and Mees (1964) to wear his glasses by the following procedures:

First, using edibles (candy or fruit) and a click from a noisemaker as an S^D, the trainers reinforced Dickie for successive approximations of picking up his (lenseless) glasses frames from different places in the room and bringing them closer and closer to his eyes. Progress was slow because Dickie didn't like having the trainers touch his head when they tried to put the frames on him properly.

Two weeks later the trainers increased deprivation by using Dickie's breakfast food as a reinforcer, and training continued. However, progress remained slow.

After two more weeks larger, adult earpieces were added to the frames, and a "roll bar" was added to the top of the frames. This roll bar guided the frames onto Dickie's head, so that the earpieces fit over the top of his ears. A second rear roll bar was added so that the frames fit like a cap, and lunch was included in training as well. By the fifth week progress was still slow.

During an afternoon session when Dickie hadn't eaten much all day, both ice cream and Dickie's full prescription glasses were introduced. The ice cream appeared to be a powerful reinforcer, and reinforcements were given when Dickie placed the earpieces correctly over his ears and when he looked through the lenses. After about 30 minutes both behaviors were strong, and he was presented with interesting things to look at (a ring, a clicker) as long as he wore the lenses. From then on, his progress was rapid.

Not only were operant acquisition procedures (differential reinforcement and successive approximation) used in this example, but also deprivation to enhance the reinforcers, artificial and natural reinforcers (different foods and interesting visual objects), and finally, a prosthetic modification (the specially designed glass frames).

EXAMPLE 2

Children with severe behavior disorders attended a child center. The goal of the center was to develop stronger appropriate performances in these children. Rather than use food or drink to strengthen behavior, Ferster and Simons (1966) used natural reinforcers successfully, as follows:

Kathy was strongly inclined to play on the rocking horse, but she needed adult help because she couldn't climb onto the horse. Also, when she wanted to dress herself, she couldn't put on or take off her clothes. Sequences of performances, like these, that lead to rewarding activity provide a chance to increase the child's repertoire. For example, to add climbing onto the horse to the repertoire of a child who enjoyed rocking, the therapist lifted Kathy up so that one foot was in a stirrup, held her hands, and left the final step of swinging one leg over the rocking horse to her. This first approximation was carefully chosen as one that was clearly within the child's potential behavior. Successive approximations resulted in her taking responsibility for more and more of the behavior needed to get onto the horse until, finally, she climbed on by herself. Being on the horse was the reinforcer.

One time when the therapist was taking off Kathy's sweater, the therapist stopped when she had one hand in the sleeve and said, "Now you take your hand out of the arm." Kathy withdrew her hand. This contingency reinforced undressing because it actually "took the sweater off." On later days Kathy did more as the therapist withdrew his support, and Kathy acquired performances farther back along the chain of behaviors leading to the sweater's coming off. In this case we do not know why getting the sweater off was reinforcing. Kathy might have been too warm; the sweater might have been restrictive; or she might have taken it off because in her experience with the therapist she had found that nothing else could happen until she complied. Given the removal of the sweater as a reinforcer, the procedure was functionally parallel to animal-training procedures where the last member of the chain is brought under the control of a reinforcer and the antecedent members are added one at a time. In the present case the whole chain of performances is executed each time, but only the last performance occurs under the control of the natural reinforcer. The earlier members, although not in the child's repertoire, are supported by the therapist as he helps the child take her hand out of the sweater sleeve.

In the first part of this example putting-through procedures (lifting the child up onto the rocking horse so that she had one foot in the stirrup) were effectively combined with the natural reinforcement that occurred during rocking. In the second part of the example the therapist took advantage of the previously discriminated operant behavior controlled by his verbal instructions ("Now you take your hand out of the arm"). He also strengthened individually the links of the chain, and the links were chained into a sequence once they were strong.

EXAMPLE 3

An applicant for admission to Day Top Village must convince the regular members of his sincerity to join them. Most of all, he must convince them of his recognition of the fact that he needs help, as the following description attests:

Member 1: "So you want to join our group, eh?"
Applicant: "Yeah. I guess so."
Member 2 (heating up): "Look man! Forget the B.S. Why don't you just say it?"
Applicant (hesitatingly): "Say what?"
Member 2 (heating up even more): "You know! Say what you mean!"
Applicant: "Well, you know, I need your help to keep clean."
Member 2: "Then God damn it, why in the hell don't you say so?"
Member 1: "Yeah man. Let me hear you say it. Say you need help."
Applicant (in ordinary conversational voice): "I need help."
Member 1: "Oh, come on, man, say it like you mean it!"
Member 2: "Yeah, say it right."
Applicant (hesitatingly but louder): "I . . . need . . . help."
Member 1: "You know—that's phony. Not at all convincing. Like man —maybe you're afraid to say it. Like maybe you don't really believe it yourself. Do you?"
Member 2: "Yeah. If you really want in, you better say it like you mean it or forget it." (Other members nod their heads in agreement.)
Applicant (louder this time): "I need help!"
Member 1: "That's better. Now say it again."
Applicant (still louder): "I need help!"
Member 2: "That's good. Now again, but this time let the whole world know about it!"
Applicant (even louder): "I need help."

Member 1 (looking at member 2, the rest of the group, and then back at the applicant with an air of disbelief): "Hey man, did you ever see anybody who was really in trouble yell for help just once?"

Applicant (takes a long look at the members with whom he has been talking, then scans the group somewhat struck down, finally screams out very loud): "Help! God damn it! I need help! Let me in! Help! I need help!"

At this point all of the members move in on the applicant and pick him up bodily, carrying him in a reclining position above their heads saying: "That's it man!" (He has been accepted into the program.)

The group presentation consisting of both verbal instructions and social consequation seems especially powerful, as it had significant impact on the magnitude of the applicant's speech. (Initially, the applicant spoke in an ordinary conversational voice, but at the end of the interview he was screaming out.) Although the content of the applicant's verbal behavior in the situation changed significantly (from "Yeah. I guess so." [guess I want to join the group] to "Help! Help! I need help!"), the response events or links in the chain had already been differentiated and discriminated. The effect of the interview procedure, through verbal instructions, group-presented positive reinforcement ("That's better"), and punishment ("Forget the B.S.," looking away from the applicant), was to change the links in the verbal chain and possible concurrent operants (gestural responses) and respondents occurring during the interview.

EXAMPLE 4

A 36-year-old married male complained of having premature ejaculation during sexual relations with his wife and other women. Ejaculation usually occurred 15 seconds after intromission. Management of his problem consisted of wife-presented penile stimulation, gradual advances toward coitus under the direction of the verbal instructions given to the patient by the behavior specialist during office calls, and progressive relaxation. (Progressive relaxation will be described later.) The patient kept a daily record of the frequency and duration of his pre-ejaculatory behavior (reaching peak sexual excitement during presented sexual stimulation without ejaculation). Wolpe (1969) reported that by the eighth session his treatment progressed as follows:

Ninth occasion (Wednesday)   Penile stimulation while astride: 5, 12, and 9 minutes.

Tenth occasion (Wednesday)   Penile stimulation while astride: 12 and 11 minutes.

Eleventh occasion (Thursday)   Penile stimulation while astride: 12½, 12, and 23 minutes. After the last, Mr. I. inserted just the glans of his penis into the vagina, maintaining it there for 5 minutes. In the course of this time Mrs. I. became excited. Thereupon he withdrew and they both had orgasms digitally.

Twelfth occasion (Friday)   Partial insertion (glans penis) for 20 minutes during which Mrs. I. alone moved and in this way gradually manipulated the penis deeper. At the end of the period, Mr. I. withdrew as he felt ejaculation was imminent.

Thirteenth occasion (Friday evening after meeting with therapist)   Partial intercourse lasted 30 minutes—partial insertion 80 percent of the time and full insertion about 20 percent, for about a minute at a time. During this minute Mr. I. would move constantly without feeling any danger of ejaculation, but when Mrs. I. moved 5 to 10 times ejaculation would become imminent.

Fourteenth occasion (Saturday)   Partial intercourse as above, 23 minutes, and then Mr. I. ejaculated during an attempt to reverse positions.

Fifteenth occasion (Saturday)   Fifteen minutes, much the same as the thirteenth occasion.

Sixteenth occasion (Sunday)   Ejaculation after 4 minutes.

Seventeenth occasion (Monday)   Forty minutes, varying between one-quarter and one-half insertion of penis. Ejaculation was imminent several times, but Mr. I. averted it by relaxing each time.

Now the therapist directed Mr. I. to concentrate first on prolonging full intromission, and then gradually to introduce movement, but to prevent excessive excitation by avoiding stimulation of Mrs. I. He was told to keep well within his capacity of control. After a few minutes of this, it would be permissible to go on to orgasm, concentrating then on coital pressure by the penis.

Eighteenth occasion (Monday)   Orgasm after 15 minutes of complete insertion with small movements.

Nineteenth occasion   Orgasm after 29 minutes of small movements. Mrs. I. said that she too had been on the point of orgasm.

Further sexual occasions enabled Mr. I. gradually to increase excursions of movement, and finally a major breakthrough occurred after the thirteenth therapeutic interview. While Mr. I. retained his erection, Mrs. I. had four orgasms, and he ejaculated during the last of them. From this time onward there was mutually satisfactory sexual performance that gradually improved. There were fourteen therapeutic interviews in all, over 5 weeks.

As in example 3, complex contingencies were involved in this example. Noteworthy, however, was the gradual increase in the duration of pre-ejaculatory behavior from 15 seconds to 29 minutes under increasing conditions of penile stimulation. The orgasm, as an automatically reinforcing event, was made contingent on longer periods of pre-ejaculatory behavior. Not explicitly stated but probably important was the social reinforcement the patient received from his wife for more and more adequate sexual performances like those described after the thirteenth interview. It was important, too, that the procedure primarily dealt with the behavior in the natural environment, and that natural consequation functioned in both the acquisition and the maintenance of behavior. The procedure also employed self-control to the extent that the patient controlled the penile stimulation he was receiving through his own verbal report of the imminence of ejaculation.

These examples give some idea of how and where the operant acquisition, maintenance, and suppression procedures given in Table 13-2 may be used. When they are used in combination, they are particularly effective, since every relevant element of the individual's environment can be brought to bear on his problem.

Stimulus Control Procedures

There are several procedures available that involve changes in the stimulation occurring immediately prior to an operant and that have either an enhancing or a suppressing effect on that operant.

When the behavior problem consists of the occurrence of discriminated operant behavior, the following procedures aimed at operant behavior suppression may be useful:

1. *Complete removal of stimuli possessing stimulus control over the behavior to be eliminated.* (This procedure is essentially the same as that described on page 358.) Such is the case when the excessive drinking of an alcoholic is eliminated by placing him in an environment (usually an institution) in which alcoholic beverages are not available. Obviously, the success of such a procedure depends entirely on the degree to which such environmental control can be arranged. In many respects this is an extremely poor solution to such behavior problems, since its success depends entirely on intensive surveillance and control by others, and a change in the environment may reinstate the behavior. Moreover, even in institutional settings, the S^D controlling the problem behavior may be made available through bribery and the like. For example, incarcerated drug addicts often regain access to drugs by buying off prison guards.

2. *Reducing the availability of stimuli possessing stimulus control of the behavior to be suppressed.* For example, a chain smoker may only get his cigarettes from a cigarette case that delivers them one at a time and then only at certain times. The availability of the smoking stimuli may then be gradually reduced until smoking occurs infrequently.[5]

[5] Azrin and Powell (1968) report that initially the smokers they studied were given a cigarette from the cigarette case every 6 minutes (the time it takes to smoke one cigarette), and they smoked twenty to forty-four cigarettes a day. Gradually, the time interval between cigarette availability was increased to 65 minutes, and there was a reduction in smoking to eight to fifteen cigarettes per day. The training period ranged from 9 to 13 weeks.

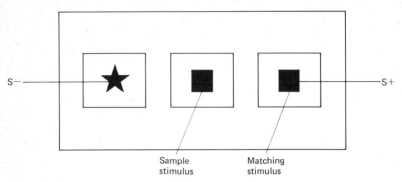

(a) *Ferster and DeMyer's Classical Operant Discrimination Training*

S—   ★   ■   ■   S+

Sample
stimulus

Matching
stimulus

Procedure:

1. The child is magazine-trained and learns to exchange coins for back-up reinforcers.

2. On each trial the child must first press the sample stimulus. This assures he'll look at sample stimulus before choosing a matching stimulus.

3. Initially, presses on either S⁻ or S⁺ are reinforced with coins.

4. Subsequently, only presses on S⁺ are reinforced.

5. Presses on S⁻ turn the machine off for 1 to 20 seconds.

FIGURE 13-1 Two procedures for the acquisition of an operant discrimination. (a) From C. B. Ferster and M. K. DeMyer. A method for the experimental analysis of the behavior of autistic children. *American Journal of Orthopsychiatry*, 1962, **32**, 92. (b) From S. Sidman and L. T. Stoddard. The effectiveness of fading in programming simultaneous form discrimination for retarded children. *Journal of the Experimental Analysis of Behavior*, 1967, **103**, 3–15.

3. *Narrowing or restricting the range of stimuli possessing stimulus control over the behavior to be suppressed.* For example, Jim and John, residential inmates of a school for delinquents, normally fight in the dressing room, swimming pool, classroom, cottage, and playroom. To suppress fighting, the school officials give social reinforcements for fighting in the camp gym and never reinforce them for attacks occurring elsewhere. Once the gymnasium develops sufficient stimulus control over aggression so that it seldom occurs outside of the gym, aggression may be reduced further or eliminated entirely by merely denying them access to the gym.

4. *Behavior suppression by the introduction of an S^D that controls behavior normally incompatible with the behavior requiring suppression.* For example, it is observed that a drug addict seldom prepares a fix in the presence of others who are not addicts. The others control non-fix, going-straight behaviors, which are normally incompatible with the preparation of a fix. The continued presence of others would, therefore, tend to suppress fix preparation.

(b) *Sidman and Stoddard's Errorless Operant Discrimination Training*

A. Background-fading program

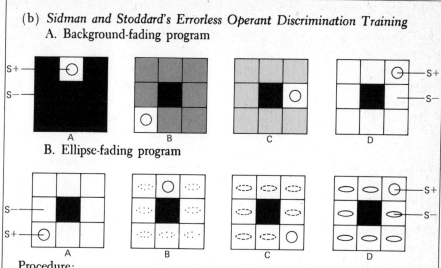

B. Ellipse-fading program

Procedure:

1. The child is magazine-trained.

2. The child is told to press the key or push the button.

3. Presses on the S⁺ close the shutter, blanking out the stimuli.

4. Release of the S⁺ key ends the trial, sounds the chimes, and actuates the reinforcer dispenser.

5. Presses on the S⁻ produce no change in the panel. (Stimuli remain the same until the child corrects his error.) Simultaneous pressing of two or more keys is counted as an error.

6. When one or more incorrect responses are made (presses of the S⁻), the child's final correct response moves the slide tray containing the last stimuli back to the start position, thus exposing the items in that tray again and allowing the child to return to an easier portion of the program.

7. First the items are presented from A to D in the background-fading program.

8. Following completion of the background-fading program, the items in the ellipse-fading program are presented from A to D.

There may also be occasions when an individual has deficits in operant discrimination. (See Table 11-5.) The remediation of such deficits can be accomplished by operant discrimination training. Figure 13-1 shows two different procedures for the acquisition of an operant discrimination. Figure 13-1(a) shows the classical operant discrimination training procedure developed by Ferster and DeMyer (1962) for the acquisition of a visual form discrimination in autistic children. Figure 13-1(b) shows the errorless discrimination training procedure developed by Sidman and Stoddard (1967) for the acquisition of a visual form discrimination in retarded children. In both cases a matching-to-sample task was used. Correct responses were reinforced, and incorrect responses were followed either by machine shutoff (from 1 to 20 seconds) or by extinction. Such machine-programmed procedures, and especially those employing errorless discrimination training, can be used to develop extremely complex discriminations quickly, with a minimum of emotional behavior, and without the necessity of training personnel.

Finally, the generalization of discriminated operant behavior may be accomplished by gradually modifying the discriminative stimulus class controlling the operant for which generalization is sought. For example, eye contact responses under the control of a single caretaker's command of "John, look at me" may gradually be shifted to the control of "John, look" and finally, merely "John." Or perhaps such commands may eventually be given by many others and in many different physical-environmental settings. The effect of this procedure, when appropriate responses are followed by appropriate consequences, would be to extend the generality of the behavior to different stimulus complexes. Behavior therapy procedures are of little value if their treatment effects are limited to the clinic or the office, and so whenever possible, the procedures should be carried out in environments that are like those of the individual's natural environment. (The remediation procedure for the elimination of stage fright described on pages 362–364 is illustrative of this.)

Other Procedures

In some cases the effectiveness of the aforementioned procedures may be enhanced by the introduction of backup procedures. Such procedures are especially useful in the remediation of serious behavior deficits, because they can be used to increase the individual's sensitivity to the common stimulus complexes occurring during social transactions. Particularly useful are:

1. *Developing the sensitivity of the individual to generalized positive reinforcers, such as praise, smiles, and nods, by pairing or making such presentations by others discriminative for presentations of the positive and negative reinforcers.* Such is the case when the psychiatric technician breaks into a broad smile, nods, and says, "good boy" as the child makes eye contact with him and receives some food.[6]

---

[6] The procedures essential for the development of conditioned reinforcers were described in Chapter 6. In actual practice the subject must make some differential response to the stimulus that is to become the conditioned reinforcer. Often such a response is merely an observing or attending response, but in the absence of such a response neither procedure (stimulus pairing or making the stimulus an S^D) will work. Lovaas and his co-workers (1966) found that sensitivity to conditioned reinforcers could not be developed until such a response occurred. In one subject, who rocked continually, such sensitivity would not develop until the rocking had first been suppressed by shock.

2. *Developing the sensitivity of the individual to gestural-verbal expressions of dislike and disapproval by pairing or making such presentations discriminative for the presentation of punishment.* For example, the psychiatric technician may say, "No!" and move the retarded child's hand away from his food tray as the child attempts to eat with his hand instead of his spoon.

3. *The use of deprivation by limiting the individual's access to unconditioned reinforcers (such as food) or social (generalized) reinforcers so as to enhance the value of these events as reinforcers when presented later during training.*

4. *The introduction of a reinforcer-sampling procedure in which the individual is given brief but non-response-contingent access to a possible reinforcing stimulus.* For example, the individual is presented with brief exposures to a filmed cartoon, and then the presentations are terminated. Subsequently, the reinstatement of such a presentation is contingent on emission of the R^D (for example, button pressing or vocalizing).

5. *The introduction of a reinforcing event menu, which is given to the individual at the beginning of training and describes or illustrates the reinforcers available contingent on behavior for that particular occasion.*

6. *The use of conjugate reinforcement in which the reinforcing stimulus is always available but its presentation at maximum intensity is contingent on emission of the R^D.* For example, the brightness of the television image may be made contingent on some response. Without the response the image is barely discernible.

7. *The introduction of a response-priming procedure in which an appropriate discriminative stimulus is presented and when an operant controlled by the stimulus is emitted, it is then reinforced.* For example, when a patient makes appropriate responses to the question: "Is there anything about the program here at the hospital you'd like to see changed?" by giving suggestions, his responses are followed by reinforcements.

8. *The use of response-building procedures that, by their nature, provide response-produced feedback in the form of additional visual, auditory, or tactual stimulation over and above that arising from the emission of the operant itself.* For example, in addition to hearing one's speech, one can feel one's vocalizations by placing one's thumb and forefinger against the pharynx and see one's mouth movements by watching oneself in a mirror.

9. *The use of a stimulus-shaping or a fading procedure in which the characteristic discriminative stimulus controlling some operant is modified or changed without interfering with its stimulus control over some operant.* For example, initially, a door may be opened only when the green light behind the plastic panel is on and the panel is pressed. Gradually, the green light on the panel is changed by fading in the lighted word *open* while presses on the panel continue to open the door.

COMPLEX DERIVATIVE PROCEDURES

There are several techniques of behavior management that derive from the procedures described in the sections on respondent and operant behavior management. As a group, these procedures involve rather complex social transactions between the therapist and the patient in which the therapist makes multiple presentations of eliciting, discriminative, and consequating stimuli.

Systematic Desensitization

Although a number of *different* procedures have been described as *systematic desensitization*, certain essential features are common to all of them. First, the procedures involve the attenuation of strong conditioned stimuli that elicit negative conditioned emotional responses in the client that are of such frequency and magnitude as to significantly disrupt other behaviors important to him or his caretakers. The following list of disturbing stimulus situations, taken from Wolpe, *The practice of behavior therapy* (1969), was made up by a patient in behavior therapy:

1. High Altitudes
2. Elevators
3. Crowded Places
4. Church
5. Darkness—Movies, etc.
6. Being Alone
7. Marital Relations (pregnancy)
8. Walking Any Distance
9. Death
10. Accidents
11. Fire
12. Fainting
13. Falling Back
14. Injections
15. Medications
16. Fear of the Unknown
17. Losing My Mind
18. Locked Doors
19. Amusement Park Rides
20. Steep Stairways

Such situations elicit disruptive behaviors that have been variously called anxiety, fear, phobias, and obsessions. In the initial interview between therapist and patient, a careful description is prepared of the physical and social stimulus complexes (situations) in which the disruptive behaviors occur. To assist in this task, some behavior therapists use questionnaires or psychometric tests in addition to the historical information reported by the patient.[7] From this list the disturbing stimulus situations may be grouped into themes or categories. For example, fear of high altitudes, fear of amusement park rides, and fear of steep stairways are all forms of acrophobia (fear of high places) and are ranked into a hierarchy. At the top of the hierarchy is the most disturbing stimulus situation, and at the bottom is the least disturbing situation.

Next, the therapist makes systematic presentations of these conditioned stimuli (CS) in attenuated form and in the absence of the unconditioned stimulus (US) with which it was originally paired. This is, essentially, an extinction procedure. The CS can be attenuated by modifying its temporal, magnitude, physical distance, or authenticity dimension, in much the same way that the CS was modified in the early phases of the treatment of stage fright described earlier. In that case, it will be recalled, the therapist presented verbal descriptions of the CS to the patient ("Imagine that you . . .") in such weakened form that they would never elicit a CEr of the magnitude elicited by the unattenuated form of the CS.

Then the behavior therapist continuously monitors the magnitude of the CEr elicited by his presentations of the CS in attenuated form and keeps it at a tolerable level. To do this, the behavior therapist often relies on the patient's subjective qualitative or quantitative descriptions of the CS intensity. The unit of measurement is called the *SUD* (subjective unit of disturbance—a measure of the magnitude of the CEr elicited by the CS). (See Wolpe, 1969.) In the SUD, 0 SUDS is designated as the *minimum* stimulus intensity, eliciting complete and utter calm, and 100 SUDS is designated as the *maximum* stimulus intensity, eliciting the "worst anxiety ever experienced." Following each presentation of the CS, the therapist may ask the patient to designate its strength in SUD units. The therapist may also use objective measures, such as the GSR (galvanic skin response—a measure of sweat gland activity) or EMG (electromyogram—a measure of skeletal muscle activity, especially tonus). As treatment progresses, the CS is presented at greater magnitude, for longer exposures, at closer distances, and in increasingly more authentic form.[8]

---

[7] Wolpe (1969) uses the Willoughby Schedule, the Fear Survey Schedule, and the Bernreuter Self-Sufficiency Inventory. When the individuals receiving treatment are sufficiently similar in the stimulus situations that are disturbing to them, a standard hierarchy of disturbing stimulus situations can be used.

[8] From a behavior theory point of view and from supporting experimental data (Litvak, 1969), maximum therapeutic (training) effect should come from presentations of the authentic CS. Wolpe (1969), however, reports a great deal of success with symbolic forms of the CS, and he is often able to terminate treatment because of significant improvement before the introduction of the authentic CS.

Finally, the therapist may choose to use *reciprocal inhibition therapy* in addition to the extinction procedure already described. Reciprocal inhibition therapy involves paired presentations of stimuli—the CS and a stimulus that normally elicits a pattern of respondents incompatible with the respondent pattern elicited by the CS.[9] Essentially, this is a counter-conditioning procedure and consists of a component of extinction, in which the CS is not followed by the original US, and a component of *respondent conditioning*, in which the CS is paired with another stimulus (either a CS or US) capable of eliciting a respondent pattern incompatible with the previously elicited negative CEr. In practice and in its classic form, as developed by Wolpe (1969), the procedure may be summarized as a series of lessons consisting of the following:

Lesson 1. The nature of the patient's problem is explored through interviews and in some cases by tests and questionnaires. For example, the patient is asked the question: "If you were confronted with such and such a situation—" (therapist inserts examples of situations, such as standing on the roof of a skyscraper), and his responses as well as those to the Willoughby Schedule, Fear Survey Schedule, and the Bernreuter Self-Sufficiency Scale are cataloged. From this historical and psychometric data, a list of those stimulus situations that are disturbing to the patient is prepared. The patient then ranks the items on the list in a hierarchy, with the most disturbing stimulus situation at the top of the hierarchy and the least disturbing stimulus at the bottom. From this initial listing, fear themes may be derived. For example, fear of being in an elevator, small room, or closet are all forms of claustrophobia. Then from this grouping, a more specific listing can be developed (including, for example, being in a particular closet).

When relaxation is chosen as the incompatible response class with which the CS will be paired, relaxation training is initiated during lesson 1, as a separate and distinct activity. Such training consists of therapist-presented verbal instruction, motor demonstrations that the patient imitates, putting-through procedures, and daily practice by the patient at home. Wolpe (1969) suggests that the therapist begin the initial instructions as follows:

[9] This stimulus pairing consists of two sets of verbal instructions that presumably elicit incompatible responses. One set consists of the therapist's suggestions to imagine or visualize the CS or other stimuli that are derivations of it, and one set consists of instructions aimed at eliciting the incompatible pattern of respondents. In reciprocal inhibition therapy, however stimulus pairing does not occur in the same sense that it occurs in the laboratory. Unlike the laboratory situation, the time intervals between paired stimulus presentations is relatively long, and the stimulus presentations really amount to complex social transactions involving verbal instructions that may possess rather complex stimulus functions. Moreover, the procedures (presentation of verbal instructions, putting-through, and though not explicitly stated, positive reinforcement from the therapist contingent on a relaxation response) and the response systems dealt with (skeletal muscle responses and the patient's verbal reports) are in some ways more obviously operant in character.

Even the ordinary relaxing that occurs when one lies down often produces quite a noticeable calming effect. It has been found that there is a definite relationship between the extent of muscle relaxation and the production of emotional changes opposite to anxiety. I am going to teach you how to relax far beyond the usual point, and with practice you will be able to "switch on" at will very considerable emotional effects of an "anti-anxiety" kind [p. 101].

Relaxation training for specific muscle groups often starts with the arms. The patient may be asked to grasp the arm of a chair, to note the differences in the sensations in his hand (touch sensations) and his forearm (muscle tension sensations), and to notice the specific sites of flexor muscle tension or extensor muscle tension. The therapist may then grasp the patient's wrist and instruct him to flex his bicep muscle by raising his arm against the resistance provided by the therapist's grasp. Once his bicep muscle is so flexed, the same instruction and therapist-presented resistance is tried with the arm extensor muscles. The therapist may then say:

> I am now going to show you the essential activity that is involved in obtaining deep relaxation. I shall again ask you to resist my pull at your wrist so as to tighten your biceps. I want you to notice very carefully the sensations in that muscle. Then I shall ask you to let go gradually as I diminish the amount of force exerted against you. Notice, as your forearm descends, that there is decreasing sensation in the biceps muscle. Notice also that the "letting go" is an activity, but of a negative kind—it is an "uncontracting" of the muscle. In due course, your forearm will come to rest on the arm of the chair, and you may then think that you have gone as far as possible—that relaxation is complete. But although the biceps will indeed be partly and perhaps largely relaxed, a certain number of its fibers will still, in fact, be contracted. I shall therefore say to you, "Go on letting go. Try to extend the activity that went on in the biceps while your forearm was coming down." It is the act of relaxing these additional fibers that will bring about the emotional effects we want. Let's try it and see what happens [Wolpe, 1969, pp. 101–102].

As relaxation training progresses, the therapist may, from time to time, palpitate the patient's muscles to determine his progress. When maximum relaxation is attained in one arm, the patient continues to practice with both arms.

Lesson 2. Relaxation training continues with emphasis on the muscles of the head, starting with the facial muscles, especially the forehead muscles. These muscles are contracted, then relaxed, every 5 seconds until further relaxation "step down" is not noticed. Then, training progresses with the muscles around the nose, the lips, and so on.

Lesson 3. The training progresses with emphasis on the muscles used in biting, the tongue muscles, neck, pharynx, and sometimes the eyeballs.

Lesson 4. Relaxation training continues with the posterior neck muscles and the deltoid shoulder muscles.

Lesson 5. Progressive relaxation training continues with the muscles of the back, abdomen, and thorax, and training in the "letting go" of the respiratory muscles is sometimes useful.

Lesson 6. Relaxation training starts with the feet and continues upward to the thorax.

By Lesson 3 or 4, usually training in relaxation is progressed sufficiently that a portion of the therapy session can be devoted to presentations initially of both neutral or control scenes and the relaxation-inducing stimuli. Following the neutral or control scenes, the CS is introduced for the remainder of the treatments. The therapist begins these presentations with the following instructions: "Let's see how well you can relax and how you react to various stimuli and images. Our main aim at all times is to keep you as comfortable as possible" (Wolpe, 1969, p. 124).

The patient is then seated. He reclines comfortably with his eyes closed and is presented these additional instructions:

> Now, your whole body becomes progressively heavier, and all your muscles relax. Let go more and more completely. We shall give your muscles individual attention. Relax the muscles of your forehead. (Pause 5 to 10 seconds) Relax the muscles of your jaws and those of your tongue. (Pause) Relax the muscles of your eyeballs. The more you relax, the calmer you become. (Pause) Let all the muscles of your shoulders relax. Just let yourself go. (Pause) Relax all the muscles of your trunk. (Pause) Relax the muscles of your lower limbs. Let your muscles go more and more. You feel so much at ease and so very comfortable [Wolpe, 1969, p. 124].

Following the patient's initial attempt at relaxation under the control of therapist-presented verbal instructions, the patient is asked to signal (using his finger) if he is not completely and utterly calm (0 SUDS). If he is not calm, further attempts to induce calm are made through the presentation of additional instructions. For example: "Imagine that on a calm summer's day you lie on your back on a soft lawn and watch the clouds move slowly overhead. Notice especially the brilliant edges of the clouds" (Wolpe, 1969, p. 125).

If the patient is still unable to remain calm following several of these presentations, training is postponed until the next session. If, however, the patient does remain calm, training may be continued in this session. The therapist will then present another set of verbal instructions to the patient. These instructions describe a "neutral" or control scene—one that the therapist believes will not be disturbing to the patient and can be used to assess (1) the patient's skill at visualizing material without disturbances and (2) the degree to which the desensitization procedure itself is provocative to the patient. The content of the instructions for such a scene is as follows:

I am now going to ask you to imagine a number of scenes. You will imagine them clearly and they will generally interfere little, if at all, with your state of relaxation. At the end of each scene presentation, I will ask you to tell me in SUDS, how much the scene disturbed you. Remember that 0 SUDS was defined as complete and utter calm while 100 SUDS was defined as the worst anxiety you ever experienced. First, I want you to imagine that you are stand-ing at a familiar street corner on a pleasant morning watching the traffic go by. You see cars, motorcycles, trucks, bicycles, people, and traffic lights; and you can hear the sounds associated with all these things. (Pause of about 15 seconds) Now stop imagining that scene and give all your attention once again to relaxing. How much in SUDS, did this scene you imagined disturb you? Now imagine that you are (therapist then presents to the patient the . . . item listed [at the bottom of] the patient's hierarchy for a particular theme). (Pause of 5 seconds) Now stop imagining the scene. How much in SUDS, did that scene disturb you? (Pause of 10 seconds) Now imagine the same scene again, the same events. (Pause of 5 seconds) Stop imagining the scene and just think of your muscles. Let go, and enjoy your state of calm. (Pause of 15 seconds) Now again imagine that you are (again, the same scene is presented). (Pause of 5 seconds) Stop the scene, and now think of nothing but your own body. (Pause of 5 seconds) How much in SUDS, did that last scene you imagined disturb you? [Wolpe, 1969, p. 126].

The therapist notes whether or not there is a reduction in SUDS over pre-ceding scene presentations, and if not, further presentations of the same scene are made. If there is a reduction, a scene from the bottom of the hierarchy of another theme is introduced, and the procedure is continued as before.

In a given session three to four hierarchies may be covered. The number of sessions required for complete desensitization is variable as are the rates of change from one item on the hierarchy to the next, the time interval be-tween scenes, and the duration of a scene. Two or three sessions a week may be scheduled. Successful desensitization may occur even when the presenta-tion of a given scene from the hierarchy is reported at 10 to 15 SUDS, al-though in some individuals the therapy may require that complete and utter calm (0 SUDS) be maintained during all scene presentations. The entire sequence can be presented mechanically with a prerecorded tape playback containing relaxation instructions and scene descriptions. The rate of pre-sentation can be controlled by the patient. In some cases drugs or carbon dioxide–oxygen may be used to suppress strong CEr's and as an adjunct to the relaxation training. In any case, therapy is continued until the patient fails to show negative CEr's (responds minimally in SUD units to the CS) to the scene presentations from the items at the top of the hierarchy.

Systematic desensitization appears to generalize well to the natural environen though the procedure seldom involves presentations of the CS in unattenuated form. However, some patients are unaffected by it for one or more reasons. First, the therapist's presentations during relaxation training, as a stimulus complex (verbal instructions, motor demonstrations to be imitated by the patient, and putting through), may fail to induce sufficient relaxation and may in fact have the opposite effect, functioning as a disturbing stimulus that is paired with the CS. Second, even when relaxation does occur, the therapist's presentation of the attenuated version of the CS (scene presentations) does not reduce the individual's sensitivity to the CS in its unattenuated form. Both of these difficulties suggest that the therapist's presentations (relaxation training and the attenuated CS procedures) are not in the same stimulus class as those occurring in the natural environment. It is often difficult to determine the reason for the failure of the procedure. Some individuals may show reduced muscle tension during relaxation training yet continue to show autonomic nervous system activation. In still other cases the therapist may not have accurately identified a functional, attenuated version of the CS. Other functional CS's from other hierarchies must then be paired with the relaxation stimuli. When it is successful, however, systematic desensitization is a highly useful procedure, because it enables the behavior therapist to deal effectively with diverse behavior problems in an artificial setting.

Finally, systematic desensitization involves a complex social transaction, the actual salient elements of which are somewhat unclear. Recent evidence shows that successful desensitization is possible without either relaxation training or the construction of an individualized fear stimulus hierarchy. This seems to point to the importance of presentations of the (verbal) instructional control of behavior (instructions to "imagine the——"), the attenuated versions of the CS, and the occurrence of the CEr without presentations of the US—that is, the extinction component, rather than the respondent conditioning component, of the entire counter-conditioning procedure.

Covert Sensitization

On occasion, taking drugs, smoking, overeating, and excessive drinking are behavior problems, because of their injurious effect on health or because of their disruptive effect on other behaviors. *Covert sensitization* may be a useful procedure for such behavior problems. Like systematic desensitization, covert sensitization is essentially a counter-conditioning process in which the relevant stimuli are paired in attenuated or symbolic form. This time, however, a stimulus capable of eliciting a strongly negative pattern of respondents is paired with those stimuli normally controlling the behavior to be suppressed. The following classic case was reported by Cautela (1966), who was the first to report the use of covert sensitization in therapy:

A 29-year-old nurse was treated with behavior therapy techniques for a number of different problems. Dating was especially disturbing to her and frequently she would drink to excess. When she had been in therapy for a while she remarked that she felt well adjusted in life except for her drinking, and this remark led the behavior therapist to the conclusion that she was disturbed more by her drinking and the way she acted on dates when she drank than she was by merely having a date. He concluded that she drank as a result of the stimulus control of the dating situation (the dance hall, the waiter, the booze, and so on) simply because in the past drinking alcohol had weakened the impact of the disturbing stimuli she had once encountered on dates. Now, even though the dating situation no longer appeared to be disturbing, she continued to drink. Initially, therapy consisted of her being told to relax and to indicate when she felt completely relaxed by raising her index finger. (She had already undergone desensitization training.) Then, she was told the following:

> Now, I want you to imagine that you ask the waitress to give you your favorite drink. Just as she brings you the drink and you reach for it, you start to feel sick to your stomach. As you hold the glass in your hand, you feel yourself about to vomit. Just as you put the glass to your lips, you vomit. It comes out of your mouth all over the table and the floor. It is a real mess. When you visualize the whole scene clearly and feel utterly sick to your stomach, raise your finger [Cautela, p. 37].

Ten seconds later the patient raised her finger. Similar instructions were presented again, only this time the scene described was at a party and she vomited all over the hostess' dress. When she signaled that she again felt sick, she was told to relax and erase the scene from her mind. She was then asked to imagine that while at a dance she started to take a drink, but when she did, she began to feel ill. This time, however, she would not try to drink and then she would immediately feel calm. Then more trials were given. During alternate trials she would imagine that she did not try to drink and felt calm. Although she had been instructed to practice the visualization procedure leading to nausea at home, she failed to do so. Nevertheless, 2 days later she excitedly reported that for the first time in 5 years she had gone dining and dancing and hadn't taken a single drink. However, she did report feeling nauseous when she thought about drinking. The patient agreed to continue visualizing herself becoming ill while drinking, although the visualization now involved beer instead of hard liquor. Subsequently, the patient reported having occasional wine coolers, which were then introduced into the procedure. One such scene was presented as follows:

You walk into your kitchen. You see a highball, a glass of beer, and a bottle of wine on the table. You start to feel sick to your stomach as you reach for one of the beverages. You vomit all over the beverages and all over the floor. (Cautela, p. 38).

Seven more training sessions occurred in the office, and the patient went through procedures daily. Drinking stopped altogether and in an 8-month follow-up, the patient reported no drinking during that period. Three additional sessions of training were given when she felt she was weakening.

Essential to this training was a stimulus pairing procedure in which verbal stimuli eliciting nausea and sickness were paired with the onset of drinking, and verbal stimuli eliciting relaxation and calmness were paired with the cessation of drinking. Note that aside from a report of induced nausea (a respondent pattern), the procedure suppressed drinking operants.

Both systematic desensitization and covert sensitization affect respondent and operant behavior. It is not clear whether these procedures involve the presentation of stimuli functional in concurrent patterns of respondent and operant behavior or if they involve chains between the two. Covert sensitization, with its component of relaxation training, its stimulus pairing procedures, its control over respondent and operant behaviors even in natural settings, is in many respects the obverse of systematic desensitization. It appears to be a powerful procedure for the suppression not only of drinking, but also of excessive eating and smoking.

Contingency Contracting

Not infrequently, the behavior control that occurs between a caretaker and an individual involves a *contingency contract* (Homme and Csanyi, 1968), or an agreement between two parties which specifies the following:

1. Response classes that each party to the contract must emit. Ordinarily, these response classes will be different for the individual and the caretaker.

2. Consequences that maintain the behavior of each party to the contract and are made available contingent on emission of the appropriate response classes by each party.

3. Discriminative stimuli in the form of (a) caretaker-presented verbal instructions or directions to the individual and (b) appropriate behavior by the individual, which is discriminative for the presentation of the consequences by the caretaker.

Although contingency contracting is widely used in behavior management, it is, perhaps, most common in parent–child situations and because of this, is sometimes called Grandma's Law. For example, the father who tells his child to "Eat your spinach first and then you can have your ice cream" is using a *positive contingency contract*, the elements of which are:

	CHILD	FATHER
Response Class	eating spinach	giving child ice cream
Consequences	ice cream	child eating spinach (a balanced diet)
Discriminative Stimuli	S^{D_1} Father says, "Eat your spinach." S^{D_2} spinach on the plate	spinach gone from plate

If the father says, "If you scream one more time, I'm going to give you a licking," he is using a *negative contingency contract*, the elements of which are:

	CHILD	FATHER
Response Class	scream	slapping child
Consequences	slap	termination of scream
Discriminative Stimuli	"If you scream one more time, I'm going to give you a licking."	hearing child scream

In general, positive contracts are used for behavioral enhancement, employ positive consequences (reinforcers), and are preferred over negative contracts. Negative contracts are more likely to be used for behavior suppression and are thus more apt to employ negative consequences (that is, punishment).

Essential in the success of such contracting in behavior control is the individual's reinforcement history. Not only must the response class specified by the contract already be part of the individual's repertoire (be differentiated),[10] but it must also be under the discriminative (stimulus) control of caretaker-presented verbal instructions or directions. Such contracts may not work with the naïve individual until the individual has been repeatedly presented with the consequences specified in the contract following emission of the appropriate behavior. In some ways this contractual relationship between the caretaker and the individual is analogous to the wise man–advice seeker relationship. That is, the wise man, like the caretaker, is able to reliably predict or specify the consequences that will follow the individual's behavior should he engage in a course of action. This is true even though the wise man usually does not present the consequences. For example, the parent's admonition: "If you play with that knife, you'll hurt yourself" acquires discriminative control over the child's knife avoidance behavior when subse-

---

[10] However, this is not to say that such contracts cannot be used to develop more complex performances. When combined with programmed instruction, the contingency contract is useful in attaining this goal.

quently he does cut himself. Likewise, "social power" based on expertise may have similar origins, as when the doctor's suggestion: "Take those pills every two hours, and your headache will go away" comes true. In the first example the consequences were mediated by the physical environment (the sharp knife), and in the second case, by the social environment (the doctor). Not uncommonly, there may be long delays between the verbal instructions or directions and the consequences. Such delays in consequences may be attenuated by additional verbal instructions, such as "Just wait and you'll see." (See Chapter 6.)

Homme and Csanyi (1968) suggest that contingency contracts are more powerful mediators of behavior control when:

1. They involve positive rather than negative consequences, that is, positive reinforcement instead of punishment.

2. The consequences involved in the contract are highly desirable and not available outside of conditions in the contract.

3. The consequences are made available *immediately* following emission of the behavior specified in the contract.

4. Initial contracts call for and reward small approximations to the final performance, which are easier for the individual to perform than the final performance.

5. The contract involves frequent but small amounts of consequences rather than infrequent or large amounts of consequences.

6. The consequences in the contract are made available only after the appropriate performance occurs and at no other time.

7. The contract is fair and involves a consequence that is proportional in value to the behavior specified and does not involve exploitation.

8. The terms of the contract, as to the kind and amount of specific, objectively verifiable behavior required and the kind and amount of specific consequences, are clear to both parties.[11]

9. The program of behavior management makes systematic use of contingency contracting.

Although the contracting procedure is often used to achieve behavior control in the context of social transactions between the caretaker and individual, it can also be used to develop self-directed or self-controlled performances—a matter to be discussed Chapter 14. And, of course, when a caretaker and a trainee have repeatedly contracted successfully, the trainee's behavior may come under such powerful control of the "contracting situation" that reported presentations of the verbal instructions in the contract are no longer even necessary.

---

[11] A parent who says, "Be a good boy, and I'll get you a present" is violating this rule. The definition of the behavior ("good boy") and the consequences ("a present"), in the absence of extensive training, is quite vague.

Contingency contracting has been used successfully in a variety of settings, including the laboratory, the clinic, the classroom, and on the street, and it has been used as a means of strengthening a wide range of behaviors including such things as abstention from cigarette smoking, punctuality, pro-social behavior, remaining in one's classroom seat, raising one's hand before talking in class, and the basic skills such as mathematics, reading, and writing.

Coverant Control Therapy

It will be recalled that behavior therapists tend to avoid dealing with private events, or subjective states, such as thinking, imagining, reveries, daydreaming, and fantasies, because of the difficulty one encounters in obtaining reliable descriptive data on the nature of the response topographies and response frequencies of such events. Behavior control that arises out of coverant control represents an interesting exception to this rule. A *coverant* is a private event that is strengthened or weakened by the consequences that follow it. The term *coverant*, first coined by Homme (1965), is a combination of the terms *covert* and *operant*. In coverant control therapy both the content and the frequency of occurrence of the coverant are manipulated, and this manipulation affects the individual's overt behavior. By carefully selecting the appropriate coverant and then following its occurrence with appropriate consequences, the therapist can modify the individual's behavior. Even though there are methodological objections to dealing with private events coverant control therapy procedures deal only with the response class dimension of frequency, and self-reporting of such frequencies is acceptable. While it might be reasonable to assume that underlying the content of a coverant is a subvocal response class having a certain topography, this is entirely speculative.

The choice of the content of the coverant depends on the nature of the individual's problem. If the behavior to be remedied merely occurs too infrequently, the therapist will choose coverants with content that is congruent with the behavior to be strengthened. On the other hand, if the problem behavior occurs too frequently and must be suppressed, coverants that are incompatible with the behavior in question are chosen. With the assistance of the behavior therapist, the individual makes up a list of appropriate coverants and selects the consequences. Most frequently, strengthening consequences are used, and they are identified as the high-probability behaviors for that individual.

Suppose, for example, a particular individual on a particular job rarely shows verbal-gestural behavior suggestive of a positive or pleasant mood. Suppose, further, that when the employee has a discussion with management, it is decided that such a mood is highly desirable and should be the rule rather than the exception. In a coverant control therapy program to obtain such behavior, the individual would first (1) prepare a list of the things that make him most happy about working on his job and (2) determine what is high-probability behavior for him. The results of the interview with management and direct observations of the employee on the job might reveal the following significant information:

STIMULUS COMPLEX OF BEHAVIOR (PHYSICAL-SOCIAL SETTING)	RESPONSE CLASS (COVERANT CLASS)	STRENGTHENING CONSEQUENCE (HIGH-PROBABILITY BEHAVIOR)
job situation	happy thoughts coverants: "My work is fun." "My boss likes me." "My colleagues are nice guys." "The girls here are really great."	drinking coffee

The employee would then be instructed to keep this list with him and to think of one of these coverants (such as "My work is fun") immediately before engaging in the high-probability behavior of drinking coffee. The individual keeps daily records of the frequency of these positive thoughts, or *pro-coverants*, and adds additional pro-coverants and high probability behaviors to the list as they occur. Presumably, as pro-coverants become more frequent, so will the individual's verbal-gestural behaviors suggestive of having a positive or pleasant mood while he is on the job.[12]

On the other hand, suppose that the individual engages in a behavior, the frequency of which should be reduced. This time, the therapy list would consist of coverants with content that is incompatible with the behavior to be controlled. Such a case was treated by the author and is summarized as follows:

At the suggestion of his wife and mother, a premed student came to the college counseling center for assistance with his problem—chronic nail-biting. He had bitten his nails since preschool days, and although he had frequently said he wanted to stop, he could not. His relatives were particularly annoyed when he bit his nails in church, because it produced a distinct and annoying sound that drew the attention of the congregation. He also bit his nails while driving, watching TV, and studying. Visual inspection of his nails revealed that all were bitten very close to the skin.

On the first session and with the assistance of the counselor, he pre-

[12] This is, perhaps, a somewhat tenuous assumption, since it is at least theoretically possible for an individual to possess concurrent behaviors that are incompatible or incongruent, as when a lover says, "Your dress is beautiful," but thinks it is ugly.

pared a list of negative thoughts or things he disliked about nail-biting. These were to be used as coverants, or thoughts incompatible with nail-biting behavior. They included:

"Nail-biting is socially unacceptable."
"Nail-biting is painful."
"Bitten nails are unsightly."
"Nails are poor tasting."

Possible strengthening consequences were discussed and eating, taking a break from studying, and eliminating (urinating) were tentatively selected. They were to be engaged in *only* after the occurrence of a coverant. Besides carrying a list of the coverants, the client was to keep a daily log showing:

1. The day.
2. The time of occurrence of nail-biting or putting finger in mouth.
3. The time of occurrence of a tendency (strong desire) to do the above.
4. The time of occurrence of a coverant followed by strengthening consequences.
5. The nature of the consequences.
6. The other incidental events he felt might be relevant.

These log sheets were collected and examined at the weekly sessions, and a visual inspection was made of the client's nails. When appropriate, the client was complimented on his progress. On the second session, a new coverant was added to the list. "Nail-biting is unhealthy" (because there are bacteria under the nails). As treatment progressed, the client reported increased sensitivity to nail-biting in others and to the stimulus situations in which he either bit his nails or had a tendency to do so. Especially provocative were studying, opening a book, and examinations. The third week he reported that chewing his nails was not as enjoyable because they had grown thicker. Toward the end of treatment (the eighth session), overt acts of nail-biting ceased entirely, although some nail-picking was reported during the seventh session. Also reported on the eighth session was the observation that merely thinking about an exam seemed to induce a tendency to chew his nails.[13] On the tenth session he reported that he seemed to think automatically of a coverant when encountering the reinforcing event. He felt he could stop keeping records, and it was agreed that he could. On the eleventh session and following the inspection of the client's nails, the counselor complimented the client on his progress and told him that at the final meeting (twelfth session), because of his progress, he would be given a nail clipper with which to

---

[13] Although those of a psychodynamic persuasion many regard nail-biting while one is taking an exam as an anxiety-reducing device, the situation can just as easily be interpreted as one having stimulus control over nail-biting, since while one bites one's nails, one avoids taking an exam.

groom his nails. In addition to the weekly visual inspections of the client's nails, the counselor and the client plotted curves from the data obtained during the first ten sessions. The curve was introduced on the fourth session and brought up to date weekly. The total number of coverants ranged seventeen to seventy-one per week. The total number of nail-biting acts (including putting fingers in the mouth and nail-picking) and tendencies to nail bite ranged from none to ten. The curves are shown in Figure 13-2. At sessions eleven and twelve the client's nails were checked, but no data were brought in. On the twelfth session it was decided that counseling could be terminated. Follow-up more than 3 years later revealed that both nail-biting and nail-picking had remained suppressed.

Although this case illustrates the procedures used in coverant control therapy, it is unlikely that the suppression of nail-biting was due to the coverant control therapy alone. As with most applications of behavior therapy, several things were going on that could have suppressed the client's behavior. For one thing, daily records were kept on the frequency of nail-biting, and this alone may have had some suppressing effect.[14] Second, at each interview the client's nails were inspected by someone normally outside of his immediate environment, which may have also had a suppressing effect. Finally, as the client's nails grew longer and thicker, they acquired new discriminative properties controlling behavior incompatible with biting.

Coverant control therapy, as a means of changing the individual's "mood" or specific behaviors by manipulating his inner thoughts, talking to oneself, fantasizing and so on, is an interesting but somewhat precarious departure from the usual behavior theory approaches to behavior management. It relies heavily on the adequacy of verbal report and self-managed or controlled contingencies; it assumes that the verbal stimulus that controls the coverants ("I'm happy today") is the appropriate stimulus for the response class of which the coverant consists (the "happiness" response), and that strengthening consequences affecting the coverant will affect the individual's overt behavior (verbal, gestural expressions of happiness) through response induction or generalization. In order for this effect to become manifest, both the coverant, as a response class, and the overt behaviors to be modified by the behavior manager must have shared some response properties together. This assumption is not entirely unreasonable, however. While one emits overt verbal and gestural expressions of happiness, he may also have covert happiness responses. Although success in the control of smoking and nail-biting has been reported in clinical settings, because of the phenomena with which

---

[14] Several observers have reported that when a smoker must keep records of his daily cigarette consumption, he seems to smoke less. Perhaps this is a manifestation of the Premack principle in which the HPB (smoking) is followed by LPB (record keeping). For example, see Whitman (1969).

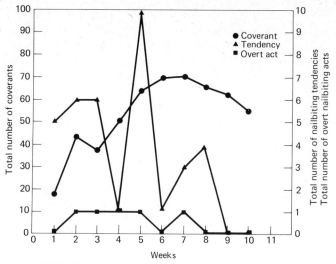

FIGURE 13-2 Coverants, nail-biting tendencies, and nail-biting acts occurring during ten weeks of coverant control therapy.

coverant control therapy deals and the nature of the procedures, further verification of coverant control therapy is needed. Meanwhile, it may be a useful procedure in the armamentarium of the behavior manager.

Other Derivative Procedures

In addition to those already mentioned, the following procedures may prove to be useful in certain cases. Although these procedures may be useful in eliminating the disruptive effect of disturbing stimuli in the individual's environment, only the first two procedures are derivatives of systematic desensitization.

EXTERNAL INHIBITION

In external inhibition the individual is first presented with several electric shocks to determine his optimum shock intensity (a shock level that is clearly felt but not aversive). Second, the individual is presented with the weakest item of his fear hierarchy, and a SUDS reading is obtained. Third, the scene is again presented, and following a signal from the individual indicating that it is "clearly visualized," two shocks are given about 1 second apart. Following a 5-second rest period, the scene is presented as before. The procedure is repeated until five to twenty shock presentations have been made. Then the scene is again presented, but this time without shock, and a SUDS reading is obtained. The treatment is continued until the SUDS reading is minimal for presentation of items in the fear hierarchy. For example,

Wolpe (1969) used such a procedure to help a patient overcome his fear of driving alone. The hierarchy items contained scene descriptions of the patient driving alone, first for half a mile, then three quarters of a mile, and so on. When the SUDS reading was zero, the next item on the hierarchy was presented, and the procedure was repeated until all items on the list were covered. In a variation of this procedure shock-induced arm flexions occur following the first scene presentation. Subsequently, arm flexions follow scene presentations in a manner like that described above.

EMOTIVE IMAGERY

Whereas in systematic desensitization positive (relaxation) and negative (fear hierarchy) stimuli are presented alternately, in *emotive imagery* the therapist constructs a single scene that contains both the positive and negative conditioned stimuli. The scene is presented only briefly at first. As the elicitation function of the negative CS weakens, it is presented for longer periods and in a more "challenging" manner. Wolpe (1969) reported the case of a 12-year-old boy who was afraid of the dark, in which he presented the following scene:

> Now I want you to close your eyes and imagine that you are sitting in the dining-room with your mother and father. It is night time. Suddenly, you receive a signal on the wrist radio that Superman has given you. You quickly run into the lounge because your mission must be kept a secret. There is only a little light coming into the lounge from the passage. Now pretend that you are all alone in the lounge waiting for Superman and Captain Silver to visit you. Think about this very clearly. If the idea makes you feel afraid, lift up your right hand [p. 160].

THOUGHT STOPPING

When an individual reports the frequent occurrence of disruptive or disturbing thoughts, *thought stopping* may be a useful remedy (Wolpe, 1969). It begins by instructing the individual first to close his eyes, then to verbalize the disturbing thought. Hearing the verbalization, the therapist suddenly shouts, "Stop!" ("Stop!" may be an S^r or an S^D, depending on the individual's history.) The therapist then points out how quickly the thought disappeared. This procedure is repeated several times. Then the individual is instructed to verbalize his thought again, but this time to say "Stop!" to himself subvocally. (Saying "Stop!" is incompatible with thinking the disturbing thought.) He is further instructed that these thoughts will return, and he is to continue the procedure of stopping the thoughts when they first occur. Thus thought stopping essentially becomes a self-control procedure useful in eliminating obsessions (such as a persistent fear of warehouse fires) and compulsions (such as frequent eyebrow plucking).

VICARIOUS EXTINCTION

When an individual avoids stimuli that are disturbing for him, a *vicarious extinction procedure* may be useful. It consists of exposing the individual to either a real-life or a filmed presentation of one or more models interacting or coming in contact with the stimulus in a manner that is not aversive to the model. The individual exposed to such portrayals must actually observe them, and observing the performances of multiple models is more effective than observing the performance of a single model. For example, Bandura, Grusec, and Menlove (1967) found that children exposed to multiple models showed more approach responses to the fear-stimulus class dogs than those who had observed a single model interact with the dogs.

CONSEQUATING REFLEXES

Procedures involving the consequation of reflexes are aimed at the remediation of certain types of respondent behavior problems (sometimes called psychosomatic disorders or organ neuroses) by systematically following them with consequences. The procedure involves four essential steps. First, the reflex or respondent behavior problem is identified, usually by means of clinical tests. For example, too rapid heart rate (tachycardia) can be detected by simply taking the patient's pulse. Second, during treatment the behavior is monitored by means of objective, reliable, and convenient observation procedures. For example, heart rate can be visually monitored by using the electrocardiogram. Third, a suitable consequence is found—one that has either a strengthening or a weakening effect on the patient's .behavior. For example, generalized or token reinforcers could be presented (for strengthening effects) or verbal aversive stimulation could be presented or token reinforcers removed (for weakening effects). Finally, when the reflex is observed, it is followed by the systematic presentation of the consequences (that is, differential reinforcement) and in some case by shaping (successive approximation) procedures. For example, not only are longer delays in heartbeat reinforced (to reduce the heart rate), but as treatment progresses, longer and longer delays may be required in order for reinforcement to occur. In some cases such training can be completely automated, and Miller (1969) suggests that it may be useful in treating a wide range of problems, including rapid heartbeat, high blood pressure, hiccough, gastrointestinal disorders, and the like.

Behavioral Counseling

Counseling refers to situations in which the behavior manager, largely through a verbal exchange (interview) process, assists a client in his pursuit of appropriate courses of action. *Behavioral counseling* refers to the use of procedures that focus on (1) the individual's overt behavior and (2) those aspects of his environment that are relevant to his vocational, educational, and marital behaviors, and to the solution of problems that result from his behavior in these areas.

The behavioral counselor's approach to a client's behavior problem is characterized by:

1. The tendency to formulate the client's behavior problems in terms of specific response classes capable of direct observation and the use of diagnostic tests that provide information about the frequency or topography of these response classes.[15]

2. The tendency to keep continuous records of the occurrence of the behavior in question so as to be able to observe the client's progress in counseling. The counselor may keep these records, or the client or his caretaker may keep them under the counselor's direction.

3. The tendency to work on only one of the client's problems at a time and to deal with new problems *only* after the old ones have been remedied.

4. The tendency to use procedures that bring about the desired behavior change in small, progressive steps.

5. The tendency to deal with the client's problems with procedures, and particularly in settings, that will facilitate generalization of the behavior modified during counseling to settings in which the problem behavior normally occurs.[16]

Behavioral counselors may make extensive use of any or all of the procedures described in this chapter, depending on their professional obligations to the client and the settings in which they work. However, inasmuch as the verbal exchange process is an essential feature of the social transactions going on between the behavioral counselor and his client, there are several essential procedures in behavioral counseling worthy of emphasis.

During the initial contacts with his client, the behavioral counselor attempts to gain empathetic understanding with his client. He does this in two ways: (1) by empathetic listening to the client so as to strengthen the client's verbal behavior of providing an accurate and detailed account of his problems as he sees them and (2) by presenting communications to the client that convince the client that the counselor understands him. This development of empathetic understanding yields two important things (Krumboltz, 1967). First, it provides an objective and relatively precise behavioral description of the nature of the client's behavior problem and the physical-environmental settings in which the problem occurs. Second, it establishes

---

[15] The behavioral counselor finds "trait" descriptions from certain diagnostic tests useless. For a discussion of why, see Chapter 11 and Bijou (1966).

[16] Consistent with this characteristic, the behavioral counselor, more than his traditionally oriented counterpart, may work with the client in such nonoffice settings as the place where the client works, the client's home, or recreational settings.

the counselor as a significant person in the client's life who has now acquired additional discriminative and reinforcing properties through his empathetic understanding of the client. However, the behavioral counselor recognizes that such a listening process may actually reinforce the client's verbal behavior in a direction antithetical to the goals of therapy. He must, therefore, carefully choose between (1) providing reinforcements for client-emitted behavior that may potentially add to the client's "bag of bad tricks" and (2) the additional social power he acquires, as a reinforcing stimulus, because of his own listening responses—a social power that he could use later to strengthen pro-therapeutic behavior in the client. Such a decision might be necessary when the counselor provides reinforcements to a misogynist whose verbal attacks of women are so vicious that his job as an office force supervisor is in jeopardy.

Following his initial contacts with the client and when sufficient empathetic understanding has developed, the counselor may introduce significant themes into the client's environment by presenting verbal directions or instructions, in the form of information-giving responses, to his client. The function of these verbal directions is to enhance or suppress the behaviors requiring modification. Such information-giving may deal with the specific response classes requiring modification and contain instructions for their modification or the possible social or physical consequences of emitting such response classes. For example, a counselor may give the client verbal instructions on the performance of specific sexual behaviors and may thus improve the client's sexual performance in marriage, or he may assist the client in his efforts to quit smoking by presenting him with recent data on lung cancer or coronary heart disease. Such information giving may cover a wide range of topics. It is a direct form of counselor intervention on behalf of his client and depends significantly on the client's sensitivity to verbal instructions.

The behavioral counselor may also consequate those behaviors of the client that require modification. This procedure would be initiated systematically only after the counselor was convinced that he had empathetic understanding with the client. Such consequation would consist of counselor-emitted verbal and gestural presentations of approval or disapproval, and would thus enhance or suppress the client's behavior. In some contexts the counselor may present tangible reinforcers to the client contingent on the occurrence of appropriate behavior. Like the presentation of verbal directions and instructions, the counselor's presentation of consequation is an active interview process. Its success in behavior modification depends on the counselor's skill in selecting and presenting, often in a subtle, indirect manner, appropriate consequences.

The behavioral counselor may also use *behavior rehearsal* when the client shows inappropriate behavior in certain social situations. This procedure combines the presentation of several essential elements. First, through role playing, the therapist portrays the other-presented stimulus complex of those with whom the client must interact and with whom he has a behavior problem. Second, the counselor presents verbal instructions to the client on the appropriate behavior to be emitted by him in that situation. Third, the counselor presents (1) consequences that are normal for the role of the other (assumed by the counselor) and (2) the consequences he normally presents as the client's counselor. For example, the counselor may assume the role of the shy client's boss and when the client asks for a raise, reply, "Why of course. I was going to give you a raise anyway." Then, the counselor might also say "That was really a good try that time." Thus behavioral rehearsal deals with the stimulus and response complexes characteristic of appropriate social transactions between the client and the other.

Finally, Krumboltz (1967) suggests that behavioral counselors continuously monitor the client's progress and use the following guides to confirm progress:

1. The counselor's understanding of the client's problem is confirmed by such client-emitted remarks as "You seem to know exactly how I feel."

2. Progress is confirmed when an inspection of the records of the client's behavior shows that the goals defined by the counselor and his client have been achieved.

3. The client's verbal reports of success, such as "Yes, I tried that and it seemed to work," may confirm success of counseling procedures.

4. Confirmation should also come from others who have an opportunity to observe the client in settings where his problem behavior is apt to occur.

5. Long-term follow-up of 1 year or more should provide confirmation of whether or not the behavior acquired in counseling is maintained in the natural environment.

In conclusion, although behavioral counseling departs radically from traditional counseling procedures in many respects, it does make extensive use of verbal exchange between the counselor and the client. Therefore, its success depends crucially on the reinforcement history of both the client and the counselor inasmuch as these communicative acts are discriminated operants.

SOME REMARKS ON THE EFFECTIVENESS OF BEHAVIOR THERAPY

Although studies on the effectiveness of behavior management procedures do not always use all of the criteria specified earlier (see Chapter 12), preliminary evidence reveals that behavior therapy is quite useful. Not only has definite improvement been reported in the patients treated with behavior therapy,[17] but the treatment takes far less time than other types of therapy,[18] the treatment effect is quite durable, and it seldom involves the appearance of other behavior problems as manifestations of symptom substitution.[19] (Symptom substitution is the occurrence of other behavior problems in the course of therapy and following occasions of definite behavior change, or improvement.) The occurrence of symptom substitution is often cited as evidence that the therapist is not dealing with the patient's real problems, only his symptoms, the real antecedents of which are in the patient's psyche (that is, his unconscious). However, a number of environmental events occurring during therapy may also create other behavior problems.[20] For example:

1. Sometimes a patient's behavior problem is avoidance behavior maintained by the termination of an aversive stimulus. Thus other problem behaviors that avoid the aversive stimulus may be reinforced even though for a time the treated behavior is successfully suppressed. For example, if nausea allows one to avoid work, then, following its successful treatment, other behaviors such as headaches may be similarly maintained.

2. New behavior problems may be due to poorly managed reinforcement contingencies, either during therapy or outside of it. For example, although a therapist may effectively suppress a juvenile delinquent's "criminal gab" and "bad talk," the juvenile delinquent's peer group may at the same time reinforce profane gestures, which begin to occur at about the same time that the bad talk is suppressed.

3. In cases of individuals with profound deficits, new behavior problems may occur simply because of the new behaviors acquired during certain phases of therapy. For example, after a retarded child learns to hold onto a spoon, he may throw it.

4. The therapist may not have isolated the controlling stimulus for a problem behavior, and the stimulus may occur somewhat unpredictably. Thus only temporary behavior-suppression is achieved. For example, aggressive attacks by a particular patient may occur on a hospital ward only when a certain staff member who reinforced them is on duty, and he may be on duty sporadically.

---

[17] Paul (1966) reports 100 percent improvement in patients with stage fright who were treated with behavior therapy (desensitization and relaxation procedures), compared with 80 percent improvement in a placebo group (that received attention from the therapist) and 45 percent improvement in a control group. Similarly, in seventeen different experiments, Ayllon and Azrin (1968) report 100 percent success in treating a mixed group of institutionalized patients.

[18] Treatment time ranges from 2 hours (see Paul, 1968) to a median number of 10 sessions per patient (see Wolpe, 1969), compared with months or even years required in other therapies.

[19] See Grossberg (1964); Paul (1968); and Cahoon (1968).

[20] Cahoon (1968) presents an interesting discussion of this problem.

It would appear, then, that a careful study of the patient's environment may reveal events that account for those occasions when symptom substitution is reported during behavior therapy.

STUDY QUESTIONS

1. Prepare a description that summarizes the essential features of the approach of specialists in behavior therapy.
2. What is the difference between flooding and implosive therapy?
3. Cite three contingencies that would make flooding procedures risky, and explain their possible consequences.
4. Based on your understanding of the procedures utilized in the hypothetical case of the individual with stage fright, choose a procedure you feel would be effective for a child who was bitten by a dog and is thus fearful of small, furry animals.
5. Suggest in detail at least two ways to manage the following:
   A man has a severe phobia of flying. He is 40 years old and has never been in an airplane.
6. What are the essential differences between respondent conditioning and respondent counter-conditioning?
7. What procedure does the author suggest to assess procedural effectiveness? Why is reliance on verbal reports described as somewhat risky?
8. Distinguish between stimulus control and consequation or schedule of consequation procedures in the management of operant behavior problems.
9. What are the three essential procedures in operant acquisition? What additional procedure may be used?
10. Why is it important to use remediation procedures that will yield generalization?
11. A treatment procedure was devised to suppress drinking in alcoholics. The patients were seated at a bar, which was set up on the hospital compound, and were shocked through a ring, which they wore on their finger whenever they imbibed. Suppression occurred almost immediately. There is some question about the generalization of the treatment to the outside world. Analyze the strengths and weaknesses of this procedure and suggest modifications or improvements that would increase the likelihood of generalization.
12. Be able to define and give examples of the following backup behavior modification procedures:
    a. Reinforcer sampling.
    b. Reinforcing event menu.
    c. Conjugate reinforcement.
    d. Response priming.
    e. Stimulus shaping or fading.
    f. Satiation.
13. Identify the following procedures:
    a. A parent quelled his child's playing with matches by requiring that his

child sit down at one time and strike the contents of an entire box of matches, one by one.

b. A retarded child was given a taste of sherbet before beginning training in which it was to be used as a reinforcer.

c. Changing the loudness of stereophonic music presentations from just audible to audible levels was made contingent on a lever-pressing response.

d. The patients were given a list of arts and crafts projects, any one of which they could work on.

e. The trainer used his hand to guide the child's grasp of the spoon and then gradually withdrew his hand.

f. A child who could talk seldom did so. The therapist showed him some pictures, said "Tell me a story about this picture," and reinforced him when he did so.

14. Describe the four essential procedures that characterize the systematic desensitization technique of behavior management.

15. What is reciprocal inhibition therapy?

16. Suggest two reasons why some patients may not be affected by systematic desensitization training and describe how you would deal with them.

17. For what types of behavior problems may covert sensitization be a useful procedure?

18. In what ways is covert sensitization similar to systematic desensitization? In what way is it dissimilar?

19. What are the essential features of contingency contracts?

20. What situations or conditions can be manipulated by the therapist to enhance the effectiveness of contingency contracts?

21. What is the origin of the word *coverant?* How does coverant control therapy work?

22. Devise a coverant control therapy procedure for:
    a. Depression.
    b. Overeating.

23. In what way does coverant control therapy depart from usual behavior theory approaches to behavior control? Why is it regarded as risky business? What are its assumptions?

24. Describe the treatment procedure in detail for the following:
    a. Overcoming a fear of being away from home using external inhibition.
    b. Overcoming a fear of being alone using emotive imagery.
    c. Overcoming fear of being in a semidarkened room using vicarious extinction.
    d. Overcoming excessive palmar sweating by consequating reflexes.

25. What is the purpose of empathetic listening? What risk does it involve?

26. What is the payoff to the counselor of establishing empathetic understanding with the client?

27. What assumption is necessary in order for information giving to work as the behavioral counselor wishes it to? (Hint: Regard information giving as an S^D presentation.)

28. Compare the approach of the behavioral counselor with traditional approaches on the following:

a. Defining, or specifying, and observing the problem for treatment.

b. Evaluation of treatment.

29. What two major classes of stimulus events does the behavioral counselor manipulate when he uses behavioral rehearsal?

30. Examine the guides used by the behavioral counselor to confirm progress and comment critically on their validity.

31. Discuss four criteria useful in evaluating a therapy program. Which ones are the most important? Why? (A review of Chapter 12 may be useful.) From the point of view of these criteria, discuss the effectiveness of behavior therapy and behavior modification procedures.

32. What is symptom substitution? In what way is it regarded as evidence of the weakness of behavior therapy and behavior modification procedures?

33. Look over the description of behavioral events and examples on page 401 that may be the basis for reports of symptom substitution and suggest a remedy for each.

REFERENCES

Ayllon, T., and Azrin, N. H. Reinforcer sampling: A technique for increasing the behavior of mental patients. *Journal of Applied Behavior Analysis*, 1968, 1, 13–20. (a)

Ayllon, T., and Azrin, N. H. *The token economy. A motivational system for therapy and rehabilitation.* New York: Appleton-Century-Crofts, 1968. (b)

Ayllon, T., and Haughton, E. Control of the behavior of schizophrenic patients by food. *Journal of the Experimental Analysis of Behavior*, 1962, 5, 343–352.

Azrin, N. H., and Powell, J. Behavioral engineering: The reduction of smoking behavior by a conditioning apparatus and procedure. *Journal of Applied Behavior Analysis*, 1968, 1, 193–200.

Bailey, J., and Meyerson, L. Vibration as a reinforcer with a profoundly retarded child. *Journal of Applied Behavior Analysis*, 1969, 2, 135–138.

Bandura, A. *Principles of behavior modification.* New York: Holt, Rinehart and Winston, 1969.

Bandura, A., Grusec, J., and Menlove, F. Vicarious extinction of avoidance behavior. *Journal of Personality and Social Psychology*, 1967, 5, 16–23.

Bandura, A., and Menlove, F. L. Factors determining vicarious extinction of avoidance behavior through symbolic modeling. *Journal of Personality and Social Psychology*, 1968, 8, 99–108.

Bijou, S. W. Implications of behavioral science for counseling and guidance. In J. D. Krumboltz (Ed.), *Revolution in counseling: Implications of behavioral science: Major papers.* Boston: Houghton-Mifflin, 1966.

Bijou, S. W., Birnbrauer, J. S., Kidder, J. D., and Teague, C. Programmed instruction as an approach to teaching reading, writing and arithmetic to retarded children. *Psychological Record*, 1966, 16, 505–522.

Cahoon, D. D. Symptom substitution and the behavior therapies: A reappraisal. *Psychological Bulletin*, 1968, 69, 149–156.

Cautela, J. R. Treatment of behavior by covert sensitization. *Psychological Record,* 1966, **16**, 33–41.

Cohen, H., and Filipczak, J. A *new learning environment.* San Francisco: Jossey-Bass, 1971.

Emery, J. R., and Krumboltz, J. D. Standard vs. individualized hierarchies in desensitization to reduce test anxiety. *Journal of Counseling Psychology,* 1967, **14**, 204–209.

Ferster, C. B. Arbitrary and natural reinforcement. *Psychological Record,* 1967, **17**, 341–348.

Ferster, C. B., and DeMyer, M. K. A method for the experimental analysis of the behavior of autistic children. *American Journal of Orthopsychiatry,* 1962, **32**, 89–98.

Ferster, C. B., Nurnberger, J. I., and Levitt, E. B. The control of eating. *Journal of Mathetics,* 1962, **1**, 87–109.

Ferster, C. B., and Simons, J. Behavior therapy with children. *Psychological Record,* 1966, **16**, 65–71.

Goldiamond, I. Self-control procedures in personal behavior. *Psychological Report,* 1965, **17**, 851–868.

Grossberg, J. M. Behavior therapy: A review. *Psychological Bulletin,* 1964, **62**, 73–88.

Homme, L. E. Perspectives in psychology: XXIV Control of coverants, the operants of the mind. *Psychological Record,* 1965, **15**, 501–511.

Homme, L. E. Coverant control therapy: A special case of contingency management. Paper read at the Rocky Mountain Psychological Association Convention, Albuquerque, N.M., 1966.

Homme, L. E., and Csanyi, A. P. *Contingency contracting. A system for motivation management in education.* Albuquerque, N.M.: Southwestern Cooperative Training Laboratories, 1968.

Karen, R. L., and Bower, R. C. A behavioral analysis of a social control agency: Synanon. *Journal of Research in Crime and Delinquency,* 1968, **5**, 18–34.

Krasner, L., and Ullmann, L. P. *Research in behavior modification.* New York: Holt, Rinehart and Winston, 1965.

Krumboltz, J. D. Behavioral counseling: Rationale and research. *Personnel and Guidance Journal,* 1965, **44**, 383–387.

Krumboltz, J. D. Behavioral goals for counseling. *Journal of Counseling,* 1966, **13**, 153–159.

Krumboltz, J. D. Changing the behavior of behavior changers. *Counselor Education and Supervision,* 1967, **6**, 222–229.

Krumboltz, J. D., and Thoreson, C. E. The effect of behavioral counseling in groups and individual settings on information-seeking behavior. *Journal of Counseling Psychology,* 1964, **11**, 324–333.

Lindsley, O. R. Direct measurement and prosthesis of retarded behavior. *Journal of Education,* 1964, **147**, 62–81.

Litvak, S. B. A comparison of two brief group behavior therapy techniques for the reduction of avoidance behavior. *Psychological Record,* 1969, **19**, 329–334.

Lovaas, O. I., Freitag, G., Kinder, M. I., Rubenstein, B. C., Schaeffer, B., and Simmons, J. Q. Establishment of social reinforcers in two schizophrenic children on the basis of food. *Journal of Experimental Child Psychology*, 1966, 4, 109–125.

Miller, N. E. Learning of visceral and glandular responses. *Science*, 1969, **163**, 434–445.

Neuringer, C., and Michael, J. L. *Behavior modification in clinical psychology*. New York: Appleton-Century-Crofts, 1970.

O'Brien, F., Azrin, N. H., and Henson, K. Increased communications of chronic mental patients by reinforcement and by response priming. *Journal of Applied Behavior Analysis*, 1969, **2**, 23–30.

Paul, G. L. *Insight versus desensitization*. Stanford, Calif.: Stanford University Press, 1966.

Paul, G. L. Two-year follow-up of systematic desensitization in therapy groups. *Journal of Abnormal Psychology*, 1968, **73**, 119–130.

Phillips, E. L. Achievement place: Token reinforcement procedures in a home-style rehabilitation setting for pre-delinquent boys. *Journal of Applied Behavior Analysis*, 1968, **1**, 213–223.

Powell, J., and Azrin, N. H. The effects of shock as a punisher for cigarette smoking. *Journal of Applied Behavior Analysis*, 1968, **1**, 63–72.

Schwitzgebel, R. *Streetcorner research: An experimental approach to juvenile delinquency*. Cambridge, Mass.: Harvard University Press, 1964.

Schwitzgebel, R. Short term operant conditioning of adolescent offenders on socially relevant variables. *Journal of Abnormal Psychology*, 1965, **72**, 134–142.

Sidman, M., and Stoddard, L. T. The effectiveness of fading in programming a simultaneous form discrimination for retarded children. *Journal of the Experimental Analysis of Behavior*, 1967, **10**, 3–16.

Stampfl, T. G., and Levis, D. J. Essentials of implosive therapy: A learning-theory-based psychodynamic behavior therapy. *Journal of Abnormal Psychology*, 1967, **72**, 496–503.

Ullmann, L. P., and Krasner, L. *Case studies in behavior modification*. New York: Holt, Rinehart and Winston, 1965.

Whitman, T. L. Modification of smoking behavior. *Behavior Research and Therapy*, 1969, 7, 257–263.

Wilkins, W. Desensitization: Social and cognitive factors underlying the effectiveness of Wolpe's procedure. *Psychological Bulletin*, 1971, 76, 311–317.

Wolf, M., Risley, T., and Mees, H. Application of operant conditioning procedures to the behavior problems of an autistic child. *Behavior Therapy and Research*, 1964, **1**, 305–312.

Wolpe, J. *The practice of behavior therapy*. New York: Pergamon, 1969.

Wolpe, J., and Lazarus, A. A. *Behavior therapy techniques*. Oxford, England: Pergamon, 1966.

CHAPTER 14

BEHAVIOR MANAGEMENT IN THE CLASSROOM

Although there have been some significant changes in education in recent years, there are still many problems. On occasion schools are still targets of vandalism and teachers victims of student aggression. Procedures designed to strengthen pro-classroom student behavior too often involve drill and negative reinforcement and less often, positive reinforcement. What is more important, procedures aimed at suppressing student behavior that is incompatible with classroom behavior too often involve punishment, either in the form of removal of positive reinforcers (as when a pupil loses his recess privileges) or in the form of presentation of aversive stimuli (as when the pupil is the recipient of ridicule, ostracism, or summary failing grades or must write his name or "thou shall not" essays several hundred times).

The purpose of formal education is the acquisition and maintenance of complex behavior repertoires that are useful to the individual in his transactions with the physical and social environment. Initially, such behaviors are acquired in artificial settings (the classroom) and strengthened by *artificial reinforcers* (praise, grades, threat). It is assumed, thereafter, that such behavior will generalize to the natural environment by operating or functioning on the individual's physical and social environment in such a manner as to produce *natural reinforcers* that maintain the behavior producing them. For example, the child in the reading class receives the teacher's praise and good grades for adequate classroom performances. Later on reading is reinforced in the natural environment by the novel stimulation or the stimulus change that frequently accompanies it (as when one reads fiction) or by the additional environmental control one obtains through reading (as when one reads an instruction manual on machine operation).

It frequently happens, however, that regardless of the conditions of acquisition, the complexity of the skill to be acquired requires intensive and prolonged training before a skill level is reached that will actually be maintained by natural contingencies. The formidable task of arranging for such conditions of acquisition falls on the classroom teacher. Like her counterpart in other specialties of behavior management, she must start her management procedures with a *preliminary observation* of the pupil's behavior in the classroom setting. This is followed by a *base-line observation* in which the pupil is required to show his skill level for those performances specified by the course outline and the school curriculum. This base-line observation reveals the characteristics of the pupil's performance and aids the teacher in formulating a *behavioral prescription* that specifies procedures for the acquisition and maintenance of certain behaviors and, in some cases, the elimination of other behaviors. It may also specify procedures aimed at eliciting positive respondent (emotional) behaviors in the pupil. Once these training procedures have been implemented, the teacher will periodically obtain additional base-line data (tests) to check the adequacy of his procedures and to identify further problems requiring remediation. The teacher's role in the management of pupils' behavior is, therefore, of singular importance for three reasons. First, teachers are best able to define precisely, "educational objectives," in the form of specific student performances required by the curriculum. Second, teachers possess the skills necessary to identify the areas of a pupil's performance that require remediation. Third, teachers are able to develop remediation procedures that will aid the pupil in acquiring those skills specified by the behavioral prescription.

Since the teacher is primarily responsible for assisting his pupils with the acquisition of skills—operant performances in one form or another—the following principles may be useful in two ways. They may provide (1) a means of developing new educational programs and (2) a means of assessing the adequacy of a program already under way, for the teacher can compare the procedures used in the program with those outlined in the following principles. The teacher is also concerned with his pupil's emotional or respondent behavior patterns in the educational situation.

THE NINE PRINCIPLES OF EFFECTIVE CONTINGENCY MANAGEMENT[1]

Principle 1 Consequence Identification

The consequences for an educational program (reinforcers and punishers), must be identified by their effects on the pupil's behavior—not on the teacher's. For example, a teacher may erroneously assume that when he gives a student the letter grade A or expressions of approval in the form of praise, he is using positive reinforcement even though the pupil's behavior remains unchanged following these presentations. The importance of this principle cannot be overstated, since it deals with the essential element in both operant acquisition and operant maintenance, namely, the consequation chosen for a training program. *In the absence of the behavioral test of a consequence, other sources of evidence of a consequence must be discounted.*

Principle 2 Automaticity

Consequences affect the pupil's behavior automatically, whether or not he can verbalize the relationship between his behavior and the consequences and whether or not he can verbalize that his behavior has been consequated. Corollaries to this principle are: (1) The pupil need not understand why his behavior is being consequated in order to learn, nor must the teacher wait until he does understand before learning can begin, and (2) if a pupil verbally reports a strong motivation in the acquisition of some skill, that does not necessarily mean that he has mastered appropriate procedures for the acquisition of that skill.

Principle 3 Relevant Criteria

When the main purpose of consequation in a training program is educational accomplishment, the consequation should be closely related to the criteria of accomplishment. This principle emphasizes the necessity of relating consequences to appropriate behavioral criteria specified in the behavioral prescription—that is, to *actual performances* and not to other criteria that might be tangentially related or even superfluous to the behavioral prescription. Thus reinforcements are presented contingent on the pupil's correctly completing

---

[1] These principles were obtained from a paper by J. L. Michael entitled *Management of behavioral consequences in education.* Inglewood, Calif: Southwest Regional Laboratory for Educational Research and Development, 1967, and appeared under the title "Principles of effective usage" in R. Ulrich, T. Stachnik, and J. Mabry (Eds.), *Control of human behavior.* Vol. 2. *From cure to prevention.* Glenview, Ill.: Scott Foresman, 1970.

a specific number of tasks, not merely working fast or merely spending time at the task.

Principle 4 Consistency

The teacher must attend to the consequences of the student's behavior at all times and in all situations. This principle simply asserts that the teacher *cannot* suspend or postpone his concern for the consequences of the pupil's behavior, wherever or whenever it occurs. If, for example, the pupil "bad mouths" the teacher on the playground his behavior should be consequated there as it is in the classroom.

Principle 5 Immediacy

The consequences must be presented immediately following the behavior responsible for them. When consequation is used in an educational program, the maximum effect can be expected when the consequation is presented *immediately* after the behavior of concern, as when the teacher immediately socially reinforces the pupil's correct recitation in class. Delayed consequation will leave the behavior of concern unaffected and will sometimes affect other behavior in a manner unfavorable to educational goals. Delayed reinforcements will not strengthen behavior desired in the behavioral prescription, but may strengthen other, later-occurring behavior that is incompatible with the desired behavior.

Principle 6 Frequency

The optimal frequency of reinforcement for either the acquisition or maintenance of a pupil's behavior is usually underestimated. Reinforcements should occur often enough to strengthen the behavior in the behavioral prescription and to offset those reinforcements that occur in the natural environment and strengthen behavior incompatible with it. For example, the frequency of reinforcement of a pupil's classroom disruptive behavior should be far below the frequency of reinforcement the pupil receives for scholastic behavior. Moreover, behavioral prescriptions that require the acquisition or maintenance of sustained, prolonged, or difficult performances or performances for which the reinforcers are weak should be fortified with additional reinforcements. Teachers should make sure that pupils are reinforced more often in such situations.

Principle 7 Small Steps

When educational work units in the behavioral prescription are too large to permit an optimum frequency of reinforcement, smaller work units should be assigned. Most educational material consists of units and subunits from which the individual tasks assigned to the pupil are derived. When assigned tasks are exceptionally difficult or made up of very large units, reinforcements may occur too infrequently to maintain the pupil's behavior, in which case easier or smaller units should be assigned. For example, teachers who provide reinforcements for completing an arithmetic work sheet containing twenty problems can, when necessary (when the pupils' behavior lags), reinforce an average of every fifth correct response (VR 5).

Principle 8   Unplanned Punishment Effects

The total effect of reinforcement that requires "prior worsening" includes the punishment effect of the worsening. "Prior worsening" refers to the common use of threat and punishment in the form of removal of positive reinforcers (as when, for example, the teacher removes playground recess privileges) and the subsequent reinstatement of these reinforcers so that they may be used to strengthen the pupil's behavior (as when playground recess activity is permitted following completion of extra or especially good work). This principle asserts that the use of such procedures contains two effects: (1) the strengthening effect of the reinstatement of the positive reinforcer and (2) the weakening punishment effect of the prior worsening procedure. This means that the effect of the positive reinforcer, in combination with the prior worsening effect, is *less* than the effect of the positive reinforcement would be if it were used alone. Moreover, in order for the threat component of prior worsening to be effective, it must, on occasion, be implemented (the positive reinforcers must actually be withdrawn), and as a result the educational situation will be paired with punishment.

Principle 9   Effective Contingency Contracting

When the teacher and the pupil engage in a contingency contract, the contract should be clear, fair, and honest. The teacher should clearly specify the amount and type of work required by the pupil and the amount and type of consequation to be given contingent on completion of the work. For example, he may say, "Do twenty of these problems, and I'll give you 20 minutes extra time for clay modeling." The teacher should also provide an amount and type of consequation that is fair in relationship to the work required. Finally, the teacher should see to it that the terms of the contract are complied with, thereby making the contract an honest one.

The actual implementation of these nine principles of effective contingency management should have a salutary effect on the pupil's behavior. Not only will the skills specified in the behavioral prescription be acquired more rapidly, but because these principles stress the use of positive reinforcement rather than punishment, the learning situation will become, through stimulus pairing with the positive reinforcers, an eliciting stimulus for positive respondent behavior.

Although these principles describe in general terms the ingredients of an effective program of contingency management, some discussion of the specific application of the principles in classroom settings is needed.

THE APPLICATION OF CONTINGENCY MANAGEMENT PRINCIPLES TO CLASSROOM SITUATIONS

The procedures used by the teacher, in the role of a contingency manager, can be roughly grouped into three areas: (1) those that involve the stimulus or instructional control of behavior, (2) those that involve consequation or schedule control of behavior, and (3) those that involve both stimulus and consequation control of behavior.

Procedures Based on the Stimulus or Instructional Control of Behavior

The classroom situation contains numerous stimuli that, it is hoped, have acquired stimulus control over the pupil's behavior or will, in the course of instruction, lead to such stimulus control. These include such things as a bell (presumably an S^D for entering the classroom and sitting down at one's desk); the mere presence of the teacher (an S^D for attention, studying, and so forth); and various manipulanda such as pencils, pens, craft materials, tools, musical instruments, and the like (presumably S^D's for appropriate classroom behavior). It is assumed that all of these stimuli have acquired their control functions through the behavioral process of operant discrimination, in which at one time or another, following emission of the appropriate behavior in the presence of these stimuli, teachers and other caretakers presented strengthening consequences. It is further assumed that following the child's acquisition of these basic skills, increasingly more complex performances were required. For example, at first, the child may have been reinforced for merely being in his seat when the bell rings; then, he may have been reinforced only for being in his seat when the bell rings, looking at the teacher, and being quiet for a certain interval of time; then, he may have been reinforced only for being in his seat when the bell rings, looking at the teacher, and remaining quiet for a longer period of time. Gradually, as more and more behavior was required, more of the student's behavior has come under the stimulus control of the bell, the teacher at the head of the class, and so on.

Often such training may start simply as a game between the teacher and the pupil. As one teacher reported:

"I was faced with the problem of my first-grade students wandering around the room during class. To solve the problem, I made the following announcement: 'Let's play a game. Anyone who is in his seat when the bell rings, gets a point!' A bell timer was used, and it went off at variable intervals, the duration of which was known only to me. Gradually, the interval was extended and extended, and more students remained in their seats for longer periods of time." Later, this teacher used the same procedure for coloring and drawing. The procedure caught on, and several of the teachers in the upper grades used it during the study of reading and arithmetic.

Besides bringing the pupil's behavior more and more under the control of ordinary classroom stimuli, the teacher can also take advantage of his students' existing behavior repertoires. He can, for example, have a child draw with crayons, a form of behavior already part of the repertoire of most preschoolers. He can also attempt to provide sufficient structure in the layout of the work environment so that it brings the child into close contact with the manipulanda and, at the same time, shuts out other stimuli that may intrude and control behaviors that are incompatible with those sought by the teacher.

Such was the case in an experimental preschool class for the retarded, where each child was assigned to a definite work area, which permitted close contact between the matron and the pupil. On each child's worktable was a large tablet and oversized crayons, and the children were seated in groups of three to four in a semicircle around the matron. The matron had direct eye contact with each child at all times and, if necessary, could manually assist the children. The work area was set apart from the rest of the class.

When classroom stimuli do possess strong stimulus control over pupils' behavior, such control is always specific to the situation involved. Changes in classroom procedures that involve the removal of stimuli normally controlling appropriate behavior will break off or disrupt the behavior those stimuli control. Students may remove these stimuli themselves (as when a pupil turns his head away from the textual stimuli in his textbook), or the stimuli may be removed under the teacher's direction (as when the teacher instructs her pupils to put their books back in their desks). During such "dead periods" the teacher may wish to introduce additional instructions (as discriminative or controlling stimuli), and perhaps consequences, to maintain classroom behavior.

The teacher may also remove controlling stimuli from the classroom when the behavior they control is disruptive. For example, a teacher may separate two talkers as a means of eliminating the disruption they cause. An interesting variation in the procedure has been reported:

One student in an eighth-grade social studies class had a reputation for talking and arguing in class, especially with those seated near him. The teacher tried changing the seating arrangement, but wherever he sat, the student invariably stirred up arguments and discussions, and excluding him from class was contemplated. As a last effort, and with the consent of the disruptive student, the teacher had him sit in the front row and to the right of the class, next to the teacher, but concealed from the other students by a two-sided screen.

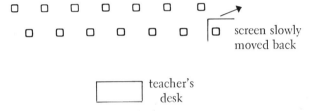

This arrangement permitted eye contact between the teacher and the pupil, but not between the pupil and the other members of the class. With the screen in place, the arguments with other students and talking out of turn stopped except for encounters between the teacher and pupil, which the teacher was able to control. Very gradually, over a 4-week period, the screen was pulled back, exposing more and more of the other students to the view of the talking student. The argumentative and disruptive behavior did not reappear. At the end of the fourth week, the screen was removed completely, and the student came up after class and thanked the teacher for his patience.

The common classroom procedure of physically relocating a student from the others with whom he talks is a stimulus control procedure but in this case, did not work. However, the screen-fading procedure was obviously superior, since it allowed for new behavior (nonargumentative, attentive behavior) to come under the control of an old stimulus (the student's classmates). Although the usual classroom procedure of changing a student's seat may work for some students, should the student be returned to his original seat, his talking could recur.

Procedures Based on the Consequation or Schedule Control of Behavior

As we have seen, the behavioral prescription specifies that some pupil behaviors should be strengthened and still others should be weakened. The teacher's control over some of these behaviors may, of course, be accomplished through the use of stimulus or instructional control procedures. However, the systematic use of consequation in the classroom provides a powerful means for the management of the pupils' behavior. The problem is in finding suitable consequences and making sure they occur promptly enough and often enough to affect the pupils' behavior.

Since most classroom situations involve groups of children, the teacher must divide his time between them and must find consequences suitable and appropriate for each child. Although praise and teacher's approval as generalized reinforcers may be extremely powerful reinforcers for some children, especially older children, they are not universal reinforcers. Even if they were, the systematic presentation of praise and approval to a class of students may become burdensome, and the style of its presentation may change radically, especially if the teacher must reinforce each pupil's behavior many, many times a day.

The nearest thing to a universal reinforcer is the token reinforcer, which can be presented both rapidly and systematically. Since the token reinforcer is not dependent on any one particular type of deprivation and since it can be changed for a wide variety of back-up reinforcers, it will function as a powerful reinforcer when it is properly introduced to the student. The token may take the more obvious form of a poker chip or the less obvious form of simply a mark on a card. If the token is to function as a reinforcer, the child must first be magazine-trained. The following example illustrates the procedure:

Over a 1-week period a group of teen-age, severely retarded youngsters were taken daily, one by one, into an area on the sheltered workshop designated as the "store." Initially, each child was taken inside the store and to a counter, which had soda pop, candy, ice cream, and chewing gum on it. Those who did not reach for any of these items were given free samples to taste. Subsequently, the pupils had to reach for what they wanted. When this reaching behavior became strong, they had to hold onto a poker chip placed in their hand by the teacher which she removed a moment later when the edible was given. Later on they had to hold the chip longer and then hand the teacher the poker chip in order to obtain the edibles. Still later, the child had to pick up a poker chip at the store door, hold on to it, then hand it to the teacher before a selection could be made. All through training, the teacher systematically presented verbal instructions to the children such as "Give me the chip" or "Go get a chip." On occasion and to facilitate learning, the teacher put some pupils through the proper responses.

Such *detailed* magazine training can be avoided in more sophisticated subjects by simply using verbal instructions such as "If you want to buy something in the store, ask Miss Smith for a poker chip." If the pupil follows the instructions correctly and subsequently makes "purchases," further magazine training is not necessary.

Once the token is introduced into the classroom, it can be presented systematically as the following two examples illustrate:

1. Each day during arithmetic, the fifth-grade teacher walked up and down each aisle, stopping momentarily by each student. The teacher watched as the student worked, and as soon as he completed a problem correctly, the teacher praised him and marked a card with a check. Each card had twenty-five spaces, and when each was filled with a check, the card could be exchanged for free time and privileges.

2. When the pupil finished his work, he approached the teacher, who then graded his paper. As he watched, the teacher marked each correct answer with a "C" written in bright red pencil. That day, each "C" was worth one minute of arts and crafts activity.

The strength of the tokens as reinforcers depends on the kinds of backup reinforcers that are available and how often the tokens can be used. From time to time it may be necessary to introduce new backup reinforcers and especially when reinforcers are expendable. Expendable reinforcers may include edibles, tickets to events, and opportunities to engage in high-probability behaviors. It will be recalled that of any two behaviors, the more probable behavior can be used to reinforce the less probable (the Premack principle). All that is required is that access to the more probable behavior be made contingent on the occurrence of the less probable behavior. Such is the case in the following example:

A teacher in a continuation high school fell on the idea of bringing into the class stereophonic rock-'n'-roll music, which was played over individual headsets. The kids really seemed to enjoy it, and they brought in their own records. Compared to other appropriate classroom performances, the listening activity was obviously more reinforcing. The teacher decided that the students would be allowed up to 15 minutes a day of listening time contingent on appropriate classroom performances. Since no more than three pupils could listen at a time, schedule requirements tended to create a shortage that made the activity even more reinforcing.

It is highly desirable to designate an area of the classroom as the "R.E. (reinforcing event) area" and even to advertise its contents:

A teacher in a lively third-grade class prepared a reinforcing event menu that listed all of the items in the store (R E. area) and their cost in points. The menu was changed once a week by the addition of one or two new items. The name of each item was printed on the menu, and the children read, with the assistance of the teacher, the items on the menu.

All of the events described so far have been strengthening events—generalized reinforcers, token reinforcers, and making the opportunity to engage in high-probability behavior contingent on the occurrence of low-probability behavior. However, there are occasions when the teacher must use consequences that will eliminate pupil behaviors. Although reinforcements can be used to strengthen behavior that is incompatible with classroom misbehavior, the misbehavior may be sufficiently disruptive so that it must be dealt with directly. One procedure involves the contingent presentation of aversive stimuli, as the following illustrates:

A high school English teacher was particularly disturbed by certain students in her class. These students frequently turned around and talked in class. Rather than lecture them on what would happen to them if they didn't behave, every time he caught them turning around or talking he sternly said: "John, shut up!" "Be quiet!" and the like. Whenever he could, the teacher also praised them for being quiet. These procedures worked quite well.

If the pupil's misbehavior has no serious consequences for classroom management, it may be worthwhile to use an extinction procedure:

A teacher in a special class gave a spelling test in which the pupil was to write the word, correctly spelled, on the blackboard. When the teacher presented the first word, one pupil misspelled it more than ten times, saying "I can't spell it." He continued writing. The teacher ignored him as he continued writing and making remarks. After about 10 minutes of this, the pupil finally spelled the word correctly, and he promptly received praise from the teacher. From then on the number of errors and remarks decreased rapidly.

Finally, group presentations of positive reinforcement and punishment can be used. For example:

The teacher promised each pupil in the class 5 minutes extra time on the playground if each arranged his desk neatly for work before lunch. The teacher also announced that if any one desk was sloppy, no one would get the extra time. Five minutes before the bell rang for lunch, she announced that the pupils should straighten out their desks. Following inspection, each child was credited with the additional play time. During clean up, some children were observed prodding others for not cleaning up fast enough or for doing a sloppy job.

This procedure is especially useful because group-managed contingencies are especially powerful and because the teacher is not systematically paired with any punishment the group may present. And, of course, it is for these very reasons that the teacher must be watchful that such contingencies are not misused.

Procedures Using a Combination of Stimulus and Consequation Control of Behavior

It is obvious that the systematic use of the procedures described so far is very demanding of the teacher. In order for these procedures to be effective, the teacher must maintain continual surveillance over the pupils' behavior, and because many of these procedures alone are weak, they must be used in combination. Moreover, it is obvious that somewhere in the educational process the pupil must become able to engage in self-directed or self-managed educational activities. There are three developments that may help the pupil accomplish this: precision teaching, programmed instruction, and contingency contracting.

PRECISION TEACHING

Precision teaching, a term used by O. R. Lindsley to describe a special method of teaching (Johnson, 1969), is a logical derivative of the principles of contingency management applied to the classroom. It involves the use of the following teacher-managed procedures:

1. *Pinpointing the behavior* (both in terms of response class and in terms of response class dimension) to be modified in the classroom.

2. *Recording the behavior* to determine its characteristics in the classroom along dimensions relevant to the curriculum.

3. *Changing something in the classroom* to change the behavior in the direction sought and specified when the behavior was pinpointed. This may include changes in teaching method, curriculum materials, motivational procedures, the classroom environment, or anything else that the teacher believes is useful.

4. *Trying again* when the classroom changes in the first plan do not produce the behavior changes sought.

Essential to the successful implementation of these procedures is the preparation of accurate measures of the pupils' classroom progress. Johnson (1967) recommends that two measures be used: the *daily performed rate* and the *daily planned rate.* The daily performed rate can be prepared by the student himself or if necessary, by the teacher. All that is necessary is that he note the task "start" and "stop" time, computing the difference between these times as the total time to complete the lesson, and then inserting them into the following formula:

$$\text{daily performed rate} = \frac{\text{total number of problems completed}}{\text{total work time}}$$

The teacher can compute the daily planned rate by means of the following formula:

$$\begin{matrix} \text{daily} \\ \text{planned} \\ \text{rate} \end{matrix} = \frac{\text{total number of problems assigned}}{\text{total time allotted}}$$

In precision teaching, assignments are individualized so that the amount of time given and the number of problems assigned to the student will vary from day to day in accordance with the teacher's specifications of the daily planned rate.[2] The daily performed rate provides a basis for studying pupil progress despite these variations because it is a measure based upon a constant unit of time (problems per minute). Hence, pupil progress (an increase in daily performed rate) can occur either because more problems are completed in the same amount of time as the previous lesson or because less time is taken to complete the same number of problems as assigned in the previous lesson. The student keeps a record of his progress (when he is able to) by making entries (plotting points) on his curve at the end of each day. The teacher may use this information in two ways: (1) as a means of assessing day-to-day the adequacy and effects of changes in classroom procedures and modifying them accordingly and (2) as a measure that can be compared with the daily planned rate to see if a student's progress is measuring up to the requirements of the curriculum. Since the pupil keeps records of his own progress, he can give his parents daily progress reports of the number of "hits" he has made for that day.

Johnson (1969) presents a good example of how these procedures can be used:

Jerry, a 14-year-old cerebral palsied child, is enrolled in a special education class. Jerry's oral reading performance is well below that expected for his age group, and he also shows poor performance in reading comprehension. In this pinpointed behavior, his recorded rate of making incorrect responses either equaled or exceeded his recorded rate of making correct responses, depending on the reading level of the test. (See Figure 14-1.) To change something in the classroom, the teacher decided to introduce a contingency contract in which she agreed to pay Jerry a nickel for every question he answered correctly—a procedure that brought quick results. (See Figure 14-1.) Following this change in classroom procedure, his rate of correctly answering the question exceeded his rate of incorrectly answering questions, suggesting that the procedure

[2] Johnson (1967) reports that even though daily planned rate and daily performed rate are positively correlated measures (an increase in one is associated with an increase in the other), an increase in daily planned rate is necessary, along with other factors, to produce an increase in daily performed rate.

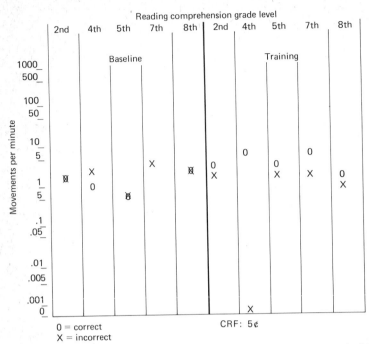

FIGURE 14-1 Jerry's progress in reading comprehension. From N. J. A. Johnson, Precision teaching: a key to the future. Paper presented at the National Society for Programmed Instruction, Annual Convention, 1969.

worked. This observation eliminated the last step in precision teaching, namely, trying again.

There are a number of advantages to precision teaching.

First, at any given time one can have immediate access to objective information about the students' progress.

Second, objective daily records based on rate can be used to study the effects of changes in the classroom procedures and may thus reveal new and functional arrangements of the environmental events occurring in the classroom.[3]

Third, objective information on the students' progress in the form of daily performance rates eliminates the ambiguity involved in communicating a student's sophistication in some skill to others and provides the groundwork for using standardized measures of accomplishment.

Fourth, objective information on the students' progress (daily performed

---

[3] When such records are plotted on special graph paper (Behavior Research Co., P. O. Box 3351, Kansas City, Kansas 66103), the teacher can determine at a glance the probability of obtaining a given rate of performance following the changes in classroom procedure.

rates) and the curriculum demands (daily planned rates) provides a basis for evaluating the skill of the teacher and may also lay the groundwork for standardized measures of teachers' accomplishment.

Fifth, giving a pupil's parents daily progress reports opens up an additional source of reinforcement for the pupil through positive parent reaction to his performance.

Finally, when the students' classroom graphs show both correct response rates and error response rates, the graphs may give the teacher clues as to the sources of difficulty in obtaining the successful management of the pupils' classroom behavior (Kunzelmann, 1968). When both the correct response rate and the error response rate are low, the low rates are probably attributable to reinforcer functions, and the teacher should look for new, more powerful reinforcers. When the correct response rate is down and the error response rate is up, this is probably due to (discriminative) stimulus functions, and the teacher should use easier, less complicated material and provide more prompts. When both the correct response rate and the error response rate are up, this is probably due to the contingencies of reinforcement, and the teacher should examine how precisely these events are being managed. And when the correct response rate is up and the error response rate is down, the teacher may wish to give serious consideration to allowing the student to continue his classroom performance with a minimum of teacher supervision (self-managed behavior).

Although precision teaching is a promising innovation in the management of classroom behavior, it requires continued teacher–pupil interaction until the pupil is able to engage successfully in self-managed behavior.

PROGRAMMED INSTRUCTION

It has probably already occurred to the reader that one solution to the problems of behavior management in educational settings is the solicitation of the services of a skilled tutor (perhaps a specialist in precision teaching) or the tutor's more recent and less expensive classroom analogue—programmed instruction (PI). Skinner (1968) suggests that such services would have the following characteristics:

1. A constant interchange between the instructional program and the student, serving to keep him alert and busy.

2. Sufficient control over the student's progress in the program so that changes in the program are not made until each point is thoroughly understood.

3. The presentation of the material to the student just when he is ready for it.

4. The provision of prompts that assist the student in making the correct response.

5. Maintenance of the student's interest and motivation throughout all phases of instruction.

Whether the program of instruction takes the form of a special textbook (software) or a teaching machine (hardware), Holland (1962) suggests that the following essential principles will be applied:

1. It will provide immediate positive reinforcement for correct answers.

2. It will require that some form of behavior be emitted by the student going through the program.

3. First smaller and easier response units are acquired; then through a gradual progression more complex ones are added until the response units become complex repertoires.

4. Through a gradual progression, more and more stimulus support is withdrawn from the program (fading) without any loss in behavior.

5. The student's observing responses (attention) and his covert behavior are continuously controlled and maintained as he carefully and silently reads the program textual material.

6. Through the presentation of many different examples of the concepts to be learned, the student learns to respond to the single stimulus property common to all of the examples and thus learns abstractions.

7. Student failure in a program of instruction is regarded as a deficiency in the way the program is written (not a deficiency in the student), and program revisions are made following an item analysis of each frame.

The application of these principles in a well-designed program of instruction possesses several important advantages besides those dealing with the acquisition and maintenance of prolonged and difficult performances. For one thing, the student can progress at his own rate and with minimum direction from others. For another, programmed instruction requires an objective, step-by-step, item-by-item operational definition of the behavior that is deemed essential to attain mastery in the subject matter in the program. As in precision teaching, this requires that the program writer decide, in detail, exactly what behaviors must occur and the order in which they must occur in order for the student to complete the program successfully. Most important of all, however, is that as the student progresses through the program, his error frequency will be down and his reinforcement frequency way up, the effect of which is to pair the learning situation with positive reinforcements and thus give it a positive eliciting stimulus function.

Although the packaging may vary, there are three major types of programs of instruction: linear, branching, and auto-elucidative. Examples of each are shown in Tables 14-1 and 14-2 and Figures 14-2 and 14-3. The programs given in Tables 14-1 and 14-2 and Figure 14-3 are useful in the acquisition of verbal skills. That given in Figure 14-2 is useful for the acquisition of motor skills. These tables and figures also give specific remarks about some of the principles involved in the design of the programs. Table 14-1 presents items from the Holland and Skinner linear program on the analysis of behavior. Inspection of this table reveals among other things that changes in both the content and the phrasing of items 5-19 to 5-23 are consistent with principle 3 de-

Table 14-1 Some Sample Items from the Holland and Skinner
Program on the Analysis of Behavior—a Linear Program.

SAMPLE ITEM	REMARKS
Electric shock, sudden loud noises, and other painful or "frightening" stimuli elicit perspiration. The very "frightened" person may break out in a "cold _____." (Answer: sweat)	The prompt "break out in a cold" is a very strong S^D for the intraverbal response of "sweat" even to those who haven't looked at this program before.

5-19

set number	item number	
A rise in temperature is a(n) (1)_____ stimulus for increase in perspiration; similarly, a painful stimulus is a(n) (2) _____ stimulus for perspiration. (Answer: 1, unconditioned; 2, unconditioned)	Changes in the wording and the content of this item compared with 5-19, make the two expressions "A rise in temperature is a(n) _____" and "a painful stimulus is a (n) _____" into S^D's for the intraverbal response "unconditioned" even though they have different content.

5-20

A special instrument (a galvanometer) is used to measure the electrical resistance of the skin. Perspiration lowers the resistance of the skin. This can be recorded by a(n) _____. (Answer: galvanometer)	This item combines old content from 5-19 and 5-20—the word "perspiration," and presents new content—the word "galvanometer," its definition (description), and the affect of perspiration on skin resistance.

5-21

A sudden drop in the electrical skin resistance is called a *galvanic skin response* (GSR). When a painful stimulus produces this effect, it is an unconditioned _____ _____ response. (Answer: galvanic skin)	The two empty spaces function as a prompt for a two-word answer. Item 5-22 combines content from 5-20—"a painful stimulus is an unconditioned stimulus" and 5-21—"a(n) galvanometer (is used to measure the electrical resistance of the skin)."

5-22

A painful stimulus elicits a GSR. This sequence of events (the stimulus and its response) is called the galvanic skin _____. (Answer: reflex)	While item 5-23 combines content from 5-22 with content presented earlier in the program about reflexes but which is not shown in this table.

5-23

Procedures: The student reads each item and then completes the sentence. This test item response requires, in some cases, more than one-word answers, thus requiring that the student compose his answer before writing it. New content is added to each frame in small increments while other content is removed. He then turns the page of the program to obtain the correct answer.

Table 14-2 Summary of Pressey's Auto-Elucidative Program.

PROCEDURE	REMARKS
1. Student is presented with any textual material (such as texts, phamphlets, articles—no special material required) along with class assignment, such as "Read Chapter 10."	Class material includes the ordinary material used in educational settings.
2. Student uses his own reading and study procedures.	Procedures capitalize on student's prior reinforcement history and current repertoire.
3. Student is given no more than thirty study questions on the important features of the material. Questions are three-part multiple choice (with only one right answer), and some of the questions give the page number where the right answer can be found.	Questions are carefully chosen to provide the student with some prompts for important facts, generalizations, and so on in the text.
4. Student answers questions in order.	Giving the student page numbers functions as a prompt, sequence not linear, however.
5. Student responds to question by either erasing a spot on an answer card, marking a spot on an answer card with special ink, or pressing a button.	Active responding is required but composing an answer is not.
6. Feedback given following the student's response when (a) spot erasure reveals either an R (right) or nothing (wrong), (b) spot marked with special ink turns black (right) or red (wrong), or (c) button press produces a point, the next item on the test, or both (right) or neither of these (wrong).	
7. Additional forms of the test may be given.	This is a remediation procedure.

scribed earlier. Similarly, Figure 14-2 illustrates items from the Skinner and Krakower linear program for the acquisition of manuscript printing. Inspection of this figure reveals among other things that correct pen strokes are immediately followed by gray ink—an example of principle 1. The reader should carefully examine the other examples of programs of instruction and become familiar with the principles used in their design.

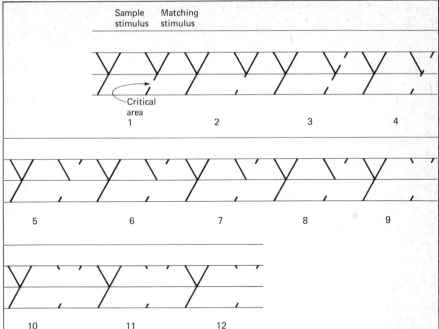

Remarks: Each critical area is bounded by an invisible ink strip about one-eighth inch wide. A special pen is used and when the strokes fall within the strip, they turn gray. Strokes exceeding the boundaries turn yellow. As the student progresses, he is required to complete more and more of the letter as more and more of it is faded from the item.

Procedures: The student makes the matching stimulus look like the sample stimulus by completing the critical area. He uses a special pen. Correct strokes produce gray, while incorrect strokes produce yellow. When the stroke turns yellow, the student is instructed to return to the point where the stroke was last gray.

FIGURE 14-2 Sample item from the Skinner and Krakower program for the acquisition of printing—a linear program. From *Handwriting by Write and See* by B. F. Skinner and S. Krakower. Copyright © 1968, by Lyons and Carnahan, a Division of the Meredith Corporation, and reprinted by permission.

Table 14-3 summarizes the characteristics of the linear, branching, and auto-elucidative programs by showing the sequence, frame size and number, stimulus and response style, response frequency, test frequency and function, error frequency, and other special features of these programs. In general, linear programs require a step-by-step, frame-by-frame progression. The student is actively prompted, responds actively to the text, and is reinforced all along the way. The acquisition of material covered later on in the program requires successful completion of the material covered earlier in the program.

Remarks:
Student writes
his first answer
here.

Student checks
his answer.

Procedures:

First, the student reads the text. He then writes his answers to the questions at the end of each section. After checking them, he moves on to the next item, which presents either new or review material.

Let's start with a definition of the relay: A RELAY IS AN ELECTRICALLY OPERATED SWITCH. The meaning of this definition is very simple. As you know, every switch has a movable contact, and that contact is moved by hand. Similarly, every relay has at least one movable contact, BUT on the relay these movable contacts are moved by an electro-magnet.

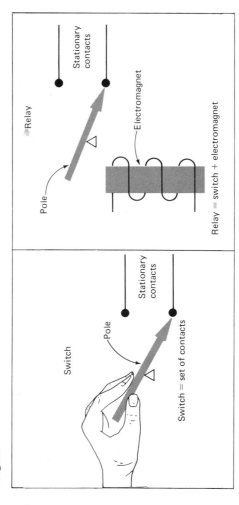

Switch = set of contacts

Relay = switch + electromagnet

Item 1   As shown in the sketches above, the switch has some sort of handle that allows you to move the pole by "fingerpower." The relay, on the other hand, has an electromagnet, which allows us to move the pole by "_____ power." (Fill in the blank and turn the page.)

Answer to Item 1   If you wrote in the word *electric*, you are correct. (If you wrote in the word *magnetic*, you are also correct. However, we prefer the word *electric* since the source of the magnetic power is the *electric* current in the coil.)

Item 2   The pole or movable contact of a relay is moved by the electric power supplied to the electromagnet. Hence, the definition of the relay. The relay is an _____ operated switch. (Fill in the blank and turn the page.)

Answer to Item 2

If you wrote in the word *electrically*, you are correct.

The function of the relay is exactly the same as that of the switch, to turn circuits on or off. You can think of a relay as being a sophisticated type of switch, but it's still basically a switch (in the same way as an electric blanket is just a fancy type of blanket).

Item 3   True or false? Relays are used to turn circuits on or off.

    (a) True . . . . Page 14.
    (b) False . . . . Page 15–1.

Answers to Item 3

You said "true." Correct! Relays, like ordinary switches, are used to turn circuits on and off. Now there are many situations where switches cannot be used but where relays are ideal. However, in order to know when to use a relay instead of a switch we must first know how a relay works.

We have said that the movable contacts (poles) on a relay are moved by an electromagnet. Just how does the electromagnet accomplish this?

New Material   Well, when electricity flows through the electromagnet, it attracts the poles from the position they are in to the other position. When electricity ceases to flow through the electromagnet, the poles return to their initial position. It's as simple as that.

Item 4   The poles of a relay flip from one position to the other position when electricity flows in the

    (a) poles . . . . Page 16.
    (b) throws . . . . Page 17.
    (c) electromagnet . . . . . . Page 18.

Page 15–1   You said "false." I'm afraid we didn't make ourselves clear. Like switches, relays are used to turn circuits on or off. The difference between a switch and a relay is that the relay is operated by an electromagnet.

Go back to Page 13 and answer the question correctly (item 3).

Review for students answering *False* to Item 3.

FIGURE 14-3 Some sample items from Kantor and Mager's program on relays—a branching program. (From R. H. Kantor and R. F. Mager, *Relays*. 2nd edition Palo Alto: Varian Associates, Copyright © 1962 by Varian Associates and reproduced by permission, pp. 11–15.)

Table 14-3 Some Characteristics of the Linear, Branching, and Auto-Elucidative

TYPE OF PROGRAM	SEQUENCE	FRAME SIZE/ NUMBER	STIMULUS STYLE	RESPONSE STYLE	RESPONSE FREQUENCY
linear program	frame-to-frame (within-frame tests)	small/many	small content units (sentences, short paragraphs)	*Study:* Student reads text. *Test:* Active— student must compose answer.	high
branching program	frame-to-test	medium/fewer	medium content units (paragraphs)	*Study:* Student reads text. *Test:* Less active—student makes multiple choice or T/F test responses.	medium
auto-elucidative program	frame-to-test	large/fewest	large content units (multiple paragraphs, sections, chapters)	*Study:* Student reads text. *Test:* Less active—student makes multiple choice test responses.	low

By contrast, in the auto-elucidative program the student reads extensive text covering a wide range of material, responds less actively, and is prompted and reinforced far less frequently. Since ordinary, nonprogrammed materials are used, the acquisition of material covered later does not necessarily depend on the acquisition of material covered earlier. The branching program lies between these two approaches and has the added advantage of moving the student forward or backward in accordance with his skill level. Forward moves ("looping forward") allow the student to skip material he has already learned, and a backward move ("washing back") provides the student with remedial instruction in material he has learned inadequately. These remedial instructional units along the way are corrective "branches" which the student completes before moving on in the program. Hence, in branching programs, errors are expected and accommodated by providing corrective feedback in the form of program branches. In the linear program by contrast, careful program writing, frame-by-frame, aims at the prevention of errors. The successful completion of the frames depends on the development and maintenance of rather

rograms

TEST FREQUENCY	TEST FUNCTION	ERROR FREQUENCY	OTHER SPECIAL FEATURES
igh	provides for immediate error detection	low	1. There is extensive use of prompts. 2. All units require responses. 3. Stimulus support is gradually faded. 4. Incorrect items are repeated.
ιedium	provides for immediate error detection and remediation by presenting student with alternative branching program material	medium	1. If certain tests are passed, student may "loop forward," (passing certain material); if he fails, he is "washed back" to learn remedial material. 2. Incorrect answers refer student to remedial material. 3. There is moderate use of prompts.
·w	provides for delayed error detection	high	1. Large amounts of material are covered. 2. Student scans the material; detailed study, then test follows. 3. Incorrect items are repeated.

complex, discriminated chain performances. Skinner (1968) suggests that a typical sequence of events might be the following:

1. Upon initial contact with materials within the program frame, the student shows precurrent behaviors consisting of initial *observing responses*. Such responses are under the discriminative control of the program content at the beginning of the units within the program, of the frames within the units, and of the sentences within the frames, and they are maintained by the reinforcements that occur sometime later, following emission of the correct test item response.

2. In programs presenting textual (reading) material, the student engages in covert behaviors consisting of *silent texts* or *reading responses*. These texts may be maintained by the textual material itself (when it presents novel stimulation or stimulus change) and by the reinforcement that follows the emission of correct test item responses.

3. In programs presenting textual materials, and immediately prior to the emission of the test item response, the student engages in either covert *echoic*

or covert *intraverbal responses*, depending on the nature of the stimulus support or prompts in the program tests. These responses are also maintained by the reinforcement that follows correct test item responses.

4. Finally, the student manipulates the program manipulandum (a pen, pencil, or button), thus registering his overt test item response, and this is followed by the presentation to the student of the correct answer to the test item. If this answer matches his answer, he receives response confirmation, which is a reinforcing event for many students.

Regardless of what behavior sequence is required for the successful completion of a given program, the program writer is concerned primarily with the student's test item response, and he uses two essential strategies to maintain it.

First, the program writer uses prompts in the form of additional stimulus support in the program content, which is presented just before the test item response is made. These prompts are systematically introduced into the program, frame-by-frame, step-by-step, and possess discriminative control over the correct test item response. In the beginning of the program, prompts that acquired their stimulus control over the correct response even before exposure to the program occurred are presented. These prompts are already functional because of the student's history of operant discrimination training. As the student progresses, more novel forms of stimulus support are added, which also acquire discriminative or prompting functions over the student's correct test behavior.

In the classic linear program these prompts take two forms—formal and thematic. The stimulus properties of the formal prompt have point-for-point correspondence with all or part of the correct answer. This is illustrated in an example taken from a portion of a high school physics program (Skinner, 1961) shown in Table 14-4. In item 15 of the program the student is presented with the partial prompt *candle*, which bears formal similarity to the correct response *incandescent* (*candle*, *incand*escent) and is therefore a formal prompt that has stimulus control over both the student's covert echoic (saying "candle" subvocally) and the correct overt test item response (writing "incandescent"). Although thematic prompts do possess stimulus control over the student's covert intraverbal responses, they do not have any point-for-point correspondence with the correct test item response. This is illustrated in item 5 of the program shown in Table 14-4. The expression *fine wire* is a thematic prompt for the correct response *filament*. The thematic prompt containing the text (*the fine wire, or*) controls the covert intraverbal (saying "filament" subvocally) and the correct test item response (writing "filament").

The design of programmed material often receives careful consideration, and other types of prompts may be introduced. For example, the use of the

Table 14-4 Some Items in a High School Physics Program of Instruction.

ITEM	CORRECT ANSWER
1. The important parts of a flashlight are the battery and the bulb. When we "turn on" a flashlight, we close a switch which connects the battery with the _____.	bulb
2. When we turn on a flashlight, an electric current flows through the fine wire in the _____ and causes it to grow hot.	bulb
3. When the hot wire glows brightly, we say that it gives off or sends out heat and _____.	light
4. The fine wire in the bulb is called a filament. The bulb "lights up" when the filament is heated by the passage of a(n) _____ current.	electric
5. When a weak battery produces little current, the fine wire, or _____, does not get very hot.	filament
13. An object which emits light because it is hot is called "incandescent." A flashlight bulb is an incandescent source of _____.	light
14. A neon tube emits light but remains cool. It is, therefore, not an incandescent _____ of light.	source
15. A candle flame is hot. It is a(n) _____ source of light.	incandescent

From *Cumulative record*, Enlarged Edition, B. F. Skinner. Copyright © 1961. By permission of Appleton-Century-Crofts, Educational Division, Meredith Corporation.

visual prompt in the layout of the following item increases the likelihood of the correct response:

The words SUBTERRANEAN and
TERRESTRIAL have the same root. The root is _____.

Of course, the answer is TERR.[4]

The sequence prompt is also quite useful. For example:

Complete the values in this set:

1 2 4 8 __ __ __

Of course, the answers are 16, 32, and 64.

Ultimately, in one sense, the multiple choice test items in a program of instruction are prompts to the extent that they prevent the occurrence of at least some incorrect answers.

Second, the program writer tries to provide frequent response confirmation (by presenting the pupil with the correct answer after he responds) under the

[4] From S. M. Markle, *Good Frames and Bad: A Grammar of Frame Writing*. 2nd ed., New York: John Wiley and Sons, Inc. Copyright © 1969 by John Wiley and Sons, Inc. and reproduced by permission.

not unreasonable assumption that such confirmation functions as a reinforcer strengthening the test response that led to it and the other responses chained to that response.

Most programs of instruction require extremely fine grain discriminations, and their successful completion depends on the maintenance of adequate precurrent behaviors and textual, covert echoic or intraverbal, and test item responses. These, in turn, are best maintained in programs that present frequent tests requiring active, overt responding and give frequent reinforcement. It is not surprising, therefore, that compared with the branching and auto-elucidative programs, the linear programs produce the lowest error rate.[5] This is not to say, however, that the branching and auto-elucidative programs are not useful. On the contrary, in students in whom the prerequisite responses (precurrent, covert, and test item responses) are already under discriminative control of the program material, behavior can be maintained with the branching and auto-elucidative programs and with a tolerable error rate.

The data of both basic and applied research and the data of real-life observation reveal that individuals can often learn complex skills from materials that apparently do not make systematic use of the principles of programmed instruction. This observation raises several issues about the essential nature of the acquisition process.

First, there is controversy over the importance of overt responding as a necessary condition of acquisition. Some evidence shows that acquisition is facilitated by frequent, overt responding to the program materials, and other evidence shows the opposite. The same is true of response style. Data comparing programs requiring that the trainee compose his answer with those in which he merely presses a button are also inconclusive.

Second, there is controversy over the relative importance of response prompting compared with response confirmation as necessary conditions for acquisition. Here, too, evidence is contradictory. Response prompting and response confirmation interact in a complex way with other important factors, such as the student's reinforcement history, the program material to be learned, and the response requirements of the program.

Third, there is disagreement over the value of programmed instruction compared to the more conventional methods of instruction. Evidence on this deals with two major types of evaluation: (1) student acquisition of the subject matter, both in terms of immediate recall and in terms of later tests of retention, and (2) student satisfaction with the mode of instruction. Although it is not possible to state categorically the superiority of all programs of instruction over other methods of instruction, for example, the lecture method or

---

[5] Error rate as a measure of the efficiency of a program of instruction seems to have a great deal of face validity. However, it is entirely possible for a student to have a low error rate on the individual frames within a section or unit of a program and to show poor overall terminal performance on an unprompted test.

mere study of a textbook, well-designed programs of instruction tend to produce equal or more acquisition than conventional methods of instruction. For example, in one study of an eleventh-grade high school history class, immediate recall of history facts was greater for students using PI either at home or in school than for those using a textbook at home and school or receiving conventional classroom instruction. On a test of retention 6 weeks later, students who had used PI showed a greater loss in acquisition. On a test of the immediate recall of history concepts, programmed methods were again superior, and there were no significant differences on the tests of retention (Jacobs, Yeager, and Tilford, 1966). Hence, the amount of acquisition shown during immediate tests of recall or later tests of retention interacts in a complex way with other things, such as the student's skills at the beginning of instruction and the subject matter of instruction. Moreover, such gains in student performance must be weighed against the costs of preparing programmed materials.[6] Furthermore, even when a program produces an amount of acquisition that is only comparable to conventional procedures, it possesses considerable merit, since the student progresses without the necessity of continuous teacher attention. Obviously, this frees the teacher to work on other aspects of the instructional program, such as the selection of additional instructional materials, providing reinforcements, and the like. Student satisfaction with programmed instruction is also variable, depending on such things as the student's skill with the subject matter in the program and the difficulty of the subject matter.

Finally, there is some question about the kinds of subject matter that can be learned best through programmed instruction. Again a definitive answer is not available. There is, however, a large number of programmed materials available, and they cover skills of varying difficulty and a wide range of subject matter, including foreign languages, reading, writing, arithmetic, algebra, calculus, statistics, social studies, psychology, counseling, interpersonal relations, piano playing, electronics, and physics, to mention but a few.

Although some of the program material at the lower levels may involve relatively simple discriminations, more often the student learns generalizations (seeing similarities between things), chains (sequences of responses that produce stimulation for subsequent responses), and concepts (decision processes or responses in which an appropriate chain must be selected from an array of branching chains). All this seems to suggest that programmed instruction is a valuable addition to the procedures available to the classroom behavior manager.

---

[6] Sometimes, a simple tabular presentation of materials to be learned provides a far more efficient means of learning than a written program. For example, students learned more material from a table of information, which was constructed in only two hours, than they did from linear programs on the same material, which took the program writer 3 months to prepare. (See Warren, 1966.)

CONTINGENCY CONTRACTING

Not infrequently, the teacher's classroom control of the student is mediated by contingency contracts. Homme and Csanyi (1968) suggest that such contracts possess the following characteristics:

1. Response classes that both the teacher and the pupil emit. The teacher's responses consist of consequating the pupil's behavior, and the pupil performs the work specified in the contract.

2. Consequences that maintain the behavior of both parties to the contract. For the teacher the consequence is an adequate performance by the pupil, and for the pupil it includes various forms of teacher-presented consequation.

3. Discriminative stimuli consisting of (a) teacher-presented verbal instructions concerning the amount and type of work to be completed and the amount and type of consequences contingent on completion of that work and (b) the work, specified in the contract, that is to be completed by the pupil.

As we have seen, in order for such contracts to work, the pupil must have had a reinforcement history that gives the teacher-presented verbal instructions discriminative control over appropriate pupil behavior. As with other forms of discriminated operant behavior, the pupil would have to have been reinforced for emitting appropriate contract-specified behavior in the presence of the teacher-presented verbal instructions. Moreover, the pupil must have already acquired the behavior specified in the contract or at least be able to do so. In fact, successful contracting between the teacher and the pupil requires that all contracts be consistent with principle 9—that all contracts between the teacher and the pupil be clear, fair, and honest.

When a pupil has had a history of contracting under such conditions, the possibility exists that he can be trained to work on his own—to develop self-directed or self-controlled classroom appropriate behavior. Such a training program has been developed by Homme and Csanyi (1968). Their program consists of three phases. In phase 1 the teacher as the behavior manager determines the relevant features of the contract, namely, the tasks or response classes to be performed by the pupil and the consequences to be presented to him for those performances. When the pupil's behavior becomes strong under these conditions, phase 2 follows in which the teacher and the pupil *share* in determining the relevant features of the contract (that is, response classes or tasks to be performed and the consequences). Finally, in phase 3 the pupil becomes the sole contract manager and thus contracts with himself, determining the tasks or response classes to be performed, the consequences to follow them, and the presentation of these consequences, all of which are forms of self-directed or self-controlled behavior. The procedure is outlined in detail as follows:

PHASE 1: *Teacher-Controlled Contracting*

1. The teacher, as the behavior manager
   (a) determines the amount of task (response classes) to be performed by the student and the amount of reinforcement to be presented and (b) presents the contract to the pupil and provides the reinforcement.
2. The pupil accepts the contract and performs the task.

PHASE 2: *Transitional Contracting:* BOTH TEACHER AND PUPIL DETERMINE THE TERMS OF THE CONTRACT.

1. In step 1 either (a) The teacher determines the amount of task to be performed by the student, and he and the pupil assume joint control over the amount of reinforcement or (b) the teacher retains full control over the amount of reinforcement, and he and the pupil assume joint control over the amount of task requirements. (c) Although either form may be utilized initially, the alternate form must be practiced before going on to the next step.
2. Step 2 requires three forms of contracting. (a) The teacher and the pupil share joint determination of the amounts of task and reinforcement. (b) The teacher controls the amount of task and the pupil determines the amount of reinforcement. (c) The teacher controls the reinforcement, and the pupil determines the amount of task. (The roles are reversed.)
3. In step 3, the pupil becomes involved in determining both the task requirements and the reinforcement. (a) The pupil determines the amount of reinforcement while sharing joint control with the teacher over the amount of task. (b) The pupil determines the amount of task and shares with the teacher the control over the amount of reinforcement. (c) Although either form may be utilized initially, the alternate form *must* be practiced before going on to the next phase.

PHASE 3: *Pupil-Controlled Contracting:* PUPIL ASSUMES COMPLETE CONTROL OF THE CONTRACTING CONTINGENCIES.

1. The pupil determines the requirements of the amount of task and reinforcement.
2. The pupil performs the task and provides the reinforcement.

The student's acquisition of self-directed or self-controlled behavior may be facilitated by the introduction of macro-contracts in addition to the micro-contract negotiated for the completion of individual tasks. A micro-contract might be, for example, "For each ten problems you get correct, you'll get 10 minutes extra recess time," whereas a macro-contract might be "For each ten (micro) contracts you complete, you'll get to listen to the stereo for a half hour."

The success of such a program critically depends on the selection of tasks the pupil must perform and the strength of the consequences used in the contract. The use of programmed instruction containing tasks of graded difficulty and built-in consequation, combined with a token system, may be especially useful in getting such pupil-controlled contracting under way. Later on, the pupil may pick out his own work assignments, perform them, and reinforce himself. At the beginning of such programs, the teacher plays a critical role in the selection of the tasks and in the selection of the consequences. Later on, her time may be spent in the development of new tasks and in trouble-shooting old ones.

Unlike many educational programs, those described here tend to emphasize the use of programmed instructional materials, the systematic use of positive reinforcement rather than punishment, and the modification of the physical features of the educational environment. In a sense, the aim is to make the acquisition of complex skills easier and more pleasant and, ultimately, to make the pupil a manager of his own affairs without the necessity of directions or consequation from others. Moreover, the skills acquired in the classroom under the control of classroom stimuli will ultimately be controlled and maintained by the events in the natural environment. This is, of course, a Herculean task, but contingency management procedures present a fresh and promising approach to the problem.

CONTINGENCY MANAGEMENT IN THE COLLEGE CLASSROOM

Besides the more formal programming procedures (that is, the use of soft-or hardware programmed instructional materials), there have been some interesting new developments in the management of behavior contingencies in the college classroom. As always, the goal of these programs has been the acquisition of behavior repertoires specified by the course requirements and the various curricula. It is a characteristic of these developments that they make extensive use of (1) contingency contracts between the professor and the college student and (2) numerous response-prompting and response-confirmation devices in the form of selected and partially or totally programmed course materials.

The procedural details of one such program are outlined in Table 14-5, which shows the number of the class meetings, the day of the activity described, the total class duration, individual activity duration, the scheduled activities, and the exam and subject matter unit grading criteria. This program was designed to handle students having heterogeneous backgrounds and to ensure a high level of accomplishment.

Although teaching apprentices aid the students as an integral part of this procedure, the professor has the following rather critical functions:

1. Specifying objectives for each unit in the course. This usually consists of a weekly assignment sheet that presents descriptive narrative outlining the technical language and concepts to be learned for that unit. Each unit consists of twenty to thirty specific behaviors (written answers to questions) that the student should be able to perform following the completion of his study.

For example: "The necessity that contingency contracts be clear seems an obvious contradiction to the principles of automaticity. State and resolve this contradiction." *or* "Use the relevant principles of effective usage to analyze the following situations: (A) A parent promised a child a bicycle for improving his school grades, but the grades did not improve. (B) A teacher who has heard about the importance of consequences tries to improve the effectiveness of his mathematics instruction by arranging this instruction to always be followed by a free activity period. Children are told that when the math period is over (it always lasts 30 minutes), they can read, draw, work with clay, or do whatever they wish (with some limitations of course). This did not seem to improve his math instruction. (C) A music teacher punishes his pupils for inattentiveness by terminating the lesson early, but the effect seems to be an increase in attentiveness.[7]

2. Discovering or producing written materials from which the students can acquire the behavior specified in the unit objectives. Typically, this consists of textbook materials, articles, and on occasion, laboratory exercises.

3. Preparing written directions on where such material can be found and how it can be used. For example, in preparing the answers to the questions on contingency contract clarity and the principle of automaticity, the professor refers the student to the text on specific pages of the original article.

4. Preparing keys for the unit exam and instructing both teaching assistants and student graders (teaching apprentices) on the exam scoring criteria.

5. Serving as a referee in disputes over the scoring of unit exam items scored by the teaching apprentices.

6. Engaging in discussions (individual, when possible) with "questionable passing," "rotten," or "failing" students on the specific items failed on the quizzes.

7. Studying the success of the procedures, using the objective data available from the exams, and devising new remediation procedures when needed.

The graders, or teaching apprentices, provide valuable assistance in the administration and scoring of exams. They also prepare wall charts showing students' progress by code number, perform an item analysis of the quizzes, and to a much lesser degree, provide tutoring services to the students.[8]

It is obvious that this approach to college instruction departs radically from ordinary college-teaching procedures—most notably in the behavior of the

---

[7] These questions were obtained from Dr. J. L. Michael, who prepared and used them in a course in which the students were required to read, among other things, his paper entitled *Principles of effective usage* (1970) from which the section entitled *The Nine Principles of Effective Contingency Management* of this chapter was obtained. The author gratefully acknowledges Dr. Michael's cooperation in obtaining these questions.

[8] In order to qualify as an apprentice, the student must have completed the course with an A in the preceding semester. In such programs students acting as apprentices receive special studies credit and a letter grade for their performance.

Table 14-5 Essential Features of One Course of Study Employing the Principles of Contingency Management in the College Classroom.*

MEETING	DAY	TOTAL CLASS DURATION (hrs.)	INDIVIDUAL ACTIVITY DURATION (hrs.)	CLASS ACTIVITY	POINTS LOST	EXAM LETTER GRADE	UNIT PERFORMANCE GRADING CRITERIA (POINTS EARNED)
1	Mon.	2	1½	Optional Meeting 1. Introductory lectures covering material not available in text, initial material in the text that can be presented in a way that is clearer than the text, material of interest value, discussion of misconceptions.			
			½	2. Students who took quiz B on Thursday remain to receive previous week's quiz results and to appeal their grade. (See below.)			
2	Tues.	2	¼	Required Meeting—all students** 1. "Warm up"—students may review their notes, but no questions are answered by professor or teaching apprentices.			
			1¾	2. Quiz A administered—students given original question sheet, carbon, and blank undersheet. Quiz contains six questions (24 possible points). Students turn in original sheet and keep carbon. As they leave, they are given answer key.	0–5 6–12	P (pass) Q (questionable)	10 2
				3. Teaching apprentices are prepared by professor re the quiz. Each is given four to seven quizzes and the key. Quizzes are to be graded in the afternoon and returned in the morning.	12+	F (fail)	0

Table 14-5 *(Continued)*

3	Wed.	2		Optional Meeting—all students		
		⅙	1. Quiz A returned—passers leave immediately.			
		⅚	2. Questionable and failing students look over quizzes and the answer key; student may fill out "regrade request form"; professor and teaching apprentice answer questions informally; individual attention given.			
		⅔	3. Professor leaves room to look over regrade requests and the quizzes and evaluates them.			
			4. Professor returns before the end of the hour and announces results of regrade requests, moving some students into the pass category.			
		1	5. Remedial lecture for those remaining in class.			
				0–5	P (pass)	8
				6–8	Q (questionable)	6
				9–12	R (rotten)	4
				12+	F (fail)	0
4	Thurs.	1		Required meeting—students failing Quiz A**†		
		1	1. Quiz B administered as above except that it contains nine questions (36 possible points)			
5	Fri.	2		Optional meeting		
		1	1. Special makeup quiz for students missing quiz B for excused absence. Quiz contains nine questions (36 possible points). Letter grade–point equivalents are the same letter grade designations as quiz B.	0–6	P	8
				7–13	Q	6
				14–20	R	4
				21–36	F	0
		1	2. Tutorial for those students wishing it.			

Table 14-5 *(Continued)*

Additional Features and Remarks

1. There are fifteen units in the course, and each unit quiz is 1 hour long. The quizzes are made up from the instructional material given to the student at the beginning of each unit and stress conceptual knowledge. Students must be able to (1) *describe* or *define* a term or concept without the use of examples, (2) *recognize* examples that illustrate a term or concept, and (3) *give* examples that illustrate a term or concept (abbreviated DRG).

2. Students are given extensive supportive course material, including written behavioral objectives (the technical language and concepts to be learned), written directions on where and how to find the technical language and the concepts to be learned, and the study questions appearing on tests. Students are also given supporting services, including tutorials, the opportunity to retake an alternative form of a unit quiz. For these reasons, students who are found cheating are given a summary 'F' in the course, and an effort is made to expel them from the university.

3. The main thrust of the course is to provide the student with written materials from which he can learn the repertoires desired by the professor. Lectures, then, are supplementary in that they (1) provide additional information that is not in the text and (2) explain critical materials in the text until the professor has time to write additional material that is clearer than the original text. When giving lectures, the professor assumes *only* that the student has acquired the knowledge in the preceding unit, for which he has taken the quizzes and passed. In other words, students are *not* expected to read and learn the material prior to the lecture on it.

4. Students are allowed to keep a carbon copy of their answers to the quiz questions, the quiz questions, and the answer key for review. The progress is recorded on a wall chart with the student's name coded.

5. Quiz make-ups are for excused absences only, and there are only two legitimate excuses: illness (confirmed by a doctor's letter) and a death in the family (confirmed by an obituary notice).

6. Final course grades are assigned by the total points earned for the fifteen quizzes, as follows:

$$A = 140+$$

$$B = 130{-}139$$

$$C = 120{-}129$$

$$D = 110{-}119$$

$$E = 109 \text{ or less}$$

* This table was prepared from descriptive material obtained from Dr. Jack L. Michael, whose generosity is gratefully acknowledged.

** Unexcused absence from this meeting results in the student's receiving zero points on this quiz.

† Students who pass (P) quiz A earn the maximum points possible for that unit (10) and are thus exempt from quiz B.

professor. The majority of his nonclass time is spent in selecting and specifying behavioral objectives (in the form of study questions and exercises), finding materials from which they can be learned, and preparing quizzes and answer keys, and the majority of his class time is spent in testing. There is a minimum of lecturing, and what verbal exchanges occur are in the form of discussions with individual students or with small groups. Although the procedure described in Table 14-5 is rather elaborate and means that the student having difficulty must spend twice as much time in class as he would in an "ordinarily taught" three-unit lecture course, most of the student's time is spent in taking exams and in receiving individual attention—*not* in listening to lectures. Moreover, the professor using this procedure believes that this additional time is needed only because he has not yet been able to prepare sufficient supportive textual materials (sources and directions, particularly) necessary for the acquisition of the course objectives for which these procedures were developed. Once this is accomplished, three meetings a week will be sufficient.

Then, too, there are variations in the sequence and the nature of other events going on in courses taught through contingency management. For example, one professor uses lectures and demonstrations as a kind of reinforcing event (with optional attendance), but only *after* the student has successfully passed in *sequence* two or three unit readiness quizzes, which prepare him for the professor's presentation. Or the student himself may pace the rate at which he completes the course requirements. Or the graders may score the exam immediately after it is completed and present oral probes to the student, requesting him to clarify his answers, in order to check the strength of his oral as well as his written responses, even when the latter are correct. Or under certain conditions the student may be permitted to take unit quizzes several times until he passes one. Or the student may be given weekly 10-minute interviews in which he makes an oral presentation of the salient points (based on study questions) covered in a reading selection. The interview is administered by the professor or a student who has already successfully passed the interview.

Regardless of which style or form such instructional procedures take, they all have the following features in common:

1. The precise specification of behavioral objectives and the extensive use of written directions as to where these objectives can be learned.

2. Primary emphasis on student utilization of textual materials and secondary emphasis on the lecture and the tutorial.

3. Typically, student contact with the lecture and the tutorial *only after* he has made contact with the textual material (the latter being measured by his at least taking the unit quiz).

4. The infusion into the procedure of frequent reinforcements in the form of points, response confirmation, and social consequences (from the professor

and teaching apprentices), which are presented immediately or a relatively short while after the quiz performance.

5. The presentation of additional consequences (for example, more points credit for passing an exam the first time it is offered) when needed to avoid the occurrence of "cumulative failure" (as when a student repeatedly shows inadequate preparation for quizzes or skips them).[9]

6. The basing of the student's grade for the course on absolute objective criteria of his accomplishment of the behavioral objectives for the course and *not* on how well he competes with other students in the class or on a priori percentages assigned to grade equivalents (that is, grading on a curve).

7. Frequent interpersonal contacts between the teaching staff (professors and teaching apprentices) and the students, so that they get to know one another and can partake of a mutually reinforcing situation.

Procedures comparable to those described in this section have been used in classes as large as 150 students and in courses ranging from statistics, general psychology, experimental analysis of behavior, developmental psychology, behavior modification, art, and botany, to mention but a few. Moreover, compared with students in traditional college lecture courses, students exposed to such instructional procedures obtain higher grades (reflecting greater acquisition at the conclusion of the course), show greater retention on tests after the completion of the course, study for and enjoy such a course more, and feel they have learned more.[10]

In summary, arranging an appropriate educational environment through the manipulation of behavioral contingencies in the college classroom represents an interesting and promising innovation in higher education having widespread applications to different courses of study and different levels of student sophistication. Moreover, it brings together *again* the teacher and the student under conditions in which there are mutually reinforcing social transactions. This may very well be the first approximation of reform in an educational system in which reform is long overdue. And there is no reason why these techniques cannot be modified and adapted to fit many of the courses offered in the secondary schools.

---

[9] Jack Michael, in a personal communication (1971), reports a controlled study using a matched group design in which students were assigned to one of two conditions. In one condition students lost points for not taking quiz A on time. In the other condition students were allowed to do their thing (be responsible for maintaining their own behavior without the consequences of losing points for taking the exam late). They could, if they wished, wait and take quiz B. Students assigned to the latter condition consistently did poorly on quiz B and showed overall greater cumulative failure than those assigned to the former condition.

[10] This was true even when the students exposed to such behavior management procedures at a southwestern state university were compared with students enrolled in an Ivy League college. See Keller (1968). Similar results have been reported by McMichael and Corey (1909), Cooper and Greiner (1970), Sheppard and McDermot (1970), and Lloyd and Knutzen (1969).

STUDY QUESTIONS

1. What two basic assumptions seem to be characteristic of formal education?
2. What types of reinforcers maintain the students' behavior following completion of their formal education?
3. Distinguish between novel stimulation, stimulus change, and environmental control as reinforcers occurring in the natural environment. In what kinds of situations might these different types of reinforcers occur?
4. Distinguish between base-line observation and behavioral prescription and give an example of each from an educational setting.
5. As stated on page 408, why is the teacher of singular importance in the management of the pupil's behavior?
6. An elementary school teacher in special education visited a hospital ward for the severely retarded. The children were given a token after going potty, after dressing, and from time to time as they played games. The teacher asked the psychologist in charge what the tokens were for, and he replied that they were a kind of reinforcer or reward for good behavior. To this, the teacher replied, "Oh, they won't work. These children are not bright enough to understand what they are for." Of which principle of effective contingency management was the teacher unaware?
7. A cute sixth-grade girl, quite mature for her age, talked in class incessantly. She seldom studied quietly during math, social studies, and English study periods. How could the Premack principle be used to improve her scholarship. (Hint: Look over Chapter 13.)
8. When is the effect of consequences on the behavior preceding them the greatest?
9. About six to eight times a day, Mary seems to get the teacher's attention by talking in class. She seldom receives the teacher's attention for good work. Which behavior is apt to be stronger? Why?
10. What is prescribed by principle 7 when the frequency of reinforcement falls below the optimum level?
11. Describe two distinct disadvantages of using prior worsening. (Hint: What is the effect on the presentation of a positive reinforcer and what is required in its use?)
12. What features of an effective contingency contract must be clear, fair, and honest? Give an example of such a contract.
13. Describe some of the behaviors that are presumed to be controlled by the following:
   a. The ringing of the school bell.
   b. The teacher entering the room.
14. What kind of training is required in order for them to be functional as S^D's (discriminative stimuli).
15. Describe the characteristics of a "game" you might use to strengthen pro-classroom behavior.
16. In what kind of a situation is a dead period apt to occur? What actually happens during such dead periods? Suggest a procedure for its remediation. (Hint: Review carefully the concept of stimulus control.)

17. Describe two different procedures employing the stimulus control principle as a means of suppressing disruptive classroom behavior (such as talking and turning around).
18. Explain why the fading procedure described on page 414 is superior to the physical relocation of a student.
19. Assuming a teacher's praise and approval are reinforcers for all of the students in a particular class, give two rather important limitations in their use.
20. In what way is praise as a generalized positive reinforcer comparable to token reinforcer re:
    a. Deprivation states?
    b. Training required for their effective use?
21. Suggest three reasons why token reinforcers may be superior to generalized positive reinforcers.
22. Define the term *back-up reinforcer* and give three examples of *back-up reinforcers* suitable for classroom use.
23. Suggest a procedure that guarantees each pupil at least one occasion of response-contingent reinforcement in the course of daily classroom instruction.
24. In the example on page 417, in what way was the teacher using a concurrent schedule?
25. Describe two situations that may limit the usefulness of an extinction procedure as a means of suppressing some behavior.
26. Suggest two reasons why group contingencies may be particularly powerful sources of behavior modification.
27. Pick out a classroom behavior of interest to you and describe how it can be dealt with using the four teacher-managed elements of precision teaching. Be specific as to the response class and the response class dimension.
28. Distinguish between daily performed rate and daily planned rate in terms of the following:
    a. Who prepares the measure.
    b. Who may be particularly interested in each measure.
    c. Why the measures are useful.
    d. How the measures can be used as a form of reinforcement or to produce reinforcements.
    e. The source of reinforcements they may produce.
29. Study the case of Jerry, given on page 419, and answer the following questions:
    a. What behavior was pinpointed? (Name both the response class and the response class dimension.)
    b. What behavior was recorded? (Name both the response class and the response class dimension.)
    c. What change in the classroom was introduced?
    d. What was done about the last step (try again) in precision teaching?
30. Suggest three advantages of precision teaching.
31. Study carefully the four records below and suggest an appropriate course of action for each subject.

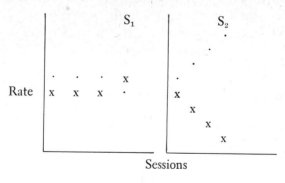

Sessions

· correct R's
x incorrect R's

32. Suggest some reasons why either the services of a tutor or programmed instruction may be particularly useful in the acquisition of prolonged and difficult performances.
33. What are the major benefits of programmed instruction?
34. Look over Table 14-1 and answer the following:
   a. What kind of response must the student make?
   b. Give an example of a prompt in the program that takes advantage of the student's preexisting repertoire.
   c. What are the effects of the slight rewording of the sentences in the frames that follow one another?
   d. Why is the sentence wording changed from one frame to the next?
   e. What probably serves as a reinforcing event in this program?
35. Look over Figure 14-2 and answer the following:
   a. What kind of response must the student make?
   b. Describe the type of prompt used in this program and how it is faded.
   c. What probably serves as a reinforcing event in this program?
   d. When the prompt is completely faded, what becomes the S^D for the printing response?
36. Look over Figure 14-3 and answer the following:
   a. What kind of response must the student make?
   b. Find an example of sentences in two successive items in the program that, because of changes in wording, are (1) somewhat different in meaning but (2) at the same time control the same response.
   c. Find an example of a question for which the answers are branching.
   d. What form does the branching material take?
   e. What probably serves as reinforcing event(s) in the program? (Hint: There are possibly two or more reinforcing events.)
37. Look over Table 14-2 and answer the following:
   a. What kind of response must the student make?
   b. What form do the program items take?
   c. What probably serves as a reinforcing event in this program?

38. Look over Table 14-3 and study carefully the characteristics of the linear, branching, and auto-elucidative programs. Be able to give brief descriptions of the following characteristics for each of them:
    a. Sequence.
    b. Frame size.
    c. Frame number.
    d. Stimulus style.
    e. Response style.
    f. Response frequency.
    g. Test frequency.
    h. Test function.
    i. Error frequency.
    j. Other special features.

39. Describe the behavior sequence that is typical for successfully completing an item in a program of instruction. What discriminative and reinforcing stimuli maintain such a performance?

40. What two major strategies are used by program writers to maintain the behavior of the student? When do these strategies occur?

41. Give a definition of a formal prompt. Give a specific example of one from the material presented in Table 14-4. Limit your example to only those elements of the program that are illustrative of a formal prompt.

42. What kind of covert verbal behavior is the formal prompt said to control?

43. Give a definition of a thematic prompt. Give a specific example of one from the material given in Table 14-4. Again, limit your example to only those elements of the program that are illustrative of a thematic prompt.

44. What kind of covert verbal behavior is the thematic prompt said to control?

45. Suggest a reason why overt responding, particularly when such responding requires that the student compose his answer, may facilitate learning more than covert responding.

46. The successful use of response prompting, rather than response confirmation, depends rather heavily on what historical factors?

47. From your experiences with the lecture method and from what you now know about behavior theory and contingency management, prepare a brief, itemized description of the weaknesses of the lecture method.

48. Suggest some criteria that may be used in deciding whether or not one should use programmed instruction.

49. What maintains the behavior of the pupil in a contingency contract? The behavior of the teacher?

50. What two basic assumptions underlie successful contracting?

51. In the developing of self-directed or self-controlled classroom behavior in students, who specifies the relevant features of the contract at the beginning of training? At the end of training? What are these features?

52. Why is phase 2 called transitional contracting?

53. Distinguish between a micro- and a macro-contract.

54. Describe the behaviors of the professor in a traditional college lecture course and of the professor in a course in which systematic use is made of contingency management.

55. What functions are carried out by the teaching apprentices in the system described in Table 14-5?
56. In what activities does the professor using a contingency management system spend most of his time inside of class? Outside of class?
57. Look over the material shown in Table 14-5 and then study the seven essential features or principles of PI as presented on page 422. Find one example of each of as many of these principles you can from the procedures described in Table 14-5.
58. Pick out the points of similarity between the seven essential features of PI and the essential features of contingency management in the college classroom as described on Table 14-5.
59. Offer a behavioral account for the observation that terminal performance on an unprompted test may be poor when the performance on sections or units of the program may be good.
60. Suggest at least two important reasons why grading on a curve is a poor procedure from the point of view of good behavior management in the classroom. (Hint: Review the nine principles of effective contingency management.)

REFERENCES

Addison, R. M., and Homme, L. E. The reinforcing event (RE) menu. *National Society for Programmed Instruction Journal*, 1966, **4**, 8–9.
Bijou, S. W., Birnbrauer, J. W., Kidder, J. D., and Teague, C. Programmed instruction as an approach to teaching reading, writing and arithmetic to retarded children. *Psychological Record*, 1966, **16**, 505–522.
Cheney, C. D., and Powers, R. B. A programmed approach to teaching. *Improving College and University Teaching*, 1970.
Cooper, J. L., and Greiner, J. M. A learning theory approach to teaching. Unpublished manuscript, 1970.
Gagné, R. M., and Rohwer, W. D., Jr. Instructional psychology. In P. H. Mussen and M. R. Rosenzwieg (Eds.), *Annual Review of Psychology*, Palo Alto, Calif.: Annual Reviews, 1969.
Gilbert, T. F. Mathetics: The technology of education. *Journal of Mathetics*, 1962, **1**, 7–73. (a)
Gilbert, T. F. Mathetics: II. The design of teaching exercises. *Journal of Mathetics*, 1962, **2**, 7–56. (b)
Hall, R. V., Lund, D., and Jackson, D. Effects of teacher attention on study behavior. *Journal of Applied Behavior Analysis*, 1968, **1**, 1–12.
Hewitt, F. M., Taylor, F. D., and Artusco, A. A. The Santa Monica Project: Evaluation of an engineered classroom design with emotionally disturbed children. *Exceptional Children*, 1969, **36**, 523–529.
Holland, J. G. Teaching machines: An application of principles from the laboratory. In W. I. Smith and J. W. Moore (Eds.), *Programmed learning*. New York: D. Van Nostrand Company, Inc., 1962.
Holland, J. G. Research in programming variables. In R. Glaser (Ed.), *Teaching*

machines and programmed learning. Vol. 2. *Data and directions.* Washington, D. C.: National Education Association, 1965.

Holland, J. G., and Skinner, B. F. *The analysis of behavior.* New York: McGraw-Hill, 1961.

Homme, L. W., and Csanyi, A. P. *Contingency contracting. A system for motivation management in education.* Albuquerque, N.M.: Southwestern Cooperating Training Laboratories, 1968.

Homme, L. E., deBaca, P. C., Devine, J. F., Steinhurst, R., and Rickert, E. J. Use of the Premack principle in controlling the behavior of nursery school children. *Journal of the Experimental Analysis of Behavior*, 1963, 4, 544.

Homme, L. E., and Tosti, D. T. Contingency management and motivation. *National Society for Programmed Instruction Journal*, 1965, 4, 14–16.

Jacobs, J. N., Yeager, H., and Tilford, J. An evaluation of programmed instruction for the teaching of facts and concepts. *Journal of Programmed Instruction*, 1966, 4, 29–38.

Jacobson, J. M., Bushell, D., Jr., and Risley, T. Switching requirements in a head start classroom. *Journal of Applied Behavior Analysis*, 1969, 2, 43–48.

Johnson, N. J. A. Acceleration by a student teacher of both planned and performed rates of primary, learning-disabled pupils. Research Training Paper No. 2, Bureau of Child Research and School of Education, University of Kansas, September, 1967.

Johnson, N. J. A. Precision teaching: A key to the future. A paper presented at the National Society for Programmed Instruction Annual Convention, April, 1969.

Kantor, R. H., and Mager, R. F. *Relays.* (2nd ed.) Palo Alto, Calif.: Varian Associates, 1962.

Keller, F. S. Good-bye teacher. *Journal of Applied Behavior Analysis*, 1968, 1, 78–89.

Kunzelmann, H. P. Data decisions. Paper read at the annual convention of the Association for Children with Learning Disabilities, Boston, 1968.

Lloyd, K. E., and Knutzen, N. S. A self-paced programmed undergraduate course in the experimental analysis of behavior. *Journal of Applied Behavior Analysis*, 1969, 2, 125–135.

Madsen, C. H., Jr., Becker, W. C., and Thomas, D. R. Rules, praise, and ignoring: Elements of elementary classroom control. *Journal of Applied Behavior Analysis*, 1968, 1, 139–150.

Markle, S. M. *Good frames and bad: A grammar of frame writing.* (2nd ed.) New York: Wiley, 1969.

McAllister, L. W., Stachowiak, J. G., Baer, D. M., and Conderman, L. The application of operant conditioning techniques in a secondary classroom. *Journal of Applied Behavior Analysis*, 1969, 2, 277–285.

McMichael, J. S., and Corey, J. R. Contingency management in an introductory psychology course. *Journal of Applied Behavior Analysis*, 1969, 2, 79–93.

Mechner, F. Behavioral analysis and instructional sequencing. In R. C. Lange (Ed.), *Programmed instruction—The sixty-sixth yearbook of the National Society for the Study of Education.* Part 2. Chicago: University of Chicago Press, 1967.

Michael, J. L. *Management of behavioral consequences in education.* Inglewood, Calif.: Southwest Regional Laboratory for Educational Research and Development, 1967.

O'Day, E., Kulhavy, R., Anderson, W., and Malczynski, R. *Programmed instruction: Techniques and trends.* New York: Appleton-Century-Crofts, 1970.

Packard, R. G. The control of "classroom attention": A group contingency for complex behavior. *Journal of Applied Behavior Analysis,* 1970, **3**, 13–28.

Pressey, S. L. Basic unresolved teaching machine problems. *Theory and Practice,* 1962, **1**, 30–37.

Pressey, S. L. Re-program programming? *Psychology in the Schools,* 1967, **4**, 234–239.

Pressey, S. L. Education's (and psychology's) disgrace: And a double-dare. *Psychology in the Schools,* 1969, **4**, 353–358.

Pressey, S. L. Personal communication, 1970.

Sheppard, W. C., and MacDermot, H. G. Design and evaluation of a programmed course in introductory psychology. *Journal of Applied Behavior Analysis,* 1970, **3**, 5–11.

Skinner, B. F. The science of learning and the art of teaching. *Harvard Educational Review,* 1954, **14**, 86–97.

Skinner, B. F. Teaching machines. *Science,* 1958, **128**, 969–977.

Skinner, B. F. *Cumulative record.* (Enlarg. ed.) New York: Appleton-Century-Crofts, 1961.

Skinner, B. F. *The technology of teaching.* New York: Appleton-Century-Crofts, 1968.

Skinner, B. F., and Krakower, S. *Handwriting with write and see.* Chicago: Lyons and Carnahan, 1968.

Staats, A. W., and Staats, C. K. *Complex human behavior.* New York: Holt, Rinehart and Winston, 1963.

Taber, J. I., Glaser, R., and Schaeffer, H. H. *Learning and programmed instruction.* Reading, Mass.: Addison-Wesley, 1965.

Thomas, D. R., Becker, W. C., and Armstrong, M. Production and elimination of disruptive classroom behavior by systematically varying teacher's behavior. *Journal of Applied Behavior Analysis,* 1968, **1**, 35–45.

Ulrich, R., Stachnik, T., and Mabry, J. (Eds.) *Control of human behavior.* Vol. 2. *From cure to prevention.* Glenview, Ill.: Scott, Foresman, 1970.

Warren, A. D. To program or not to program: a multiple choice. *Journal of Programmed Instruction,* 1966, **3**, 41–44.

Zimmerman, E. H., and Zimmerman, J. The alteration of classroom behavior in a special classroom situation. *Journal of the Experimental Analysis of Behavior,* 1962, **5**, 59–60.

CHAPTER 15

SOME AFTERTHOUGHTS

Now that you've studied some of the principles of behavior and how they have been applied by others in the solution of some behavior problems, you're probably eager to try them out yourself. And, of course, you can and should. It doesn't matter that you're not a professional or a specialist. The fact that you are around people means that you'll have numerous opportunities for the social practice of behavior principles.

And, of course, you may become so excited by the success of your attempts, that you will consider further study leading to a professional level of sophistication either in research or the practice (application) of behavior principles to solve human problems in a field known as behavioral engineering or behavioral technology. When such practice is used in the remedy of behavior deficits and behavior deviations it is called behavior therapy and when it is used to solve educational problems it is called educational technology. Either way, as a beginner or as a professional practitioner or researcher, you should be warned, however, that your work will not be without criticism from various quarters. For this reason, a brief review of some of the current criticisms of those who engage in the social practice of behavior principles would seem to be in order.

There is the old argument that specialists in behavior management are not scientists, but rather pipe fitters whose contribution to psychology is insignificant. The reader will undoubtedly recognize that this criticism is a derivative of the controversy described earlier in Chapter 1 on basic versus applied research. The difficulty is in deciding what is basic research and what is applied research.

How does one characterize, for example, the brilliant work of David Premack in teaching Sarah, the chimpanzee, to read and write sentences as forms of receptive and expressive language? (See Chapter 7.) Is he a scientist studying language development in the chimpanzee, or is he a very sophisticated animal trainer? And suppose he decides to go commercial and develop training programs for the mongoose and the gorilla, so that they can be sold to carnivals and circuses for display? Obviously, it is not easy to decide, because for each new species, he would have to develop appropriate procedures, thereby adding to our knowledge.

Added to this defense is the point that well-trained behavior managers, as part of their craft, engage in systematic and objective observation of the behavior of concern (the base-line observation) and its treatment (the behavioral prescription)—in what might be called a *microexperiment*. Although such procedures do not permit the actual verification of laws of the kind one can obtain from a well-controlled laboratory study,[1] successful application in the natural environment does provide other kinds of information. For example, it gives us some idea of the *power* and *generality* of the variables specified in the laws of behavior. For if we can make a successful application (change behavior in a desired manner by manipulating a particular variable, for example, present response-contingent reinforcement) in an uncontrolled setting this not only shows that the variable is powerful, but that it also possesses extensive generality, despite the intrusion of other variables.

On the other hand, when applications in natural settings fail, new and significant "boundary" variables are often discovered, which can be studied and verified in subsequent laboratory study. What is more, when these failures occur, they force us to try out other, perhaps new procedures, which may also lead to significant discoveries and stimulate further research aimed at verification in well-controlled laboratory study. In short, besides helping to solve

---

[1] In ordinary applications, it is not customary to remove the treatment (the behavioral prescription), return to base line, and then reinstate the treatment as demanded by the reversal paradigm. It is not possible, therefore, to state that the observed behavior change is solely attributable to the treatment. (See Chapters 1, 11, and 12 for discussions of this.)

human problems, applications of the behavior principles add significantly to our knowledge about human behavior.

Although such criticism is more likely to be heard from academic psychologists (especially the experimental psychologists), criticism also comes from the more speculative and philosophically oriented psychologists, and of course, from the laymen whom they indoctrinate.

Consider the following episode:

An attractive girl about 20 years old, gave an informal, brief talk on the usefulness of behavior therapy in the solution of one's personal problems. She spoke to a group of professionals from various fields including psychology, who were interested in, but not necessarily committed to, her approach. The problems of concern to her were her orgasms, her feelings of depression, and her risky driving maneuvers (such as turning without giving a signal and changing lanes suddenly).

As a means of controlling these problems, she kept track of their daily frequency by means of a simple wrist counter, and at the end of each day she plotted points on a curve for the total frequency of each. To increase her orgasm frequency, she made sure that she spent a certain amount of time each day in sexual activity, and the mere act of record keeping seemed to help. Whenever she felt depressed, she noted the situation in which the depression occurred and immediately removed herself from that situation. Using her compiled list, she was often able to avoid depressive situations. The frequency of risky driving maneuvers also seemed to be decreased by her merely keeping a daily record of their frequency of occurrence.

As she told of her experience with these procedures, her excitement and enthusiasm seemed to be contagious, at least judging by the questions and requests from the audience for information on where the wrist counters could be purchased. There were, however, some hostile reactions to her presentation. Some felt that her approach was too contrived, too manipulative, too mechanistic and dehumanizing, too limited to tics and twitches, and not concerned with what was really important—her emotional needs. As her talk ended, the author even overheard one critic suggest that the speaker had been so well programmed that she herself was not even mindful of the social and philosophic implications of her own behavior!

Of course, the author was struck by these critical remarks even though he had heard them before. It didn't matter that the young lady had improved her sex life through her own ingenuity,[2] was much happier, and was much

[2] The author recognizes that she left much unsaid in the description of her treatment procedure. He did feel, however, that her excitement and joy suggested that there was considerable spontaneity and pleasure involved in her sex life.

less of a peril to her fellow drivers. Rather, one got the feeling from the conversations to follow that some professionals felt that the young lady would have been better off if she had sought professional help from a psychotherapist, who would have been able to make sense of (or interpret) what one of them described as her frigidity, depression, and accident proneness—that is, she should have sought help from someone who could help her get insight into her real problem. It didn't matter to these critics that the girl was happy, excited, and enthusiastic about her own successful attempts to change her own behavior.

Another way to look at this is that in many ways, the procedures the young lady used to deal with her personal problems are not unlike those she would use to deal with a physical ailment. For example, if she had strep throat, the chances are that she would follow the doctor's orders to take her temperature every 4 hours, stay in bed, and take penicillin three times a day. From the point of view of behavior theory, such behavior as taking one's temperature, going to bed, and pill taking involves the kind of self-control she used in dealing with her personal problems.

Of course, we must admit that even though her record keeping amounted only to a momentary button press on a wrist counter and plotting a point on a curve, it was a nuisance. Maybe, too, this is where her critics got the idea that she was programmed. To them, by recording and storing data on her own behavior, she acted like a computer.[3] Perhaps one day, successful applications will be possible without the necessity of such observing and recording procedures (maybe through electrical or chemical intracranial stimulation). In the meantime, however, they are essential.

Then there is the argument that we do not as yet have sufficient knowledge to make sensible applications of behavior principles to solve human problems. Ever since man has lived with others and engaged in social transactions, however, he has from time to time been regarded as having behavior problems requiring remediation. For anyone who is concerned with the behavior of his charges—whether he is the prehistoric man who attempted to release evil spirits through the trephining of the victim's skull or the modern-day probation officer, minister, doctor, teacher, spouse, or parent—to suspend action until sufficient knowledge on the principles of behavior is available is to deprive the persons in his charge of valuable training and protection. It is, in effect, as Krasner (1965) has pointed out, to put them in peril from the hostile forces in nature—disease, pestilence, predators, weather, famine, and man.

Then there is the charge that for the controller to use reinforcements or

---

[3] Similar criticisms might have been made had she used electromechanical sensing and recording devices to monitor and perhaps consequate her own behavior. Even though such equipment is acceptable in treating physical ailments, the use of such equipment to treat behavior problems is, to many, the epitome of dehumanization.

other forms of stimulation to induce behavior is to rob the individual of his right to be an autonomous and self-determined person. Such procedures, it is argued, make the individual particularly dependent on the manipulations of the controller.

Thus the child who does his homework without parent-presented prodding or reinforcements is said to be autonomous and controlled only by his own inner need to learn. On the other hand, the child who is lacking in autonomy requires continual prodding, the effect of which is to make his behavior particularly dependent on such presentations from his controller. Skinner (1971) suggests that what is involved is the degree to which the causes of the individual's behavior are conspicuous to those about him. In the case of the first child the causes appear to be internalized and are attributed to a need system, and in the latter case they are attributed to presentations from others.

We have already learned, however, that the behavior shown by the autonomous child can just as easily be attributed to external sources of control, particularly the study situation—a feature of the physical environment that often goes unnoticed. On the other hand, the source of control in the latter case arises from the social environment and consists of presentations of verbal instructions and reinforcements from concerned parents or tutors—events that are particularly conspicuous, especially to those who must present them.

What is suggested, then, is that in both cases, there are external sources of stimulation that serve to control behavior, albeit one seems far less conpicuous than the other. Because the causes of behavior are sometimes inconspicuous, we tend to attribute such behavior to the characteristics of the individual and his psyche—that is, his needs, desires, readiness to learn, and so on—rather than to his reinforcement history.

A primary source of behavior change in organisms arises from the stimulation they receive from their physical and social environments, whether these forms of stimulation are conspicuous or not. The sources of such stimulation are the physical and social objects and events that have marked the organism's unique history. With a few exceptions, most all of us have, from infancy on, made contact with these sources of stimulation *over* and *over* again.

Although these points seem obvious enough, the question arises as to whether or not it is possible to make contact with others and yet not affect their behavior. It is as if one possessed a completely neutral stimulus function, so that neither other people's physical stimulus properties (their physiognomies, clothes, uniforms, badges, and titles) nor their social stimulus properties (their eye contact, glances, smiles and gestures, and verbal expressions) possess eliciting, discriminative, or consequating stimulus functions. It is necessary to bring this up because a rather significant number of professionals believe that they can engage in contacts with others without actively influencing their behavior. Rather these professionals prefer to describe themselves as neutral, not imposing themselves on others but only "reflecting" the individual's behavior so that he may gain insight from his behavior, as the following example, reported by Axline (1964), illustrates:

> He [Dibs] picked up the jar and read the label. "This is the red finger paint," he announced. "Red." He put the jar down on the table and circled the outstretched palms of his hands around above the paint and paper, very close to it but not touching it. Quickly, he touched the paint with the tip of his fingers.
>
> "Spread it on," he said. "Take the red paint, Dibs, and spread it on. Spread it on one finger, two fingers, three fingers. First the red. Then the yellow. Then the blue. Put it on in order."
>
> "You would sort of like to try it?" I asked.
>
> "These are all the signs of what it says it is?" Dibs said, looking up at me and then pointing to the labels on the jars.
>
> "Yes. Those are the directions."
>
> He dipped his fingers in the paint again.
>
> "Oh, take it off," he said. He picked up another paper towel and wiped the paint off vigorously.
>
> "You would sort of like to do it, and then again, you don't like it," I commented.
>
> "Now those crayons are different," Dibs said. "The American Crayon Company makes those. And this is the Shaws Finger Paint. The water colors are made by Prang."
>
> "Yes," I said [pp. 53–54].

This is an excerpt from a play therapy session with a disturbed child named Dibs, an essential feature of which was reflecting. Unfortunately, the therapist's nonverbal or gestural responses are not presented, so that it is not possible to estimate either their frequency or their character. Nor is it possible to determine the therapist's function as a model, even though the entire account reveals several occasions of modeling. The same is somewhat true of the therapist's use of putting-through procedures. Nevertheless, it seems clear that even when a therapist steadfastly attempts to merely reflect the patient's behavior, other important events may be occurring that affect the patient's behavior in a significant way. If nothing else, the reflecting seems to maintain the child's own movements and what he says about them—perhaps through the attention he receives as the therapist observes and repeats what the child says in order to reflect the child's behavior. And there are, of course, occasions when the therapist appears to be providing reinforcements—that is, "Yes, those are the directions" and "Yes" after Dibs said, "The water colors are made by Prang."[4]

---

[4] This is, of course, an assumption, since it is not possible to establish, a priori and in the absence of a critical test, whether or not such presentations are reinforcers.

It would seem, then, that it is the rule rather than the exception for contacts between individuals to involve events possessing eliciting, dicriminative, or consequating stimulus functions. The effect of this is to make us acutely aware that our presentations to others are very likely to affect their behavior. This means that when both professional and novice alike engage in transactions with others, they must be concerned with the effects of their presentations on the welfare of the individual and of society at large. If, for example, we were to contract with a parent to improve his child's reading skill, it would be because, like the parent, we have thought it over and feel that it is worthwhile for the child, his parents, and society at large to improve the child's reading skills. Similarly, if we were to *not* provide our services to a client who wishes us to develop a training program for improving pick-pocketing skill among children, it would also be because we have thought it over and we feel it is *not worthwhile* for the children, their parents, or society for our youth to become skillful at picking pockets. Everyone who applies behavior principles or who engages in related research must consider the social consequences of any program with which they are associated. And although there have been and still are despots in various political, religious, educational, and correctional positions who have, as behavior change agents of the society, readily and continuously used deprivation and punishment to induce behavior change, the charge that specialists in behavior management are simply mindless automatons controlling other controllers and the controlled is simply not true. If anything, this charge is more applicable to those workers who erroneously believe that they are immune from such influence over the client by virtue of the procedures they use. They believe that they do not impose their values upon the client because their procedures do not directly affect the behavior of the client, only his psyche. To them, it is only through the modification of these intrapsychic states (something the individual does himself) that behavior change is possible.

It is just because specialists in behavior management are aware of their influence that they must ask themselves repeatedly and searchingly the question: Is the behavioral goal of this procedure consistent with the wishes of the individual, his caretakers, and society at large? Everyone who influences others through social transactions must ask himself this question whether he is a specialist or not. And, of course, there are a number of goals on which most of us agree: that our children must learn the basic academic skills of reading, writing, and arithmetic; of personal care and hygiene; of friendliness, warmth, and respect for others; and the more complex skills that will enable them to solve the problems of living in a technological society and a changing world. Even if we cannot agree entirely on all of these, we can at least agree on some, and it is on those points of agreement that we can use the principles of behavior to our fullest advantage. And it is here that all of us, as concerned human beings and agents of behavior change in others, can look forward to better health, happiness, and interpersonal relationships, through the positive means of behavior control that the principles of behavior give us. It is through the application of such positive means of behavior control, especially positive reinforcement, that maybe our dreams of the good life with others will become a reality. And to fail to take this opportunity now is to go on as we always have—to secure behavior control through more negative means: ostracism, ridicule, verbal threat or attack, segregation, incarceration, bodily harm, even death, in short, through punishment.

STUDY QUESTIONS

1. Suggest a definition for each of the following:
   a. Behavior therapy.
   b. Educational technology.
   c. Behavioral engineering or behavioral technology.
2. Prepare two arguments with examples in rebuttal to the charge that those who apply behavior principles add little to the field of psychology.
3. Study carefully the anecdote and the discussion following it on pages 452–453 and find examples of language (terms) used in the analysis of behavior that show:
   a. "excess meaning."
   b. states or events that are not directly observable and are regarded as antecedent to behavior change.
4. Suggest some reasons why some students of behavior would not accept the author's point of rebuttal that the young lady's mental problems can be profitably approached as one would approach physical problems.
5. A couple having marital difficulties attended a special 6-day, live-in therapy program at a seaside retreat. An essential feature of the program, besides rap sessions and sensitivity training (opportunities for novel forms of sensory stimulation especially through physical contact with others), was that each partner to the marriage confess to others in the group his three most "guilty secrets." This usually happened on the second or third day (Tuesday or Wednesday). Sometimes these revelations produced motor as well as verbal attacks of the guilty spouse by the other. The psychologist running the program reports that by Thursday the couples once again showed affection to each other, and by Friday or Saturday the couples seemed to be straightened out. No follow-up information was presented. In his interpretation of the events, the psychologist suggested that each guilty party possessed psychic energy that was diverted from warm, interpersonal relationships, and love for one's spouse to suppressing the "guilty secrets"—for example, of marital infidelity. Once such a secret was made known to the spouse, the energy could be redirected toward the spouse in a positive manner. What are your impressions of the strengths and weaknesses of such a program? How could it be improved? Suggest a behavior theory interpretation of the events going on.
6. Outline the reinforcement history necessary to make a student do his work

nightly without prodding or reinforcements from his parents or a tutor. (Hint: Look over the discussion on pages 453–454 of the "autonomous" child.)

REFERENCES

Andrews, L. M., and Karlins, M. *Requiem for democracy?* New York: Holt, Rinehart and Winston, 1971.

Axline, V. M. *Dibs in search of self*. New York: Ballantine Books, 1964.

Krasner, L. The behavioral scientist and social responsibility: No place to hide. *Journal of Social Issues*, 1965, 21, 9–30.

London, P. *Behavior control*. New York: Harper and Row, 1969.

Reagan, M. C. Basic and applied research: A meaningful distinction? *Science*, 1967, 155, 1383–1386.

Skinner, B. F., *Walden two*. New York: Macmillan, 1948.

Skinner, B. F. *Science and human behavior*. New York: Macmillan, 1953.

Skinner, B. F. *Cumulative record*. (Enlarg. ed.) New York: Appleton-Century-Crofts, 1961.

Skinner, B. F. *Beyond freedom and dignity*. New York: Alfred A. Knopf, 1971.

Ulrich, R. Behavior control and public concern. *Psychological Record*, 1967, 17, 229–234.

Ulrich, R., Stachnik, T., and Mabry, J. *Control of human behavior*. Glenview, Ill.: Scott, Foresman, 1966.

Ulrich, R., Stachnik, T., and Mabry, J. (Eds.) *Control of Human Behavior*. Vol. 2. *From cure to prevention*. Glenview, Ill.: Scott, Foresman, 1970.

Tables and figures in the text are designated by *italics*. Footnotes are designated by *n*.

Absolute threshold, 101–104
Abstraction, 120
Activation syndrome, 37, 358
Adams, J. S., 246
Addison, R. M., 447
Adventitious contingencies. *See* Superstitious behavior
Adventitious stimulus pairing, 233
Affective behavior. *See* Emotional behavior
Aggression, animal vs. human, 256; and catharsis, 265; causes of, 148–149, 256–259, 261–265; child vs. adult, 259–260; and competition, 262; control of, 265; definition of, 255, 259; expectations and, 263–264; genetic factors in, 259; in the Herring Gull, 257–258; and instinctive needs, 259; and modeling, 262, 265; operant, 256; and operant conditioning, 256; operant-respondent behavior chain, 256–257; respondent (elicited), 255; respondent conditioning of, 256; and revolution, 262; social training of, 261, 264–265; stimuli discriminative for, 262; and systemic frustration, 262; territorial defense and, 258–259; and verbal community, 261
Ainsworth, M. C., 126

Akers, R., 279 n, 286, 287
Albert and the rat, 37
Allen, R. M., 126
Amaurotic familiar idiocy, 312–314
Ameen, L., 324 n, 336
Amount of reinforcement, response latency and, 54, 55; response rate and, 54; response variability and, 54, 55
Anderson, W., 449
Andrews, L. M., 458
Anonymous, 218
Anrep, G. V., 46
Antecedent-consequence relations, *13*, 16–17, 271
Application of behavior principles, criticisms of, 451–454; as microexperiments, 451; social implications of, 456–457; usefulness of, 451
Armstrong, M., 449
Artificial reinforcers, 407
Artusco, A. A., 447
Attitudes, and actions, 270–271; and audience control response, 271; behavioral analysis of, 269; and beliefs, 271; and consistency of behavior, 268; criticism of, 270–271; nature of, 267–268; questionnaire

459

73 74 75 76   9 8 7 6 5 4 3 2 1